RYOSUKE
ASAKURA

Val × Love

10

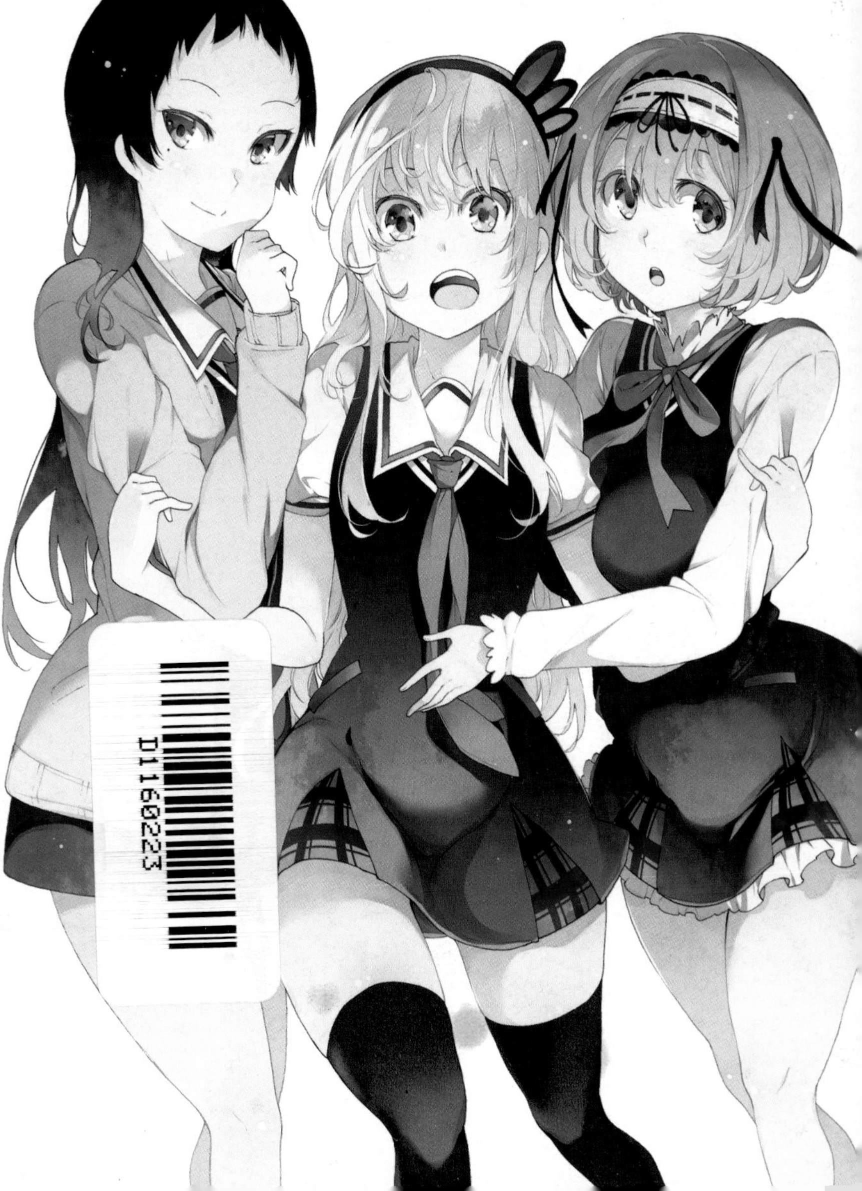

[CONTENTS]

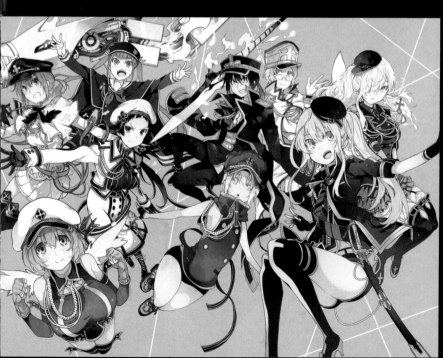

Chapter 50

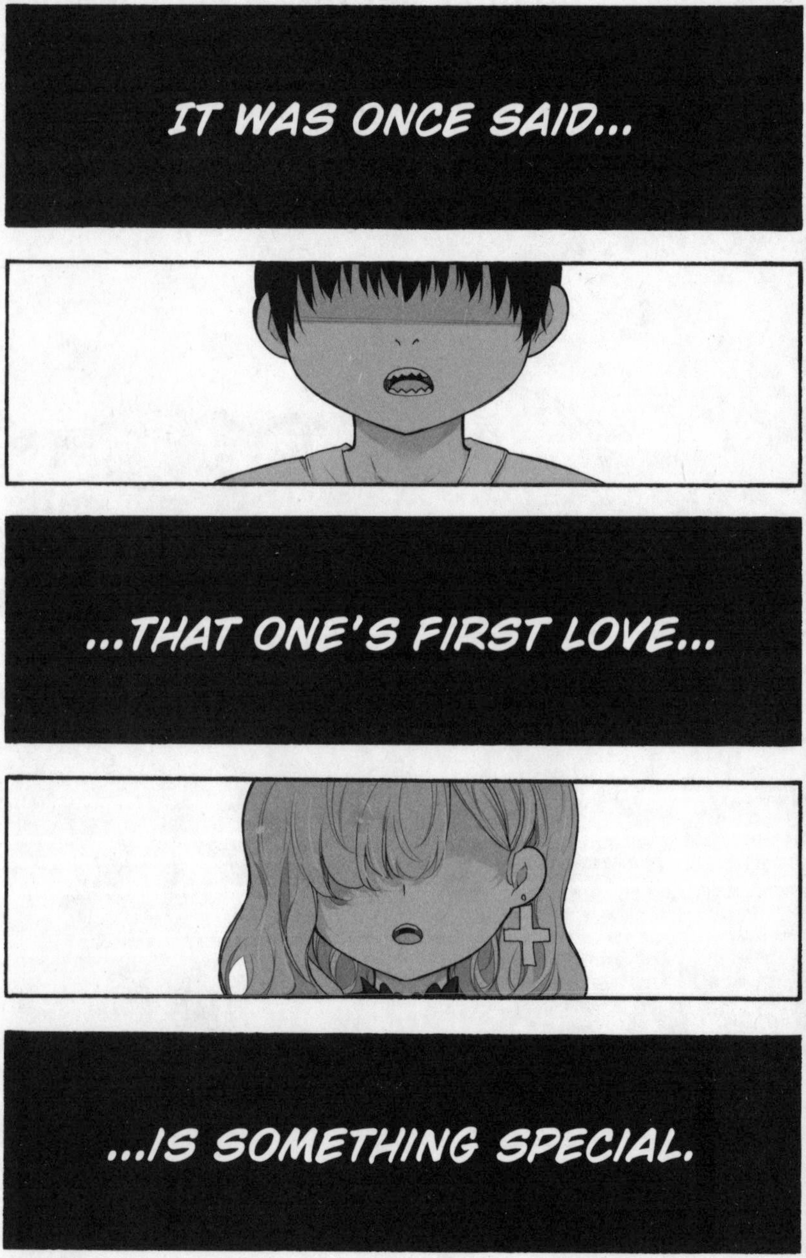
IT WAS ONCE SAID...
...THAT ONE'S FIRST LOVE...
...IS SOMETHING SPECIAL.

Chapter 50: The Special Maiden

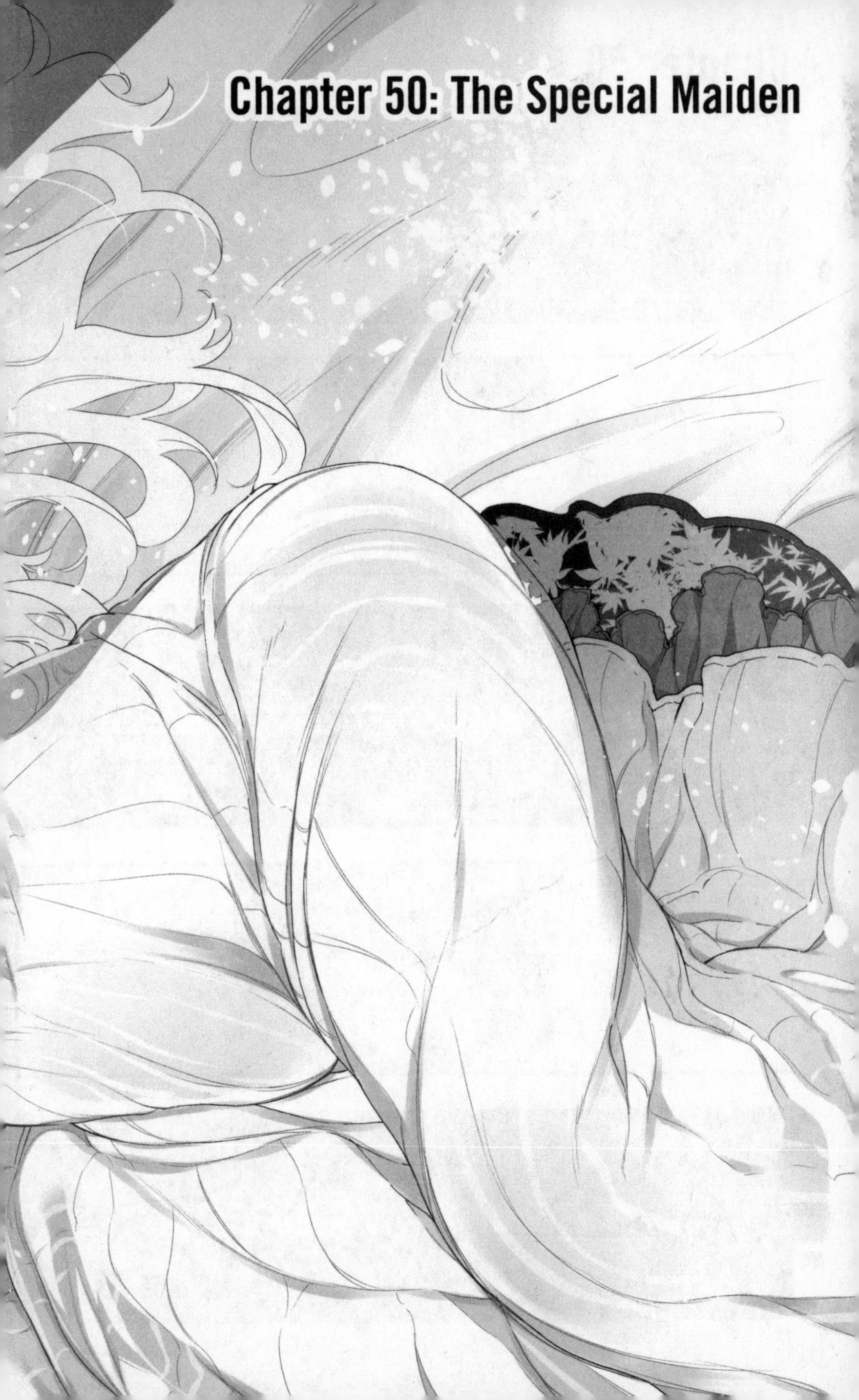

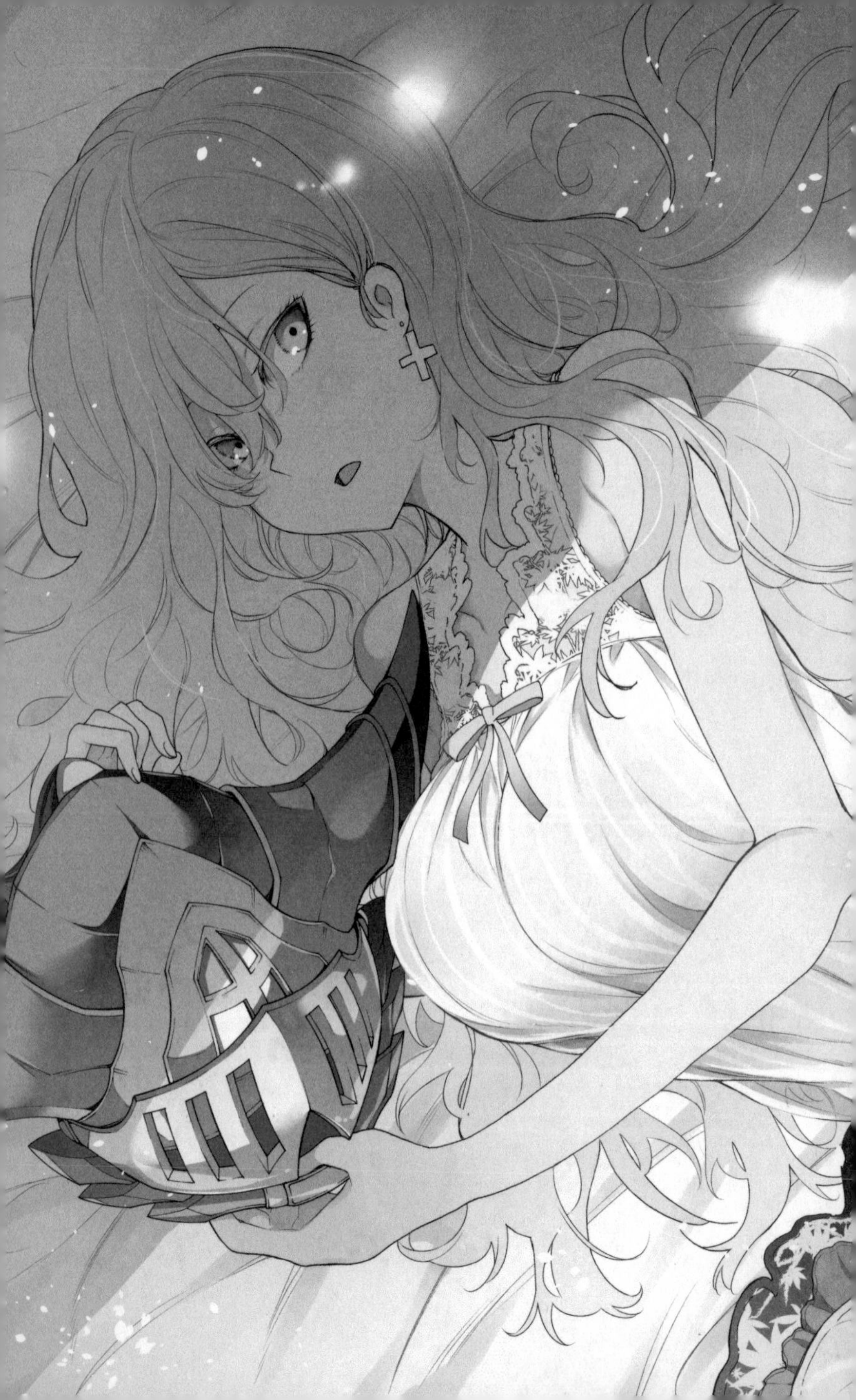

Val X Love

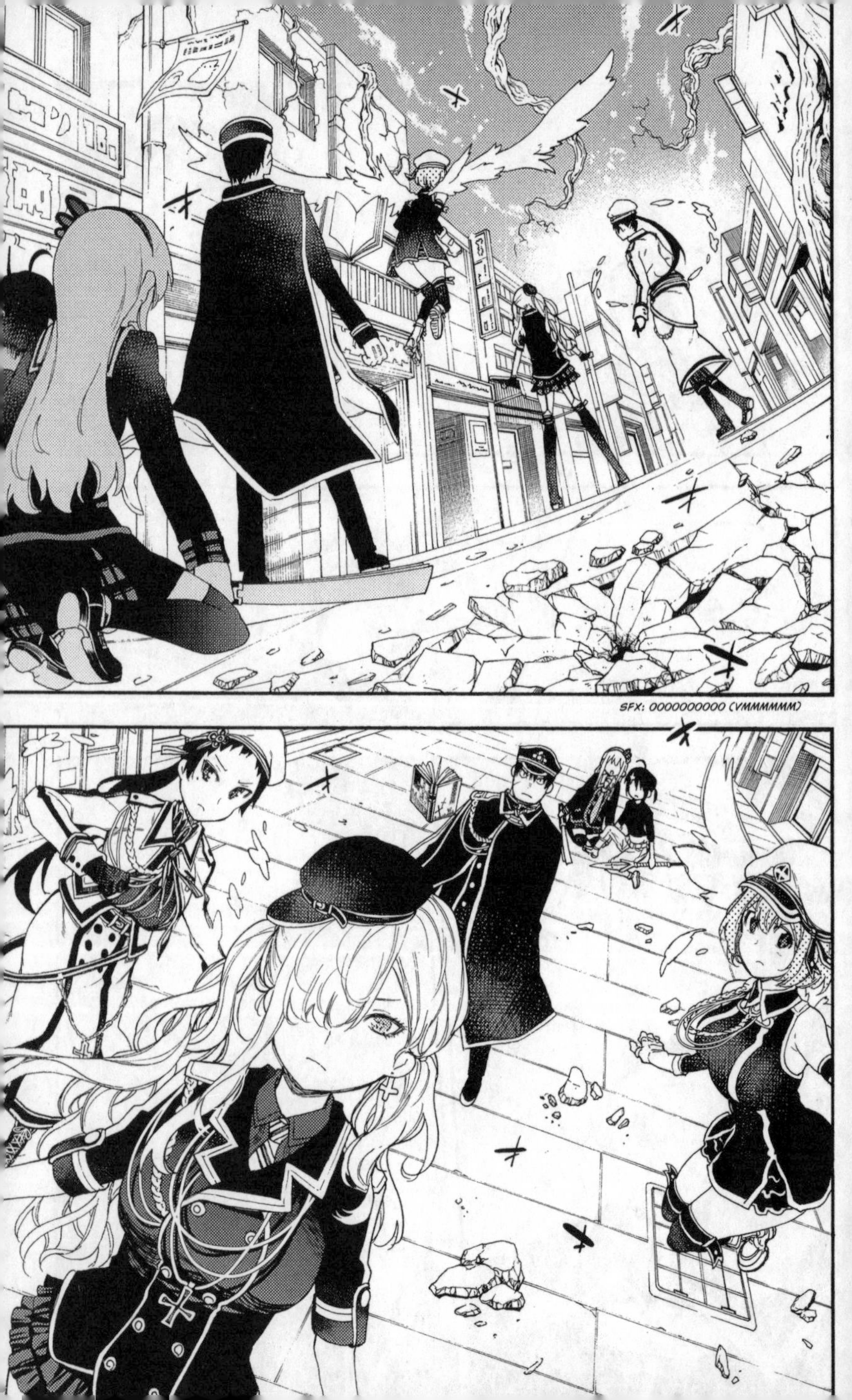
SFX: OOOOOOOOOO (VMMMMMM)

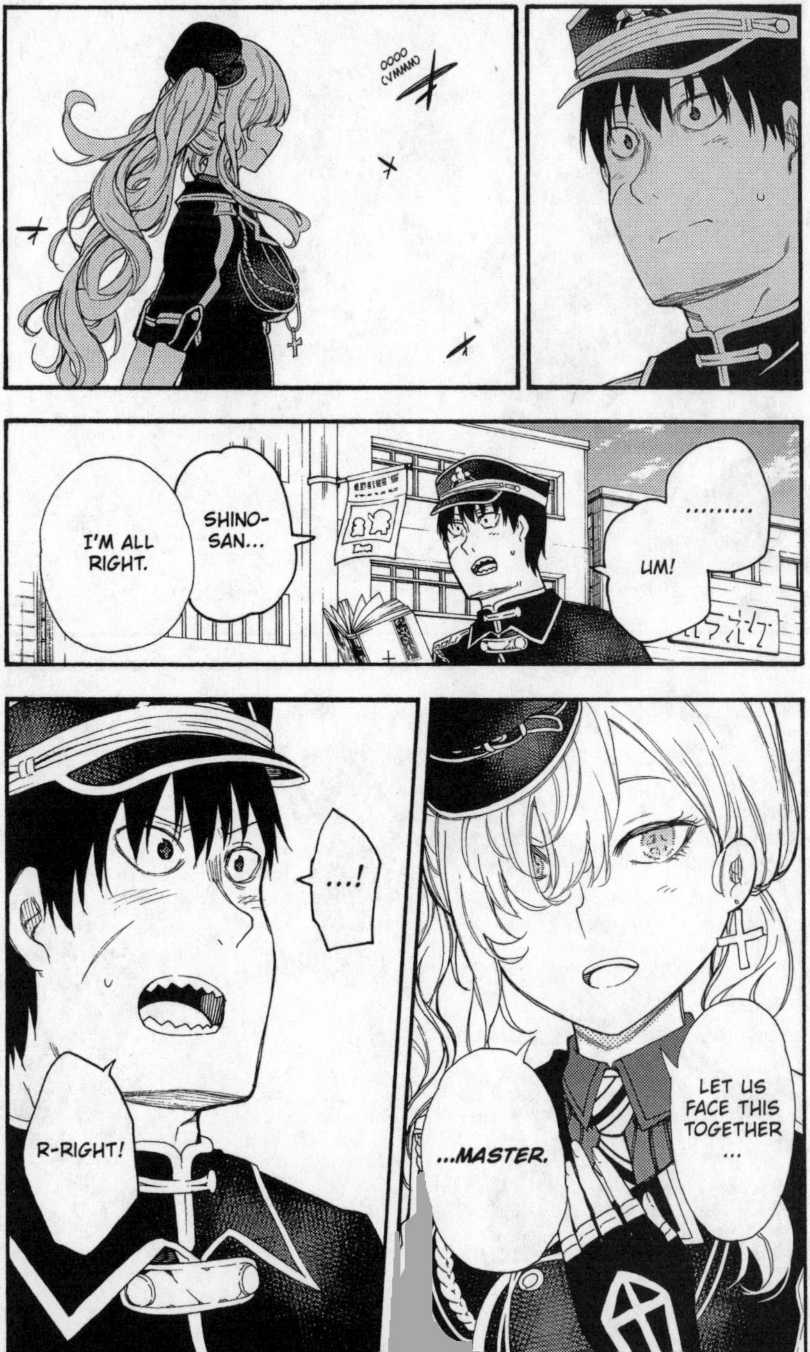
(VMMM OOOO
....
UM!
SHINO-SAN...
I'M ALL RIGHT.
LET US FACE THIS TOGETHER ...
...MASTER.
...!
R-RIGHT!

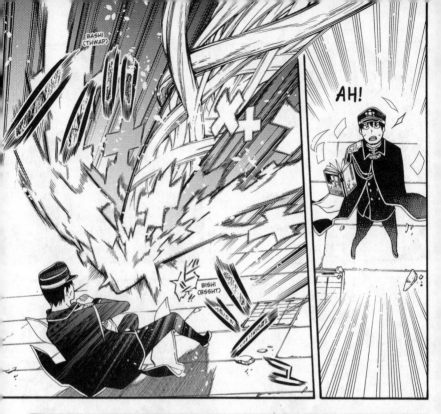

BASHI
(THWAP)

AH!

BISHI
(BSSHT)

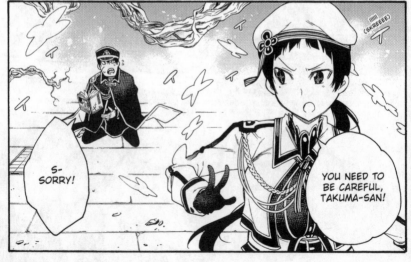

(SKREEEE)

S-SORRY!

YOU NEED TO BE CAREFUL, TAKUMA-SAN!

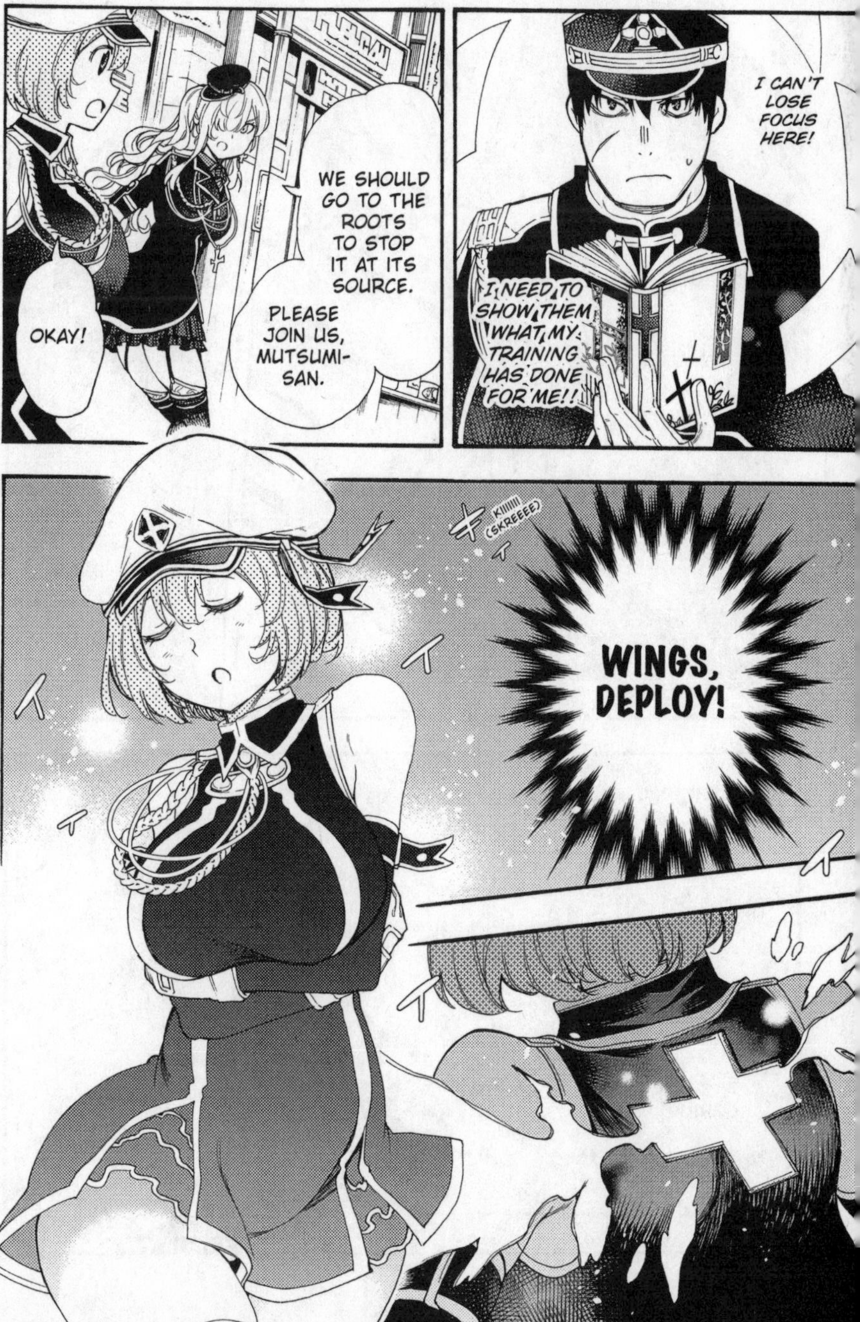
I CAN'T LOSE FOCUS HERE!
I NEED TO SHOW THEM WHAT MY TRAINING HAS DONE FOR ME!!
WE SHOULD GO TO THE ROOTS TO STOP IT AT ITS SOURCE.
PLEASE JOIN US, MUTSUMI-SAN.
OKAY!
KIIIIIII (SKREEEEE)
WINGS, DEPLOY!

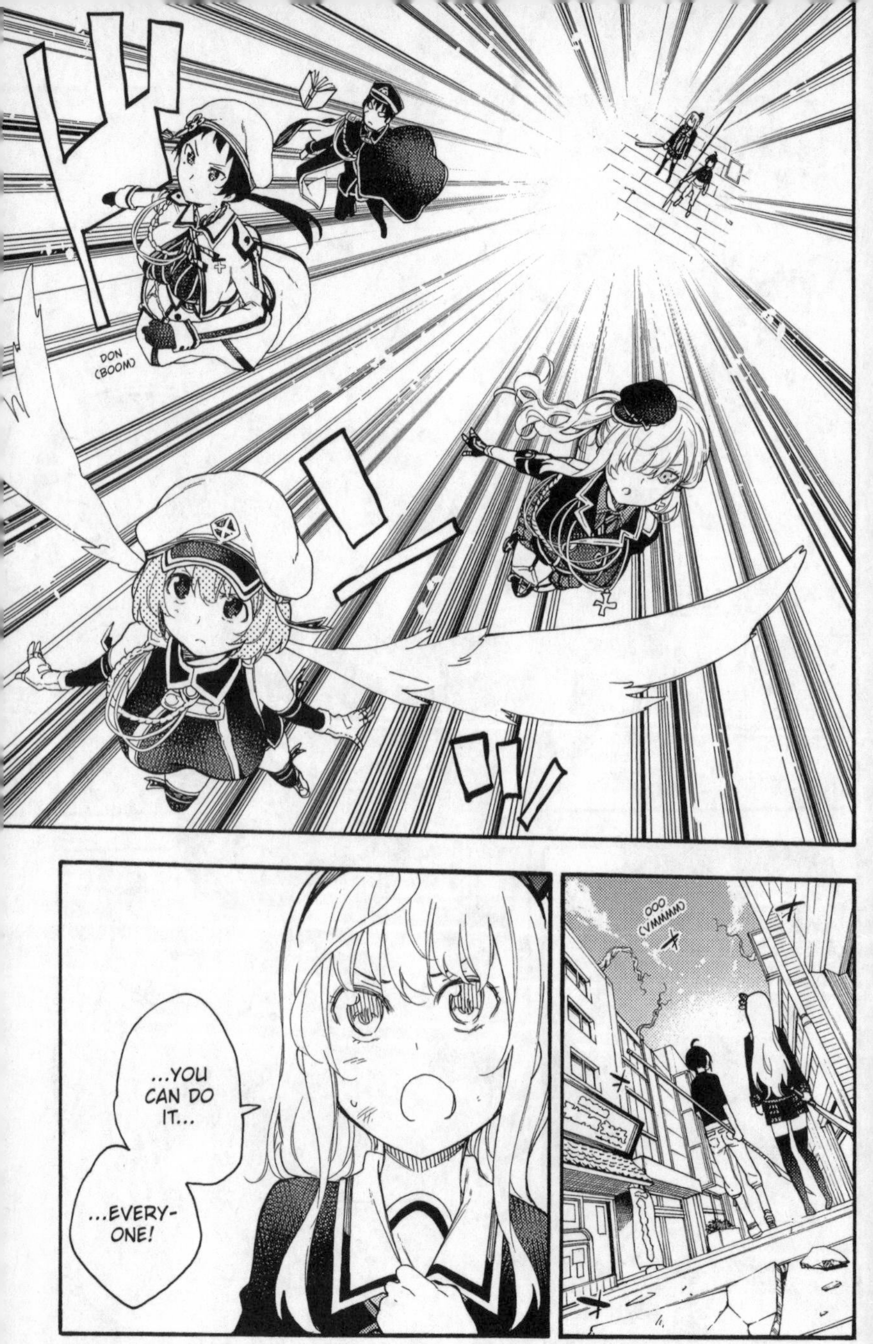
DON (BOOM)
OOO (VMMMM)
...YOU CAN DO IT...
...EVERY-ONE!

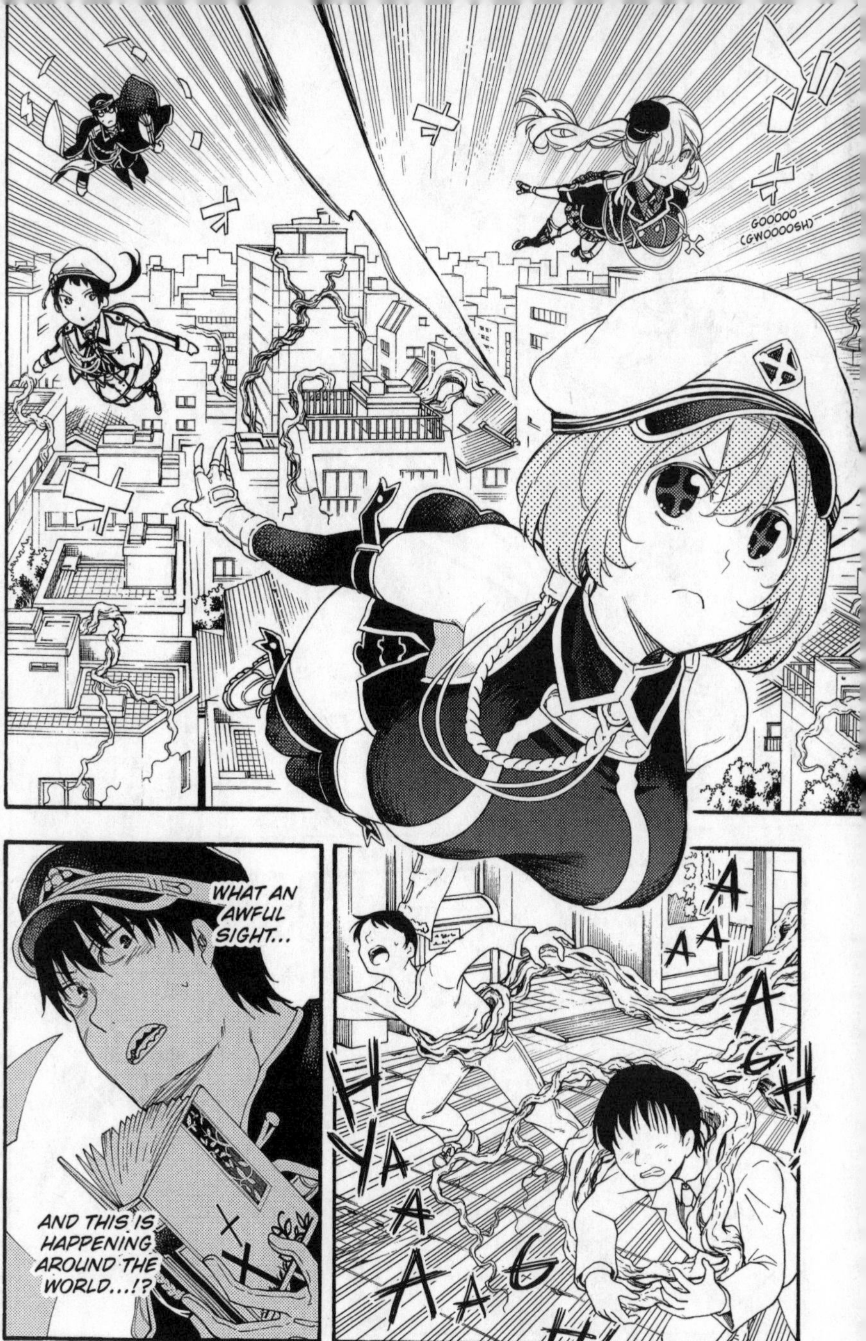
GOOOOO
(GWOOOOSH)
AAAAAGH!
HYAAAAGH!
WHAT AN AWFUL SIGHT...
AND THIS IS HAPPENING AROUND THE WORLD...!?

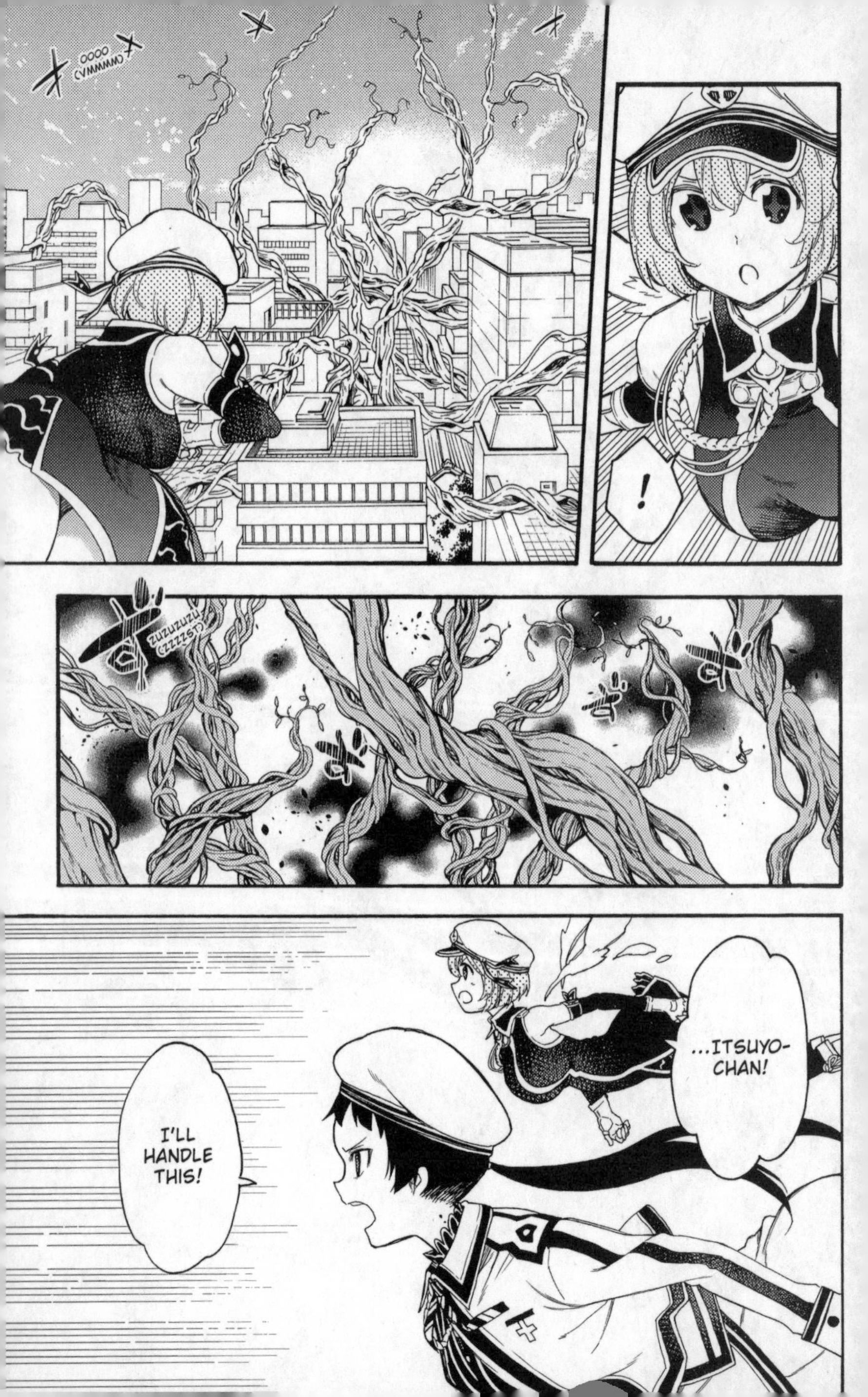
!
OOOO (VMMMM)
ZUZUZUZU (ZZZZZST)
...ITSUYO-CHAN!
I'LL HANDLE THIS!

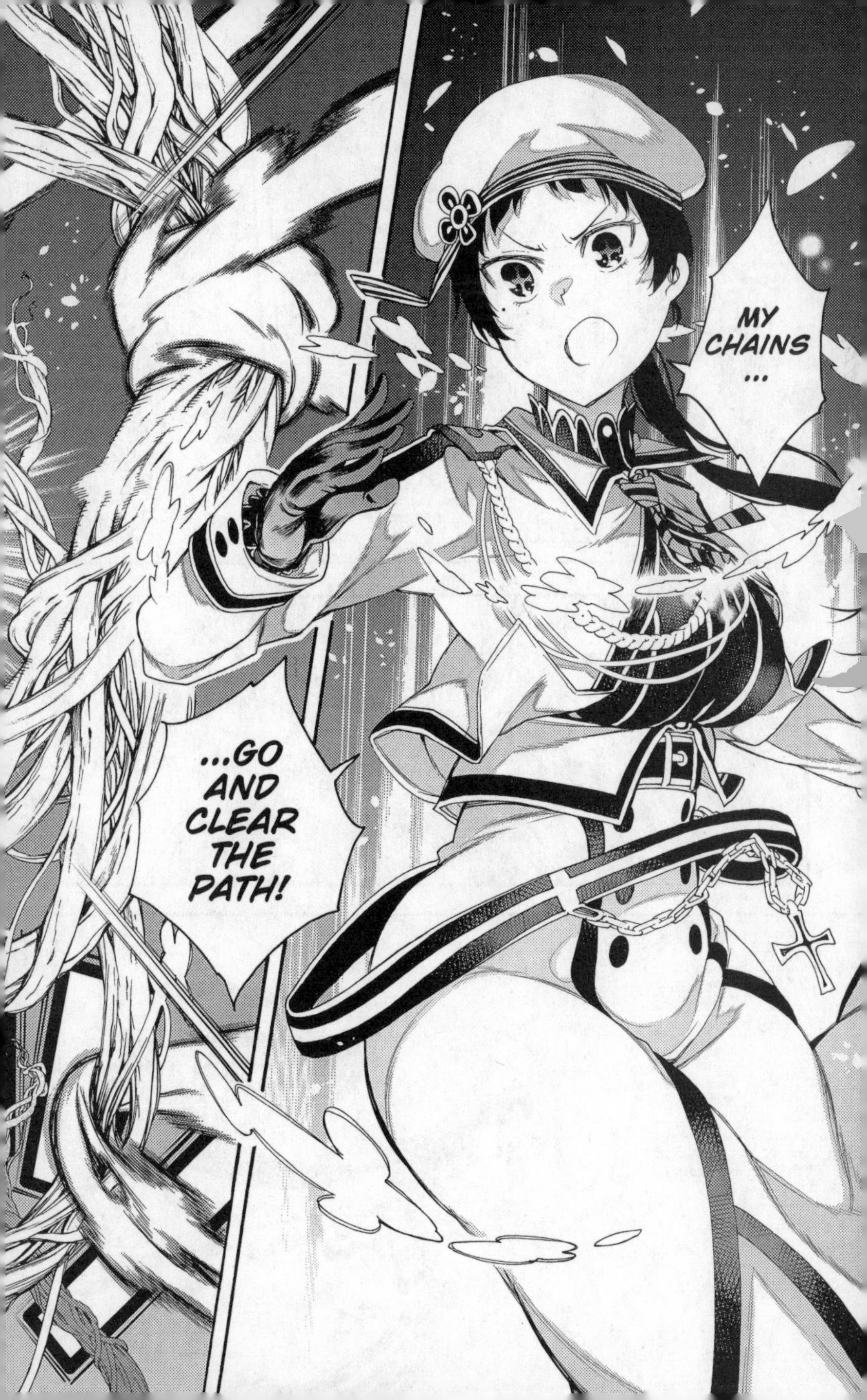
MY CHAINS ...
...GO AND CLEAR THE PATH!

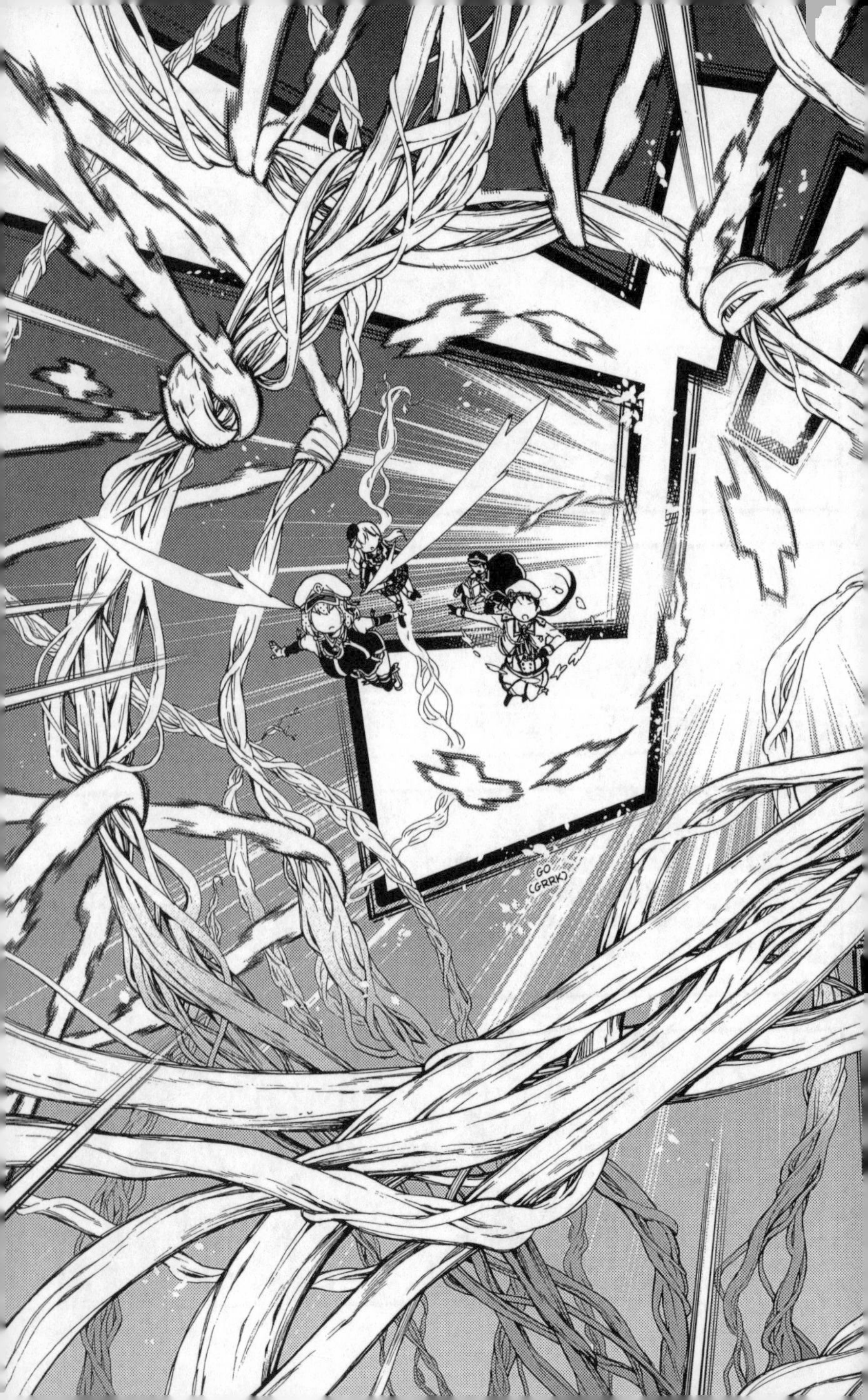
GO
(GRRK)

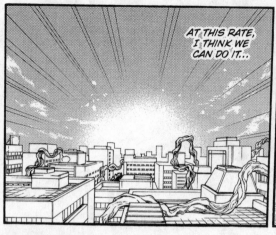

AT THIS RATE, I THINK WE CAN DO IT...

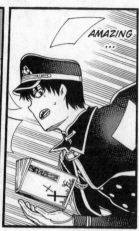

AMAZING...

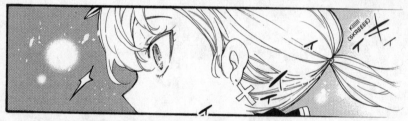

KIIIII (SKREEEE)

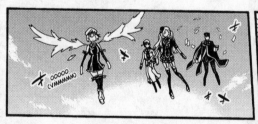

OOOOO (VMMMMMO)

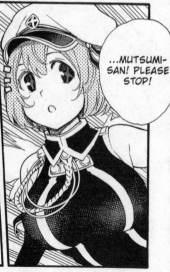

...MUTSUMI-SAN! PLEASE STOP!

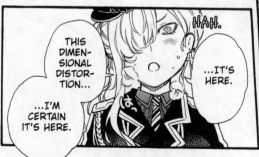

HAH.

...IT'S HERE.

THIS DIMENSIONAL DISTORTION...

...I'M CERTAIN IT'S HERE.

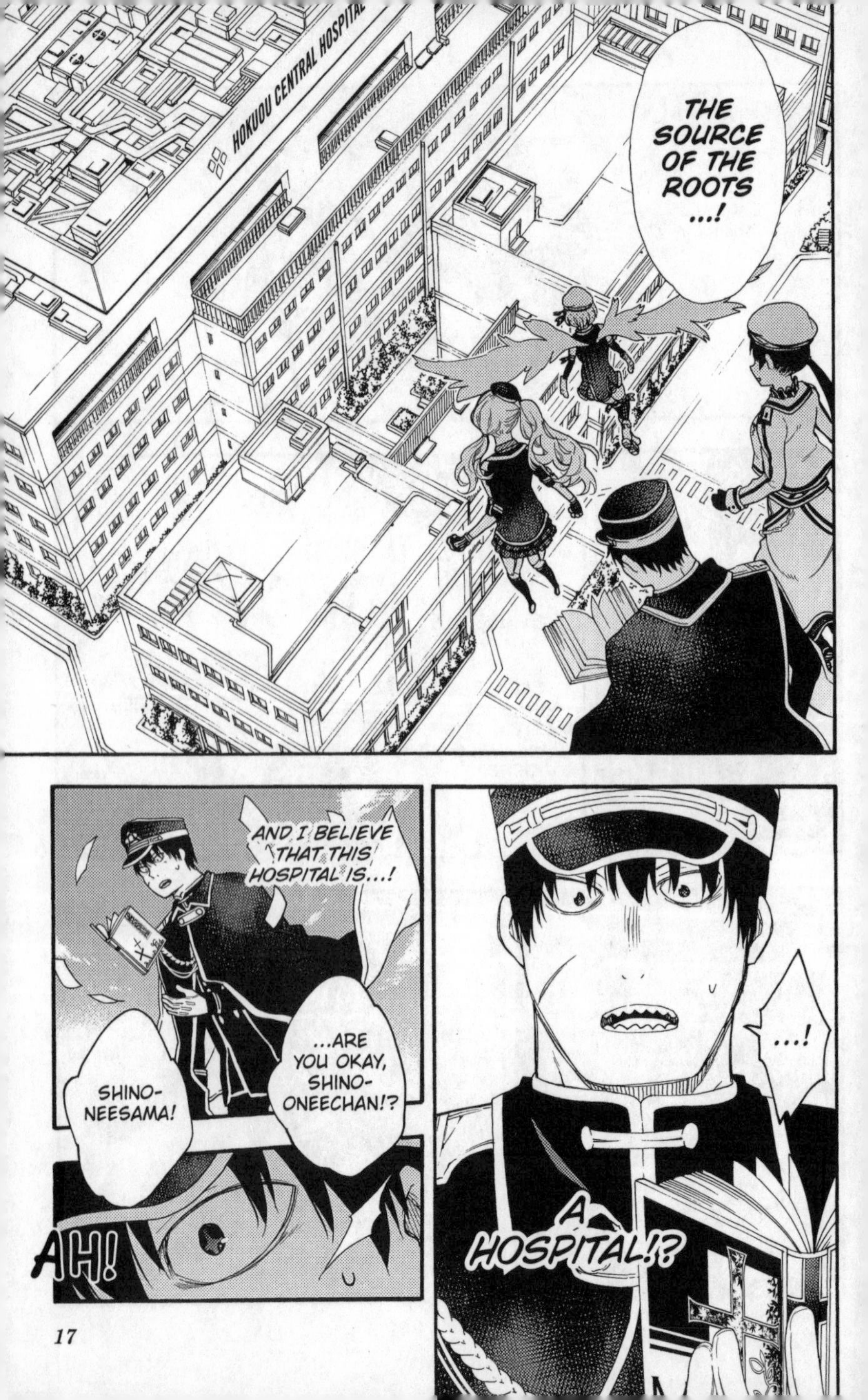
HOKUUOU CENTRAL HOSPITAL
THE SOURCE OF THE ROOTS ...!
...!
A HOSPITAL!?
AND I BELIEVE THAT THIS HOSPITAL IS...!
...ARE YOU OKAY, SHINO-ONEECHAN!?
SHINO-NEESAMA!
AH!

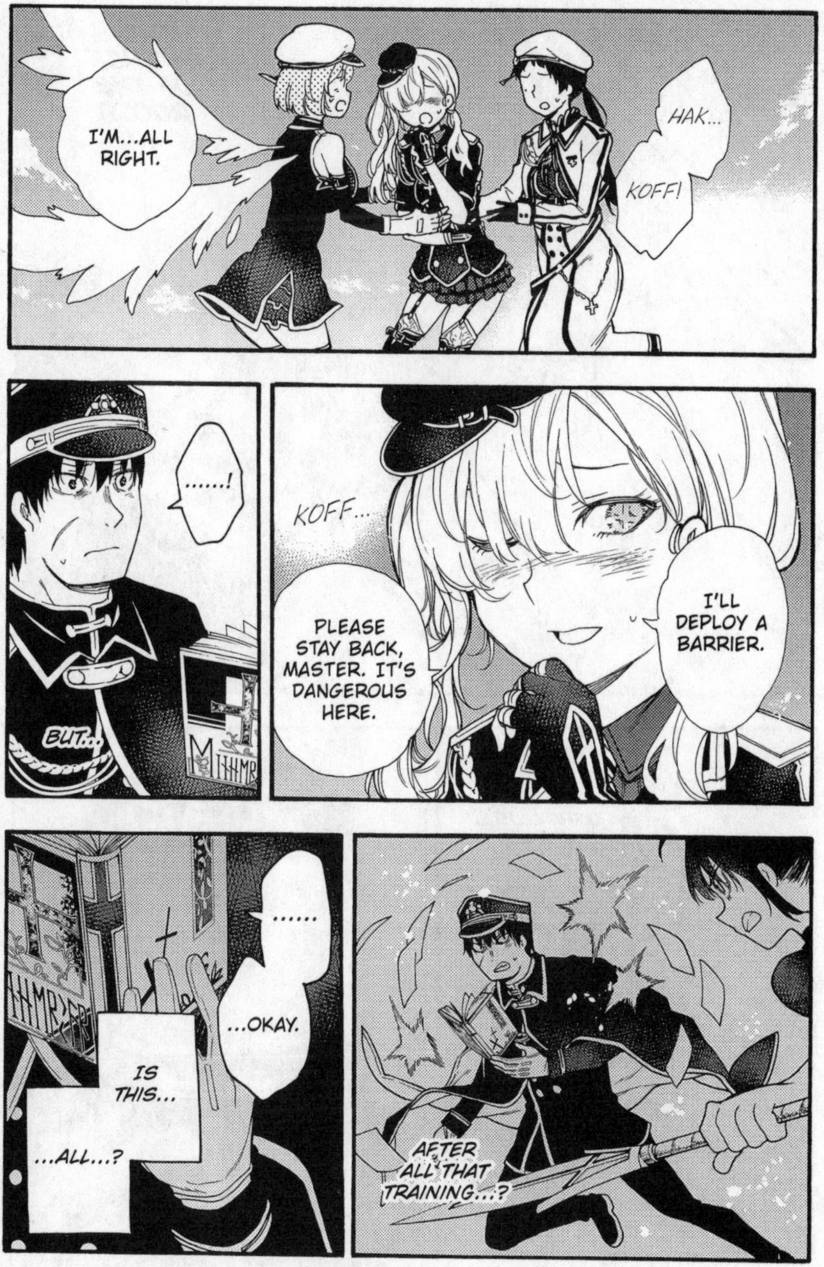
HAK...
KOFF!
I'M...ALL RIGHT.
KOFF...
I'LL DEPLOY A BARRIER.
PLEASE STAY BACK, MASTER. IT'S DANGEROUS HERE.
......!
BUT...
AFTER ALL THAT TRAINING...?
......
...OKAY.
IS THIS...
...ALL...?

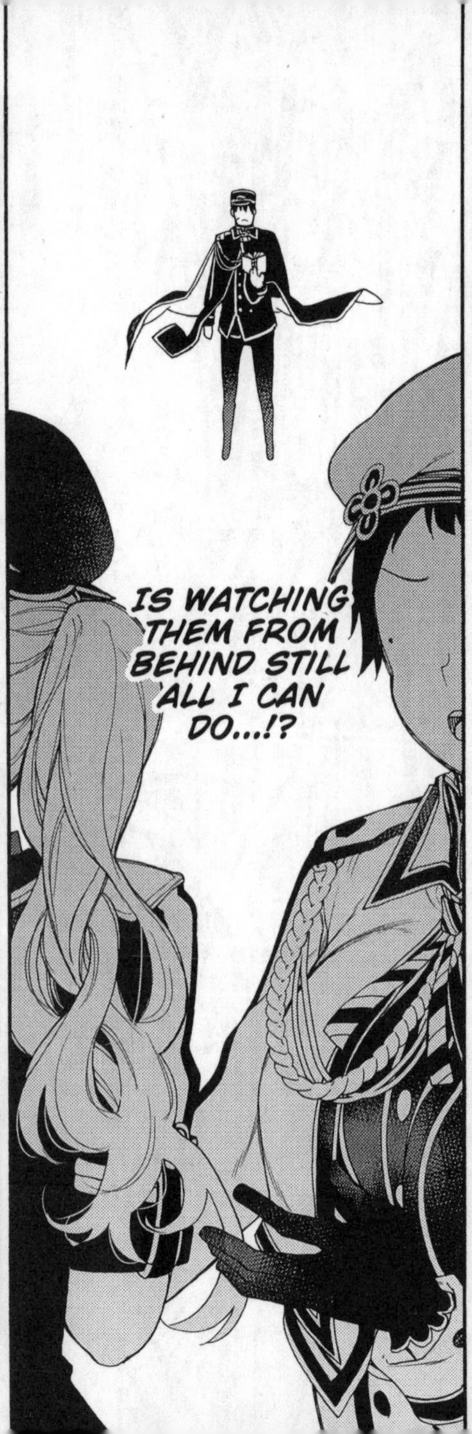
IS WATCHING THEM FROM BEHIND STILL ALL I CAN DO...!?
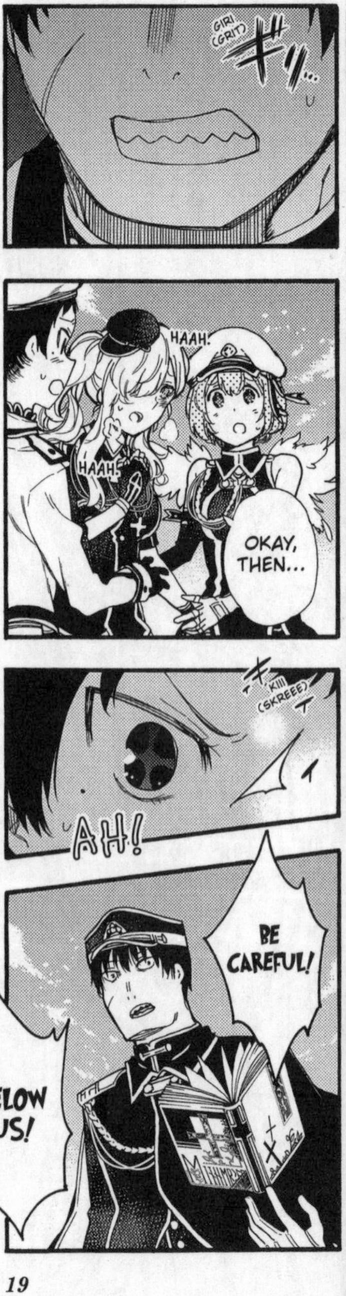
GIRI (GRIT)
HAAH!
HAAH
OKAY, THEN...
KIII (SKREEE)
AH!
BE CAREFUL!
BELOW US!

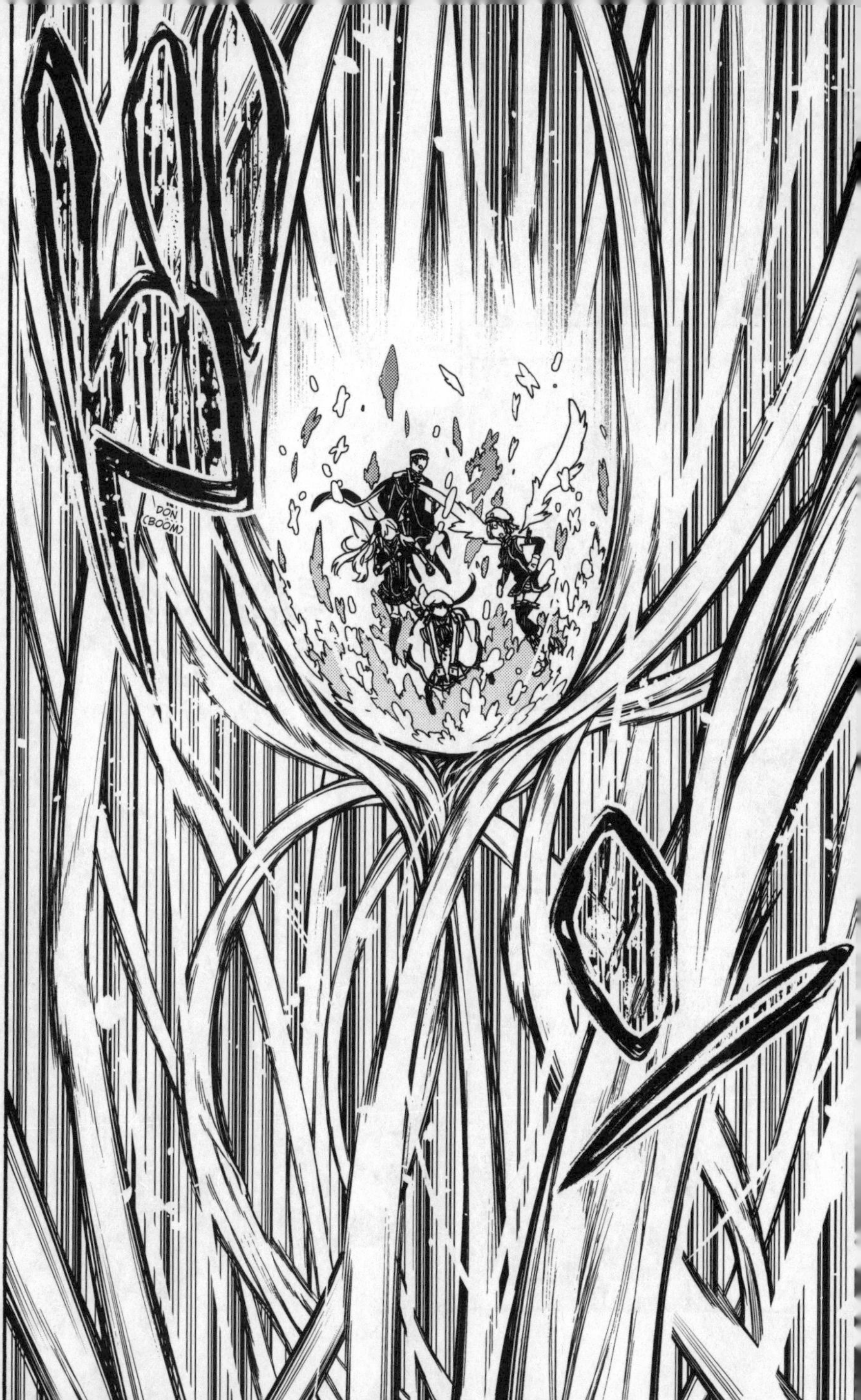
DON (BOOM)

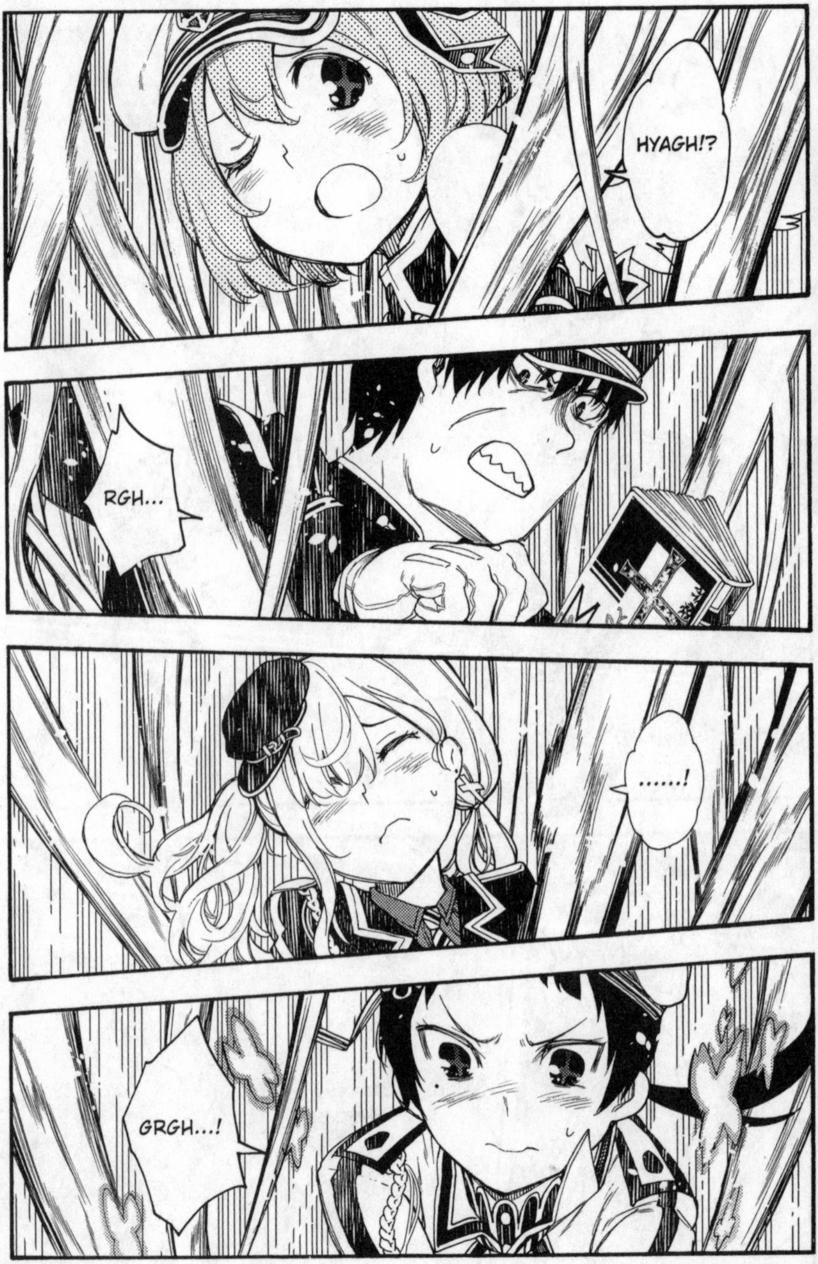
HYAGH!?
RGH...
......!
GRGH...!

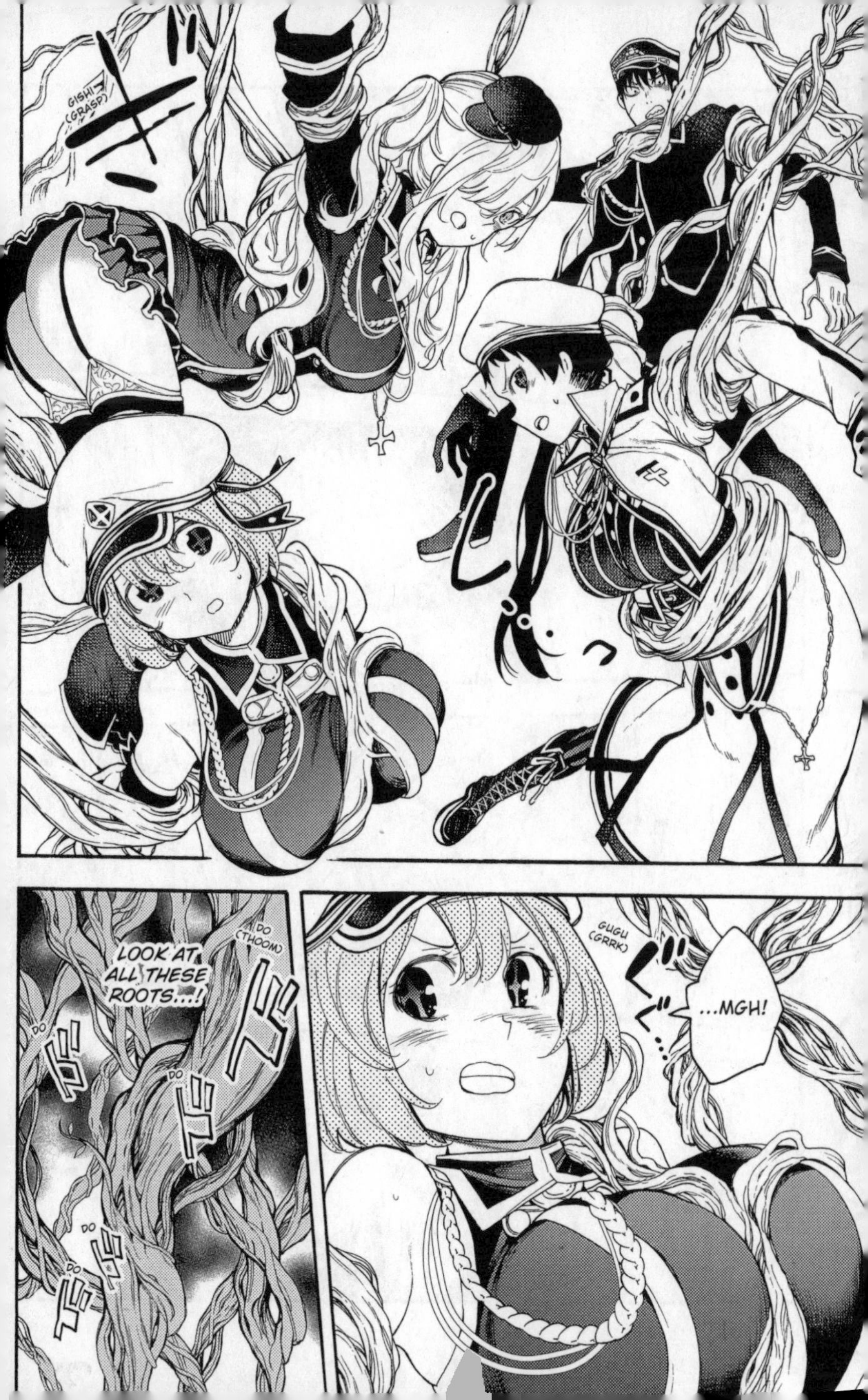
GISHI (GRASP)
GUGU (GRRK)
...MGH!
DO (THOOM)
LOOK AT ALL THESE ROOTS...!
DO
DO
DO
DO

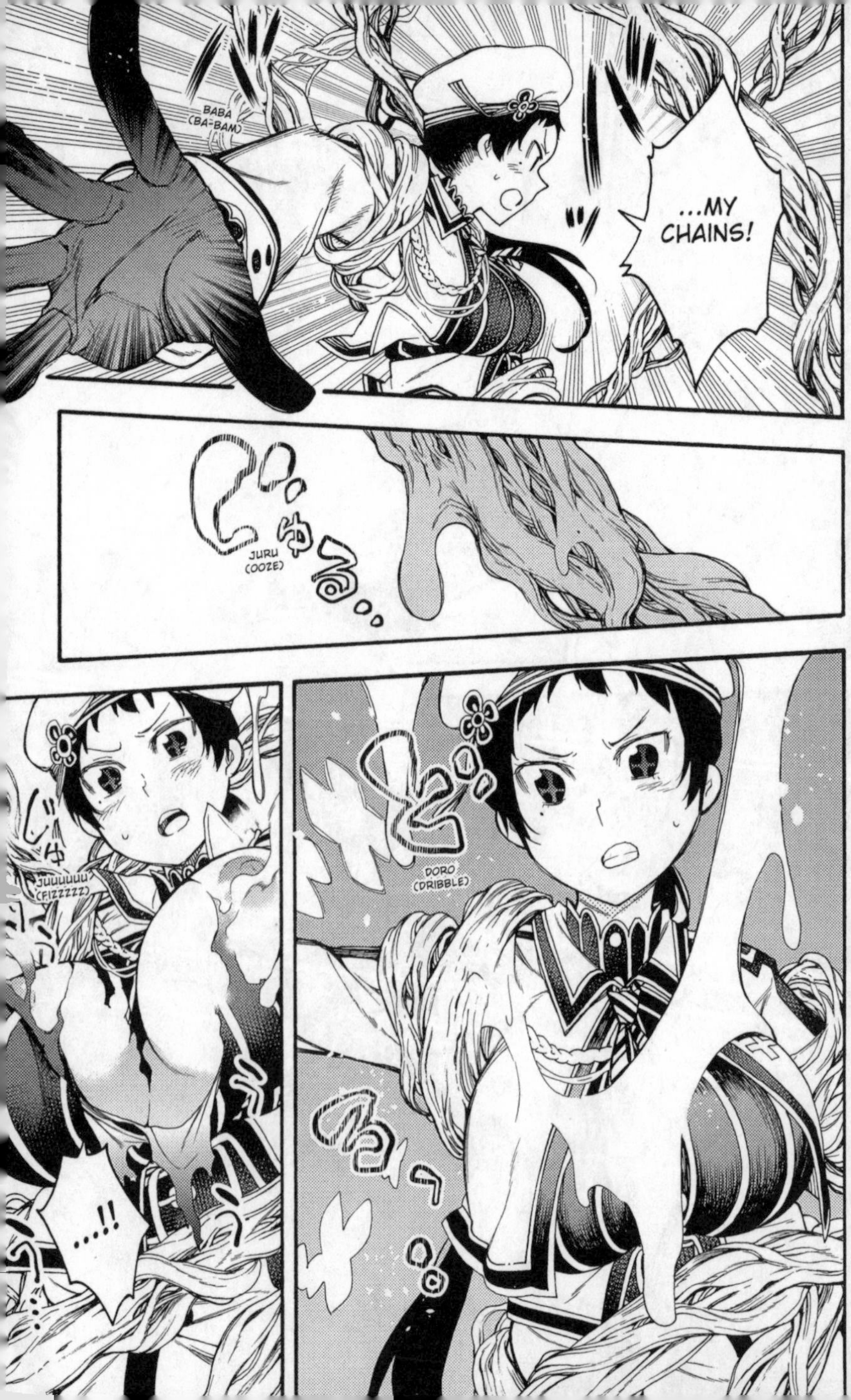
...MY CHAINS!
BABA (BA-BAM)
JURU (OOZE)
DORO (DRIBBLE)
JUUUUUUU (FIZZZZZ)
...!!

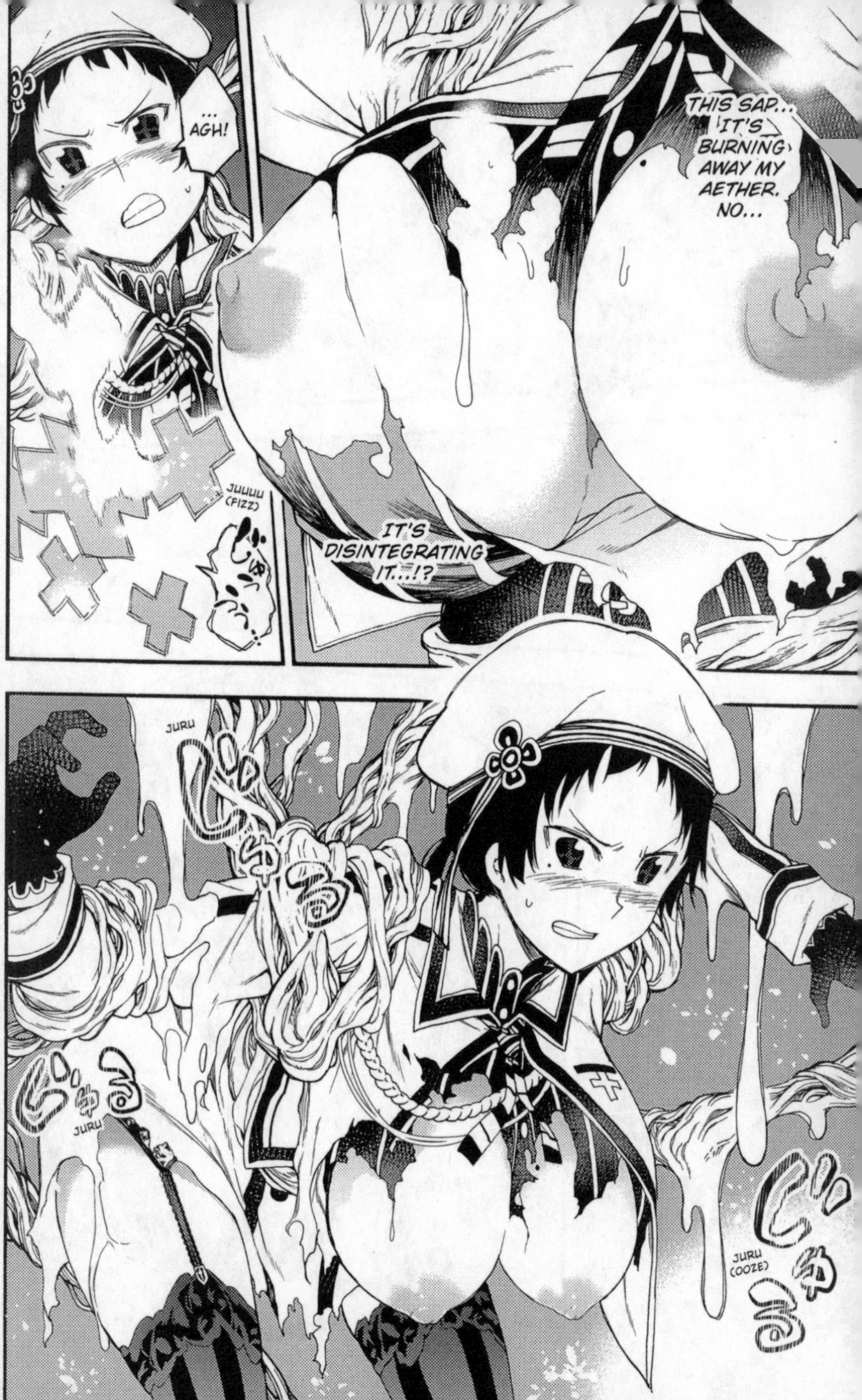
THIS SAP... IT'S BURNING AWAY MY AETHER. NO...
IT'S DISINTEGRATING IT...!?
...AGH!
JUUUU (FIZZ)
JURU (OOZE)
JURU
JURU

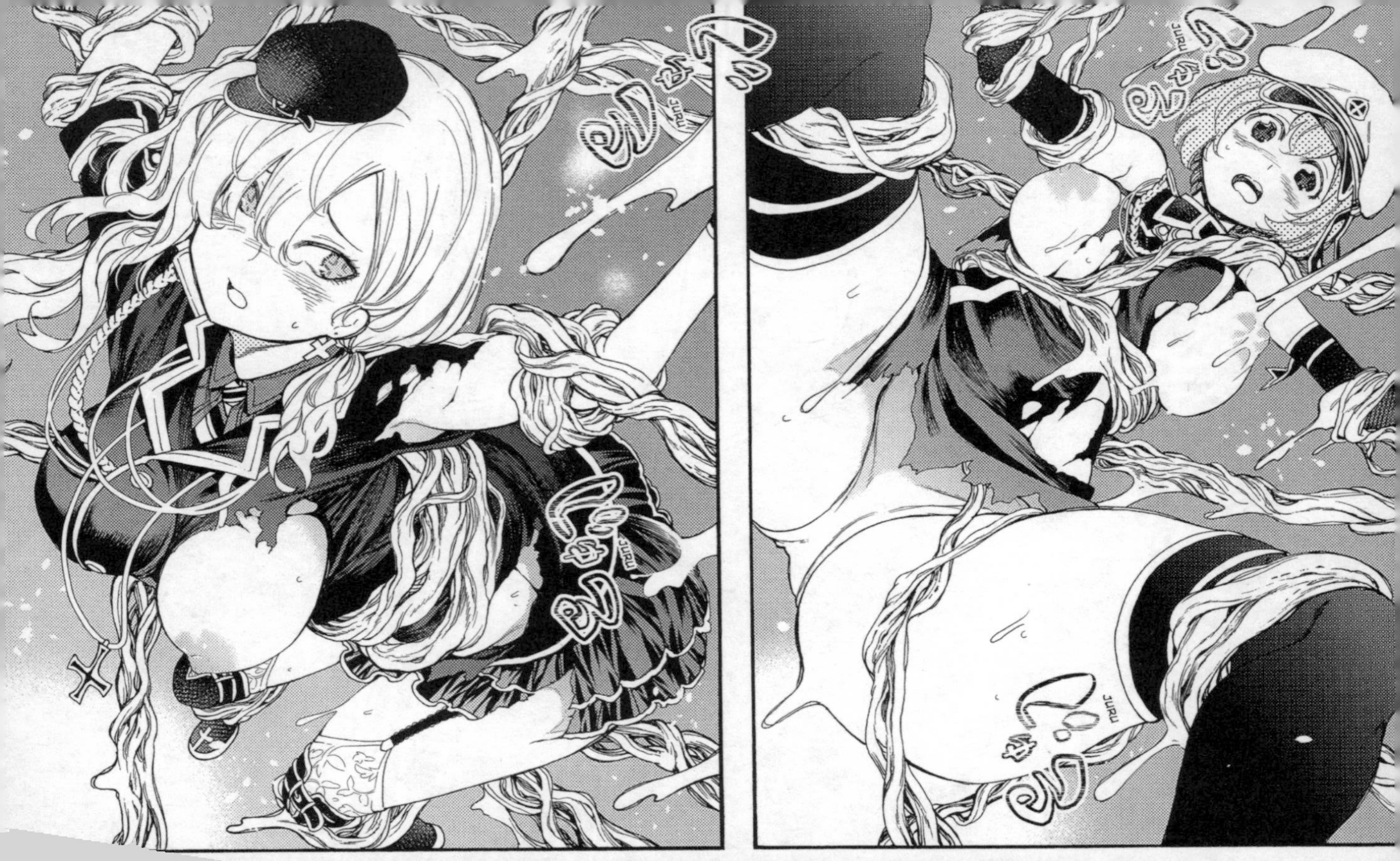
JURU
JURU
JURU
JURU

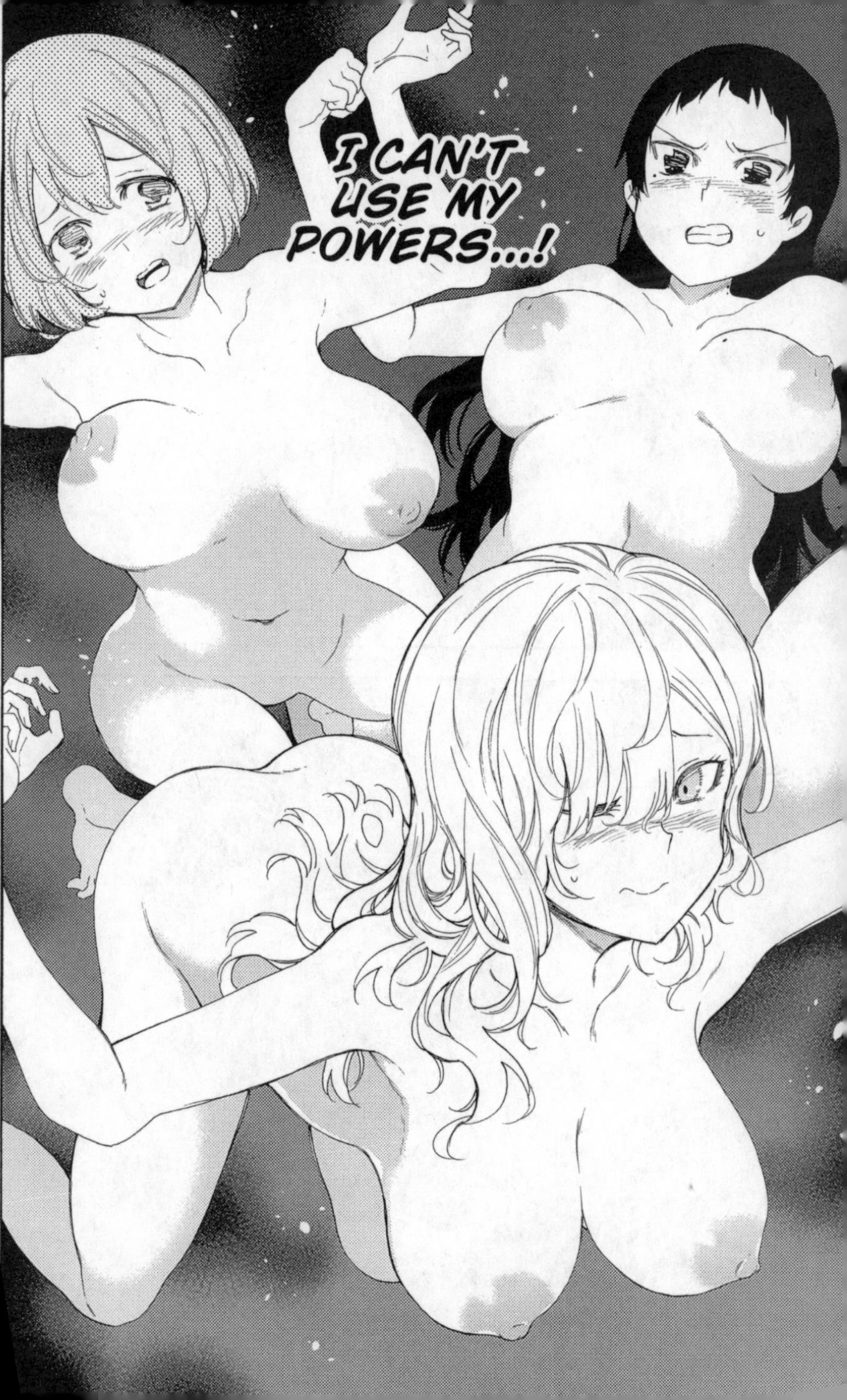
I CAN'T USE MY POWERS...!

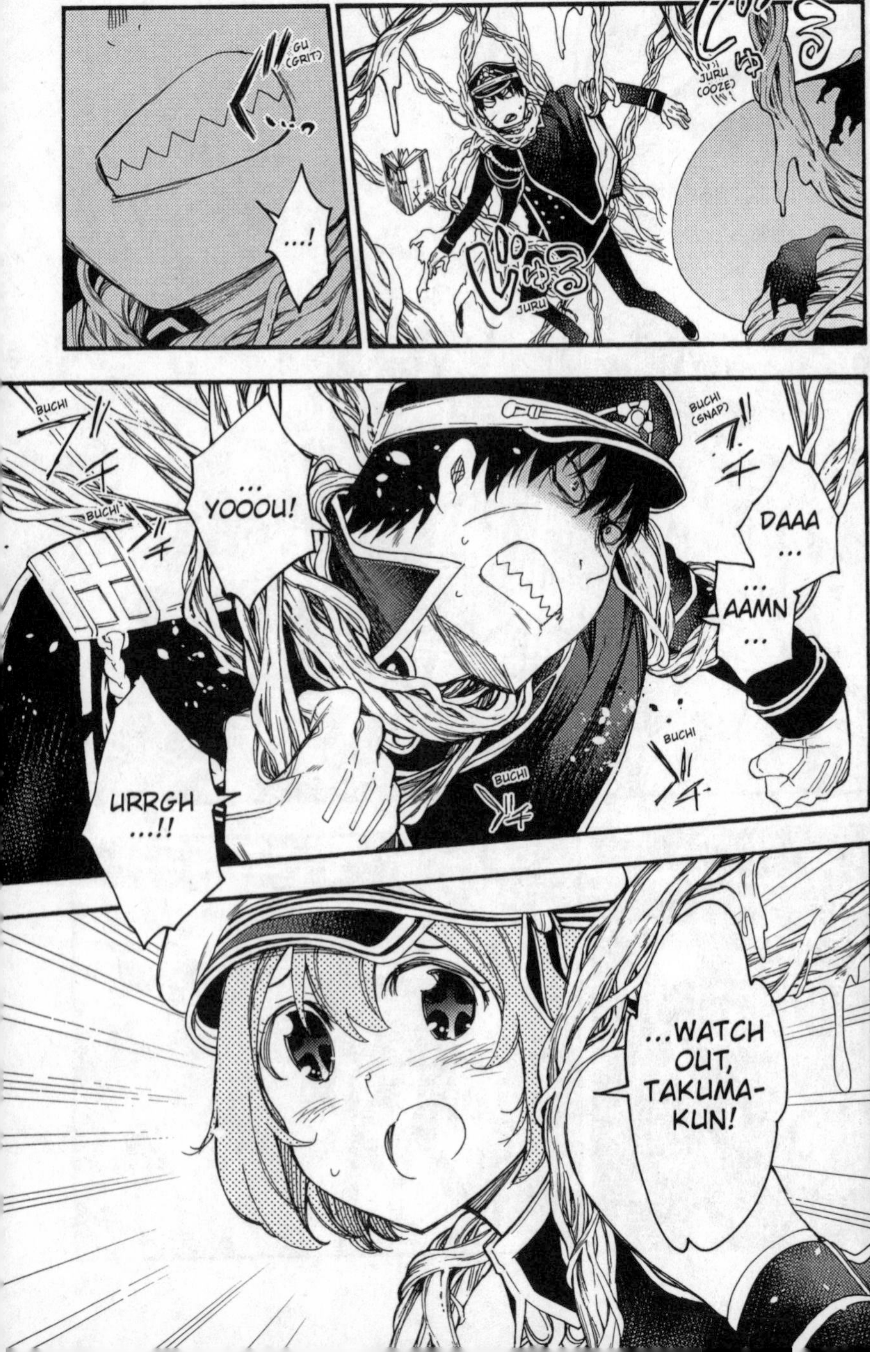
JURU (OOZE)
JURU
GU (GRIT)
...!
BUCHI (SNAP)
DAAA... ...AAMN...
...YOOOU!
BUCHI
BUCHI
BUCHI
BUCHI
URRGH...!!
...WATCH OUT, TAKUMA-KUN!

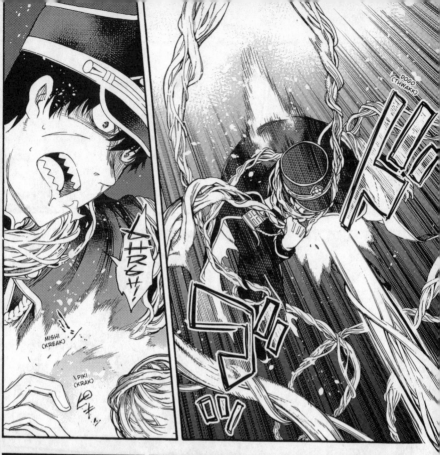

DOGO
(THWAKK)

ZHRSH!!

MISHI
(KREAK)

PIKI
(KRAK)

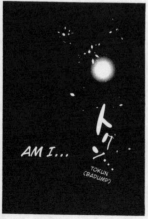

AM I...

TOKUN
(BADUMP)

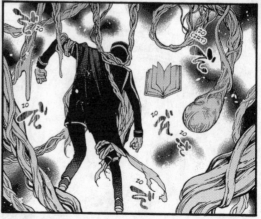

ZO
(JERT)

28

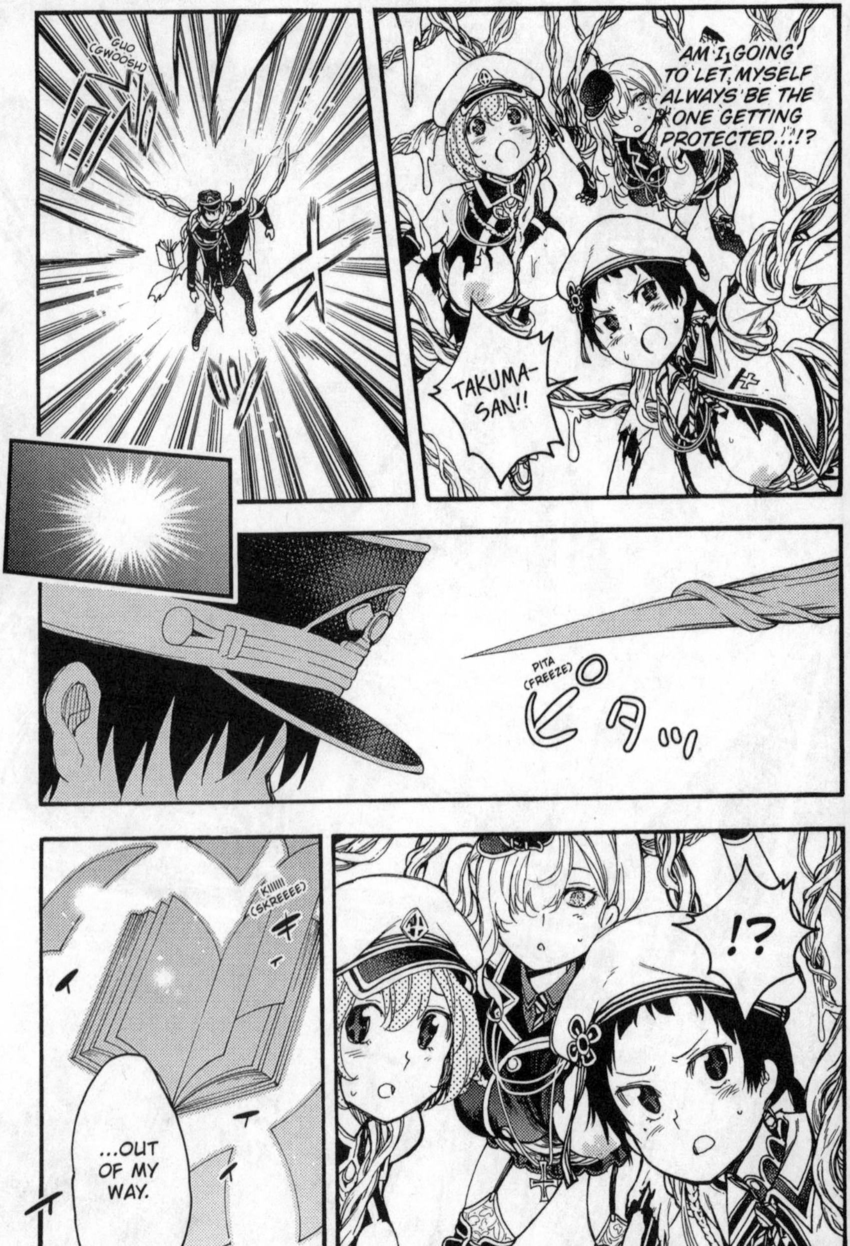
AM I GOING TO LET MYSELF ALWAYS BE THE ONE GETTING PROTECTED...!?
TAKUMA-SAN!!
GUO (GWOOSH)
PITA (FREEZE)
!?
KIIIIII (SKREEEEE)
...OUT OF MY WAY.

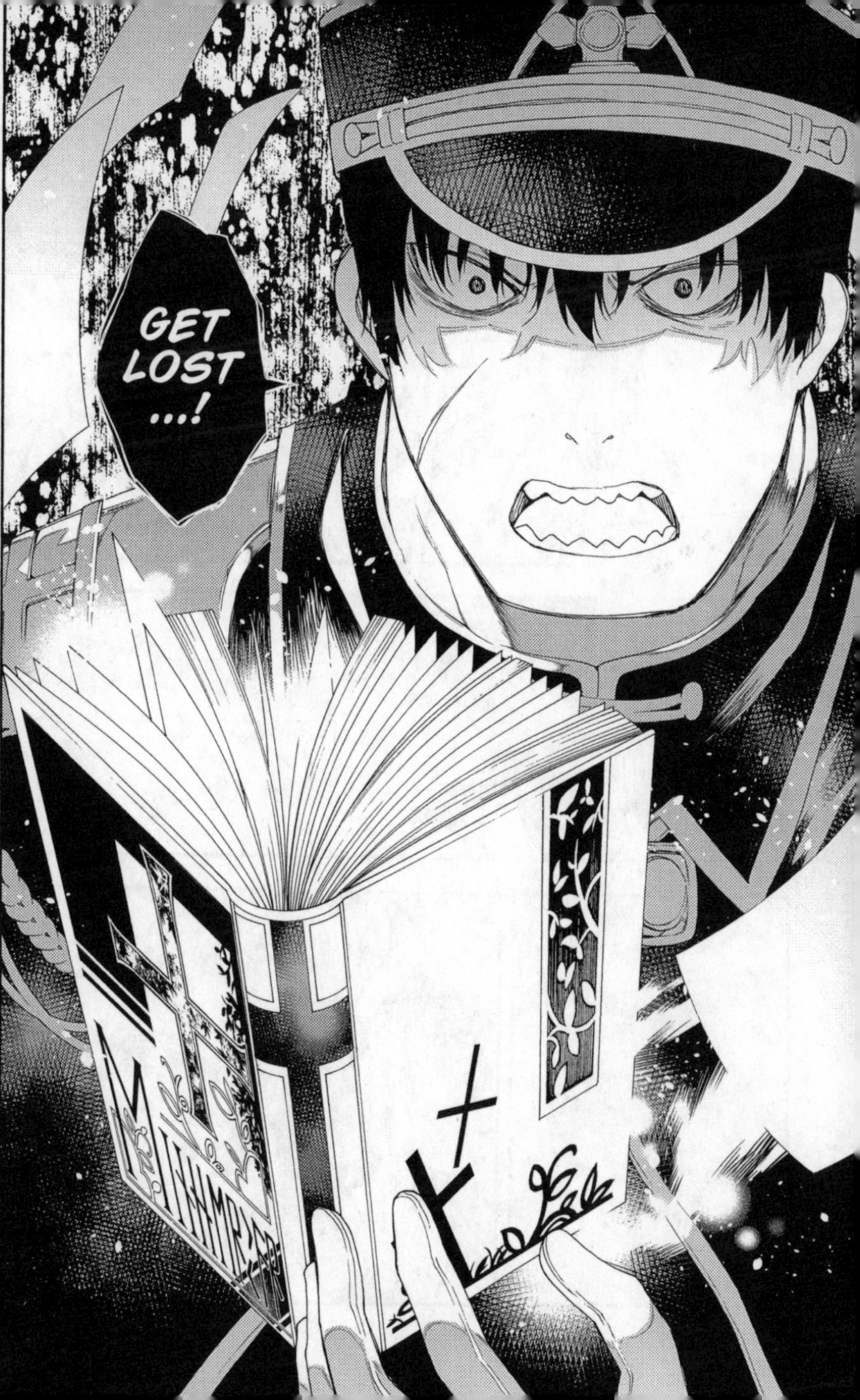
GET LOST ...!

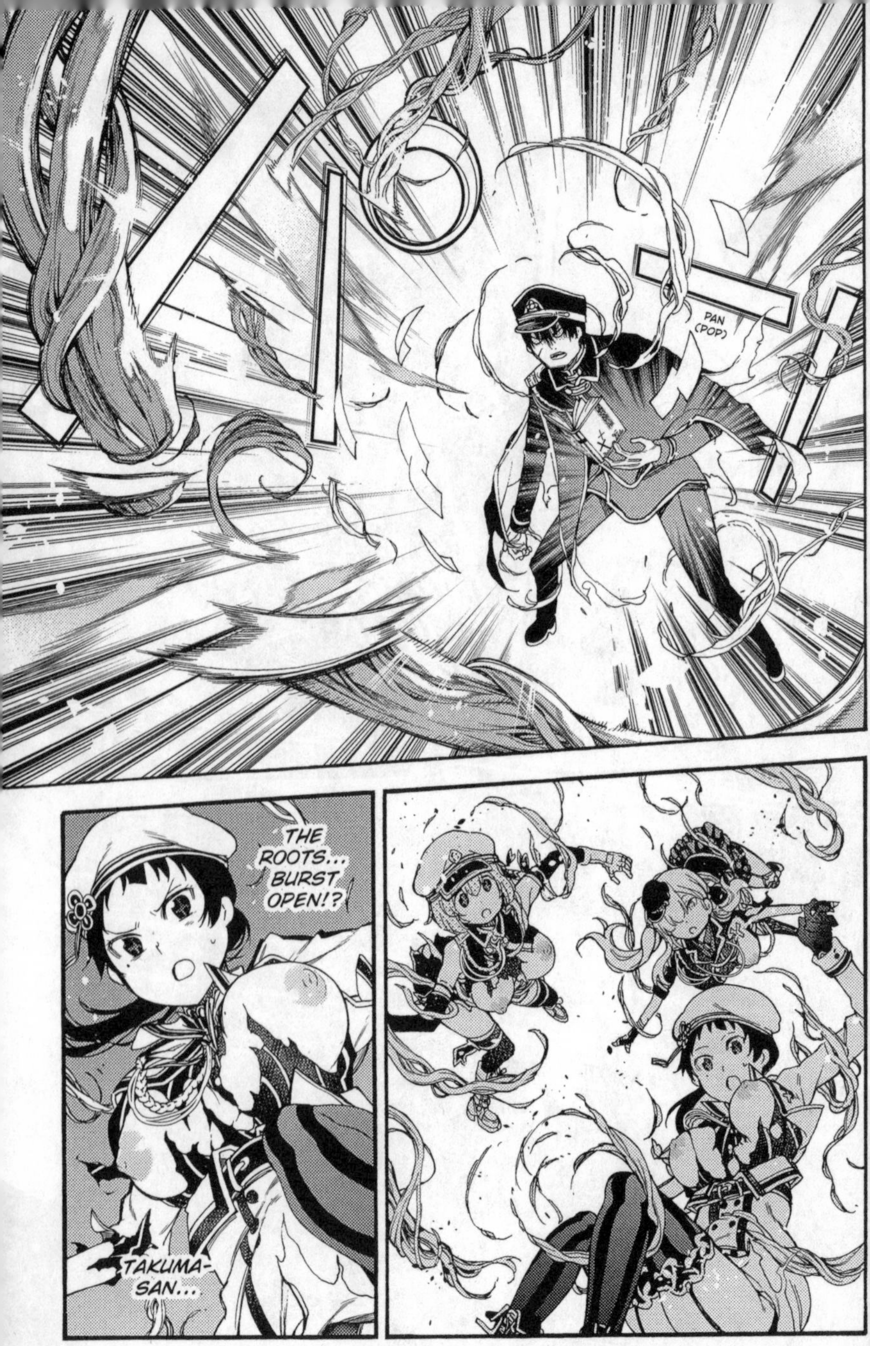
PAN
(POP)
THE ROOTS... BURST OPEN!?
TAKUMA-SAN...

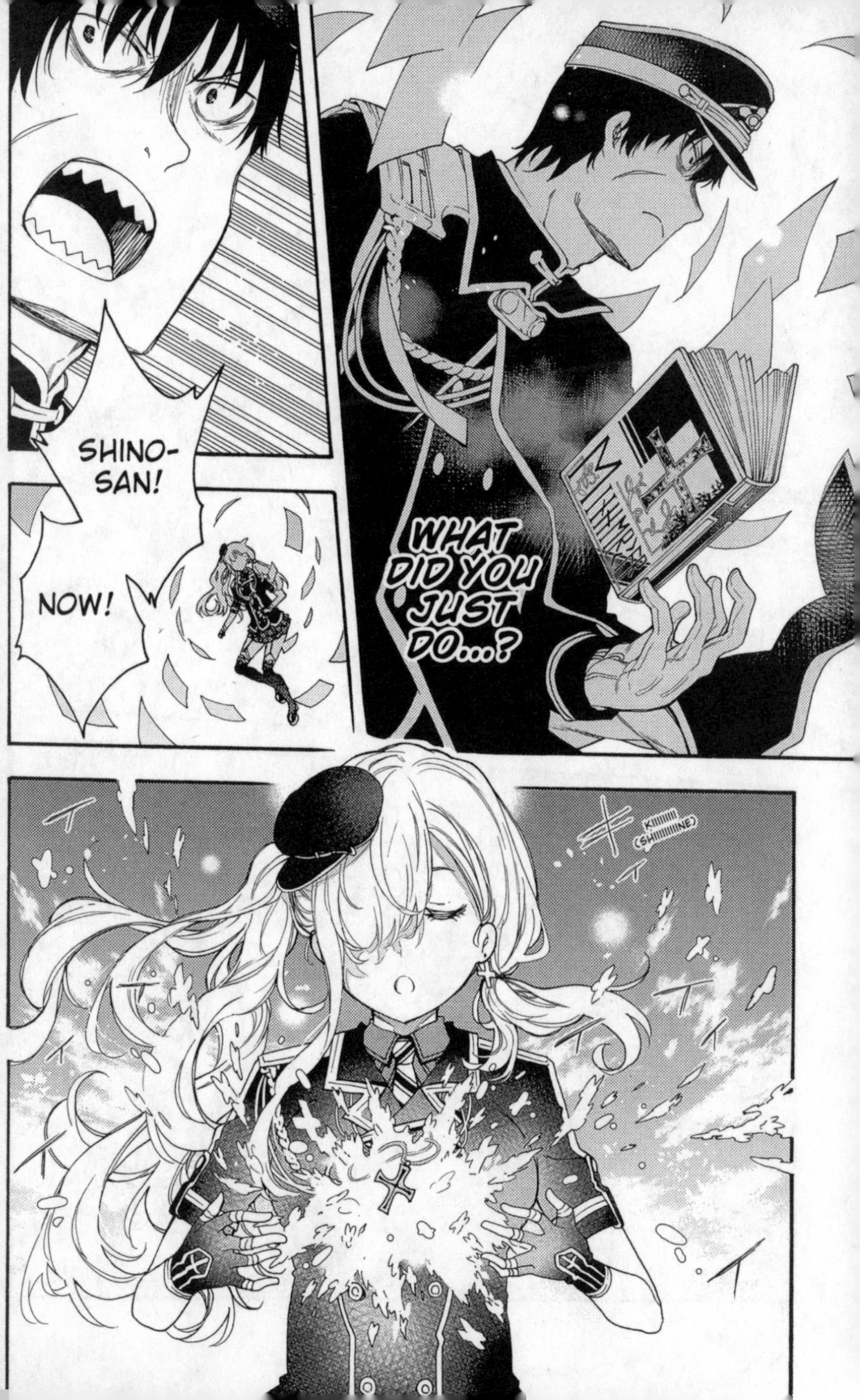
WHAT DID YOU JUST DO...?
SHINO-SAN!
NOW!
KIIIIIIIII (SHIIIIIIIIINE)

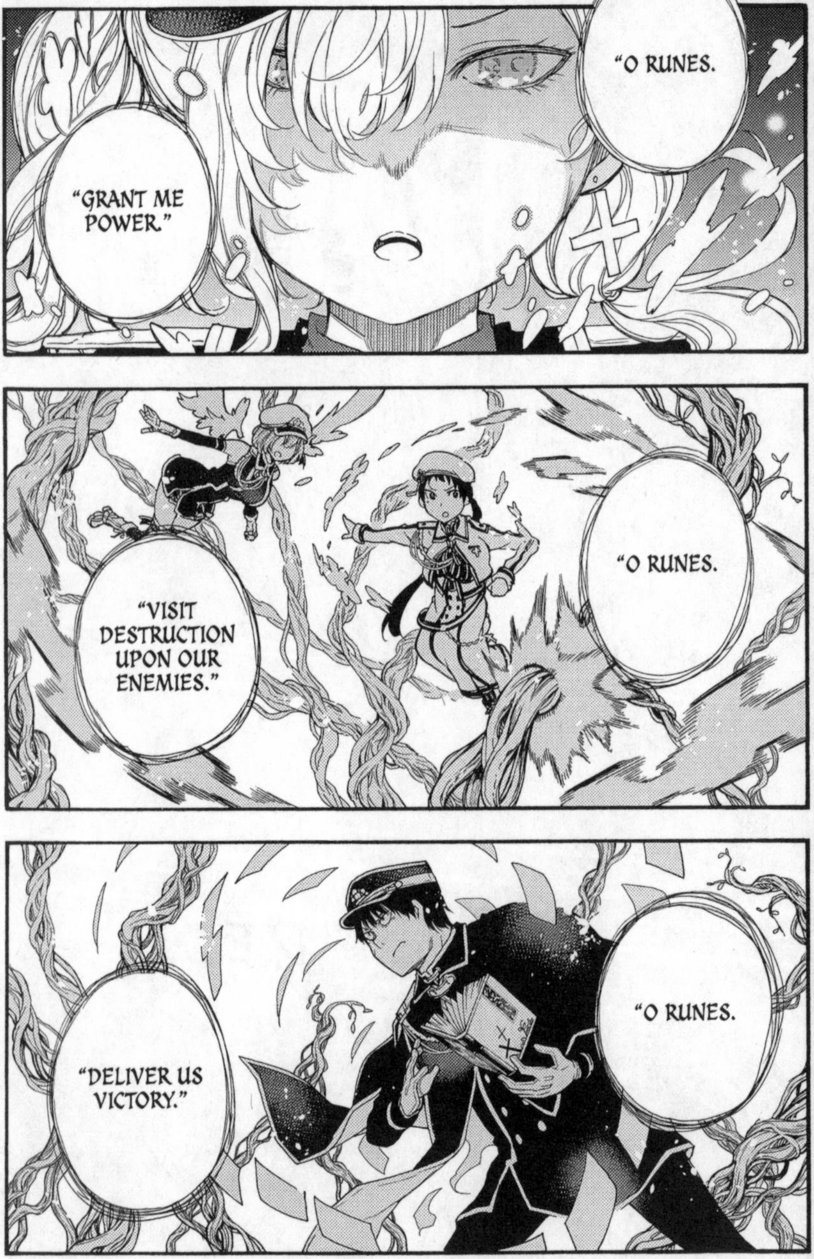
"O RUNES.
"GRANT ME POWER."
"O RUNES.
"VISIT DESTRUCTION UPON OUR ENEMIES."
"O RUNES.
"DELIVER US VICTORY."

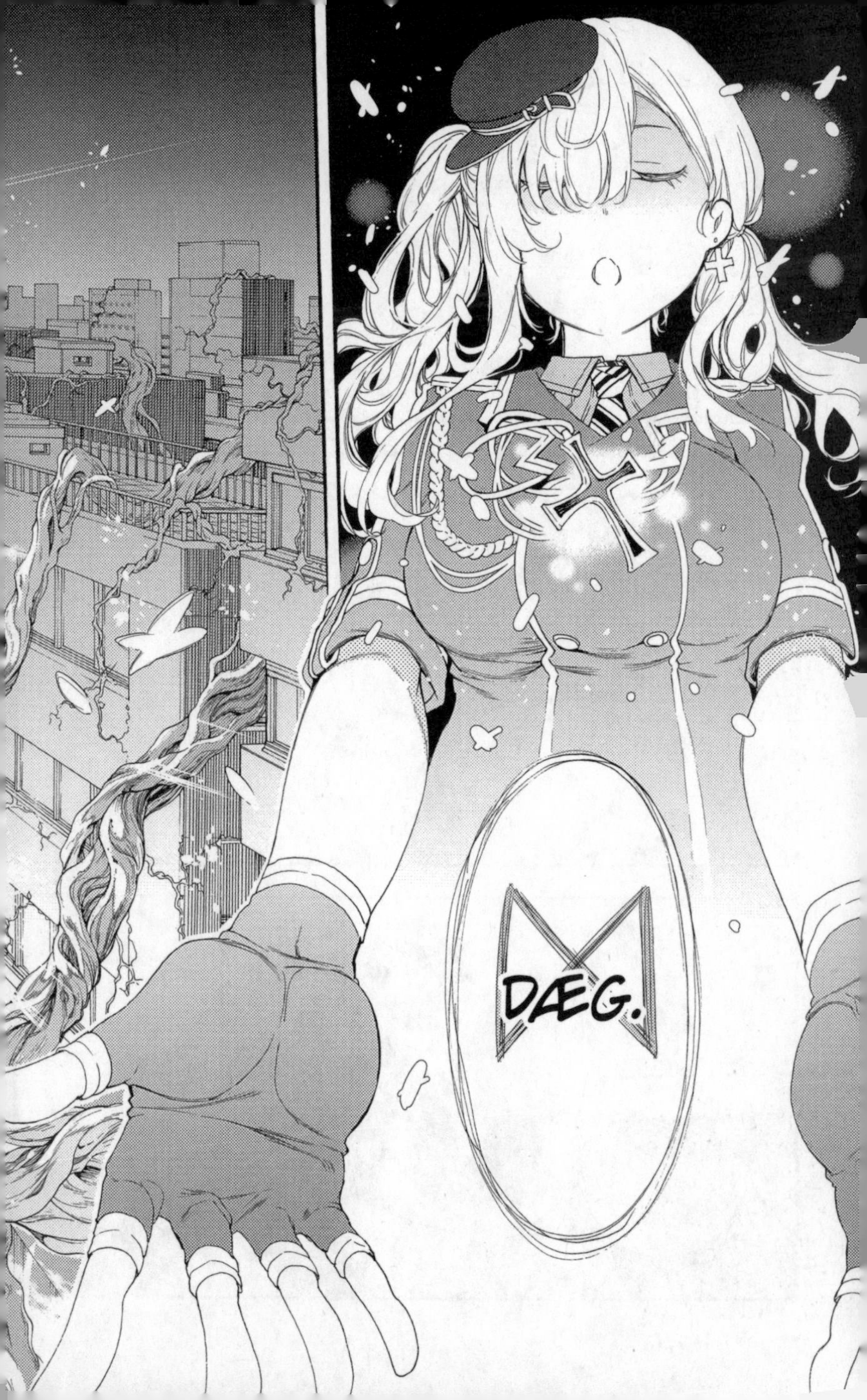
DÆG.

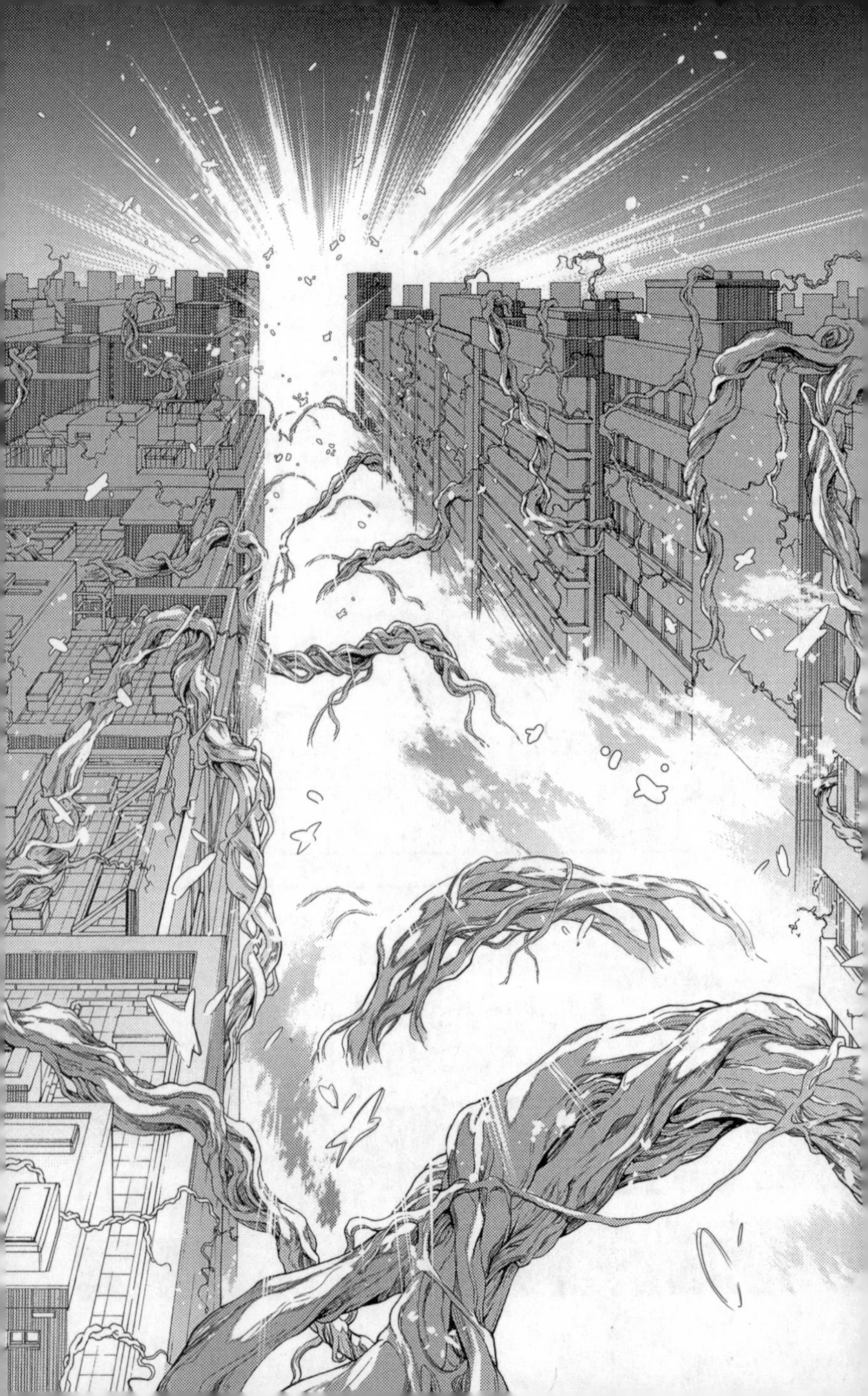

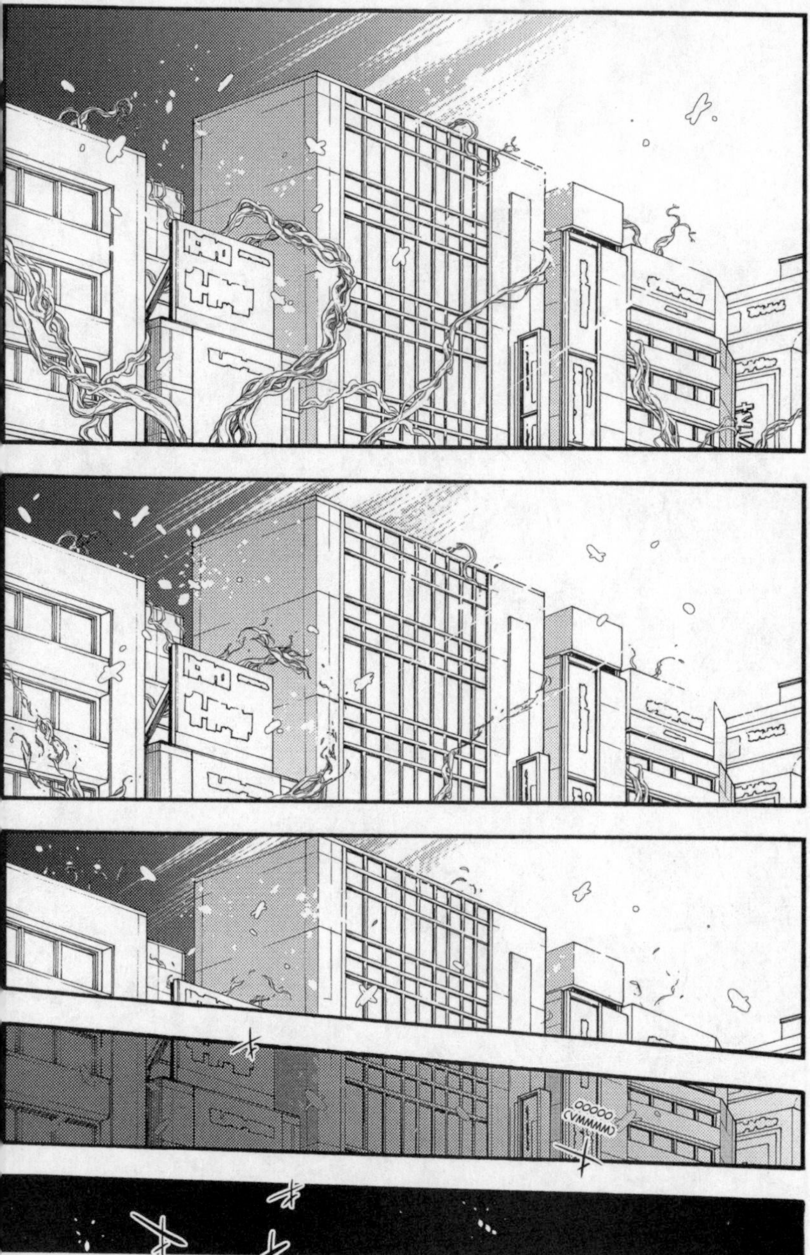
OOOOO
(VMMMM)

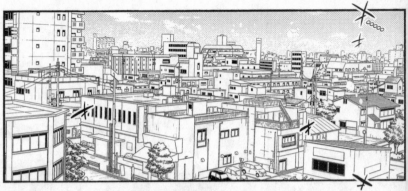

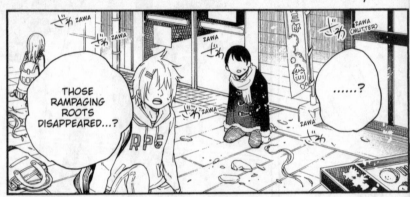

ZAWA (MUTTER)
ZAWA
......?
ZAWA
THOSE RAMPAGING ROOTS DISAPPEARED...?
ZAWA
ZAWA
HEY, OVER HERE! SOMEONE'S BEEN INJURED!
HELP ME OUT!
ZAWA
ZAWA
ZAWA
ZAWA
...LOOKS LIKE IT ALL WORKED.
JARI (GSSRT)

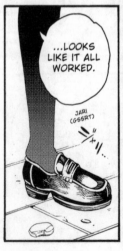

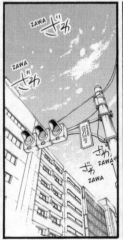

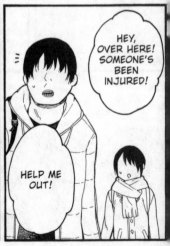

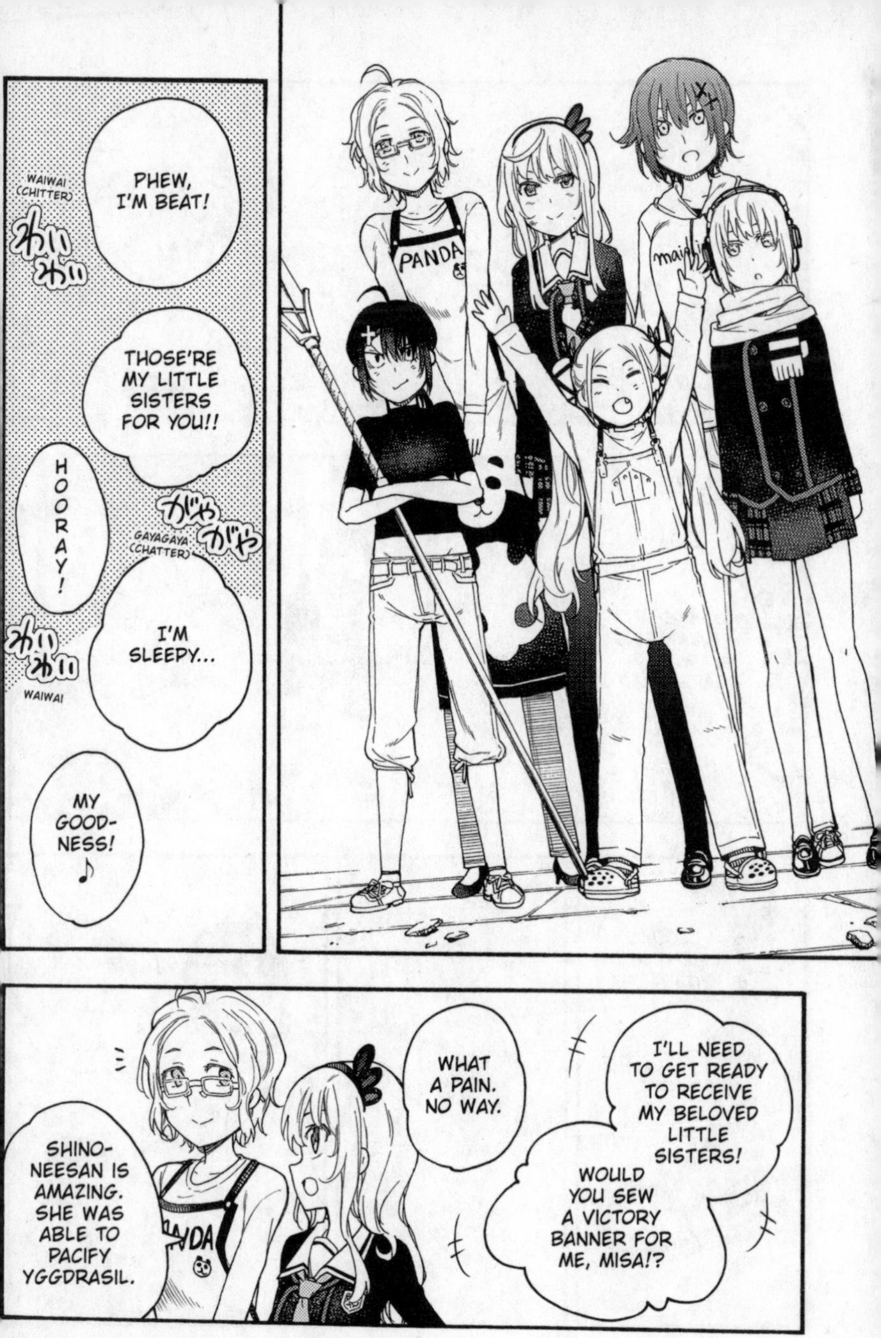
PHEW, I'M BEAT!
WAIWAI (CHITTER)
THOSE'RE MY LITTLE SISTERS FOR YOU!!
GAYAGAYA (CHATTER)
HOORAY!
I'M SLEEPY...
WAIWAI
MY GOOD-NESS! ♪
I'LL NEED TO GET READY TO RECEIVE MY BELOVED LITTLE SISTERS!
WOULD YOU SEW A VICTORY BANNER FOR ME, MISA!?
WHAT A PAIN. NO WAY.
SHINO-NEESAN IS AMAZING. SHE WAS ABLE TO PACIFY YGGDRASIL.

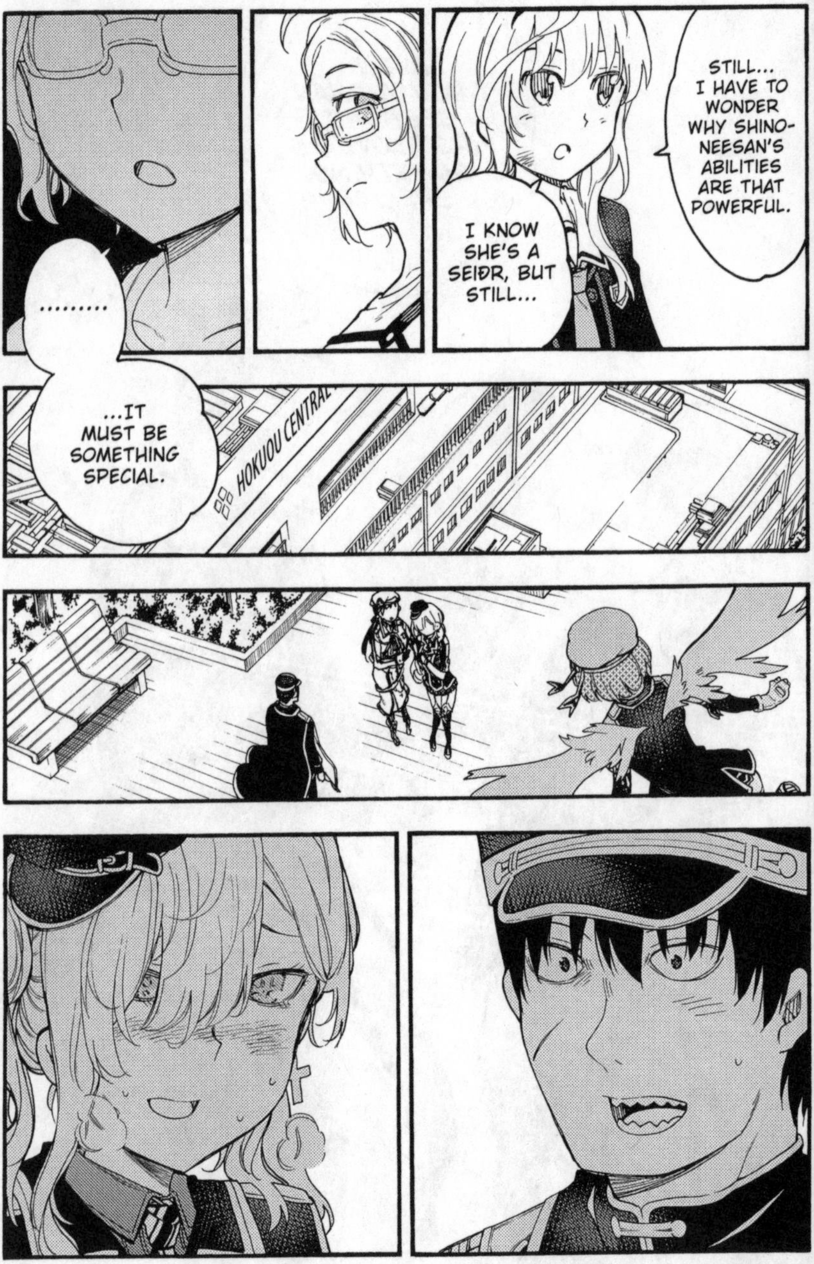
STILL... I HAVE TO WONDER WHY SHINO-NEESAN'S ABILITIES ARE THAT POWERFUL.
I KNOW SHE'S A SEIÐR, BUT STILL...
....
...IT MUST BE SOMETHING SPECIAL.
HOKUOU CENTRAL

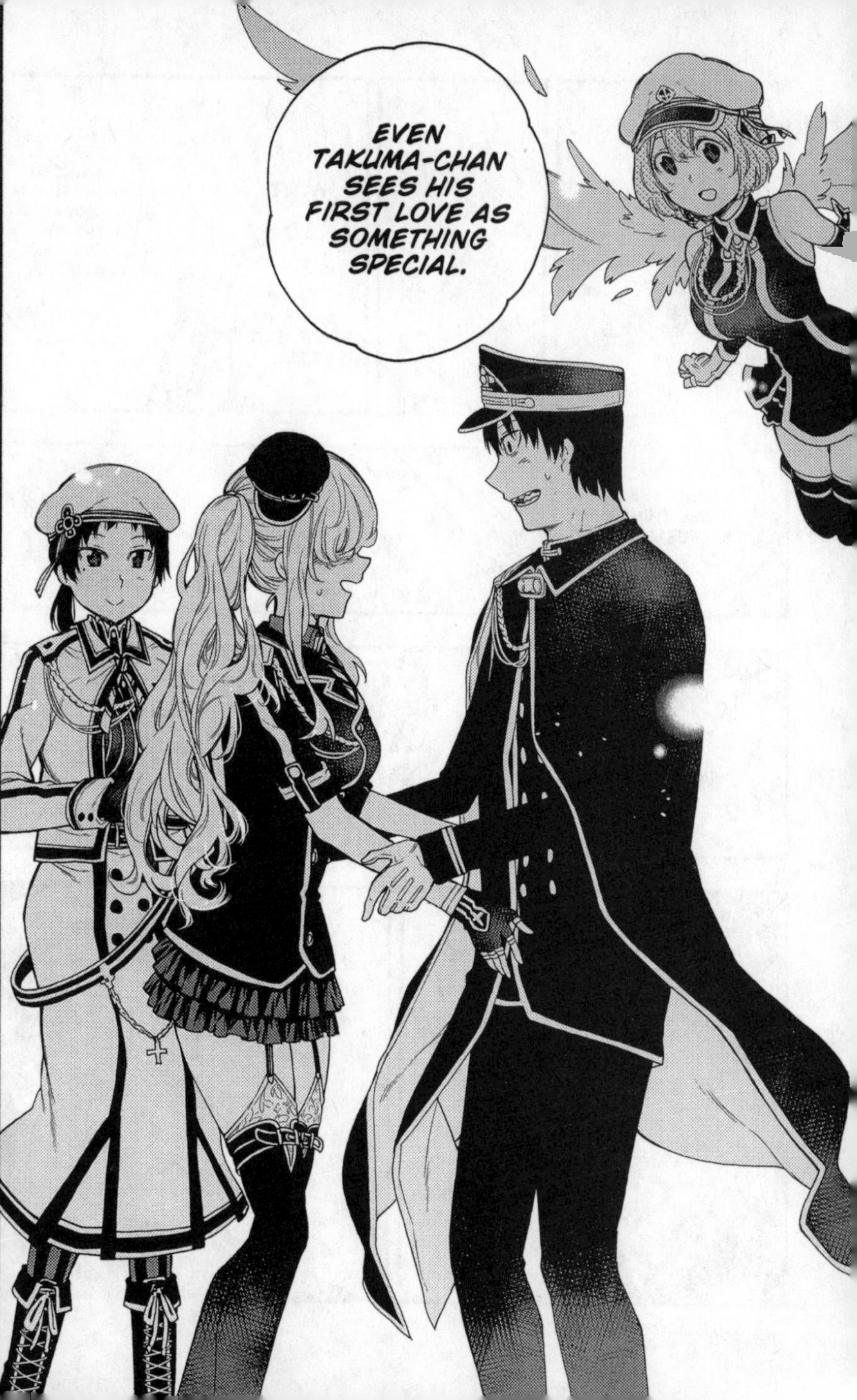
EVEN TAKUMA-CHAN SEES HIS FIRST LOVE AS SOMETHING SPECIAL.

Val × Love

PAKI
(KRAK)

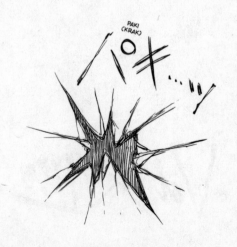

Chapter 51

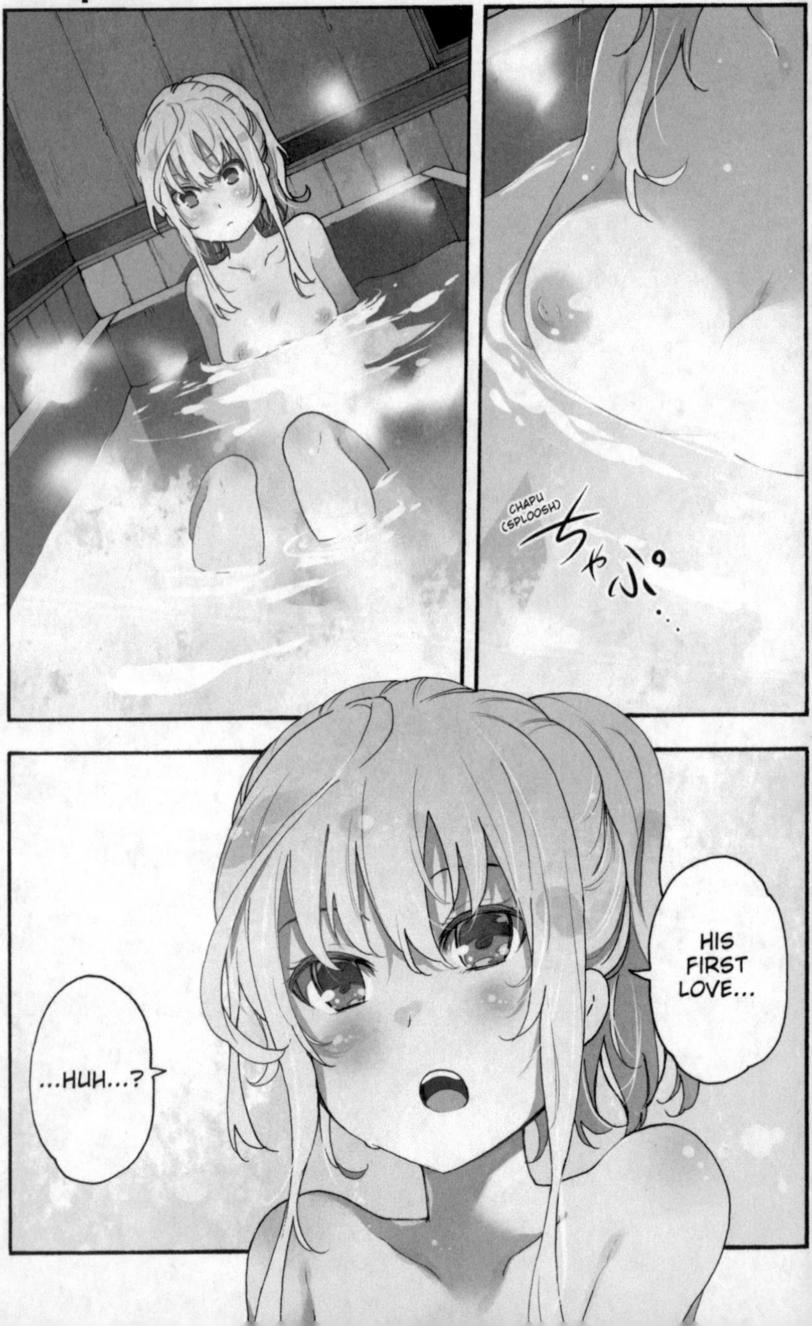
CHAPU (SPLOOSH)
ちゃぷ…
HIS FIRST LOVE...
...HUH...?

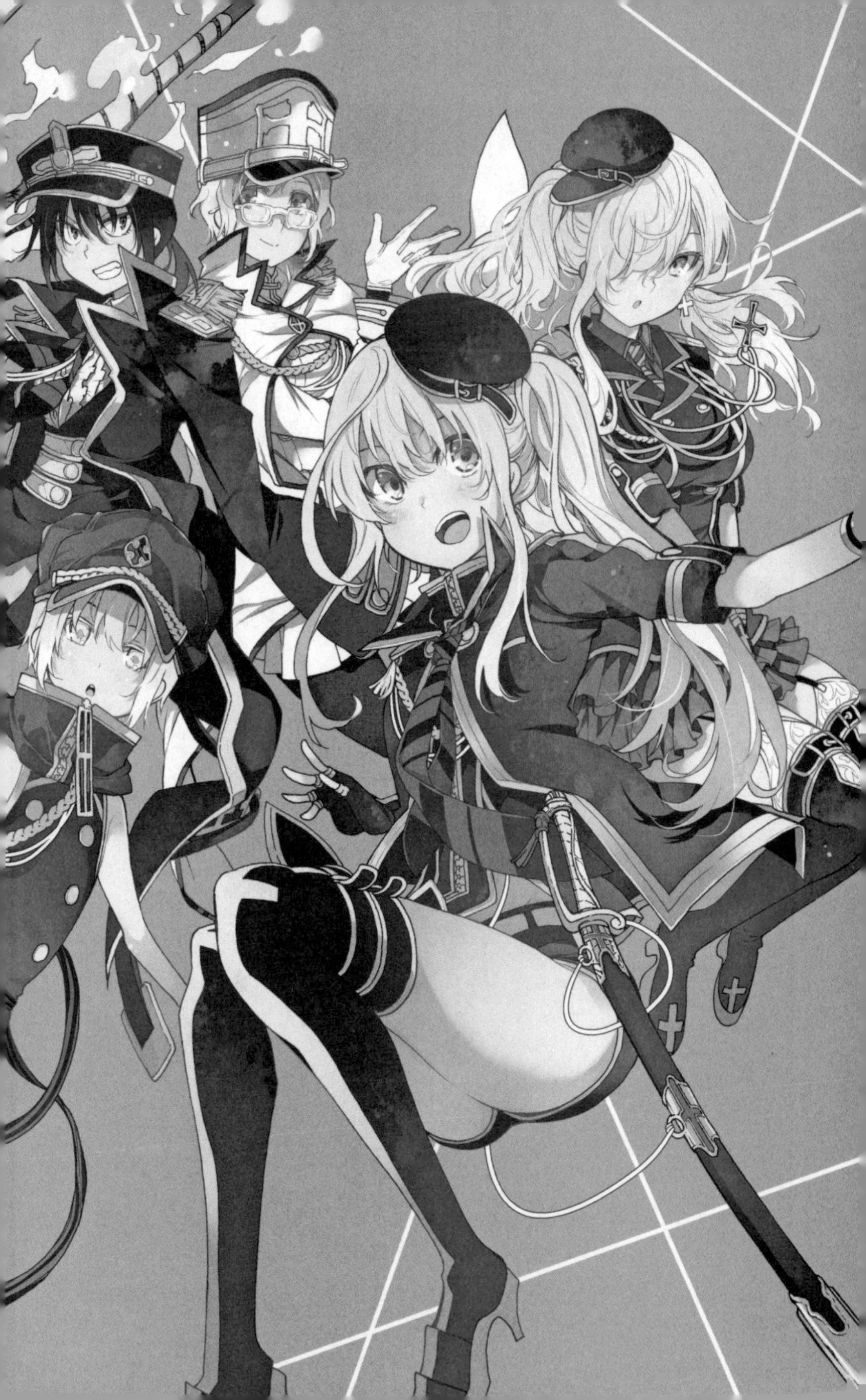

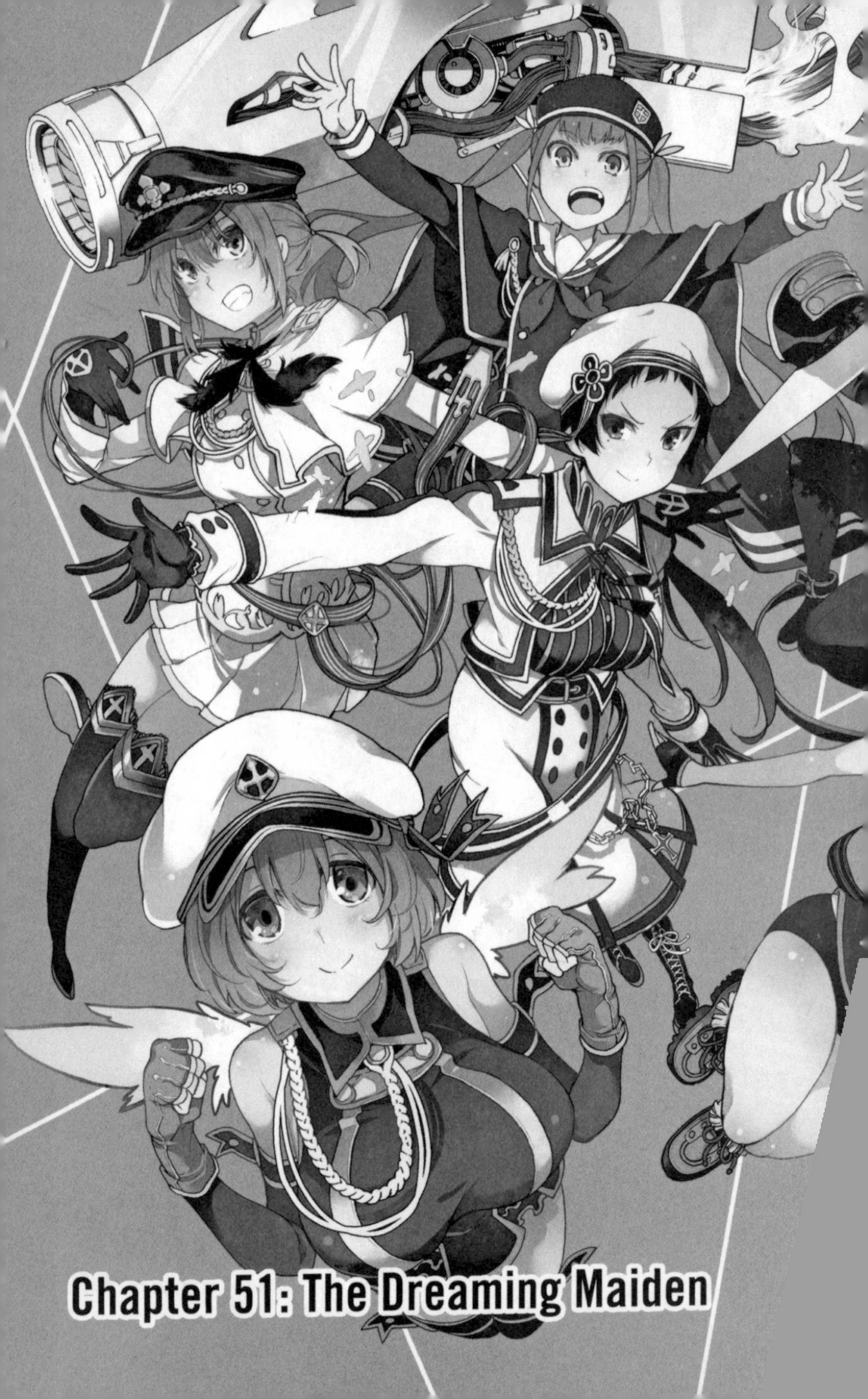
Chapter 51: The Dreaming Maiden

Val × Löve

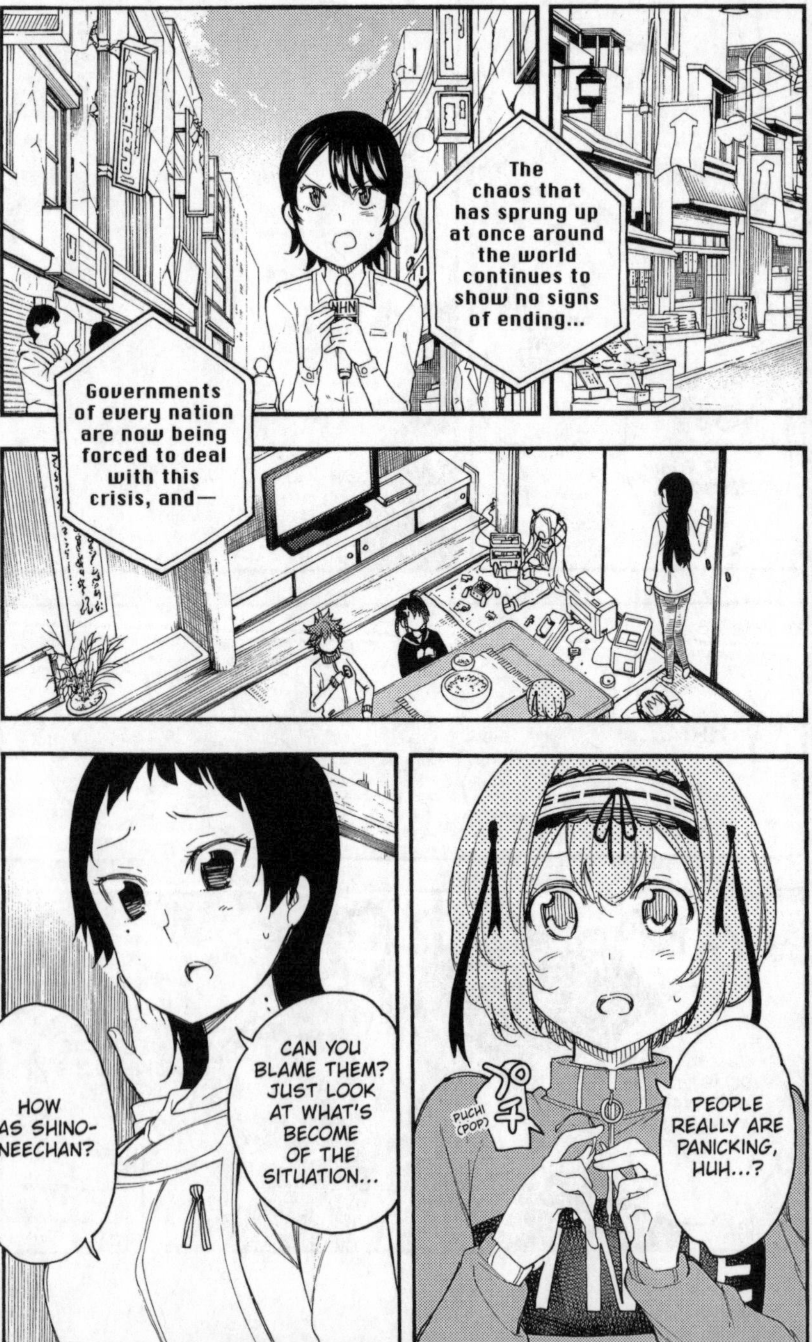
The chaos that has sprung up at once around the world continues to show no signs of ending...
Governments of every nation are now being forced to deal with this crisis, and—
NHN
PEOPLE REALLY ARE PANICKING, HUH...?
PUCHI (POP)
CAN YOU BLAME THEM? JUST LOOK AT WHAT'S BECOME OF THE SITUATION...
HOW WAS SHINO-ONEECHAN?

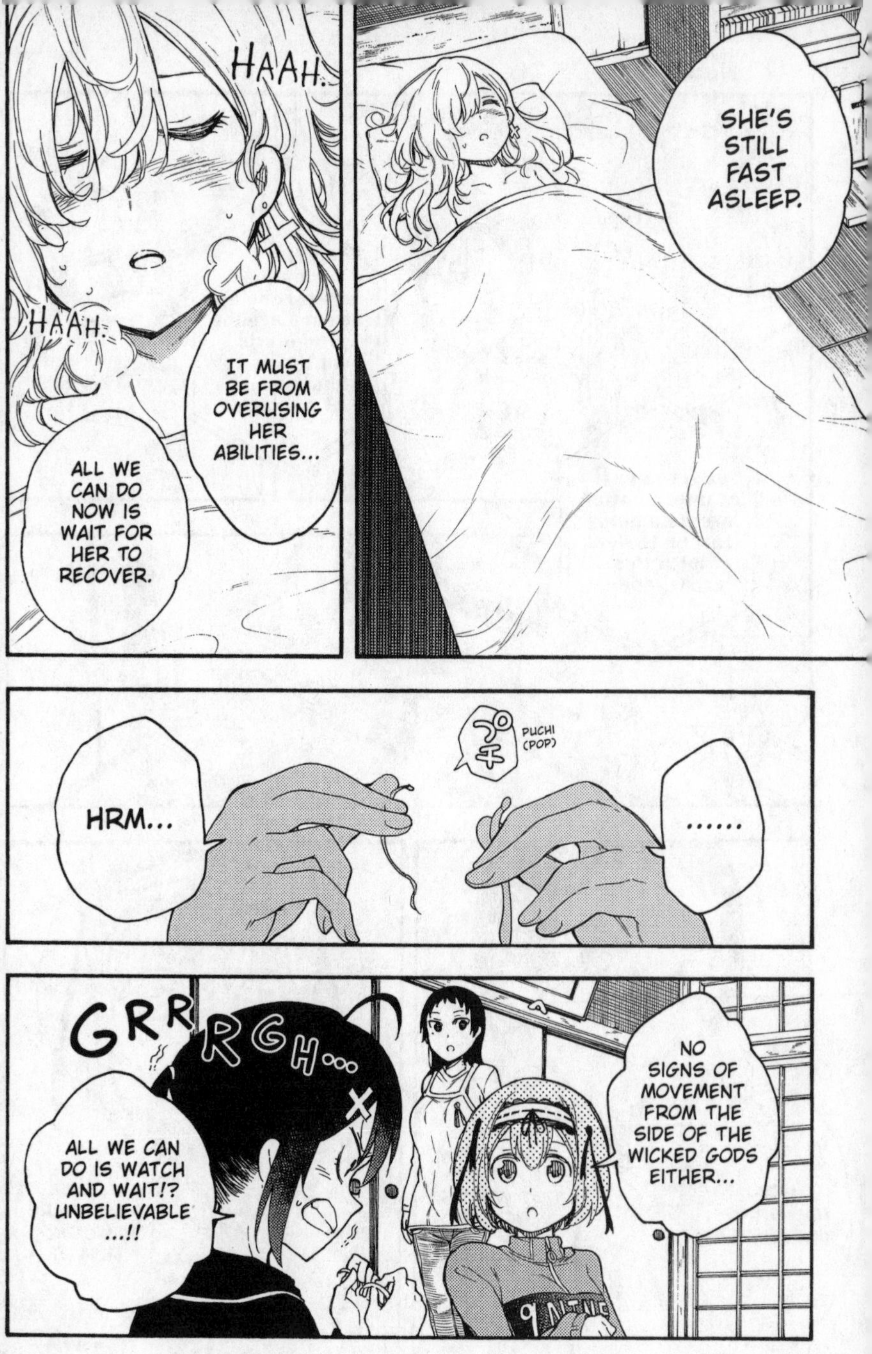
SHE'S STILL FAST ASLEEP.
HAAH.
IT MUST BE FROM OVERUSING HER ABILITIES...
HAAH.
ALL WE CAN DO NOW IS WAIT FOR HER TO RECOVER.
......
プチ
PUCHI (POP)
HRM...
NO SIGNS OF MOVEMENT FROM THE SIDE OF THE WICKED GODS EITHER...
GRRRGH...
ALL WE CAN DO IS WATCH AND WAIT!? UNBELIEVABLE ...!!

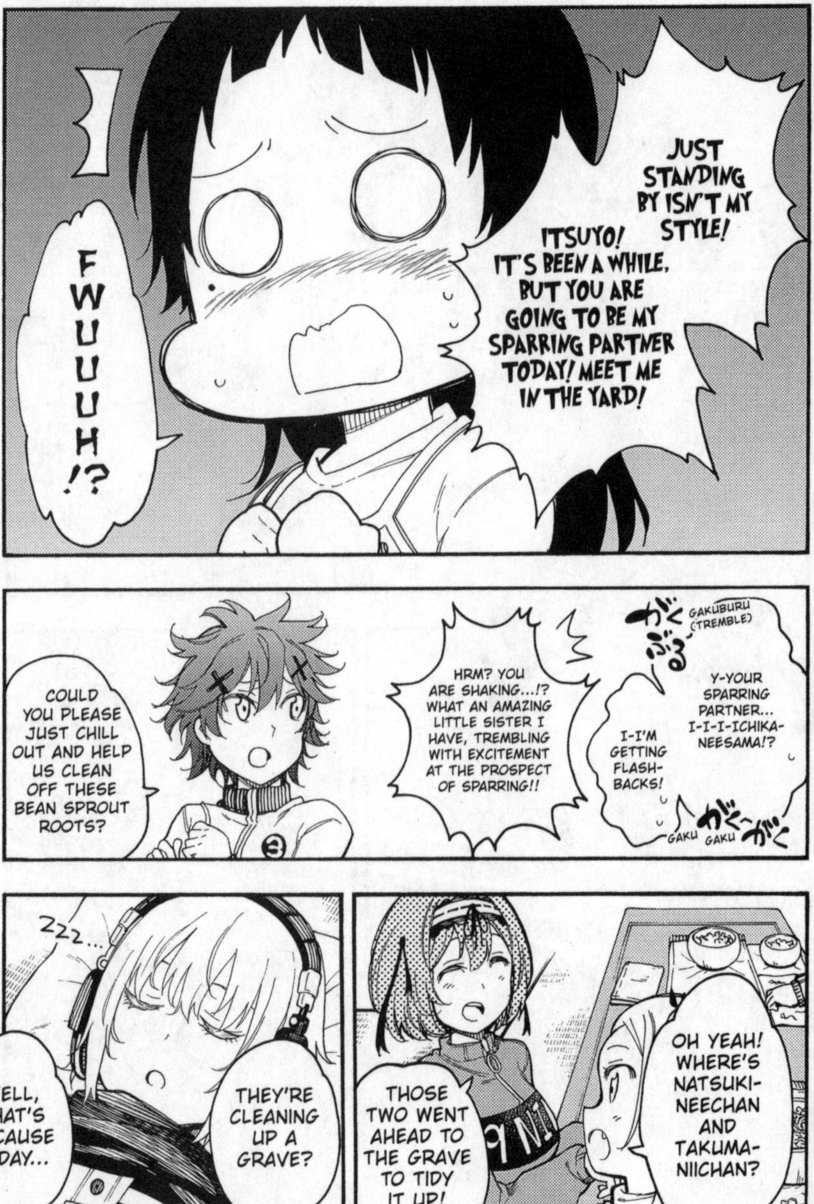
JUST STANDING BY ISN'T MY STYLE!
ITSUYO! IT'S BEEN A WHILE, BUT YOU ARE GOING TO BE MY SPARRING PARTNER TODAY! MEET ME IN THE YARD!
!
FWUUUUH!?
GAKUBURU (TREMBLE)
Y-YOUR SPARRING PARTNER... I-I-I-ICHIKA-NEESAMA!?
I-I'M GETTING FLASH-BACKS!
GAKU GAKU
HRM? YOU ARE SHAKING...!? WHAT AN AMAZING LITTLE SISTER I HAVE, TREMBLING WITH EXCITEMENT AT THE PROSPECT OF SPARRING!!
COULD YOU PLEASE JUST CHILL OUT AND HELP US CLEAN OFF THESE BEAN SPROUT ROOTS?
OH YEAH! WHERE'S NATSUKI-NEECHAN AND TAKUMA-NIICHAN?
THOSE TWO WENT AHEAD TO THE GRAVE TO TIDY IT UP! ♪
ZZZ...
THEY'RE CLEANING UP A GRAVE?
WELL, THAT'S BECAUSE TODAY...

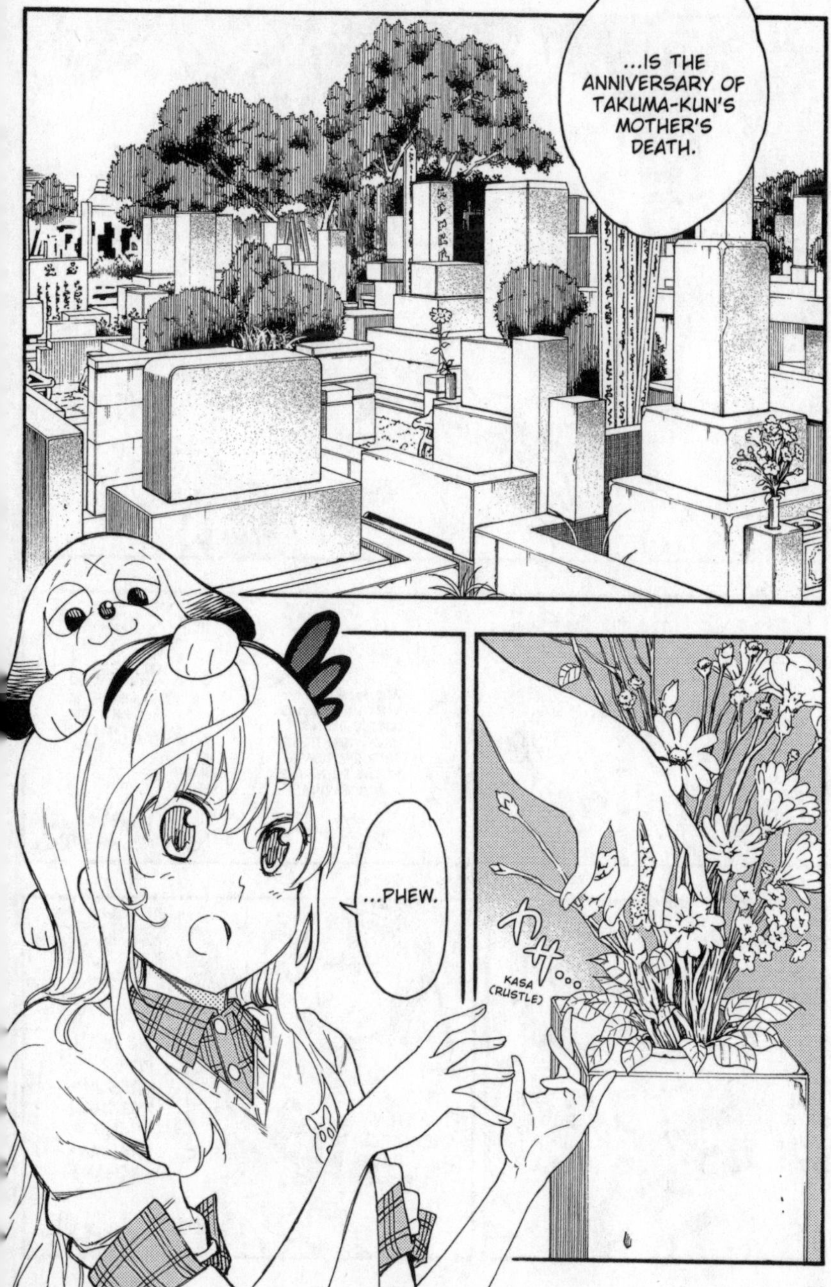
...IS THE ANNIVERSARY OF TAKUMA-KUN'S MOTHER'S DEATH.
カサ
KASA (RUSTLE)
...PHEW.

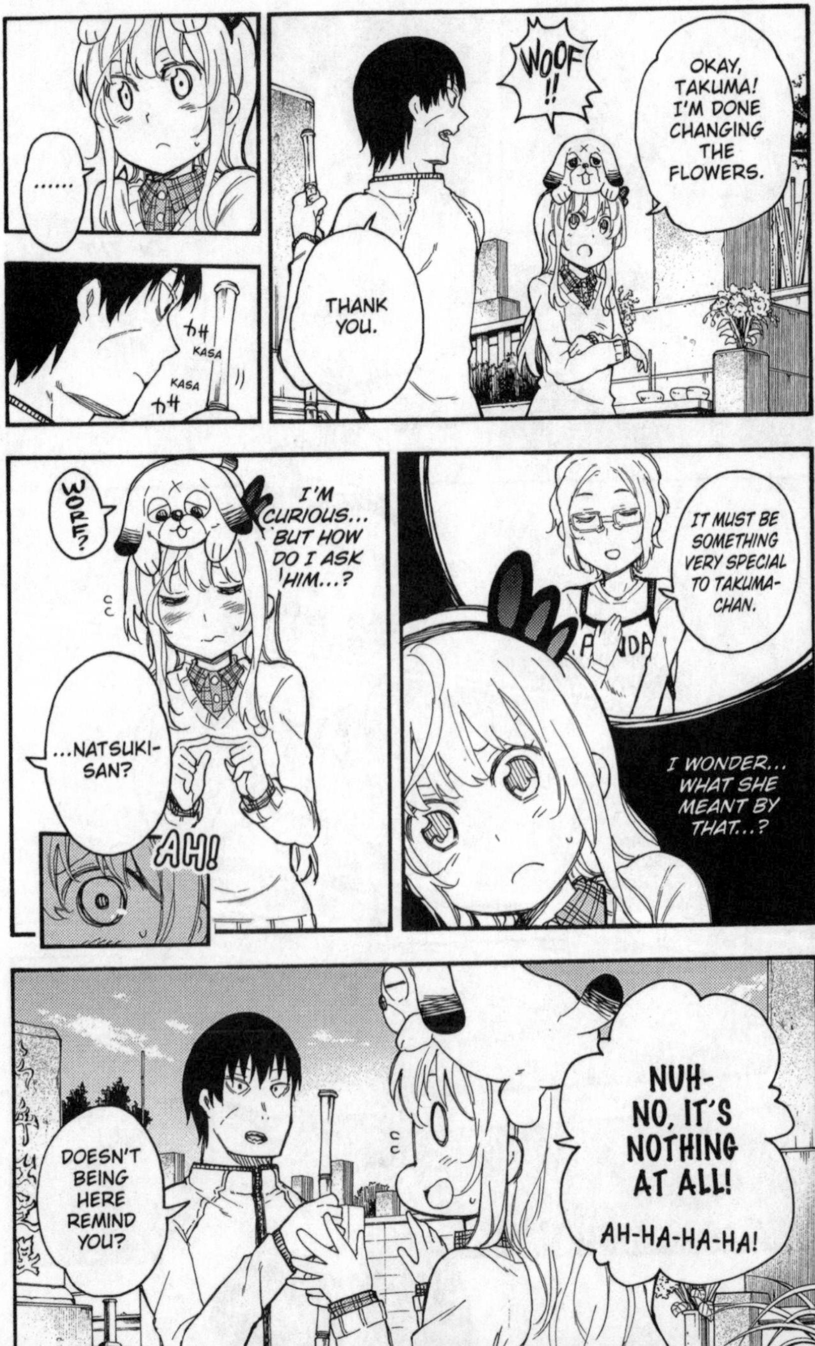
OKAY, TAKUMA! I'M DONE CHANGING THE FLOWERS.
WOOF!!
THANK YOU.
......
KASA
KASA
IT MUST BE SOMETHING VERY SPECIAL TO TAKUMA-CHAN.
I WONDER... WHAT SHE MEANT BY THAT...?
I'M CURIOUS... BUT HOW DO I ASK HIM...?
WORF?
...NATSUKI-SAN?
AH!
NUH-NO, IT'S NOTHING AT ALL!
AH-HA-HA-HA!
DOESN'T BEING HERE REMIND YOU?

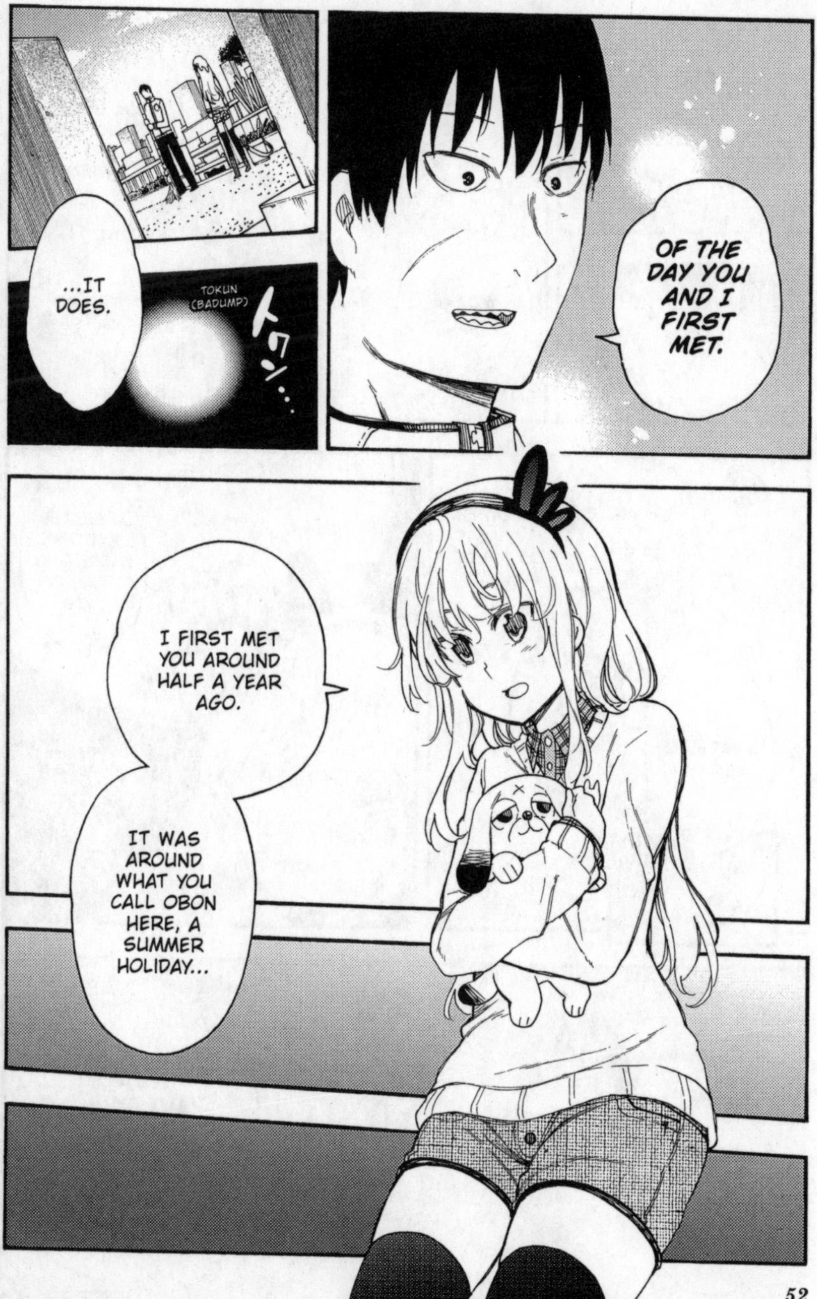
OF THE DAY YOU AND I FIRST MET.
...IT DOES.
TOKUN (BADUMP)
I FIRST MET YOU AROUND HALF A YEAR AGO.
IT WAS AROUND WHAT YOU CALL OBON HERE, A SUMMER HOLIDAY...

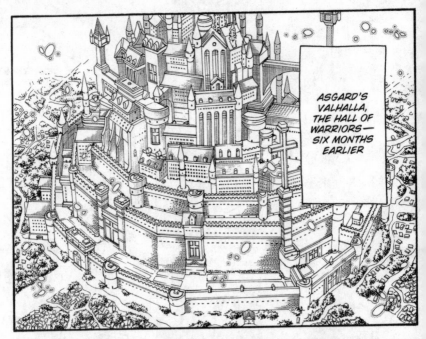

ASGARD'S VALHALLA, THE HALL OF WARRIORS— SIX MONTHS EARLIER

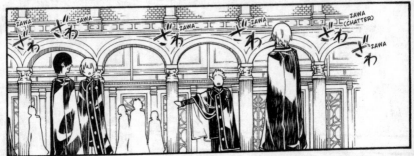

ZAWA ZAWA ZAWA ZAWA ZAWA ZAWA (ZAWA (CHATTER)) ZAWA

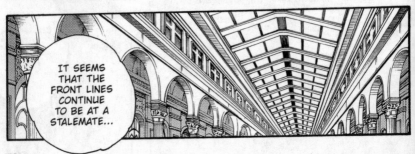

IT SEEMS THAT THE FRONT LINES CONTINUE TO BE AT A STALEMATE...

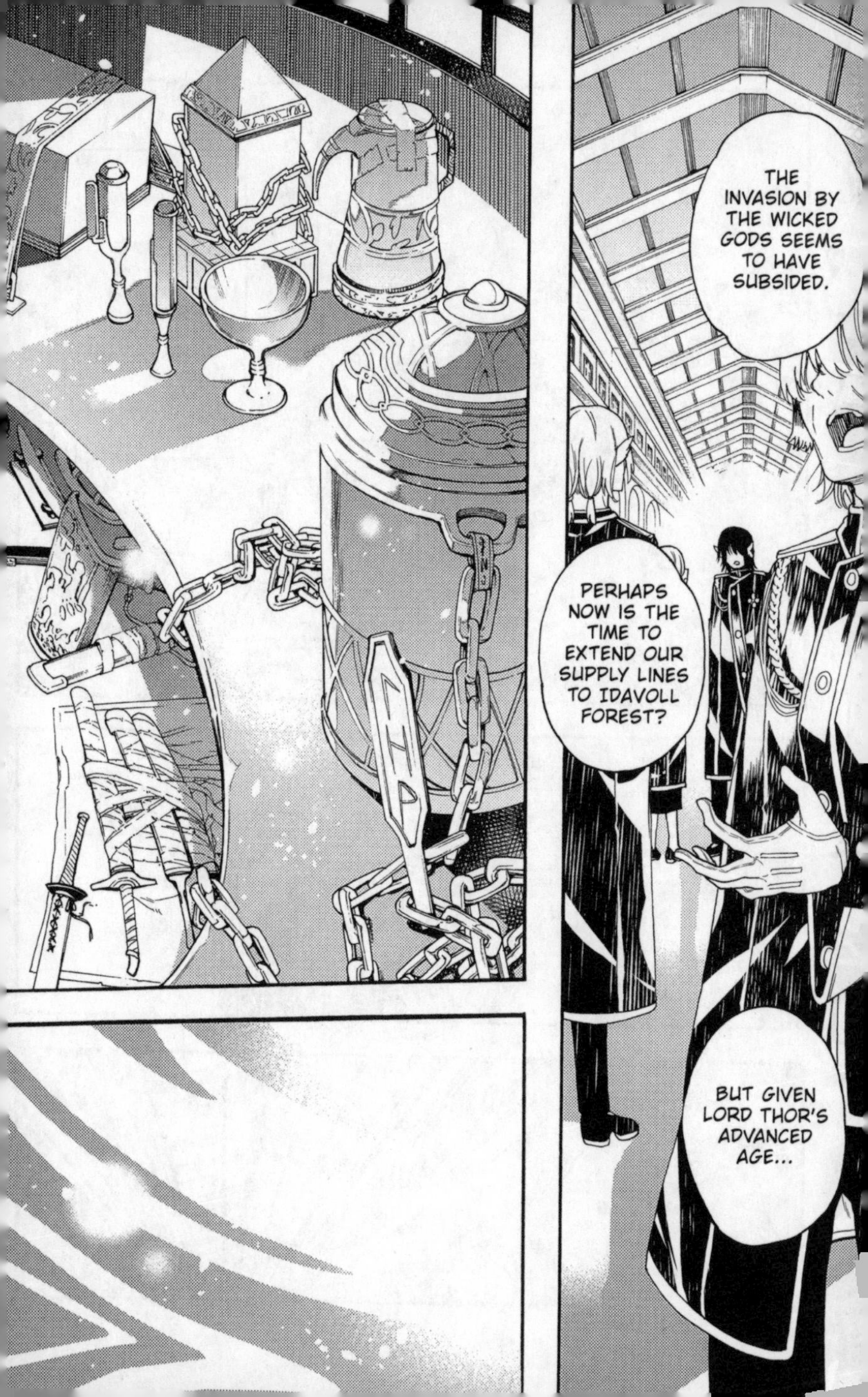
THE INVASION BY THE WICKED GODS SEEMS TO HAVE SUBSIDED.
PERHAPS NOW IS THE TIME TO EXTEND OUR SUPPLY LINES TO IDAVOLL FOREST?
BUT GIVEN LORD THOR'S ADVANCED AGE...

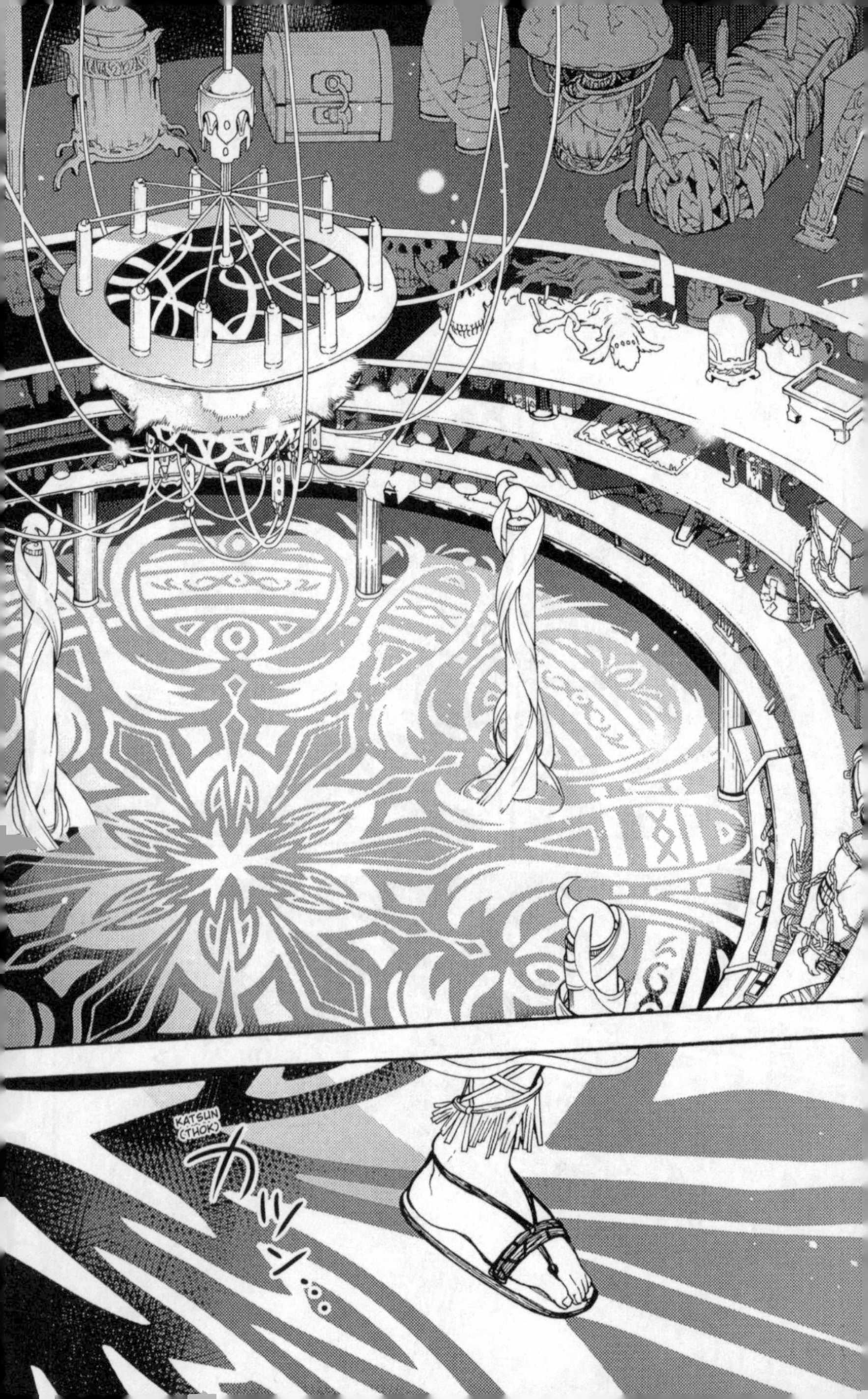
KATSUN (THOK)
カツーン…

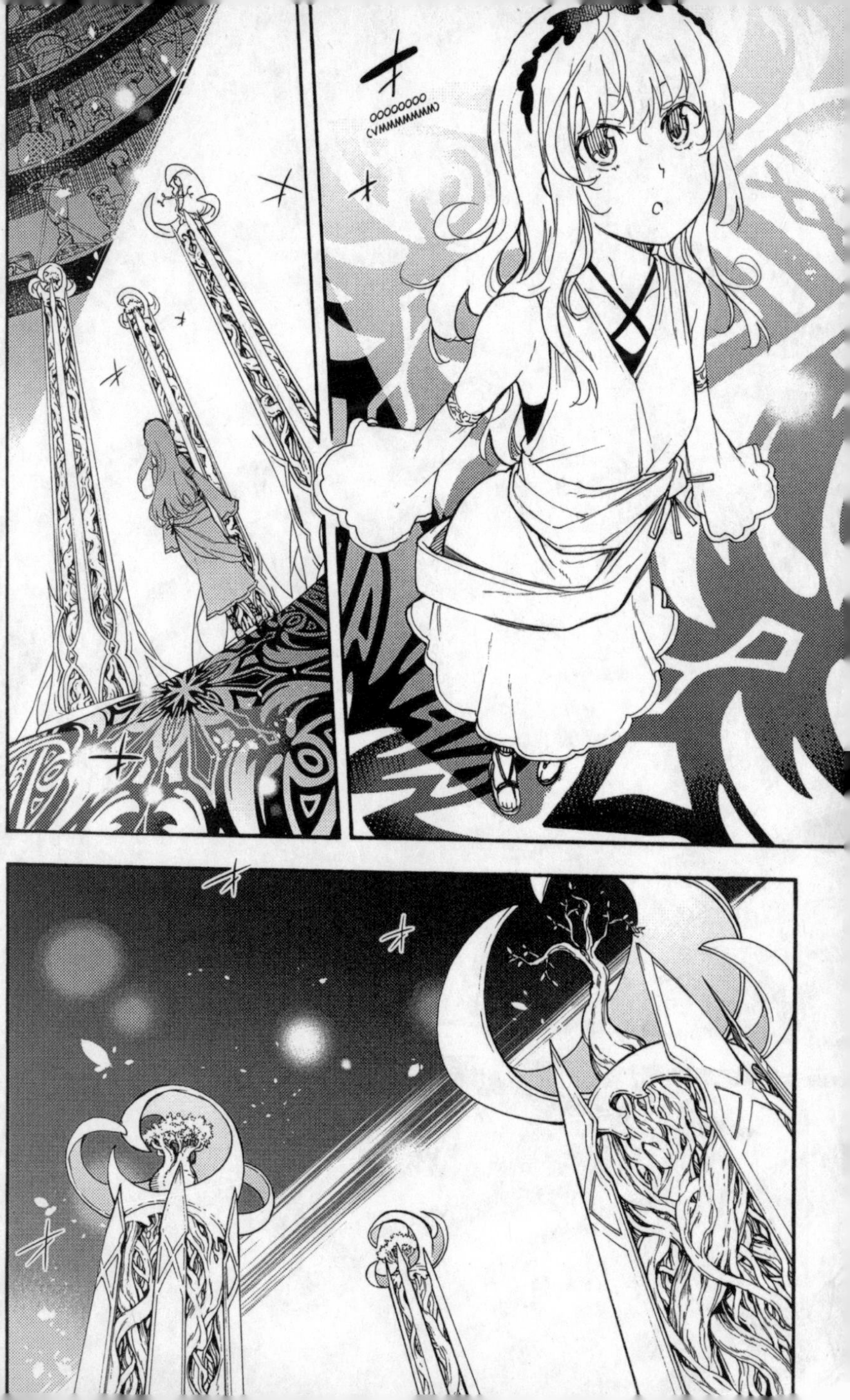
OOOOOOOO
(VMMMMMMMM)

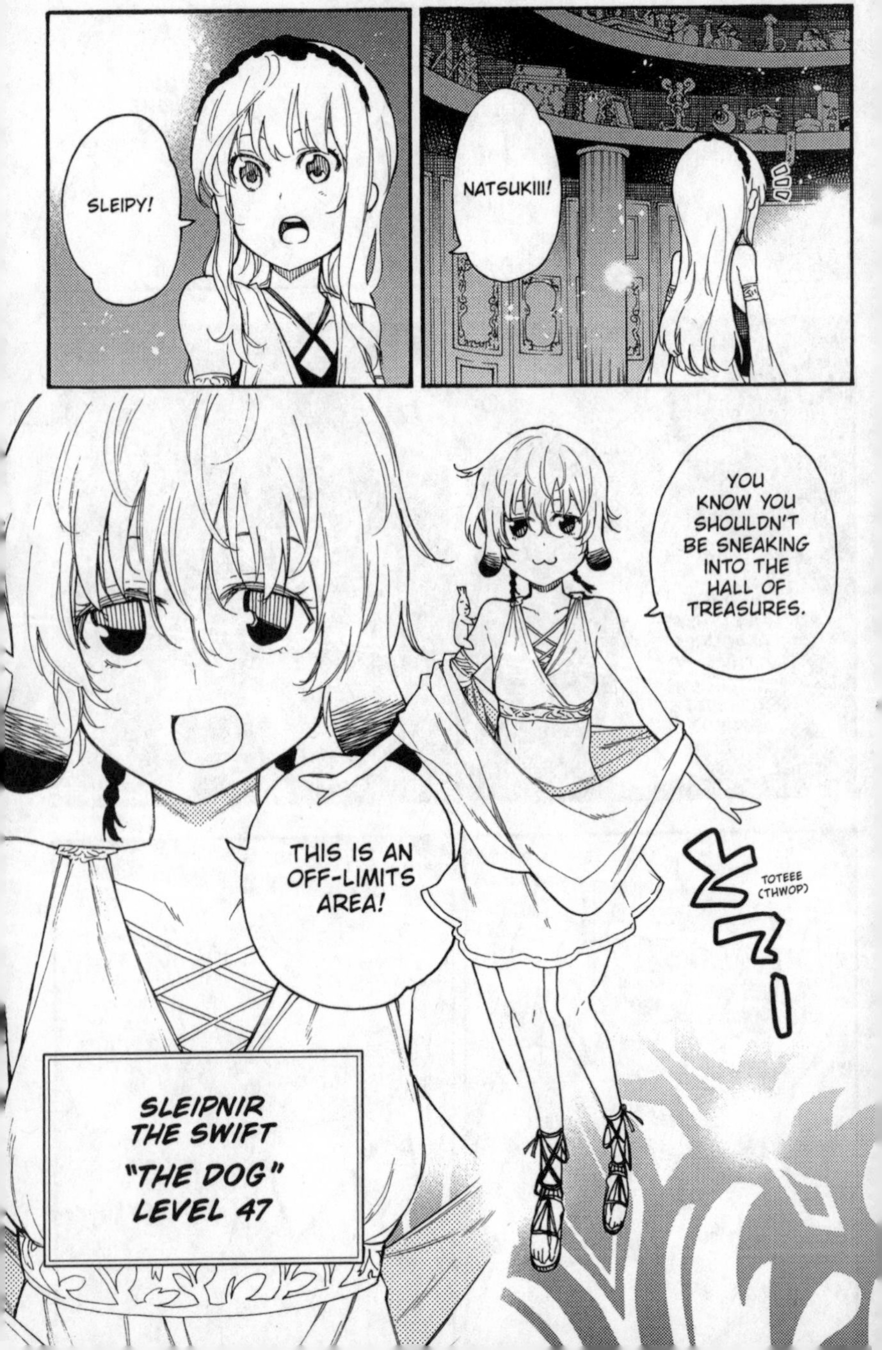
NATSUKIII!
SLEIPY!
YOU KNOW YOU SHOULDN'T BE SNEAKING INTO THE HALL OF TREASURES.
TOTEEE (THWOP)
THIS IS AN OFF-LIMITS AREA!
SLEIPNIR THE SWIFT "THE DOG" LEVEL 47

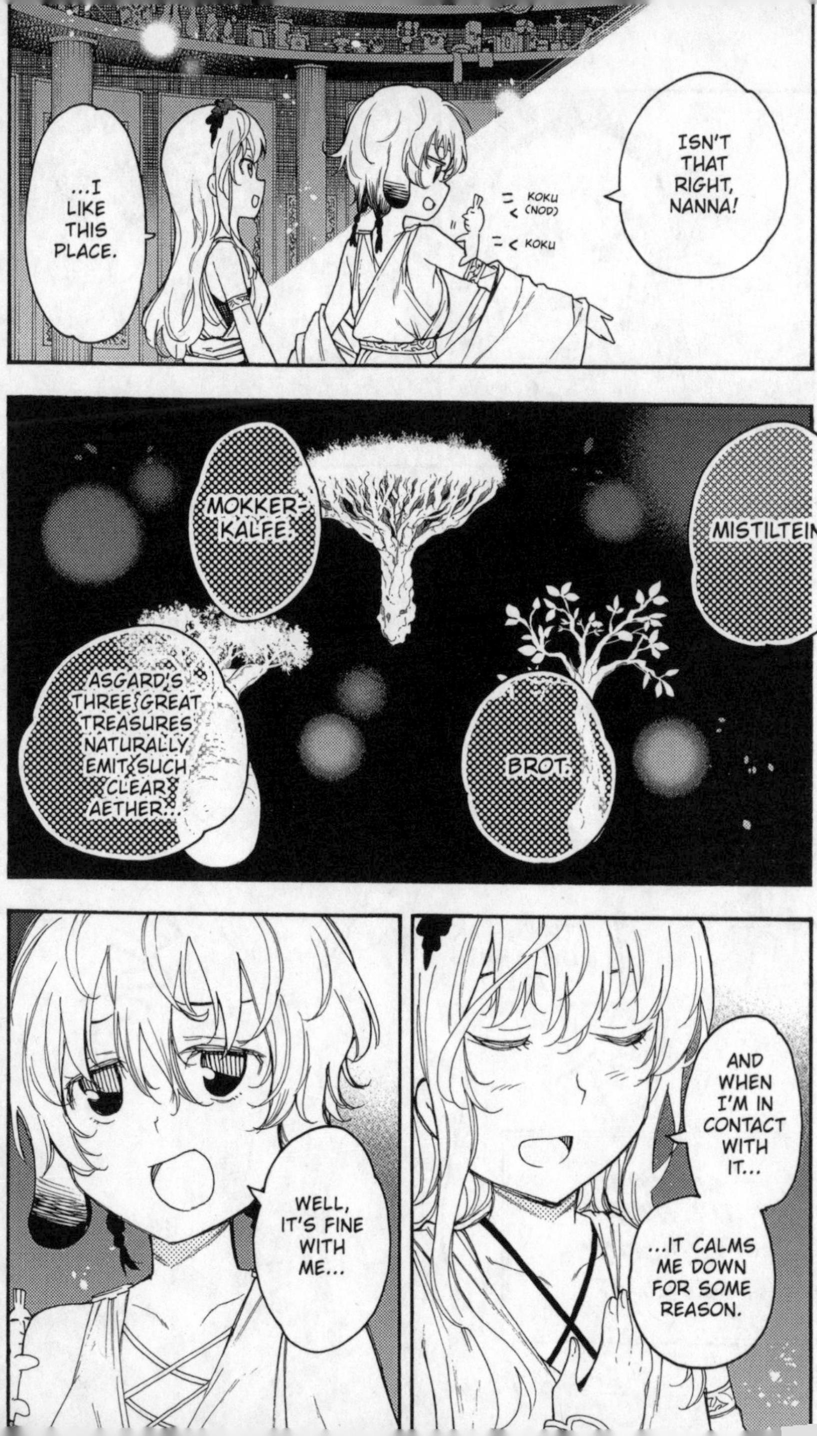
ISN'T THAT RIGHT, NANNA!
KOKU (NOD)
KOKU
...I LIKE THIS PLACE.
MISTILTEINN.
MOKKER-KALFE.
BROT.
ASGARD'S THREE GREAT TREASURES NATURALLY EMIT SUCH CLEAR AETHER...
AND WHEN I'M IN CONTACT WITH IT...
...IT CALMS ME DOWN FOR SOME REASON.
WELL, IT'S FINE WITH ME...

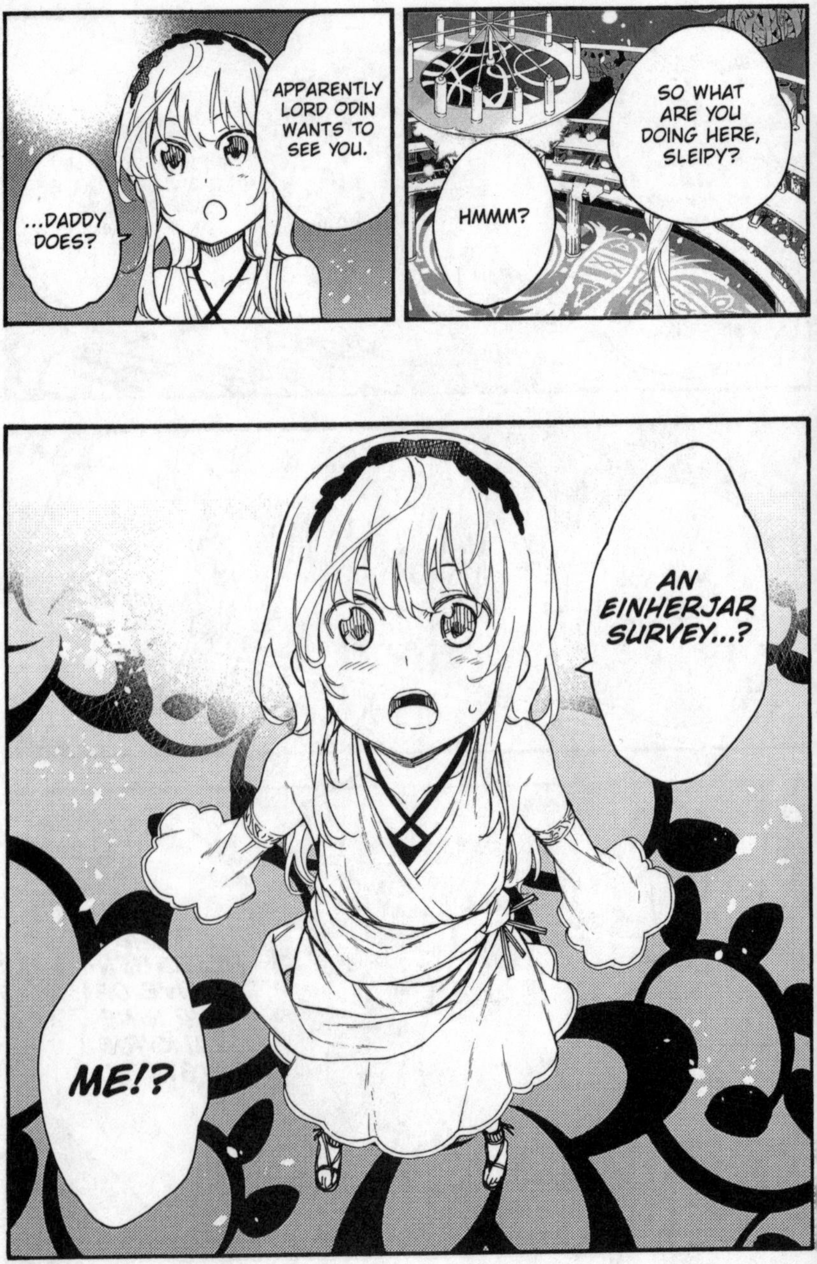
SO WHAT ARE YOU DOING HERE, SLEIPY?
HMMM?
APPARENTLY LORD ODIN WANTS TO SEE YOU.
...DADDY DOES?
AN EINHERJAR SURVEY...?
ME!?

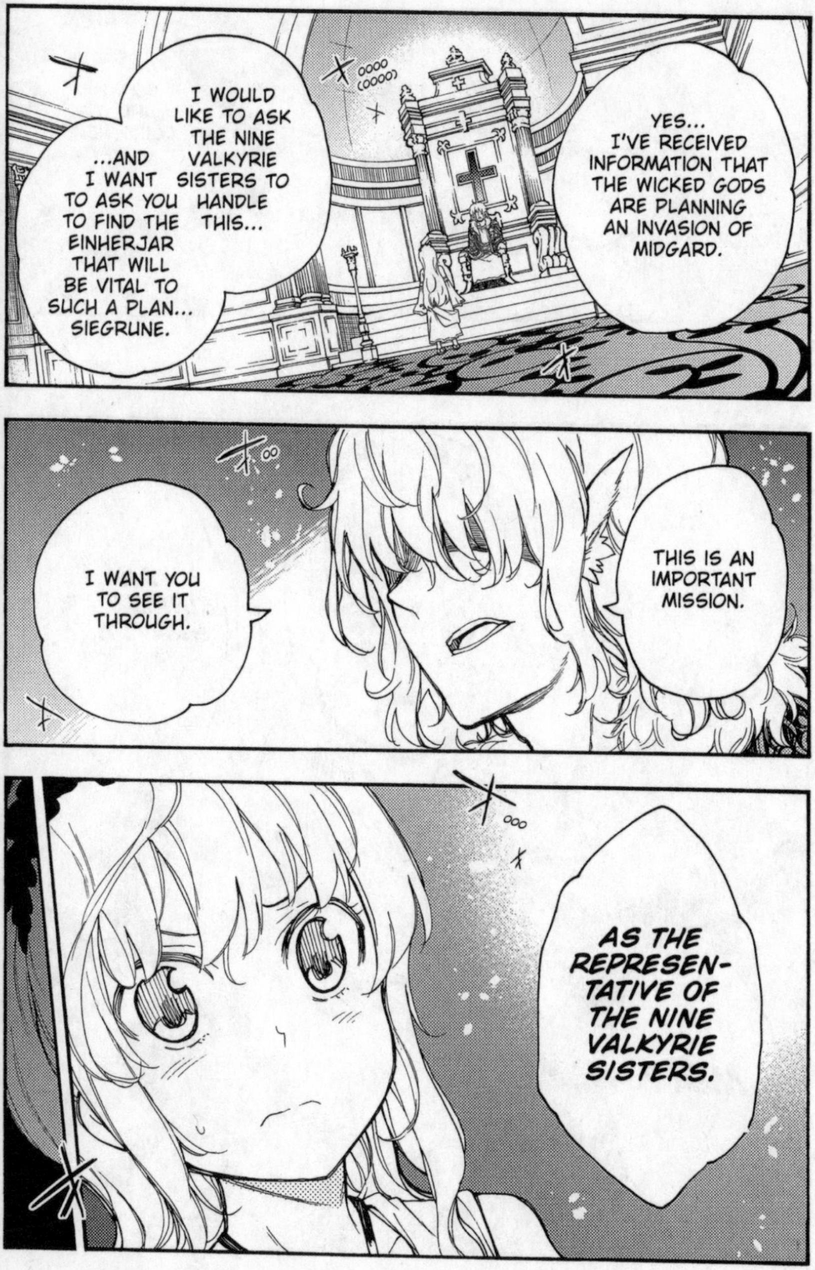
YES... I'VE RECEIVED INFORMATION THAT THE WICKED GODS ARE PLANNING AN INVASION OF MIDGARD.
I WOULD LIKE TO ASK THE NINE VALKYRIE SISTERS TO HANDLE THIS...
...AND I WANT TO ASK YOU TO FIND THE EINHERJAR THAT WILL BE VITAL TO SUCH A PLAN... SIEGRUNE.
THIS IS AN IMPORTANT MISSION.
I WANT YOU TO SEE IT THROUGH.
AS THE REPRESEN-TATIVE OF THE NINE VALKYRIE SISTERS.

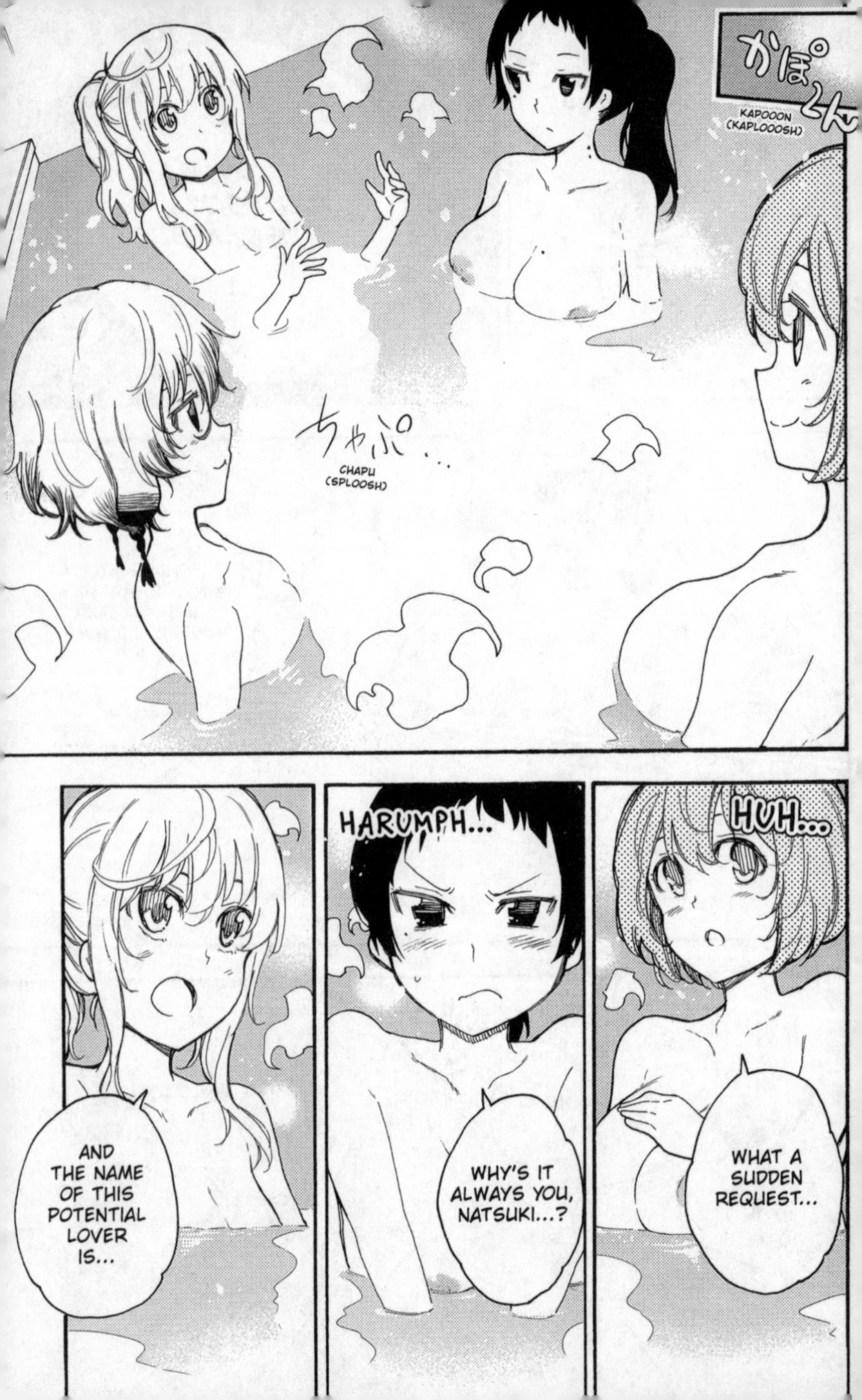
KAPOOON (KAPLOOOSH)
ちゃぷ...
CHAPU (SPLOOSH)
HUH...
WHAT A SUDDEN REQUEST...
HARUMPH...
WHY'S IT ALWAYS YOU, NATSUKI...?
AND THE NAME OF THIS POTENTIAL LOVER IS...

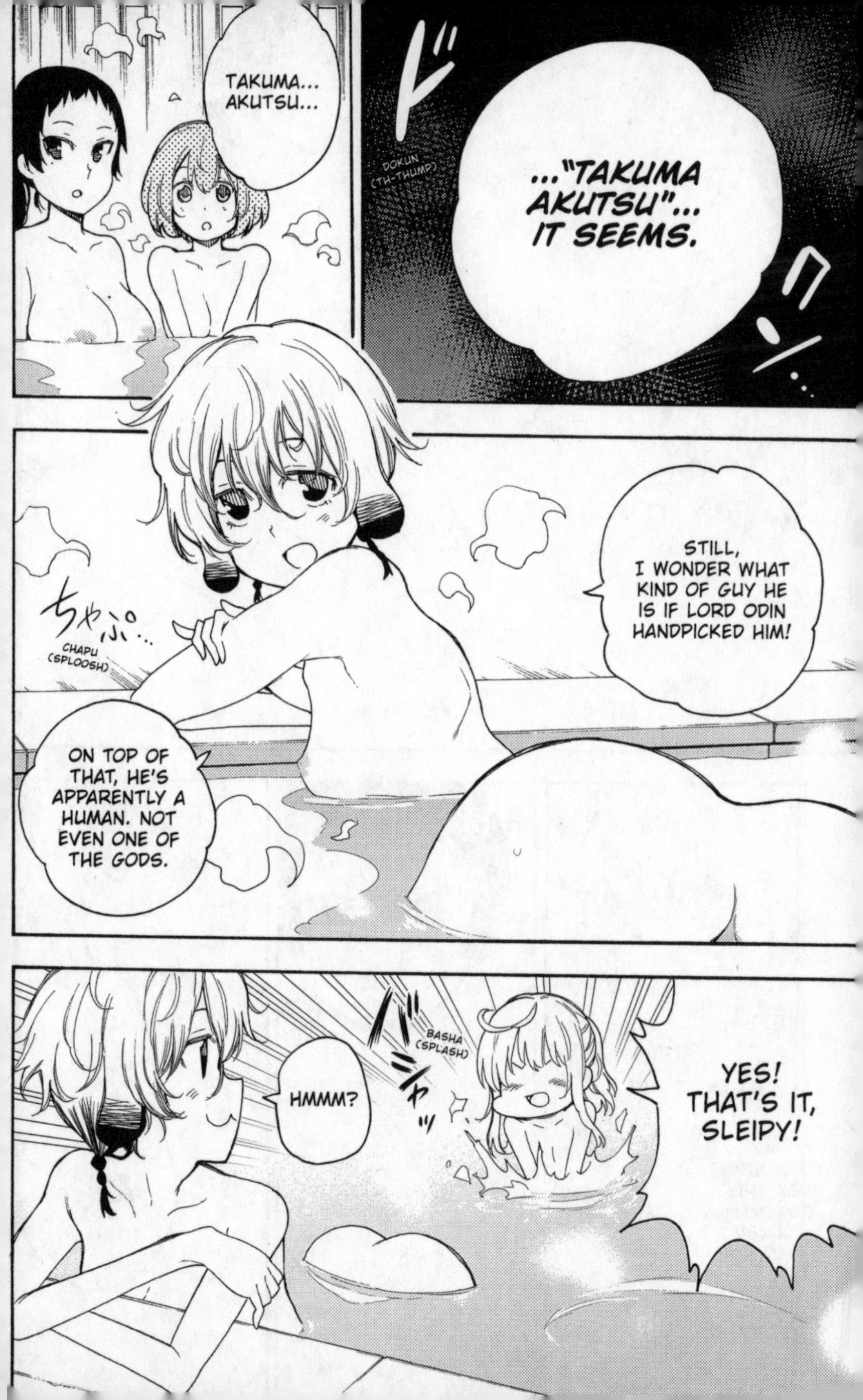
DOKUN (TH-THUMP)
..."TAKUMA AKUTSU"... IT SEEMS.
TAKUMA... AKUTSU...
STILL, I WONDER WHAT KIND OF GUY HE IS IF LORD ODIN HANDPICKED HIM!
ちゃぷ...
CHAPU (SPLOOSH)
ON TOP OF THAT, HE'S APPARENTLY A HUMAN. NOT EVEN ONE OF THE GODS.
YES! THAT'S IT, SLEIPY!
BASHA (SPLASH)
HMMM?

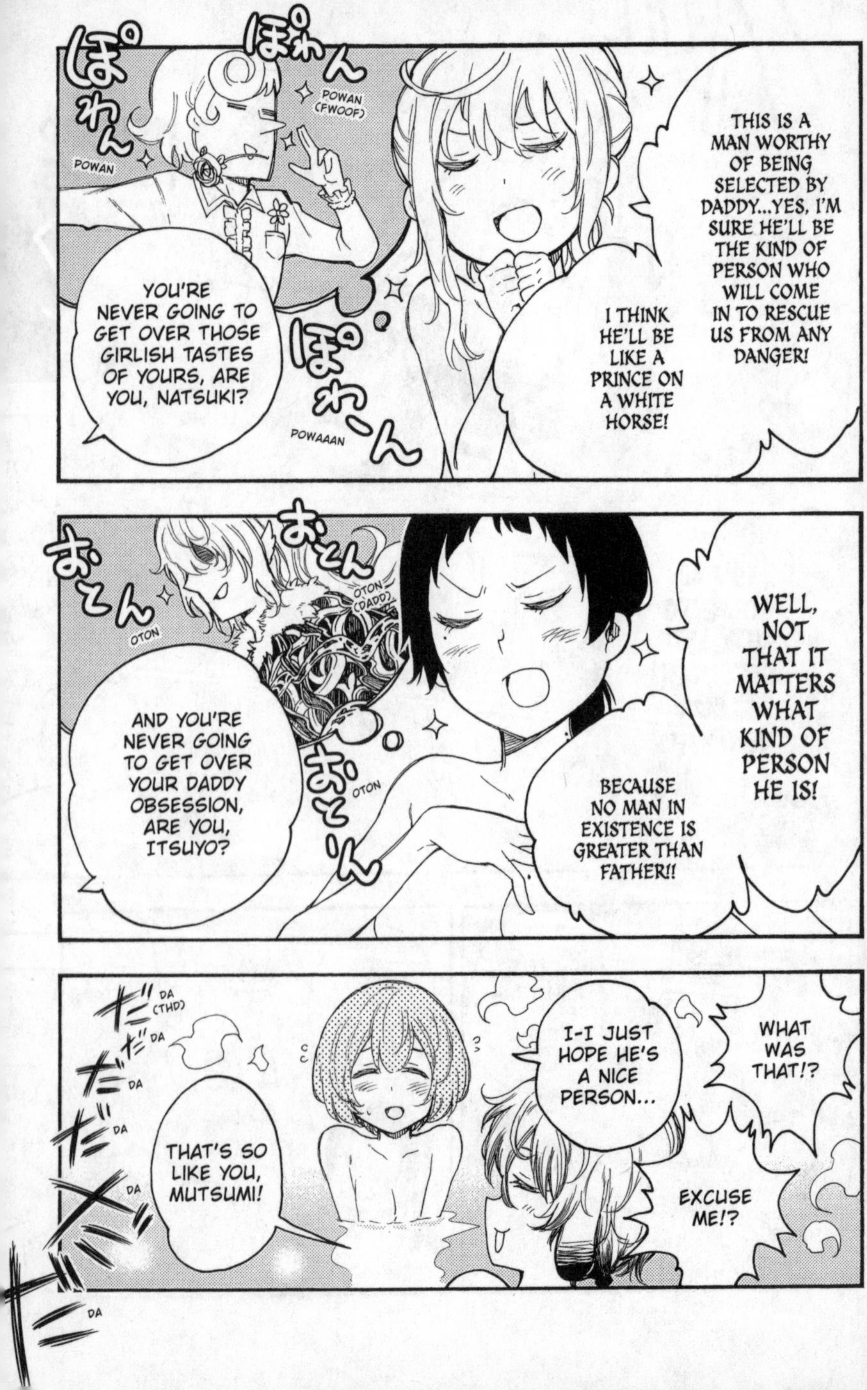
THIS IS A MAN WORTHY OF BEING SELECTED BY DADDY...YES, I'M SURE HE'LL BE THE KIND OF PERSON WHO WILL COME IN TO RESCUE US FROM ANY DANGER!
I THINK HE'LL BE LIKE A PRINCE ON A WHITE HORSE!
ぽわん
POWAN (FWOOF)
ぽわん
POWAN
ぽわ〜ん
POWAAAN
YOU'RE NEVER GOING TO GET OVER THOSE GIRLISH TASTES OF YOURS, ARE YOU, NATSUKI?
WELL, NOT THAT IT MATTERS WHAT KIND OF PERSON HE IS!
BECAUSE NO MAN IN EXISTENCE IS GREATER THAN FATHER!!
おとん
OTON (DADD)
おとん
OTON
おとん
OTON
AND YOU'RE NEVER GOING TO GET OVER YOUR DADDY OBSESSION, ARE YOU, ITSUYO?
WHAT WAS THAT!?
EXCUSE ME!?
I-I JUST HOPE HE'S A NICE PERSON...
THAT'S SO LIKE YOU, MUTSUMI!
だ DA (THD)
だ DA
だ DA
だ DA
だ DA
だ DA

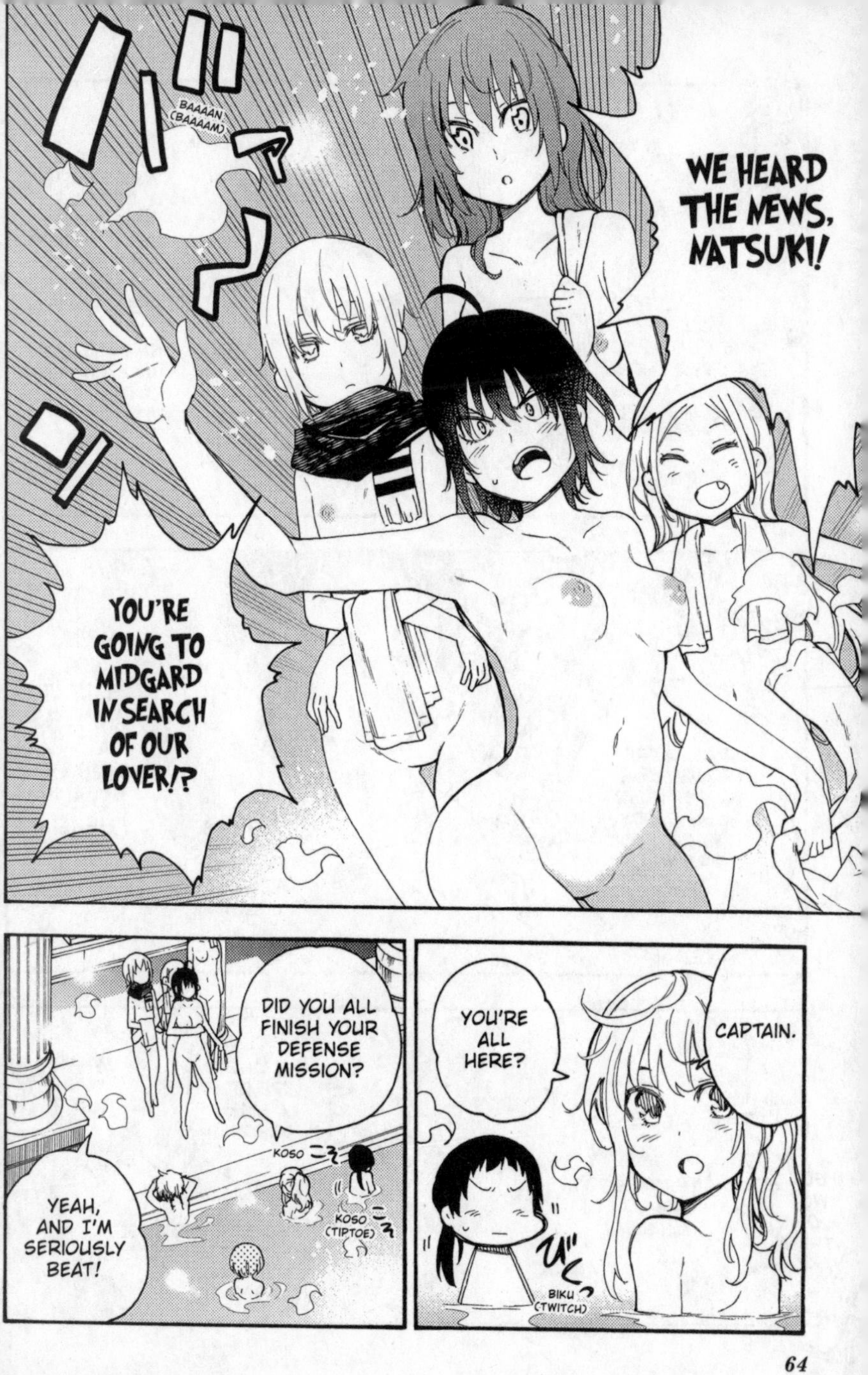
BAAAAN (BAAAAM)
WE HEARD THE NEWS, NATSUKI!
YOU'RE GOING TO MIDGARD IN SEARCH OF OUR LOVER!?
CAPTAIN.
YOU'RE ALL HERE?
BIKU (TWITCH)
DID YOU ALL FINISH YOUR DEFENSE MISSION?
KOSO
KOSO (TIPTOE)
YEAH, AND I'M SERIOUSLY BEAT!

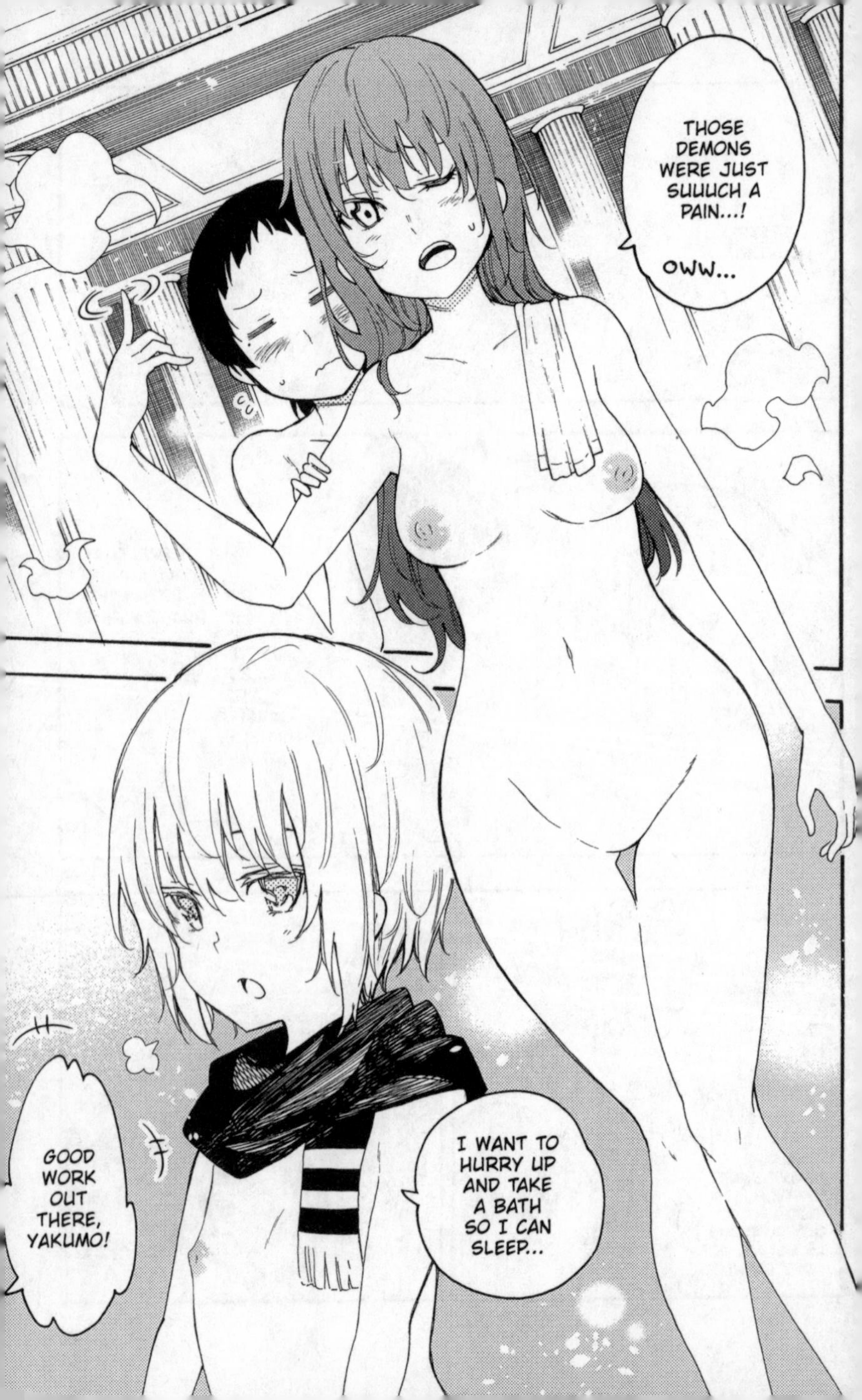
THOSE DEMONS WERE JUST SUUUCH A PAIN...!
OWW...
I WANT TO HURRY UP AND TAKE A BATH SO I CAN SLEEP...
GOOD WORK OUT THERE, YAKUMO!

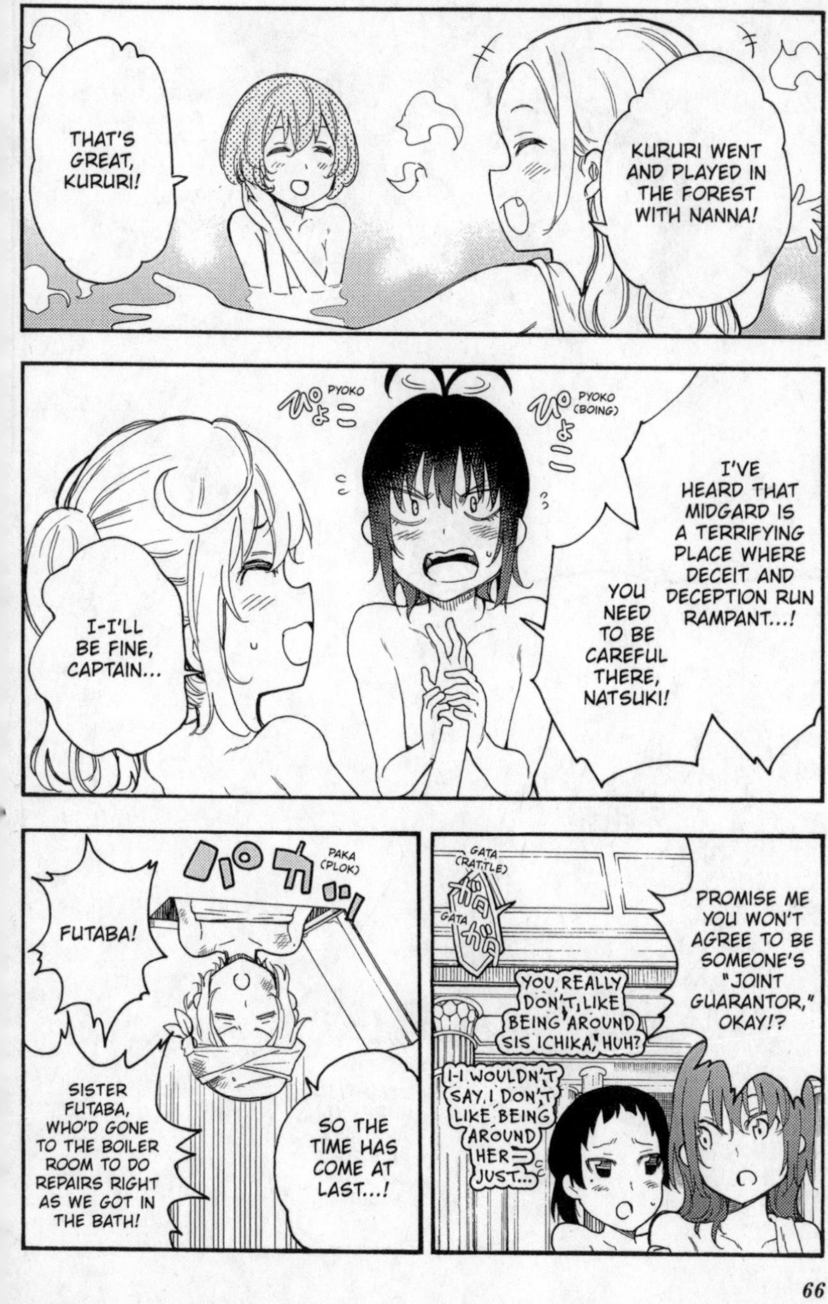
KURURI WENT AND PLAYED IN THE FOREST WITH NANNA!
THAT'S GREAT, KURURI!
PYOKO (BOING)
PYOKO
I'VE HEARD THAT MIDGARD IS A TERRIFYING PLACE WHERE DECEIT AND DECEPTION RUN RAMPANT...!
YOU NEED TO BE CAREFUL THERE, NATSUKI!
I-I'LL BE FINE, CAPTAIN...
GATA (RATTLE)
GATA
PROMISE ME YOU WON'T AGREE TO BE SOMEONE'S "JOINT GUARANTOR," OKAY!?
YOU REALLY DON'T LIKE BEING AROUND SIS ICHIKA, HUH?
I-I WOULDN'T SAY I DON'T LIKE BEING AROUND HER JUST...
PAKA (PLOK)
FUTABA!
SO THE TIME HAS COME AT LAST...!
SISTER FUTABA, WHO'D GONE TO THE BOILER ROOM TO DO REPAIRS RIGHT AS WE GOT IN THE BATH!

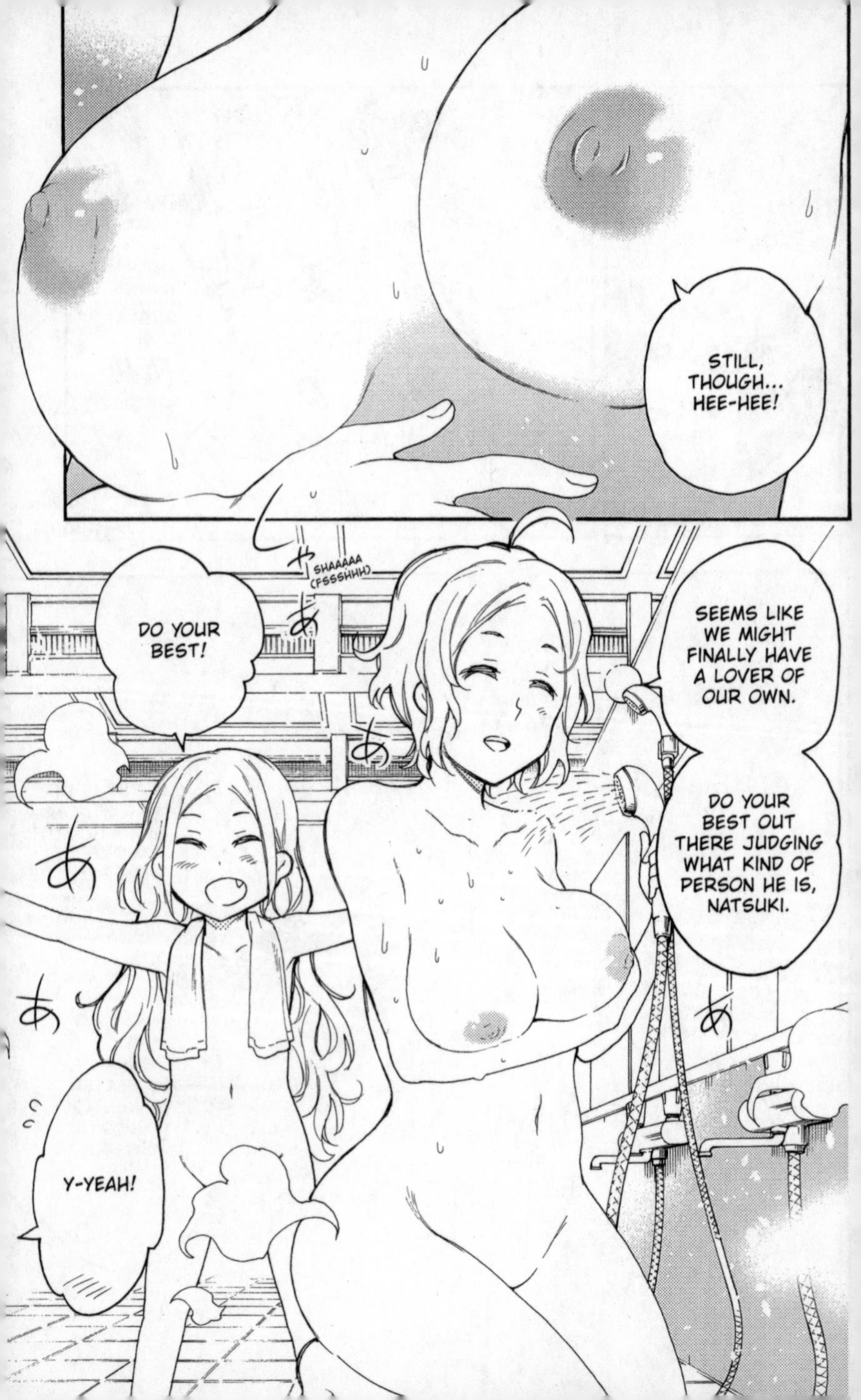
STILL, THOUGH... HEE-HEE!
SEEMS LIKE WE MIGHT FINALLY HAVE A LOVER OF OUR OWN.
DO YOUR BEST OUT THERE JUDGING WHAT KIND OF PERSON HE IS, NATSUKI.
SHAAAAA (FSSSHHH)
DO YOUR BEST!
Y-YEAH!

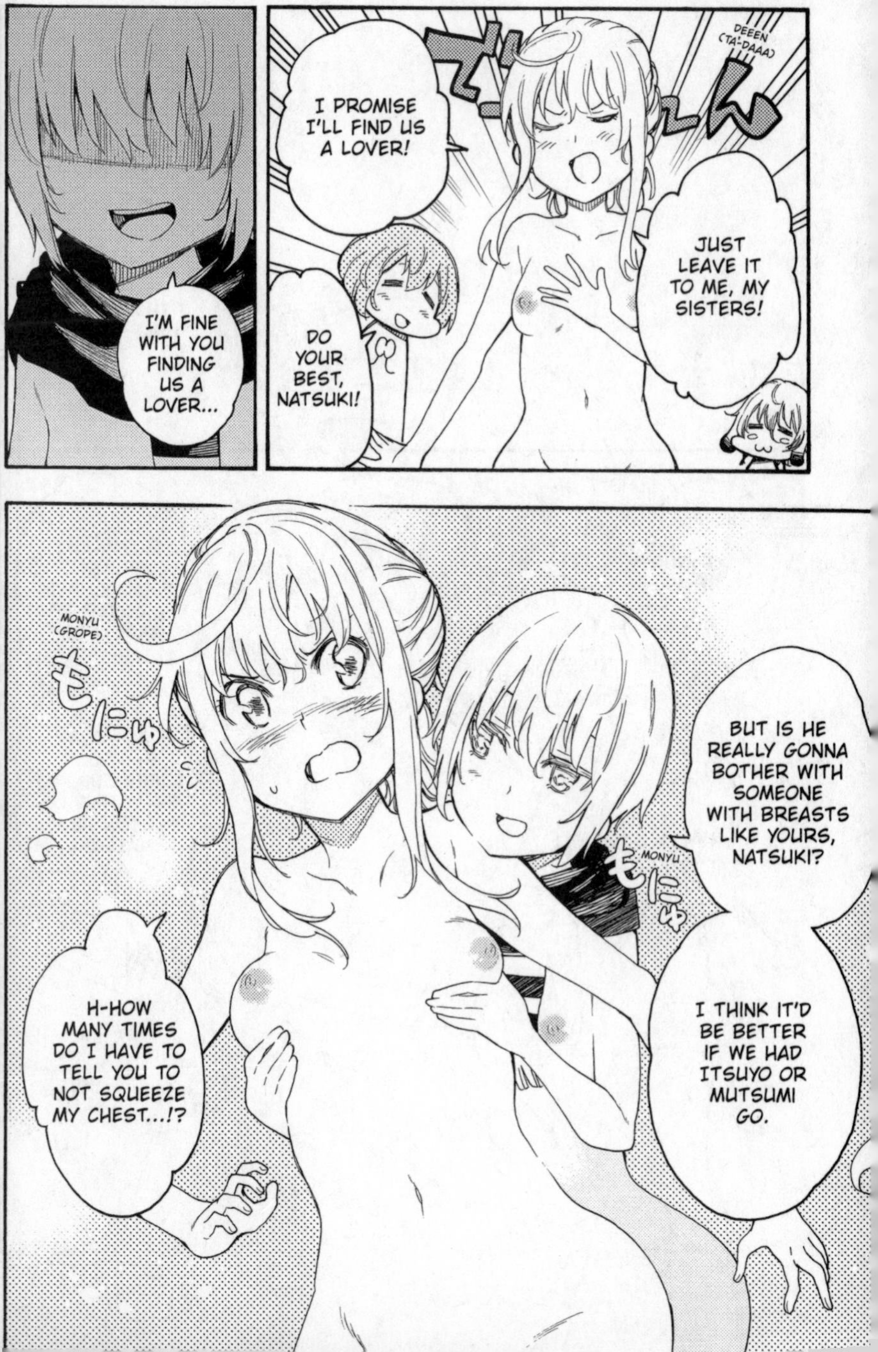
DEEEN (TA-DAAA)
I PROMISE I'LL FIND US A LOVER!
JUST LEAVE IT TO ME, MY SISTERS!
DO YOUR BEST, NATSUKI!
I'M FINE WITH YOU FINDING US A LOVER...
BUT IS HE REALLY GONNA BOTHER WITH SOMEONE WITH BREASTS LIKE YOURS, NATSUKI?
I THINK IT'D BE BETTER IF WE HAD ITSUYO OR MUTSUMI GO.
MONYU
H-HOW MANY TIMES DO I HAVE TO TELL YOU TO NOT SQUEEZE MY CHEST...!?
MONYU (GROPE)

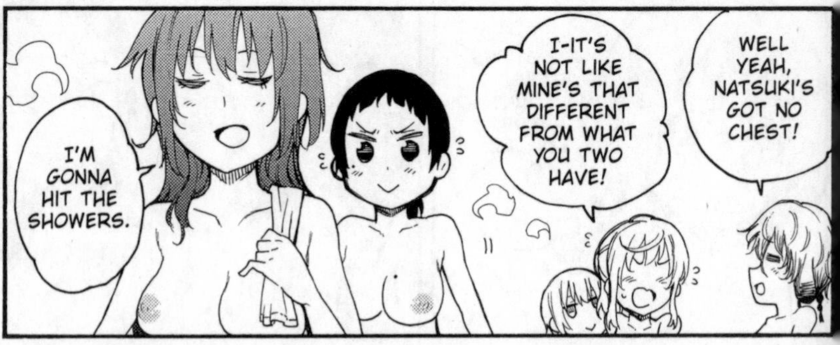
WELL YEAH, NATSUKI'S GOT NO CHEST!
I-IT'S NOT LIKE MINE'S THAT DIFFERENT FROM WHAT YOU TWO HAVE!
I'M GONNA HIT THE SHOWERS.

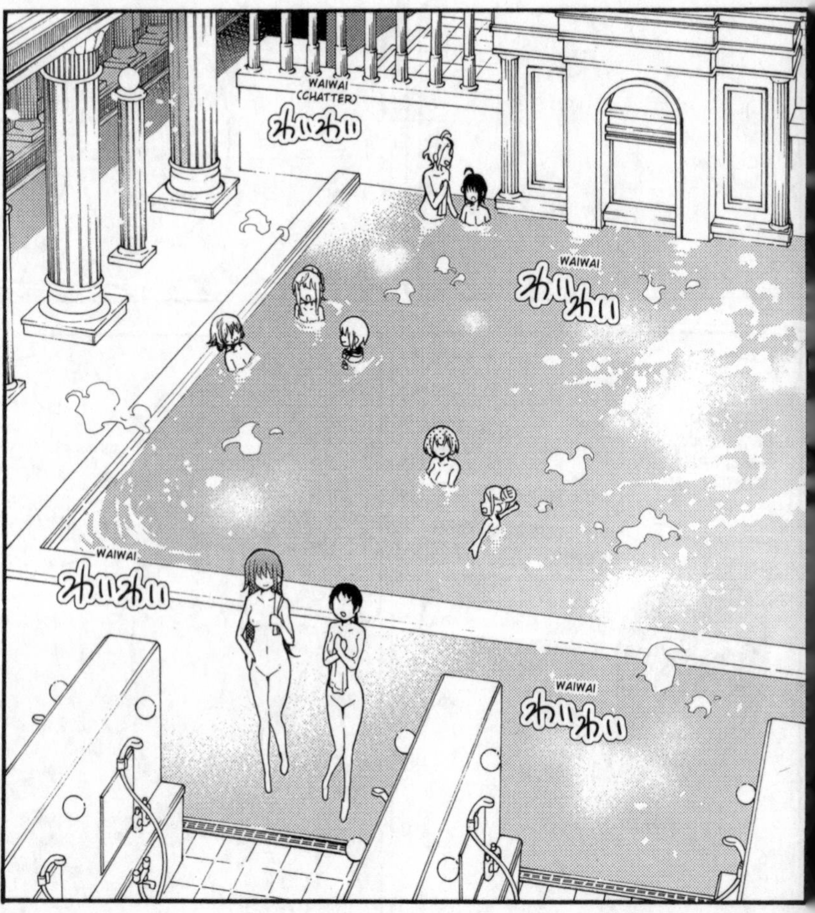
WAIWAI (CHATTER)
わいわい
WAIWAI
わいわい
WAIWAI
わいわい
WAIWAI
わいわい

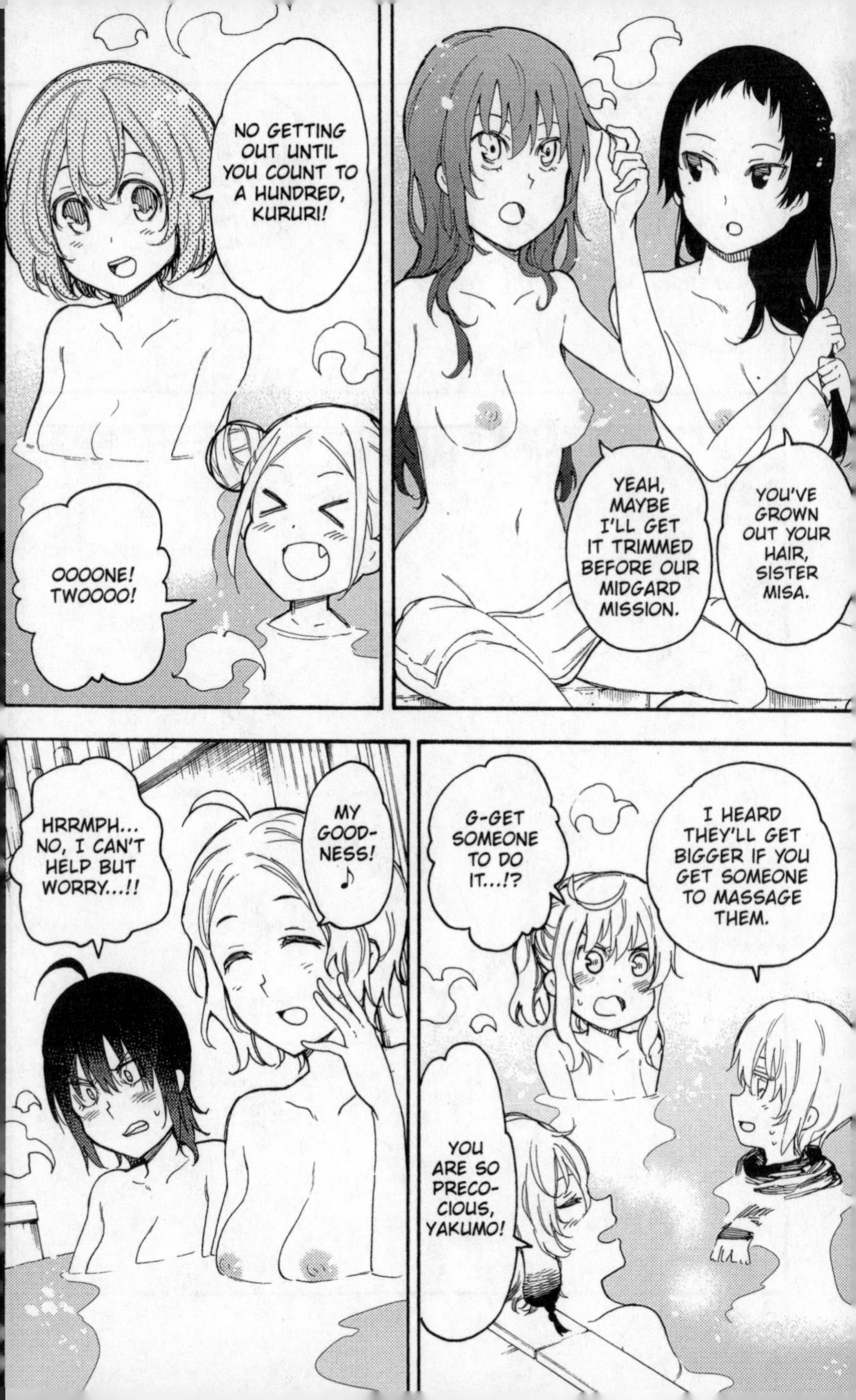
YOU'VE GROWN OUT YOUR HAIR, SISTER MISA.
YEAH, MAYBE I'LL GET IT TRIMMED BEFORE OUR MIDGARD MISSION.
NO GETTING OUT UNTIL YOU COUNT TO A HUNDRED, KURURI!
OOOONE! TWOOOO!
I HEARD THEY'LL GET BIGGER IF YOU GET SOMEONE TO MASSAGE THEM.
G-GET SOMEONE TO DO IT...!?
YOU ARE SO PRECOCIOUS, YAKUMO!
MY GOODNESS! ♪
HRRMPH... NO, I CAN'T HELP BUT WORRY...!!

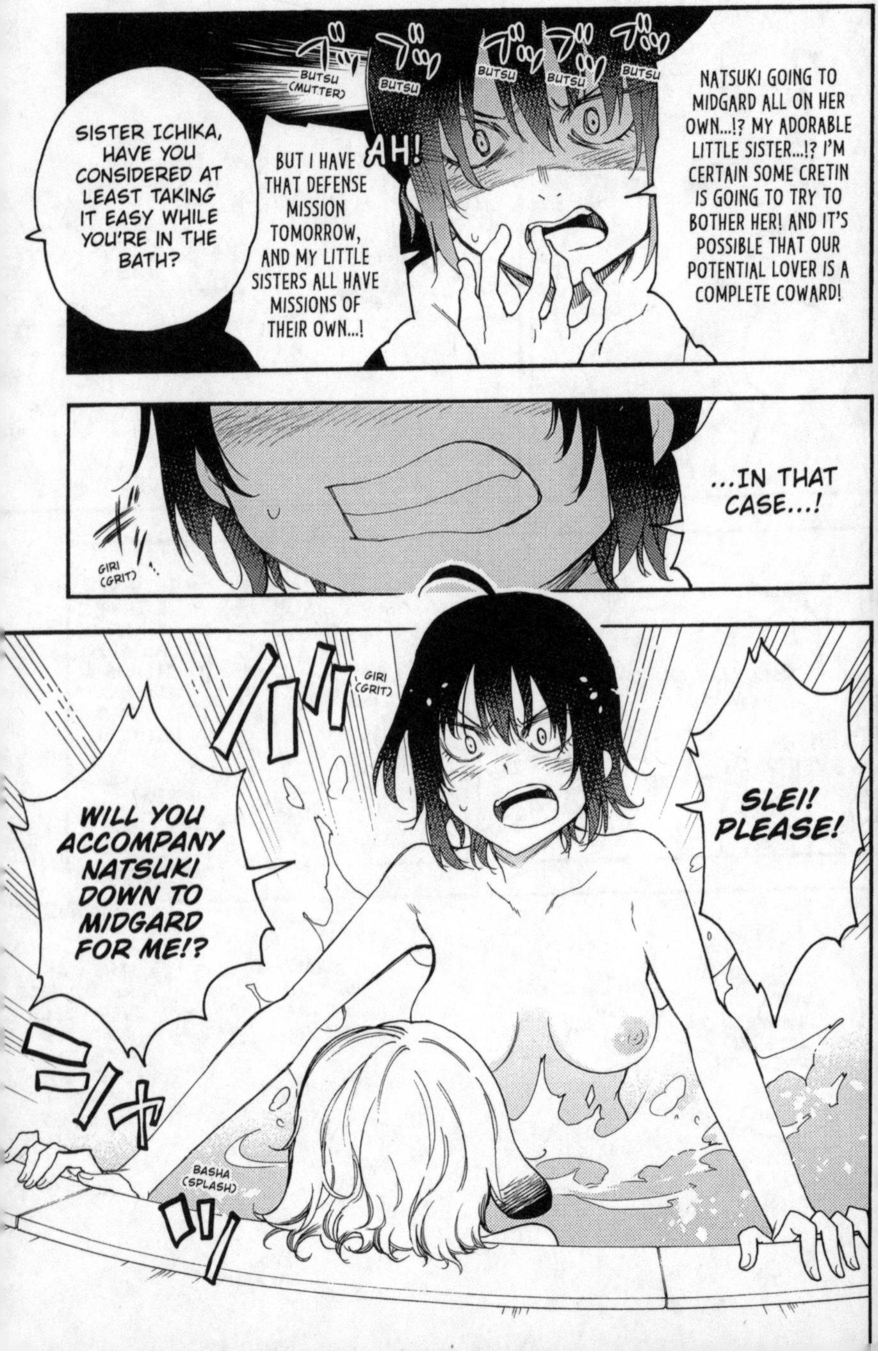
NATSUKI GOING TO MIDGARD ALL ON HER OWN...!? MY ADORABLE LITTLE SISTER...!? I'M CERTAIN SOME CRETIN IS GOING TO TRY TO BOTHER HER! AND IT'S POSSIBLE THAT OUR POTENTIAL LOVER IS A COMPLETE COWARD!
BUTSU
BUTSU
BUTSU
BUTSU
BUTSU (MUTTER)
AH!
BUT I HAVE THAT DEFENSE MISSION TOMORROW, AND MY LITTLE SISTERS ALL HAVE MISSIONS OF THEIR OWN...!
SISTER ICHIKA, HAVE YOU CONSIDERED AT LEAST TAKING IT EASY WHILE YOU'RE IN THE BATH?
...IN THAT CASE...!
GIRI (GRIT)
SLEI! PLEASE!
GIRI (GRIT)
WILL YOU ACCOMPANY NATSUKI DOWN TO MIDGARD FOR ME!?
BASHA (SPLASH)

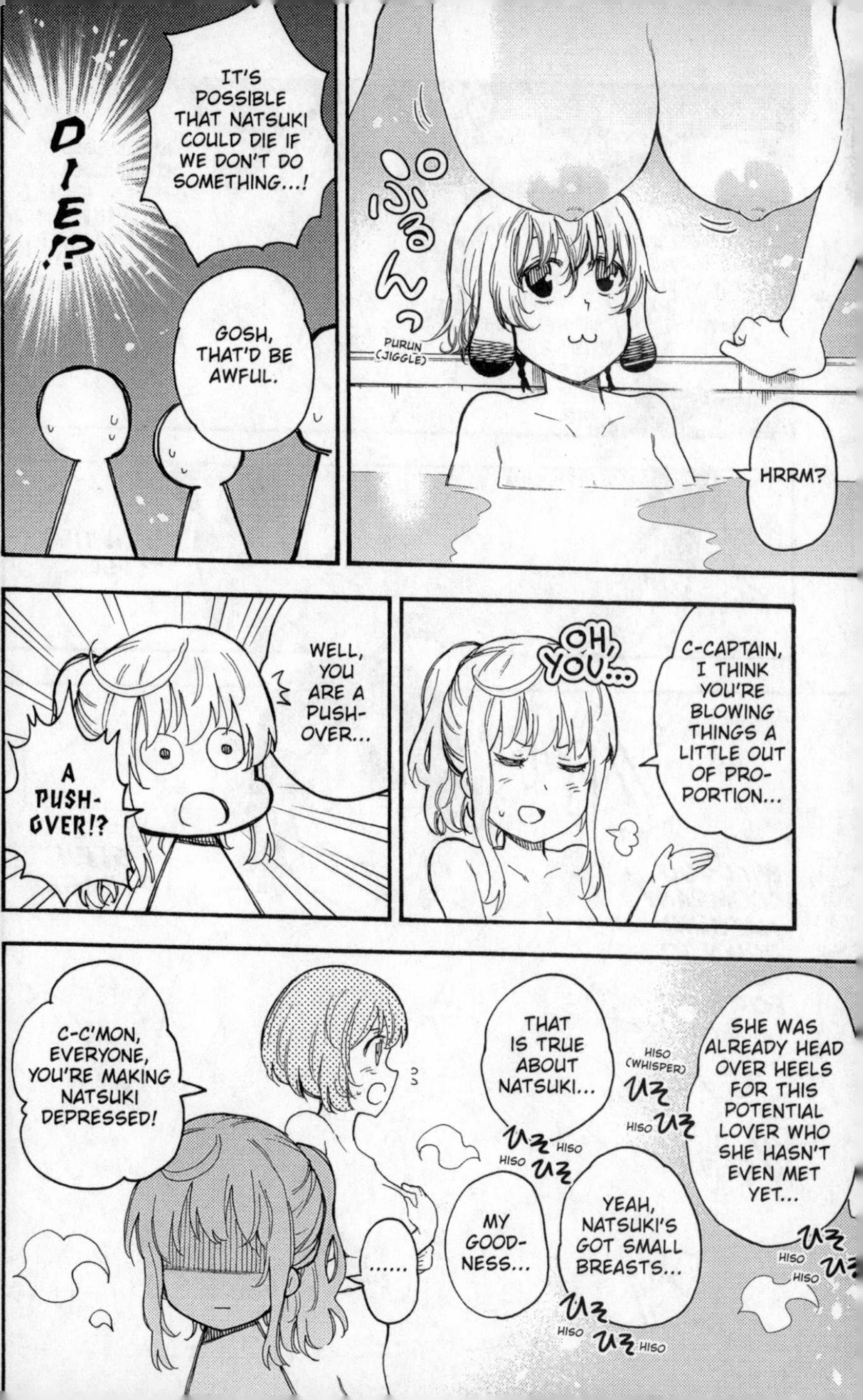
ぷるんっ
PURUN (JIGGLE)
HRRM?
IT'S POSSIBLE THAT NATSUKI COULD DIE IF WE DON'T DO SOMETHING...!
DIE!?
GOSH, THAT'D BE AWFUL.
C-CAPTAIN, I THINK YOU'RE BLOWING THINGS A LITTLE OUT OF PRO-PORTION...
OH, YOU...
WELL, YOU ARE A PUSH-OVER...
A PUSH-OVER!?
SHE WAS ALREADY HEAD OVER HEELS FOR THIS POTENTIAL LOVER WHO SHE HASN'T EVEN MET YET...
ひそ HISO ひそ HISO
HISO (WHISPER) ひそ HISO ひそ
THAT IS TRUE ABOUT NATSUKI...
ひそ HISO HISO ひそ
YEAH, NATSUKI'S GOT SMALL BREASTS...
ひそ HISO ひそ HISO
MY GOOD-NESS...
......
C-C'MON, EVERYONE, YOU'RE MAKING NATSUKI DEPRESSED!

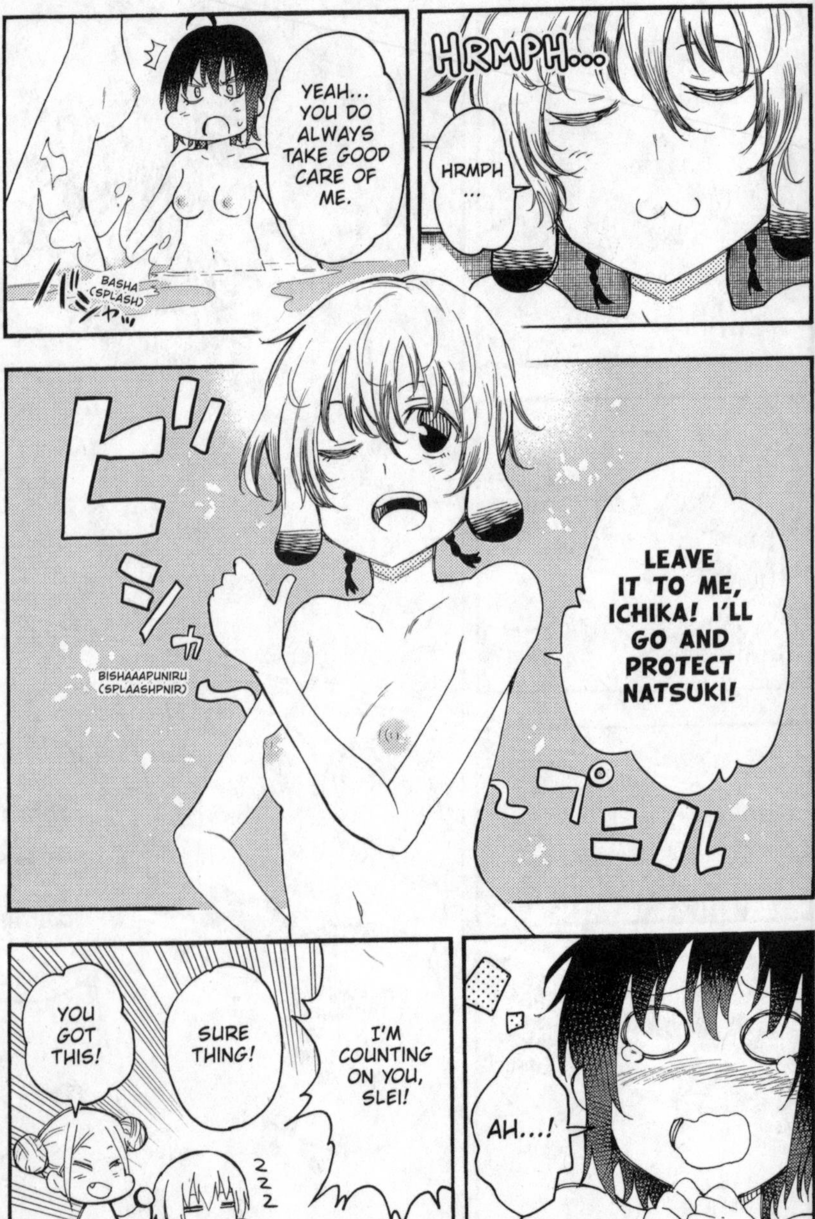
HRMPH...
HRMPH ...
YEAH... YOU DO ALWAYS TAKE GOOD CARE OF ME.
BASHA (SPLASH)
LEAVE IT TO ME, ICHIKA! I'LL GO AND PROTECT NATSUKI!
BISHAAAPUNIRU (SPLAASHPNIR)
AH...!
I'M COUNTING ON YOU, SLEI!
SURE THING!
YOU GOT THIS!

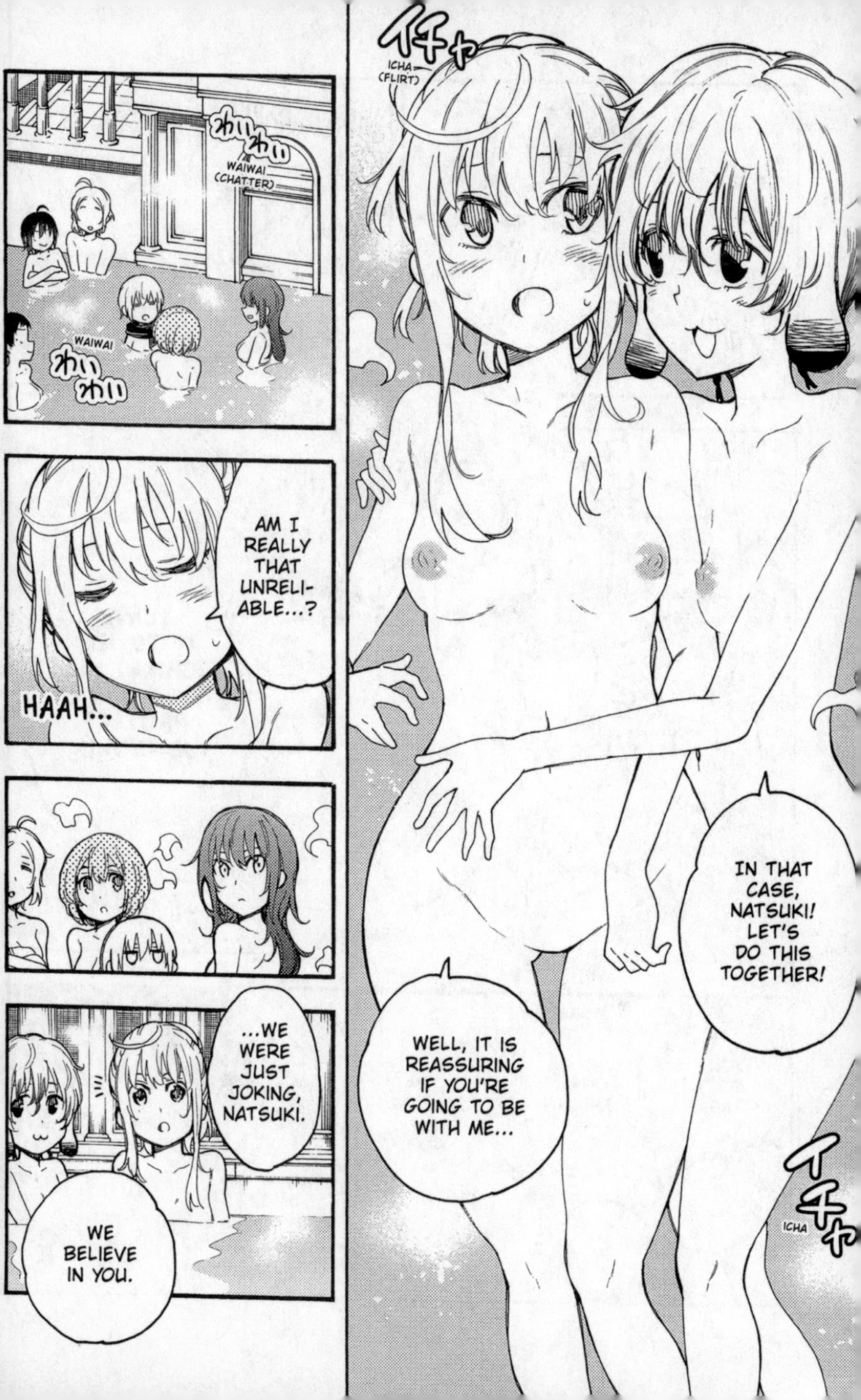
イチャ
ICHA (FLIRT)
IN THAT CASE, NATSUKI! LET'S DO THIS TOGETHER!
WELL, IT IS REASSURING IF YOU'RE GOING TO BE WITH ME...
イチャ
ICHA
わいわい
WAIWAI (CHATTER)
WAIWAI
わいわい
AM I REALLY THAT UNRELI-ABLE...?
HAAH...
...WE WERE JUST JOKING, NATSUKI.
WE BELIEVE IN YOU.

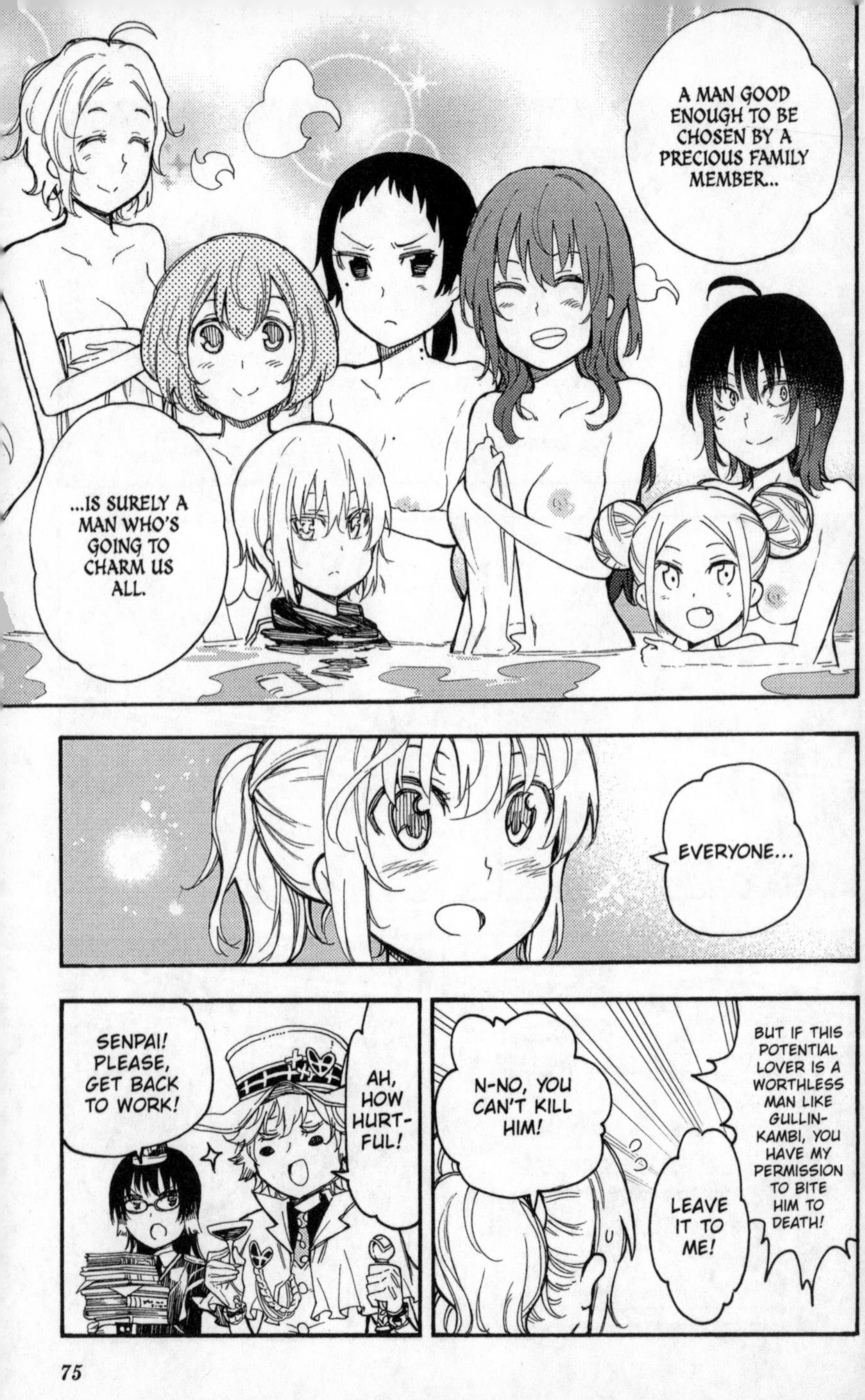
A MAN GOOD ENOUGH TO BE CHOSEN BY A PRECIOUS FAMILY MEMBER...
...IS SURELY A MAN WHO'S GOING TO CHARM US ALL.
EVERYONE...
BUT IF THIS POTENTIAL LOVER IS A WORTHLESS MAN LIKE GULLIN-KAMBI, YOU HAVE MY PERMISSION TO BITE HIM TO DEATH!
LEAVE IT TO ME!
N-NO, YOU CAN'T KILL HIM!
AH, HOW HURT-FUL!
SENPAI! PLEASE, GET BACK TO WORK!

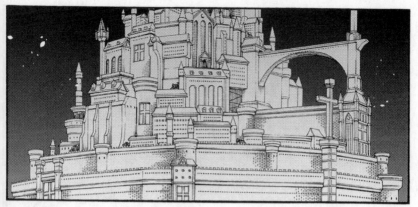

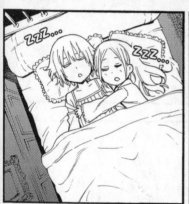

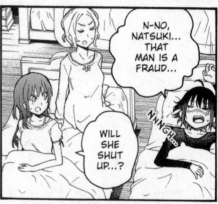

N-NO, NATSUKI... THAT MAN IS A FRAUD...

WILL SHE SHUT UP...?

NNNGH...

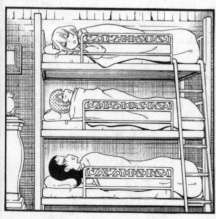

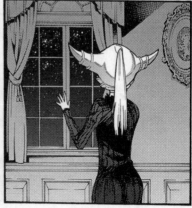

76

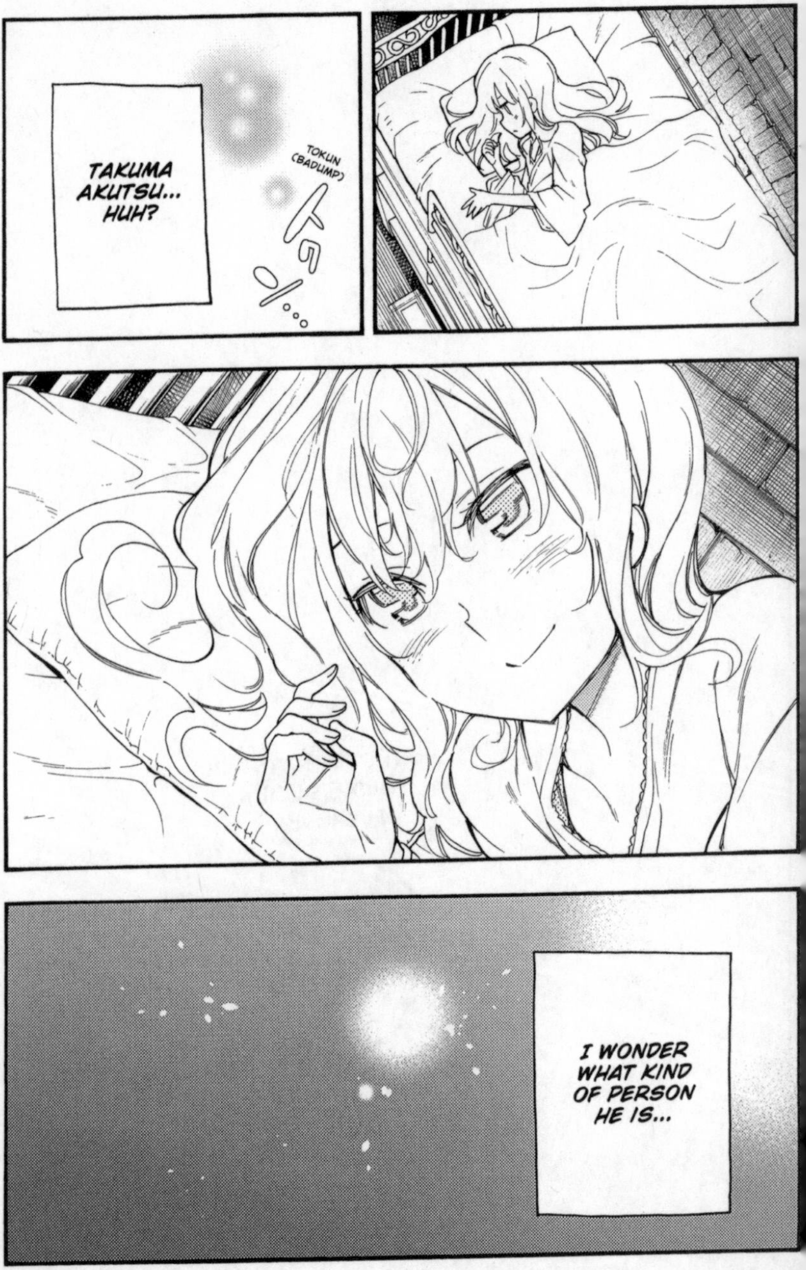

TOKUN (BADUMP)
トクン…
TAKUMA AKUTSU... HUH?
I WONDER WHAT KIND OF PERSON HE IS...

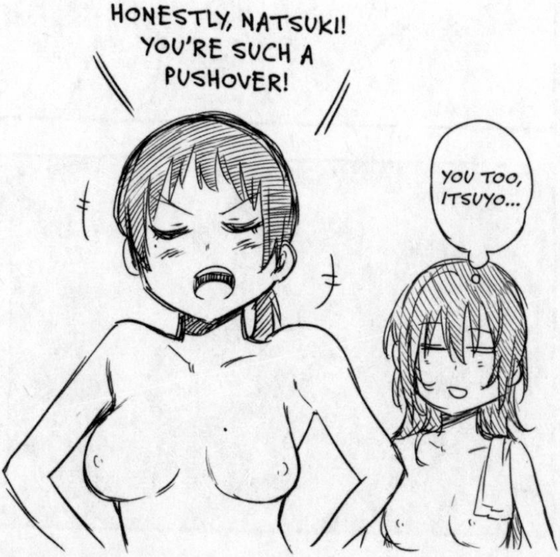
HONESTLY, NATSUKI! YOU'RE SUCH A PUSHOVER!
YOU TOO, ITSUYO...

Chapter 52

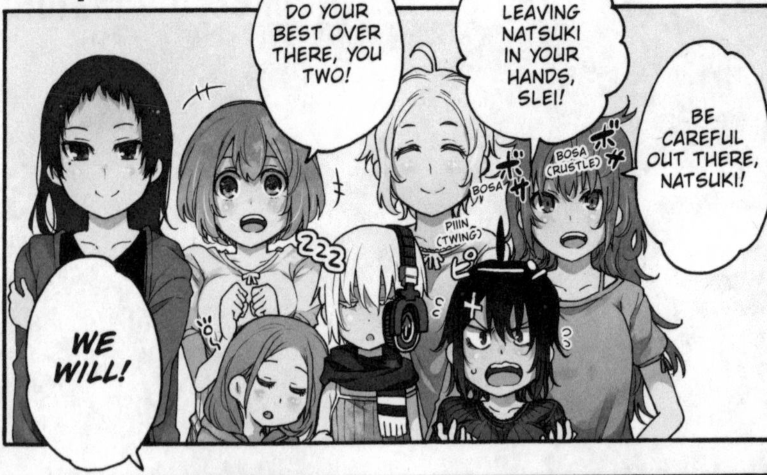
BE CAREFUL OUT THERE, NATSUKI!
BOSA (RUSTLE)
BOSA
I'M LEAVING NATSUKI IN YOUR HANDS, SLEI!
DO YOUR BEST OVER THERE, YOU TWO!
PIIIN (TWING)
WE WILL!

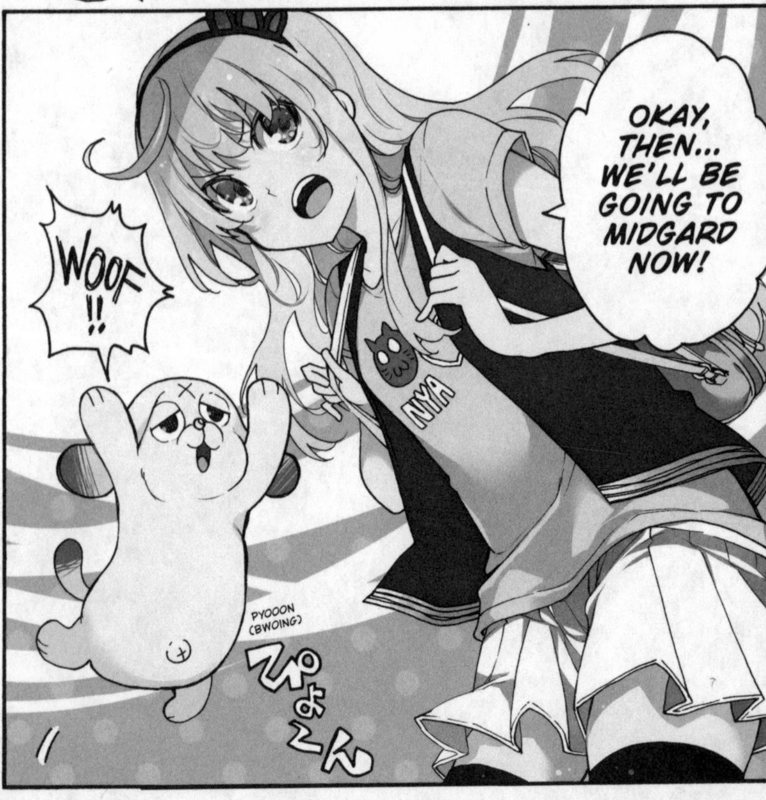
OKAY, THEN... WE'LL BE GOING TO MIDGARD NOW!
NYA
WOOF!!
PYOOON (BWOING)

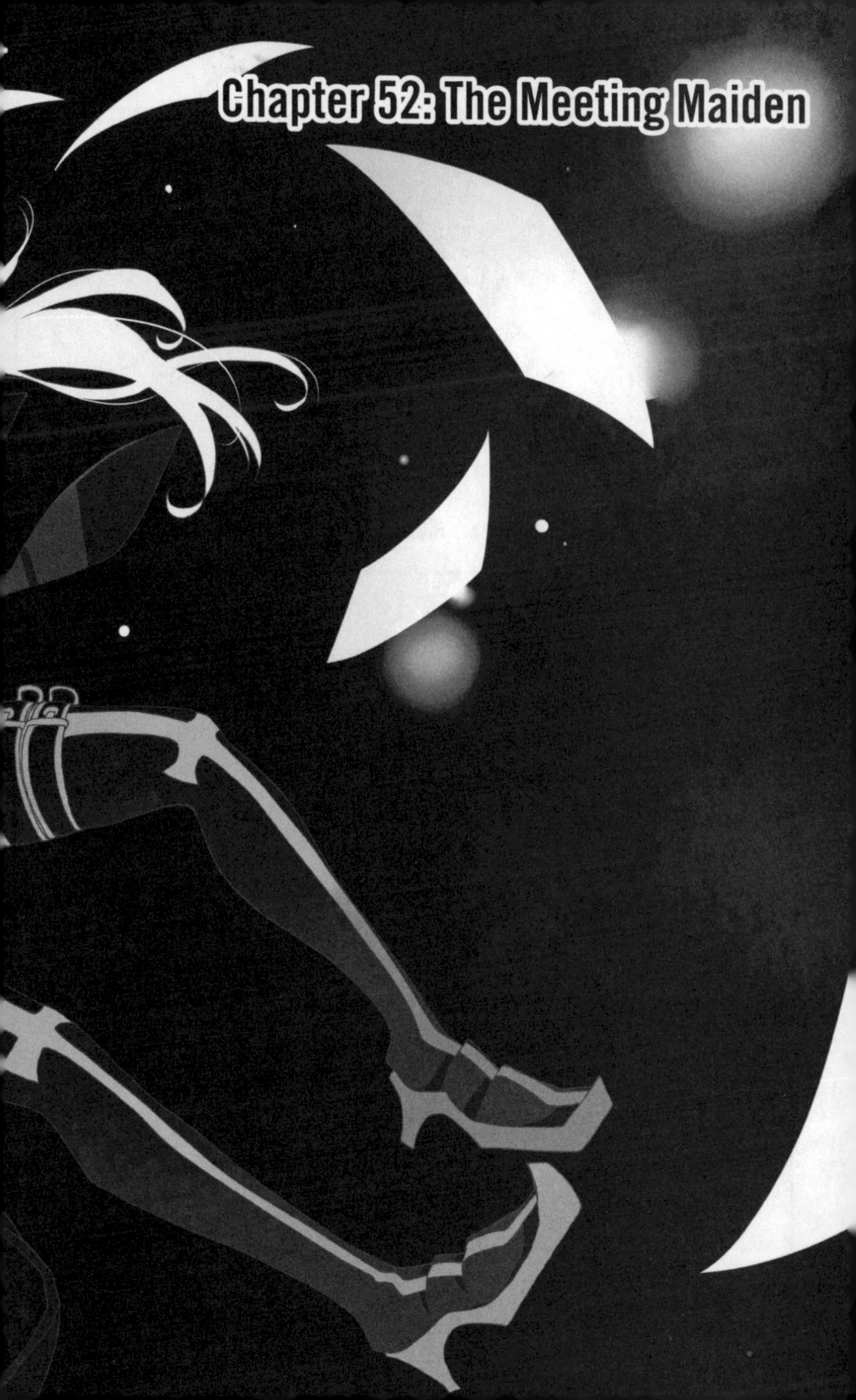
Chapter 52: The Meeting Maiden

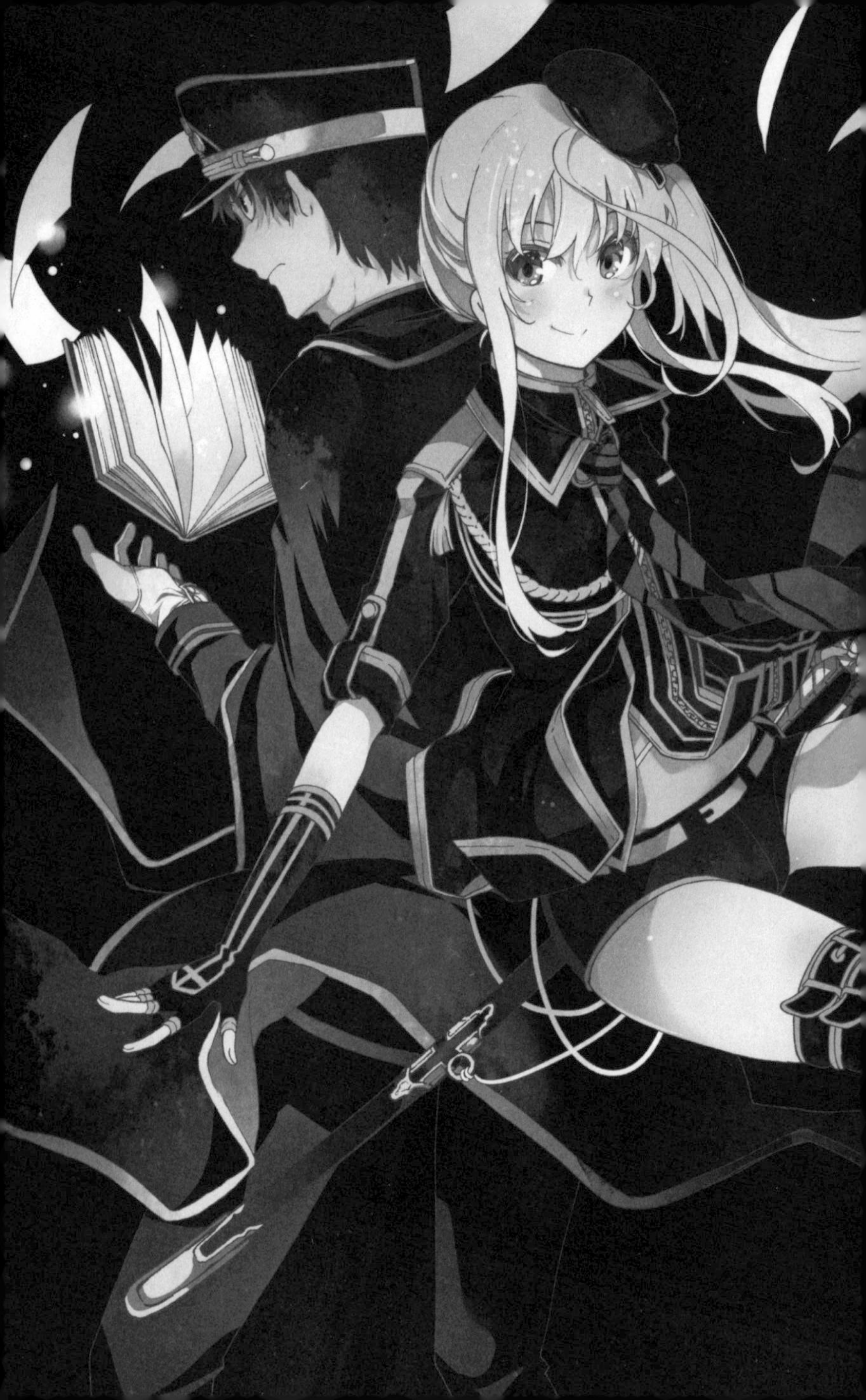

Val × Love

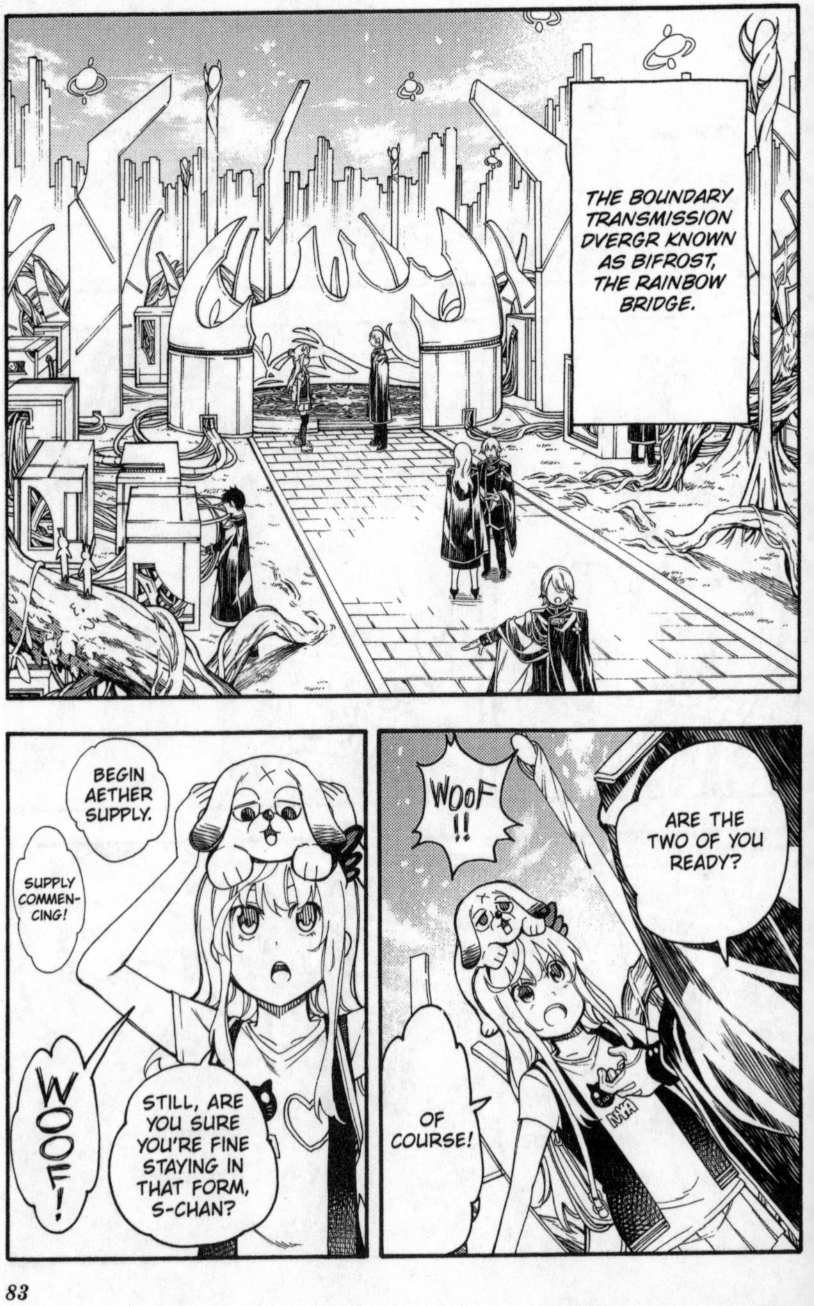
THE BOUNDARY TRANSMISSION DVERGR KNOWN AS BIFROST, THE RAINBOW BRIDGE.
ARE THE TWO OF YOU READY?
WOOF!!
OF COURSE!
BEGIN AETHER SUPPLY.
SUPPLY COMMENCING!
STILL, ARE YOU SURE YOU'RE FINE STAYING IN THAT FORM, S-CHAN?
WOOF!

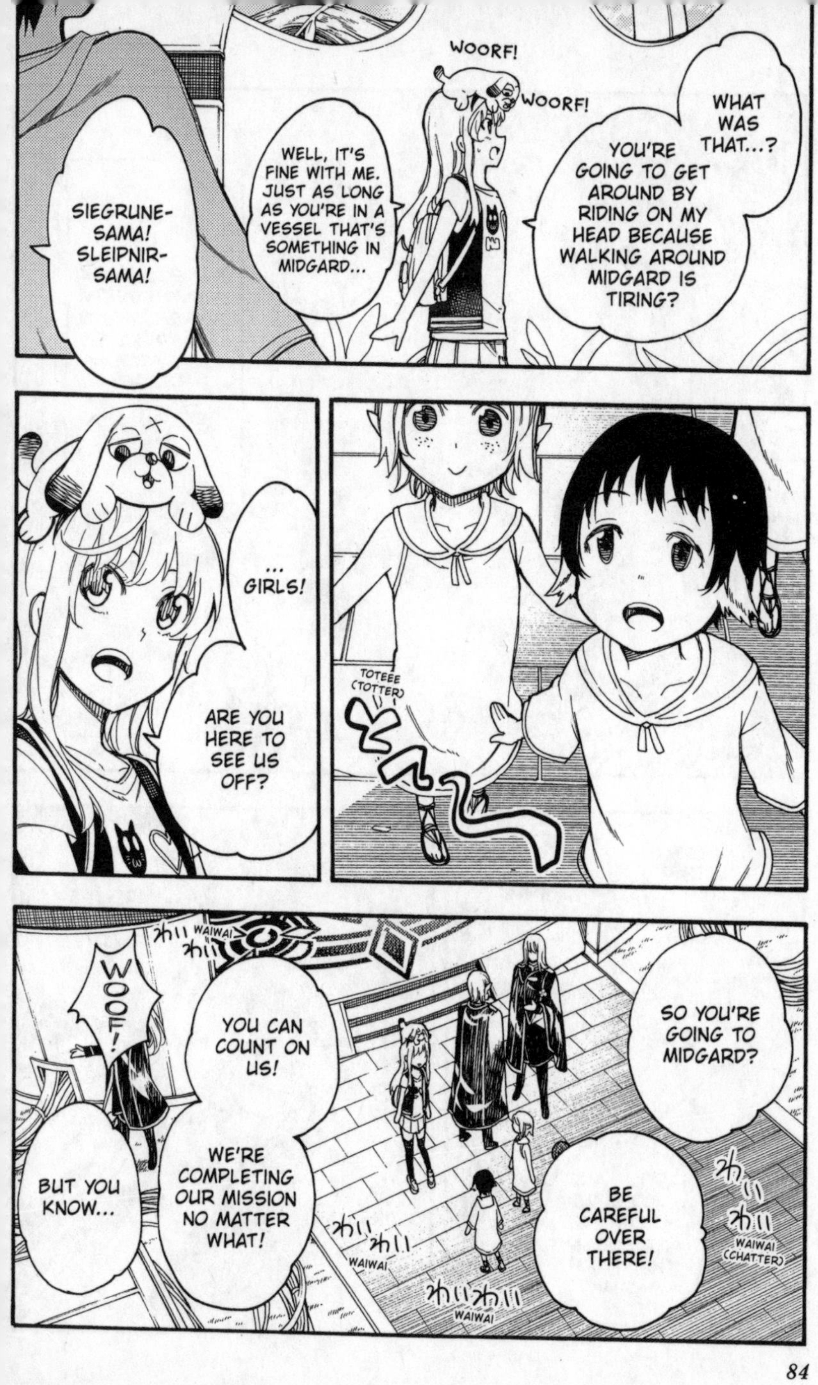
WOORF!
WOORF!
WHAT WAS THAT...?
YOU'RE GOING TO GET AROUND BY RIDING ON MY HEAD BECAUSE WALKING AROUND MIDGARD IS TIRING?
WELL, IT'S FINE WITH ME. JUST AS LONG AS YOU'RE IN A VESSEL THAT'S SOMETHING IN MIDGARD...
SIEGRUNE-SAMA! SLEIPNIR-SAMA!
TOTEEE (TOTTER)
... GIRLS!
ARE YOU HERE TO SEE US OFF?
SO YOU'RE GOING TO MIDGARD?
WAIWAI (CHATTER)
BE CAREFUL OVER THERE!
WAIWAI
WAIWAI
YOU CAN COUNT ON US!
WAIWAI
WOOF!
WE'RE COMPLETING OUR MISSION NO MATTER WHAT!
BUT YOU KNOW...

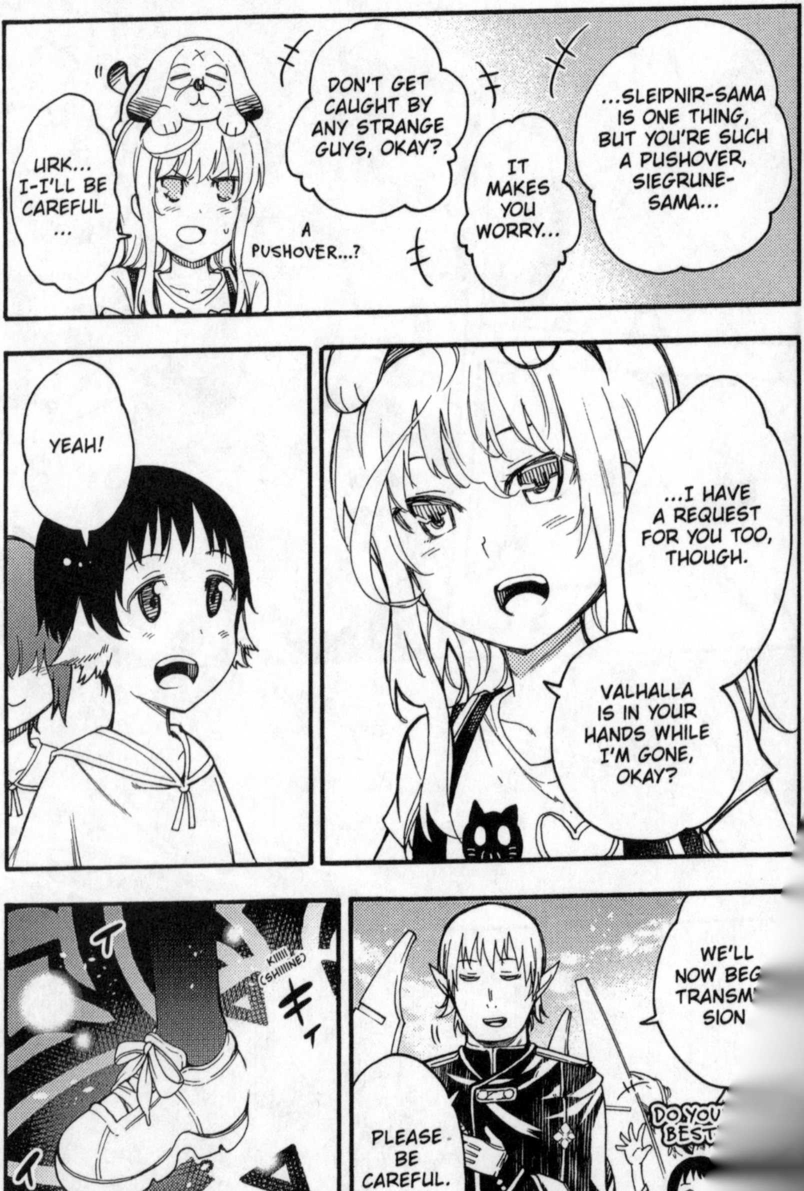
...SLEIPNIR-SAMA IS ONE THING, BUT YOU'RE SUCH A PUSHOVER, SIEGRUNE-SAMA...
IT MAKES YOU WORRY...
DON'T GET CAUGHT BY ANY STRANGE GUYS, OKAY?
A PUSHOVER...?
URK... I-I'LL BE CAREFUL ...
...I HAVE A REQUEST FOR YOU TOO, THOUGH.
VALHALLA IS IN YOUR HANDS WHILE I'M GONE, OKAY?
YEAH!
WE'LL NOW BEG TRANSM SION
DO YOU BEST
PLEASE BE CAREFUL.
KIIIIN (SHIIINE)

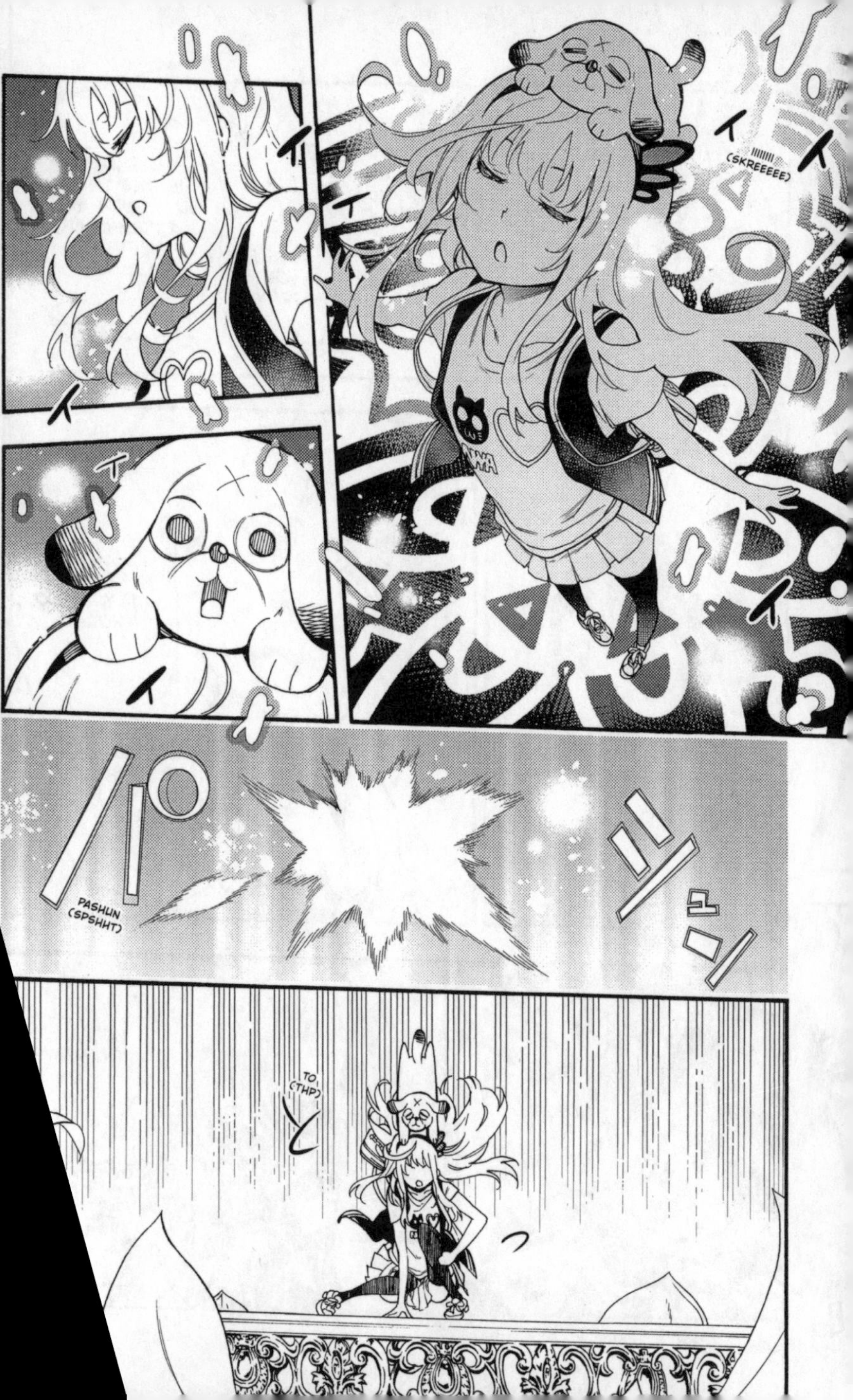
IIIIIIII
(SKREEEEE)
PASHUN
(SPSHHT)
TO
(THP)

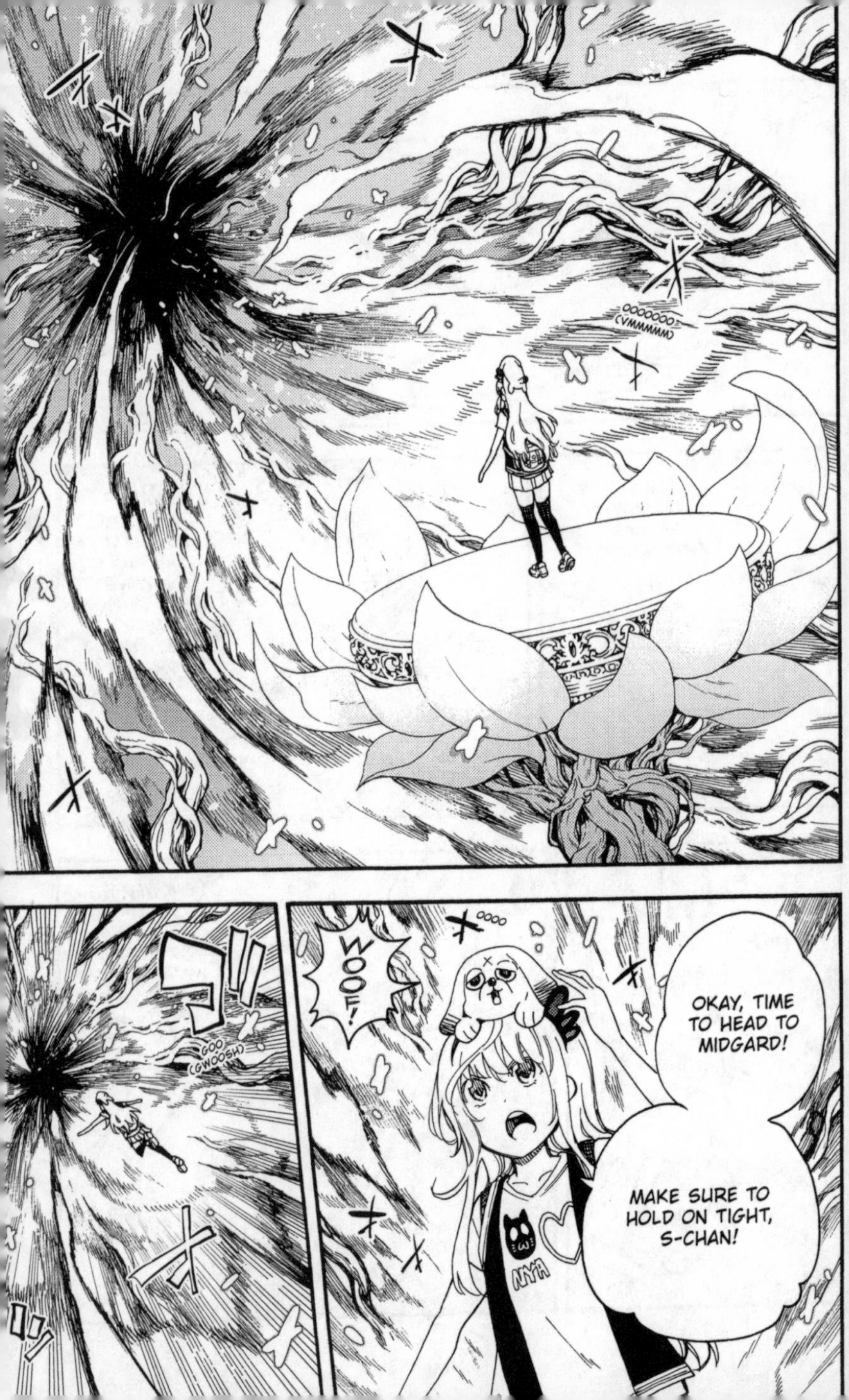
OOOOOOO
(VMMMMMM)
OKAY, TIME TO HEAD TO MIDGARD!
OOOO
WOOF!
MAKE SURE TO HOLD ON TIGHT, S-CHAN!
GOO
(GWOOSH)

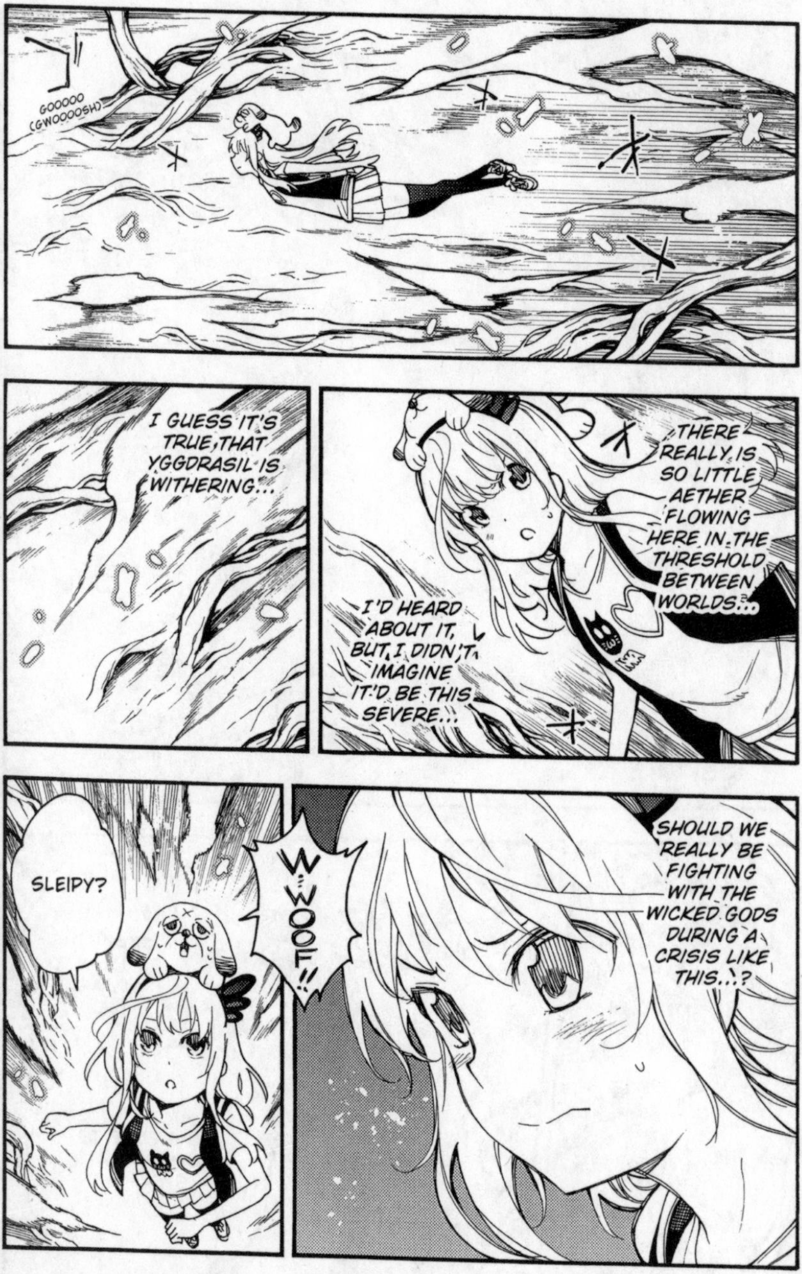
GOOOOO (GWOOOOSH)
THERE REALLY IS SO LITTLE AETHER FLOWING HERE IN THE THRESHOLD BETWEEN WORLDS...
I'D HEARD ABOUT IT, BUT I DIDN'T IMAGINE IT'D BE THIS SEVERE...
I GUESS IT'S TRUE, THAT YGGDRASIL IS WITHERING...
SHOULD WE REALLY BE FIGHTING WITH THE WICKED GODS DURING A CRISIS LIKE THIS...?
SLEIPY?
W-WOOF!!

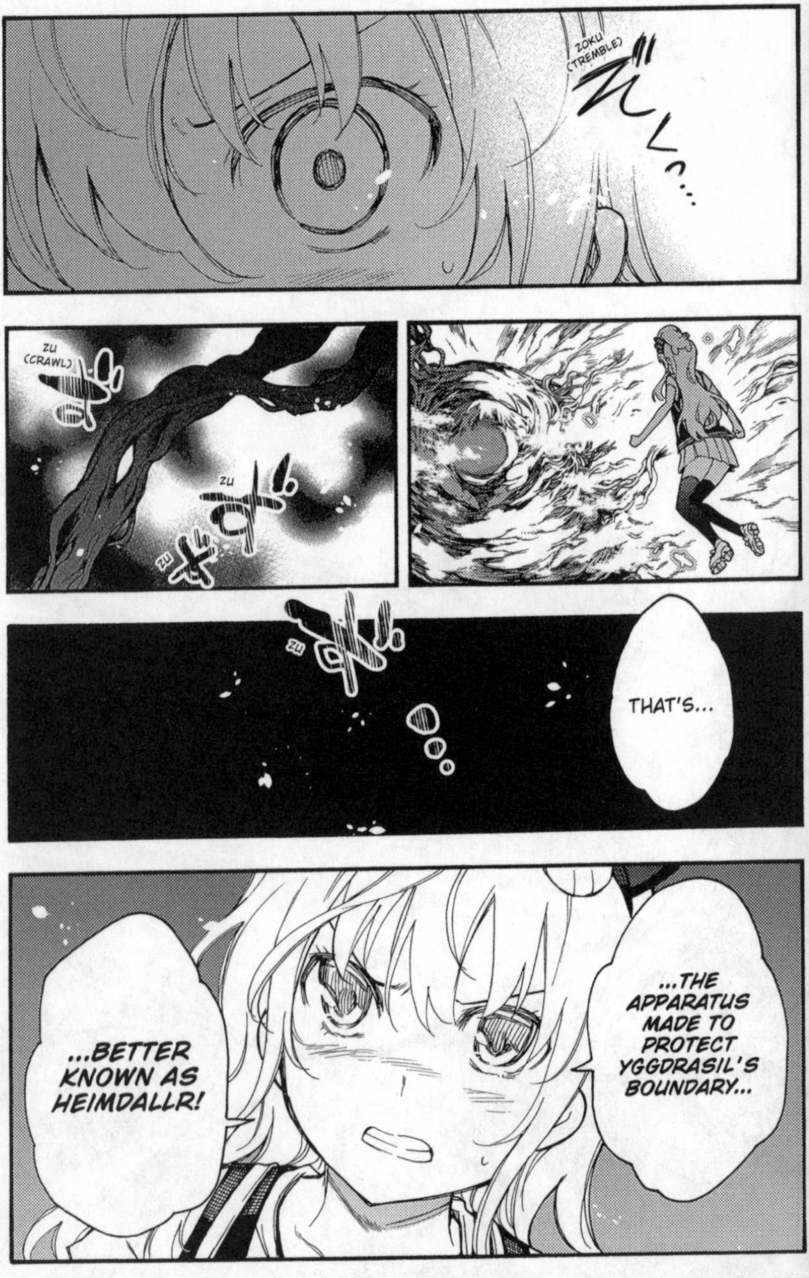
ZOKU (TREMBLE)
ZU (CRAWL)
ZU
ZU
THAT'S...
ZU
...THE APPARATUS MADE TO PROTECT YGGDRASIL'S BOUNDARY...
...BETTER KNOWN AS HEIMDALLR!

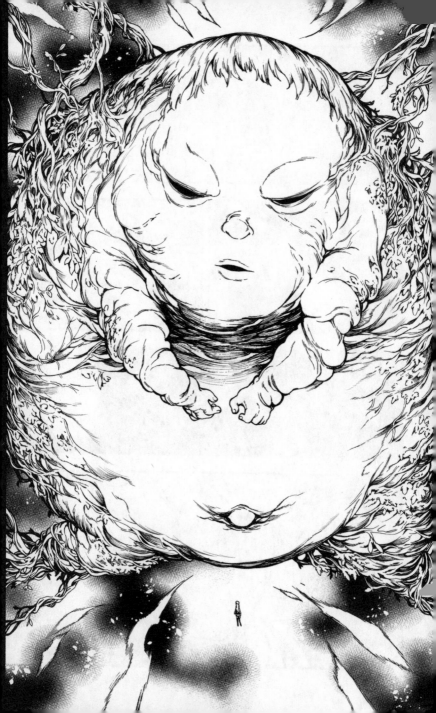

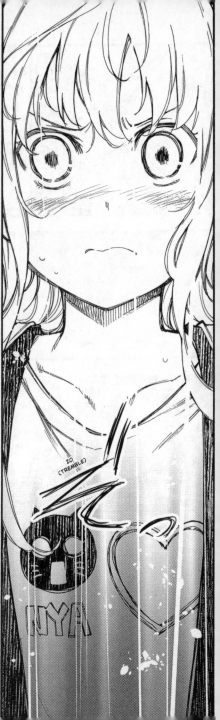

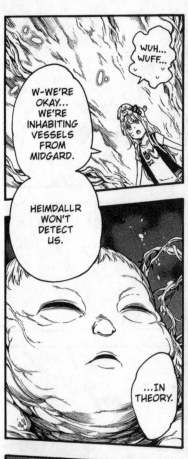

WUH... WUFF...

W-WE'RE OKAY... WE'RE INHABITING VESSELS FROM MIDGARD.

HEIMDALLR WON'T DETECT US.

...IN THEORY.

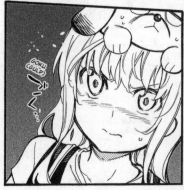

GOKU (GULP)

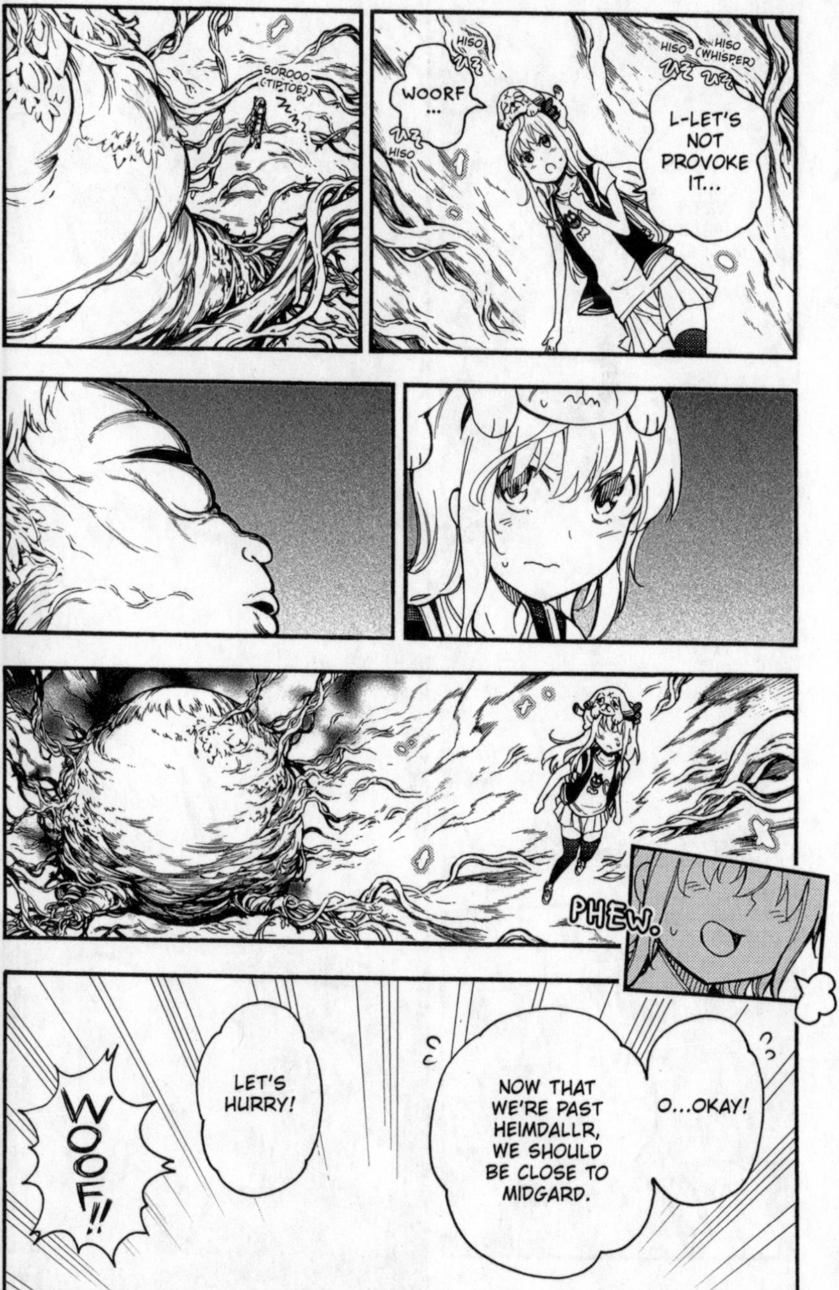
HISO HISO (WHISPER)
L-LET'S NOT PROVOKE IT...
HISO
WOORF...
HISO
SOROOO (TIPTOE)
PHEW.
O...OKAY!
NOW THAT WE'RE PAST HEIMDALLR, WE SHOULD BE CLOSE TO MIDGARD.
LET'S HURRY!
WOOF!!

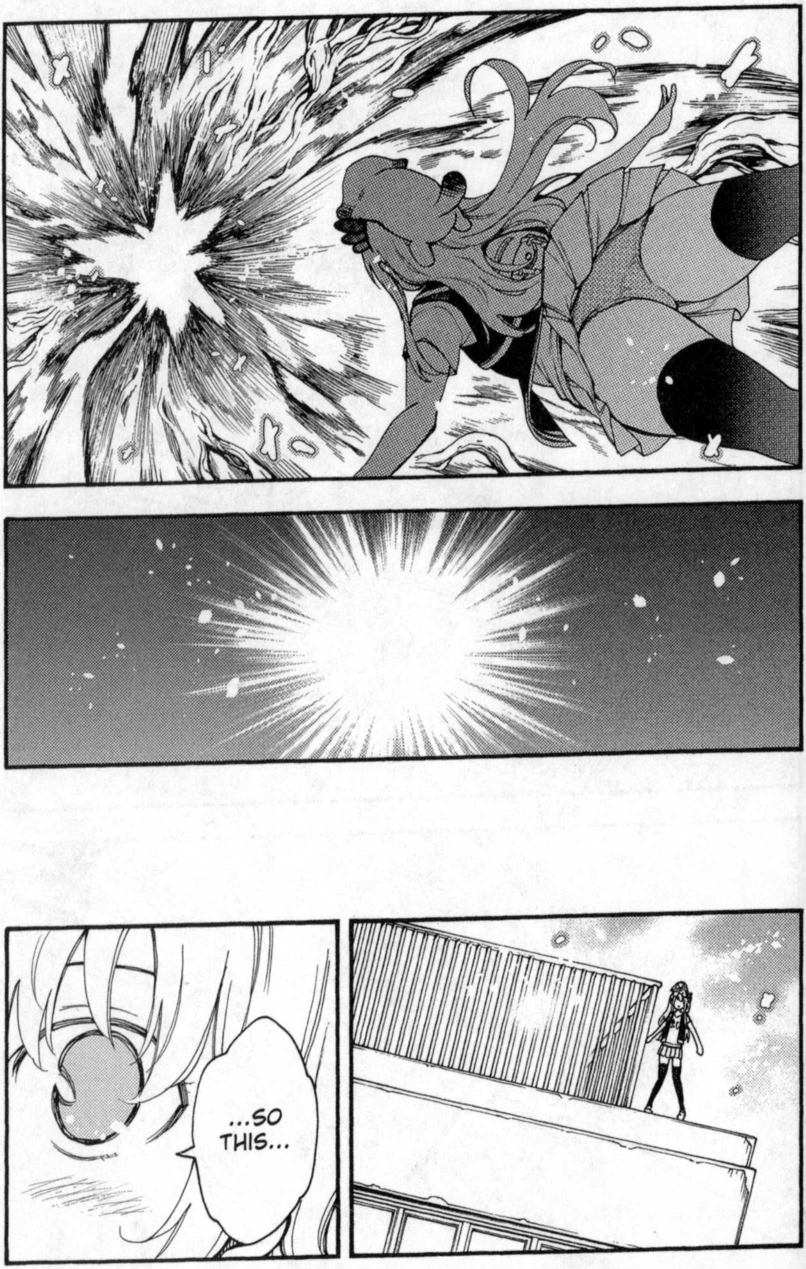
...SO THIS...

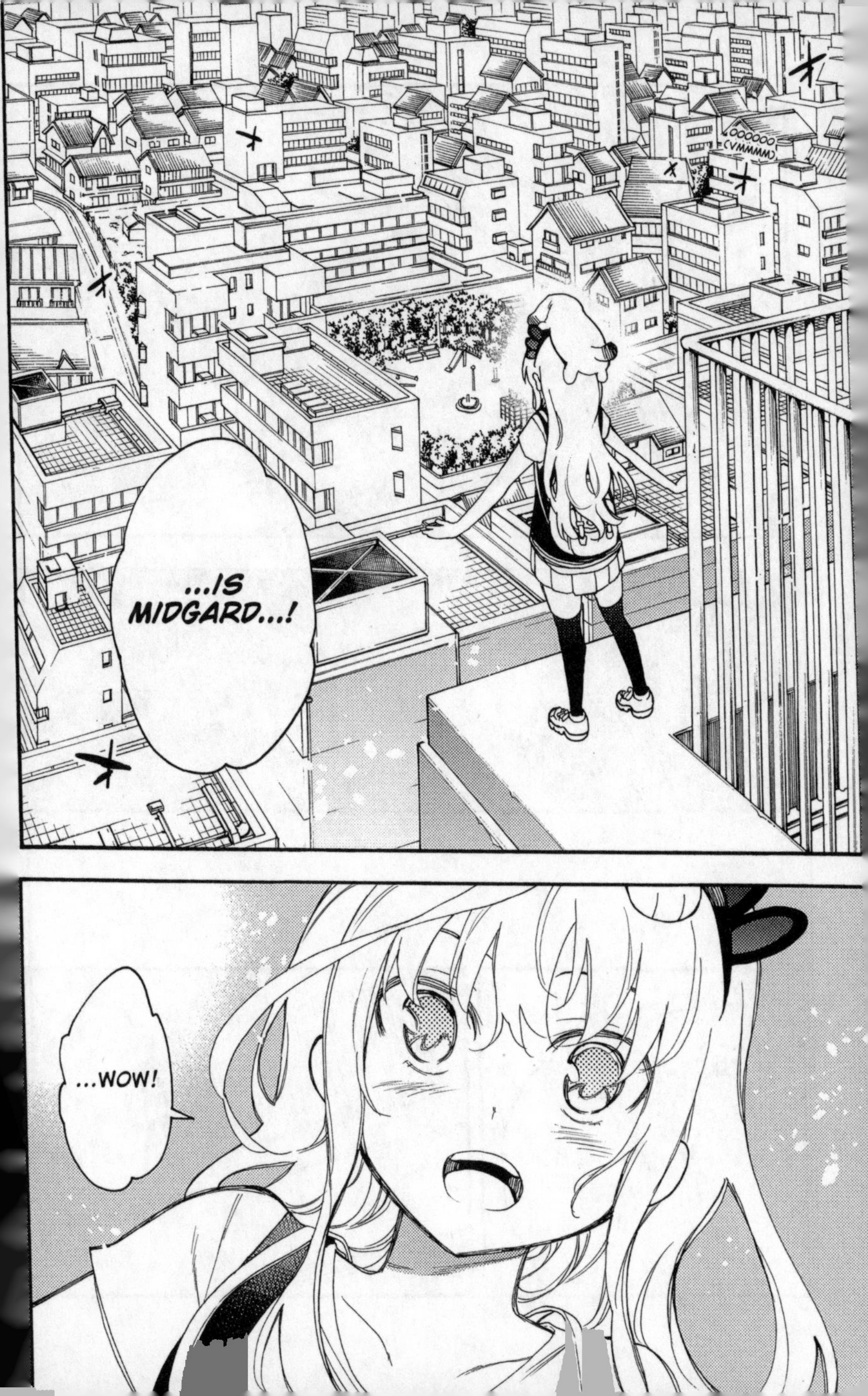
OOOOOO
(VMMMMM)
...IS MIDGARD...!
...WOW!

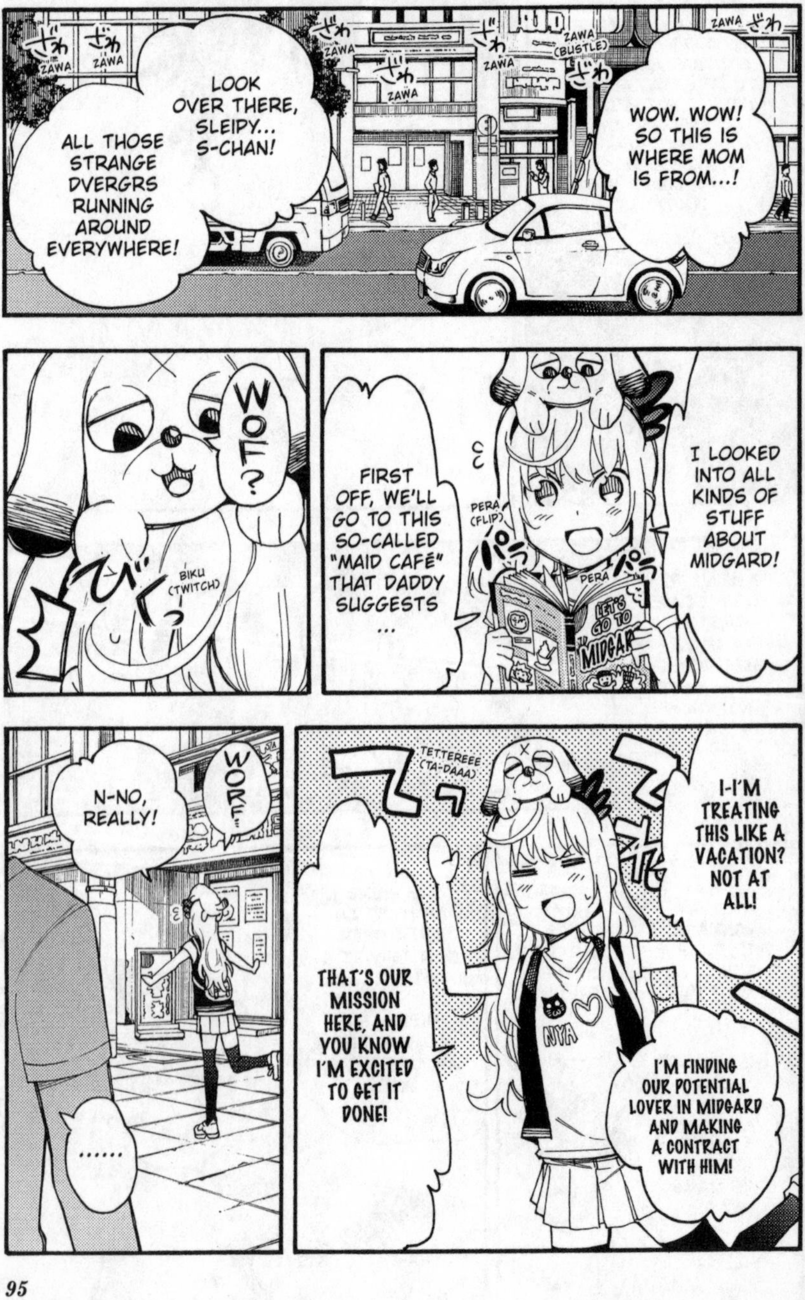
ZAWA ZAWA
ZAWA (BUSTLE)
WOW. WOW! SO THIS IS WHERE MOM IS FROM...!
ZAWA ZAWA ZAWA ZAWA ZAWA
LOOK OVER THERE, SLEIPY... S-CHAN!
ALL THOSE STRANGE DVERGRS RUNNING AROUND EVERYWHERE!
I LOOKED INTO ALL KINDS OF STUFF ABOUT MIDGARD!
PERA PERA (FLIP)
LET'S GO TO MIDGARD
FIRST OFF, WE'LL GO TO THIS SO-CALLED "MAID CAFÉ" THAT DADDY SUGGESTS ...
WOF?
BIKU (TWITCH)
I-I'M TREATING THIS LIKE A VACATION? NOT AT ALL!
I'M FINDING OUR POTENTIAL LOVER IN MIDGARD AND MAKING A CONTRACT WITH HIM!
TETTEREEE (TA-DAAA)
THAT'S OUR MISSION HERE, AND YOU KNOW I'M EXCITED TO GET IT DONE!
NYA
WORF...
N-NO, REALLY!
......

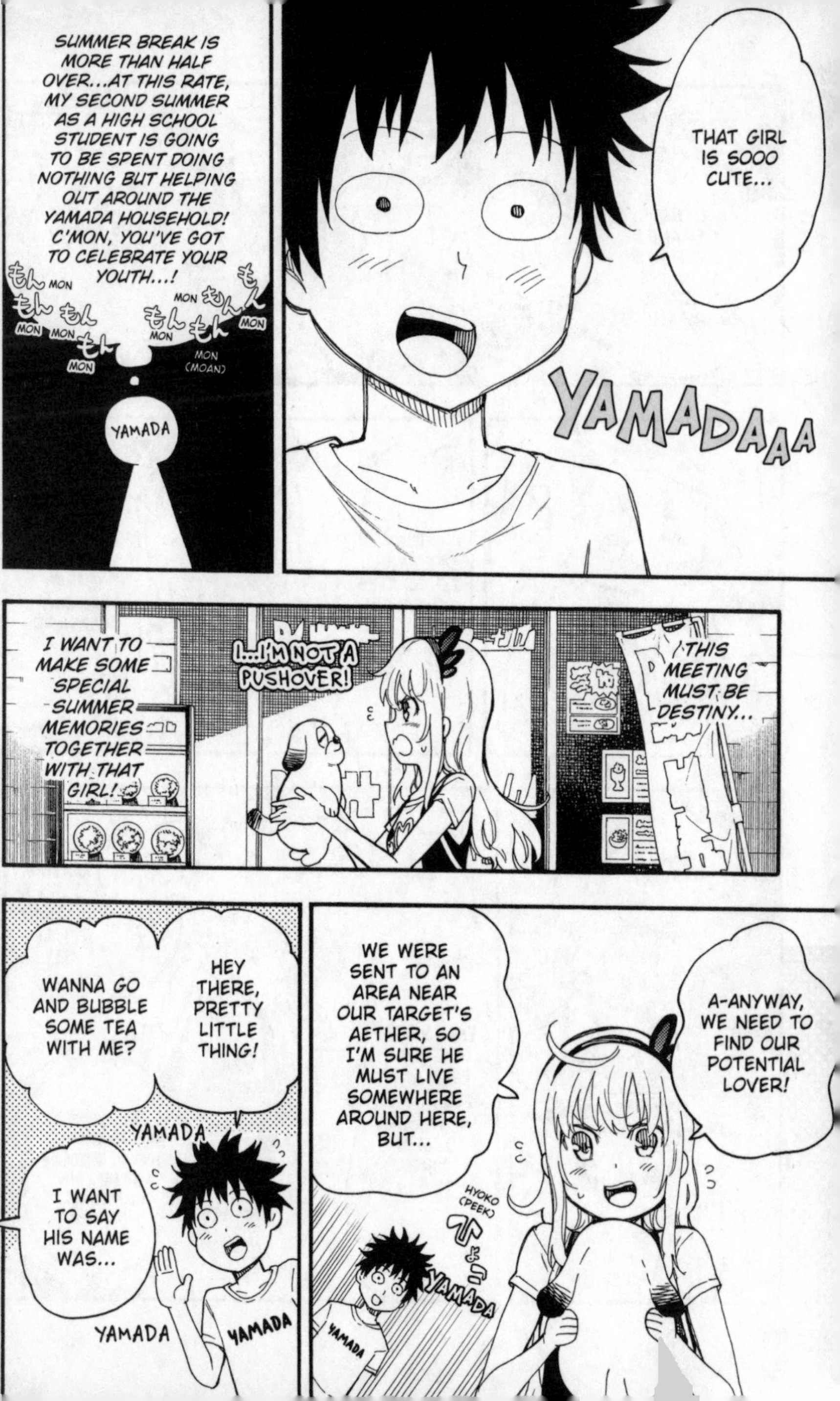
THAT GIRL IS SOOO CUTE...
YAMADAAA
SUMMER BREAK IS MORE THAN HALF OVER...AT THIS RATE, MY SECOND SUMMER AS A HIGH SCHOOL STUDENT IS GOING TO BE SPENT DOING NOTHING BUT HELPING OUT AROUND THE YAMADA HOUSEHOLD! C'MON, YOU'VE GOT TO CELEBRATE YOUR YOUTH...!
もん MON もん MON もん MON もん MON もん MON もん MON もん MON もん MON (MOAN)
YAMADA
THIS MEETING MUST BE DESTINY...
I...I'M NOT A PUSHOVER!
I WANT TO MAKE SOME SPECIAL SUMMER MEMORIES TOGETHER WITH THAT GIRL!
A-ANYWAY, WE NEED TO FIND OUR POTENTIAL LOVER!
WE WERE SENT TO AN AREA NEAR OUR TARGET'S AETHER, SO I'M SURE HE MUST LIVE SOMEWHERE AROUND HERE, BUT...
HYOKO (PEEK)
YAMADA
YAMADA
HEY THERE, PRETTY LITTLE THING!
WANNA GO AND BUBBLE SOME TEA WITH ME?
YAMADA
I WANT TO SAY HIS NAME WAS...
YAMADA
YAMADA

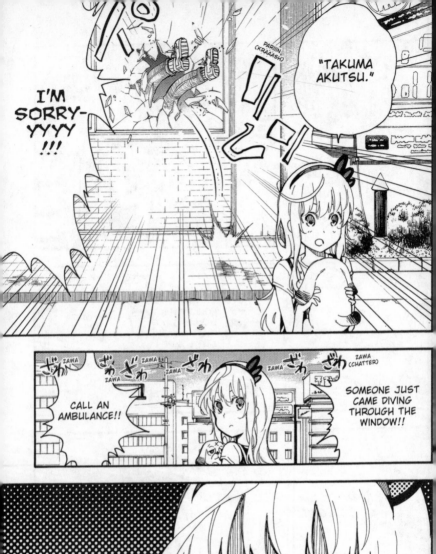

I'M SORRY-YYYY!!!

PARIIIN (KRAAASH)

"TAKUMA AKUTSU."

ZAWA ZAWA ZAWA ZAWA ZAWA ZAWA (CHATTER)

CALL AN AMBULANCE!!

SOMEONE JUST CAME DIVING THROUGH THE WINDOW!!

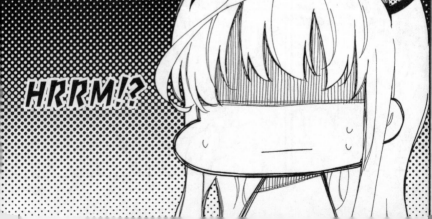

HRRM!?

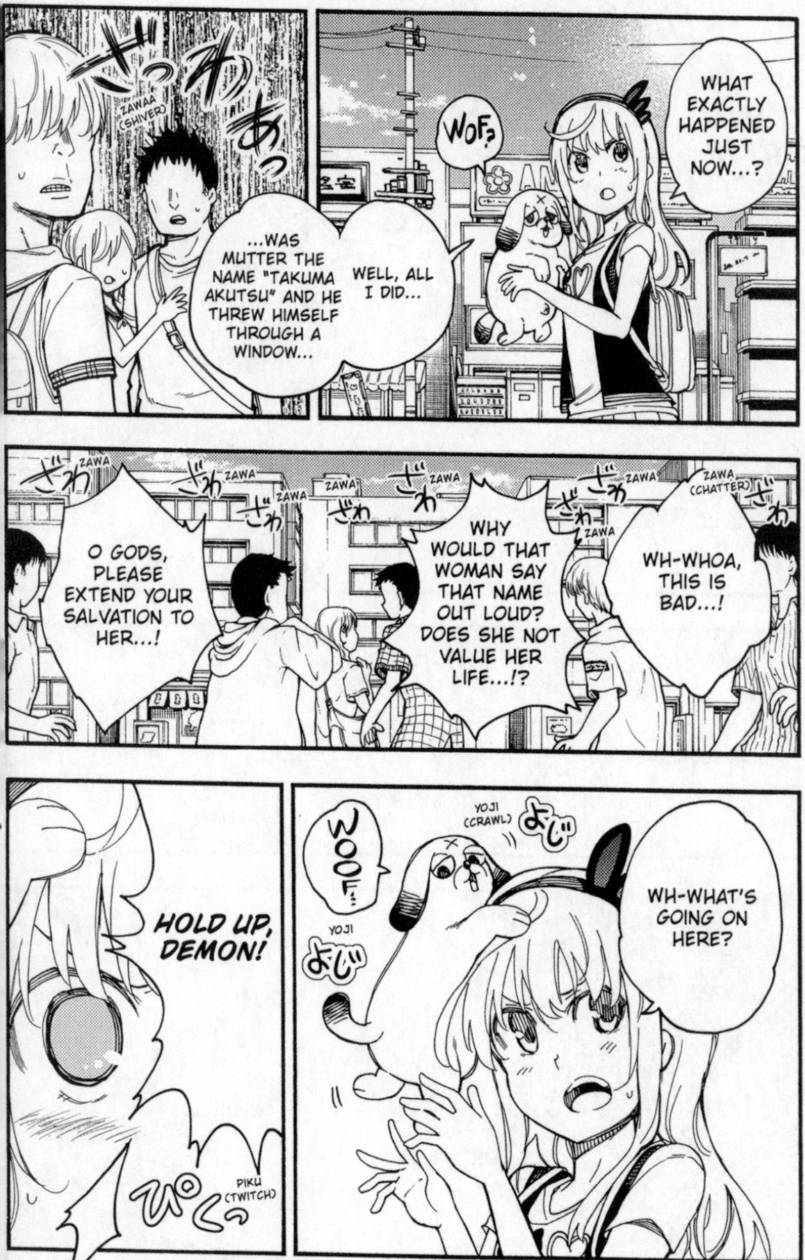
WHAT EXACTLY HAPPENED JUST NOW...?
WOF?
WELL, ALL I DID...
...WAS MUTTER THE NAME "TAKUMA AKUTSU" AND HE THREW HIMSELF THROUGH A WINDOW...
ZAWAA (SHIVER)
ZAWA (CHATTER)
WH-WHOA, THIS IS BAD...!
ZAWA
ZAWA
WHY WOULD THAT WOMAN SAY THAT NAME OUT LOUD? DOES SHE NOT VALUE HER LIFE...!?
ZAWA
ZAWA
ZAWA
ZAWA
ZAWA
O GODS, PLEASE EXTEND YOUR SALVATION TO HER...!
WH-WHAT'S GOING ON HERE?
YOJI (CRAWL)
WOOF!
YOJI
HOLD UP, DEMON!
PIKU (TWITCH)

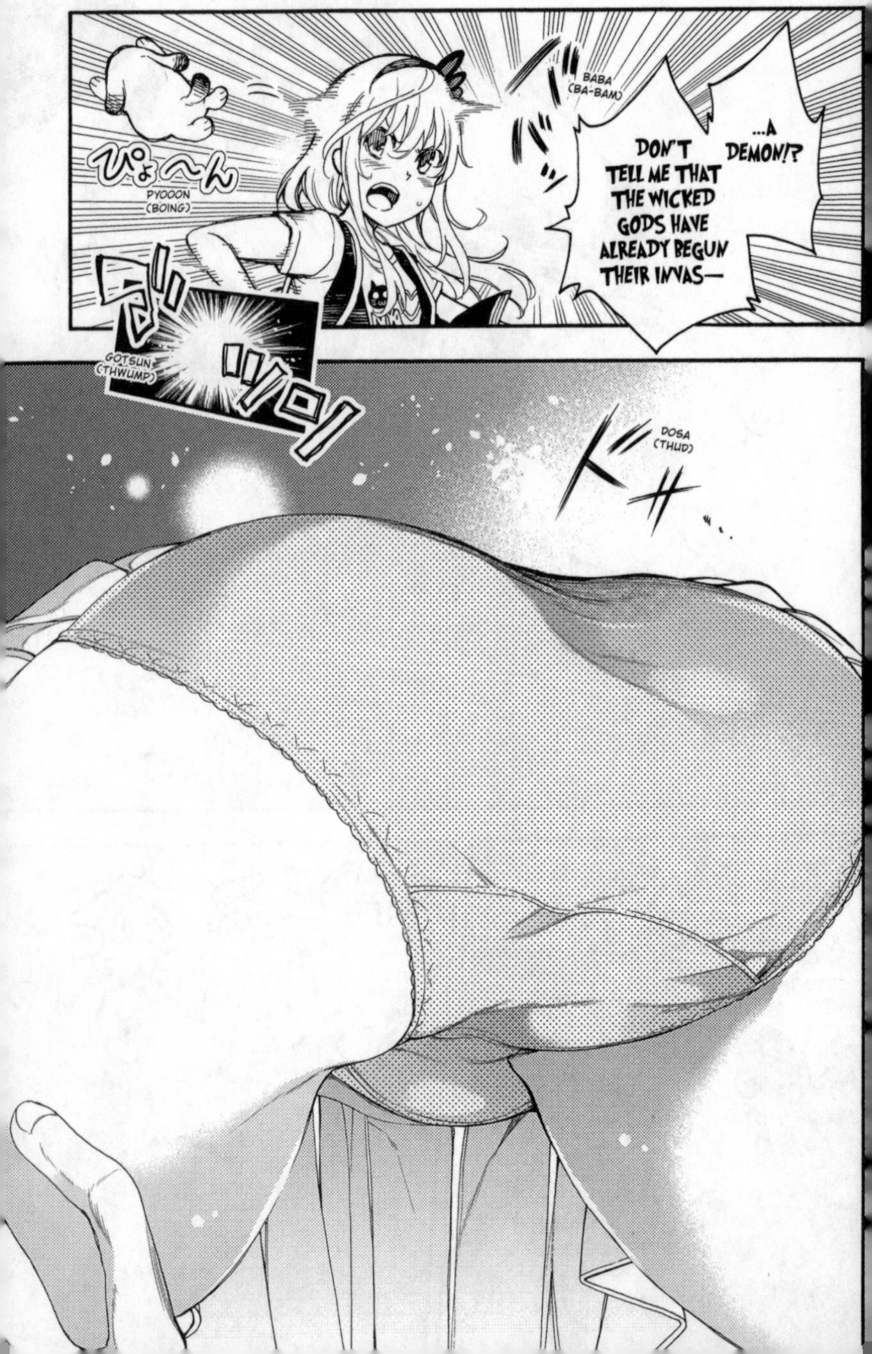
...A DEMON!?
DON'T TELL ME THAT THE WICKED GODS HAVE ALREADY BEGUN THEIR INVAS—
BABA (BA-BAM)
PYOOON (BOING)
GOTSUN (THWUMP)
DOSA (THUD)

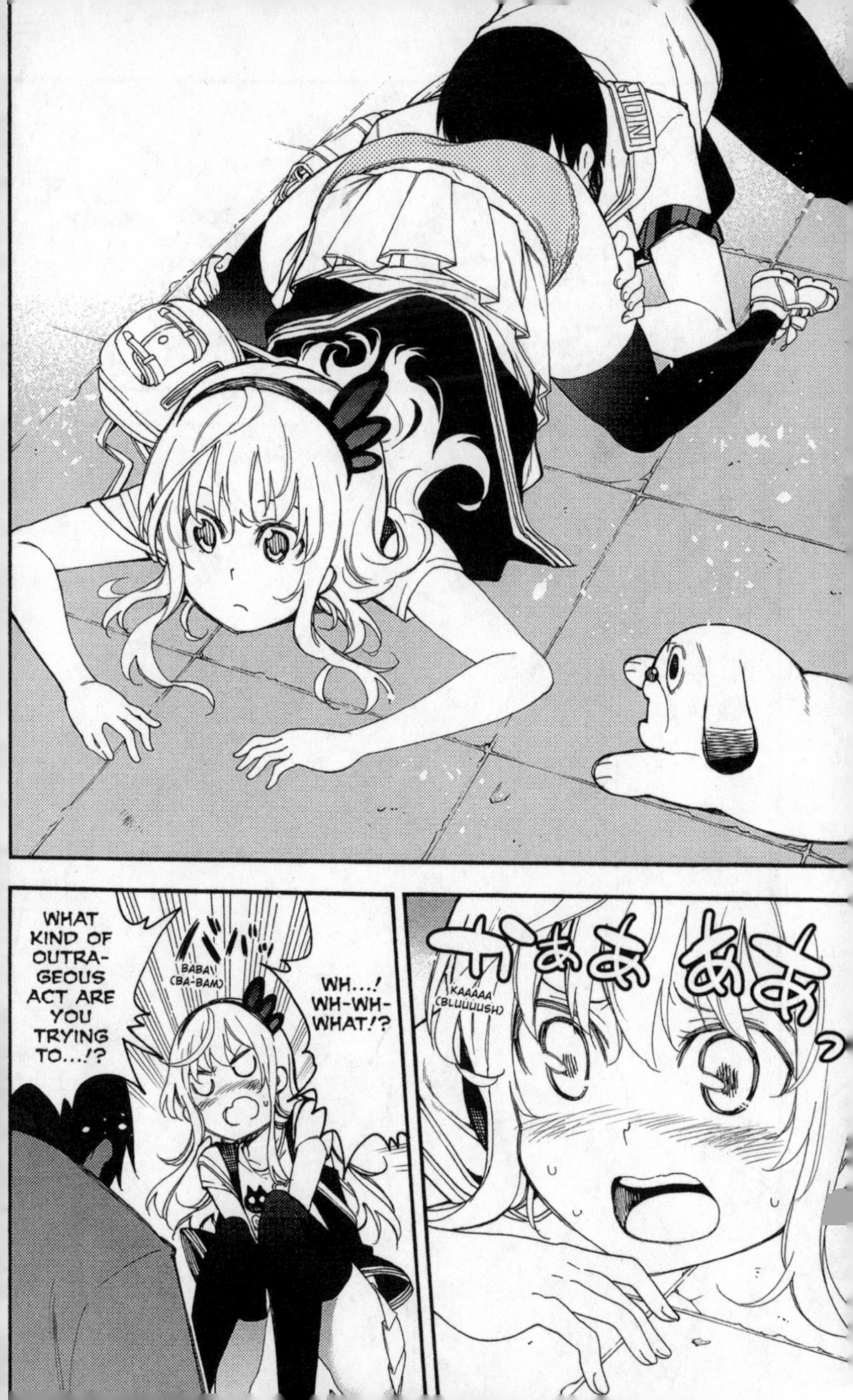
かぁぁ あぁっ
KAAAAA (BLUUUUSH)
WH...! WH-WH-WHAT!?
ババ
BABA\ (BA-BAM)
WHAT KIND OF OUTRAGEOUS ACT ARE YOU TRYING TO...!?

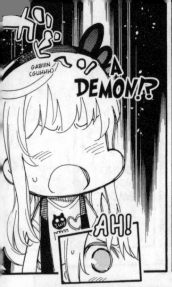

GABIIIN
(GUHHH)

A DEMON!?

AH!

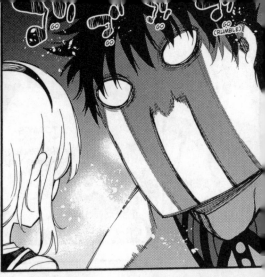

GO
(RUMBLE)

GO

GO

GO

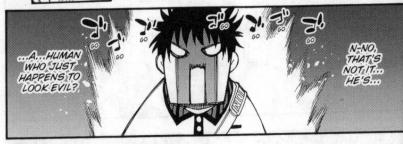

...A...HUMAN WHO JUST HAPPENS TO LOOK EVIL?

GO

GO

GO

GO

N-NO, THAT'S NOT IT... HE'S...

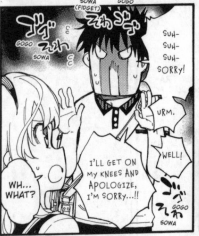

SOWA (FIDGET)

GOGO

GOGO

SOWA

SUH- SUH- SUH- SORRY!

URM.

WELL!

WH... WHAT?

I'LL GET ON MY KNEES AND APOLOGIZE, I'M SORRY...!!

GOGO

SOWA

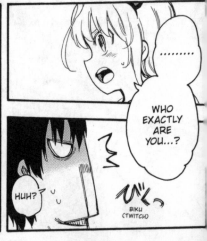

....

WHO EXACTLY ARE YOU...?

HUH?

BIKU (TWITCH)

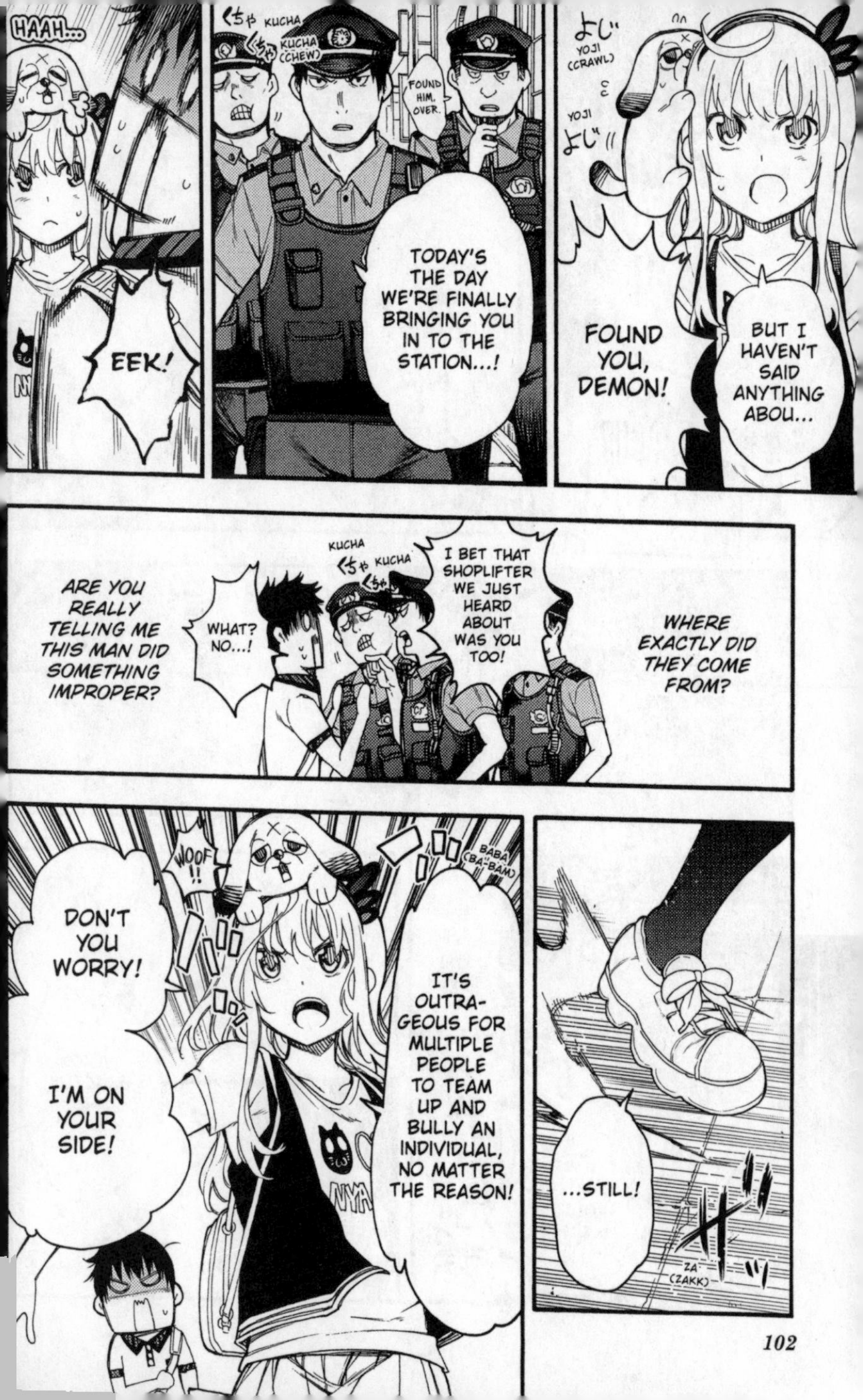
よじ YOJI (CRAWL)
よじ YOJI
BUT I HAVEN'T SAID ANYTHING ABOU...
FOUND YOU, DEMON!
くちゃ KUCHA
くちゃ KUCHA (CHEW)
FOUND HIM. OVER.
TODAY'S THE DAY WE'RE FINALLY BRINGING YOU IN TO THE STATION...!
HAAH...
EEK!
WHERE EXACTLY DID THEY COME FROM?
I BET THAT SHOPLIFTER WE JUST HEARD ABOUT WAS YOU TOO!
くちゃ KUCHA
くちゃ KUCHA
WHAT? NO...!
ARE YOU REALLY TELLING ME THIS MAN DID SOMETHING IMPROPER?
...STILL!
ZA (ZAKK)
BABA (BA-BAM)
IT'S OUTRAGEOUS FOR MULTIPLE PEOPLE TO TEAM UP AND BULLY AN INDIVIDUAL, NO MATTER THE REASON!
WOOF!!
DON'T YOU WORRY!
I'M ON YOUR SIDE!

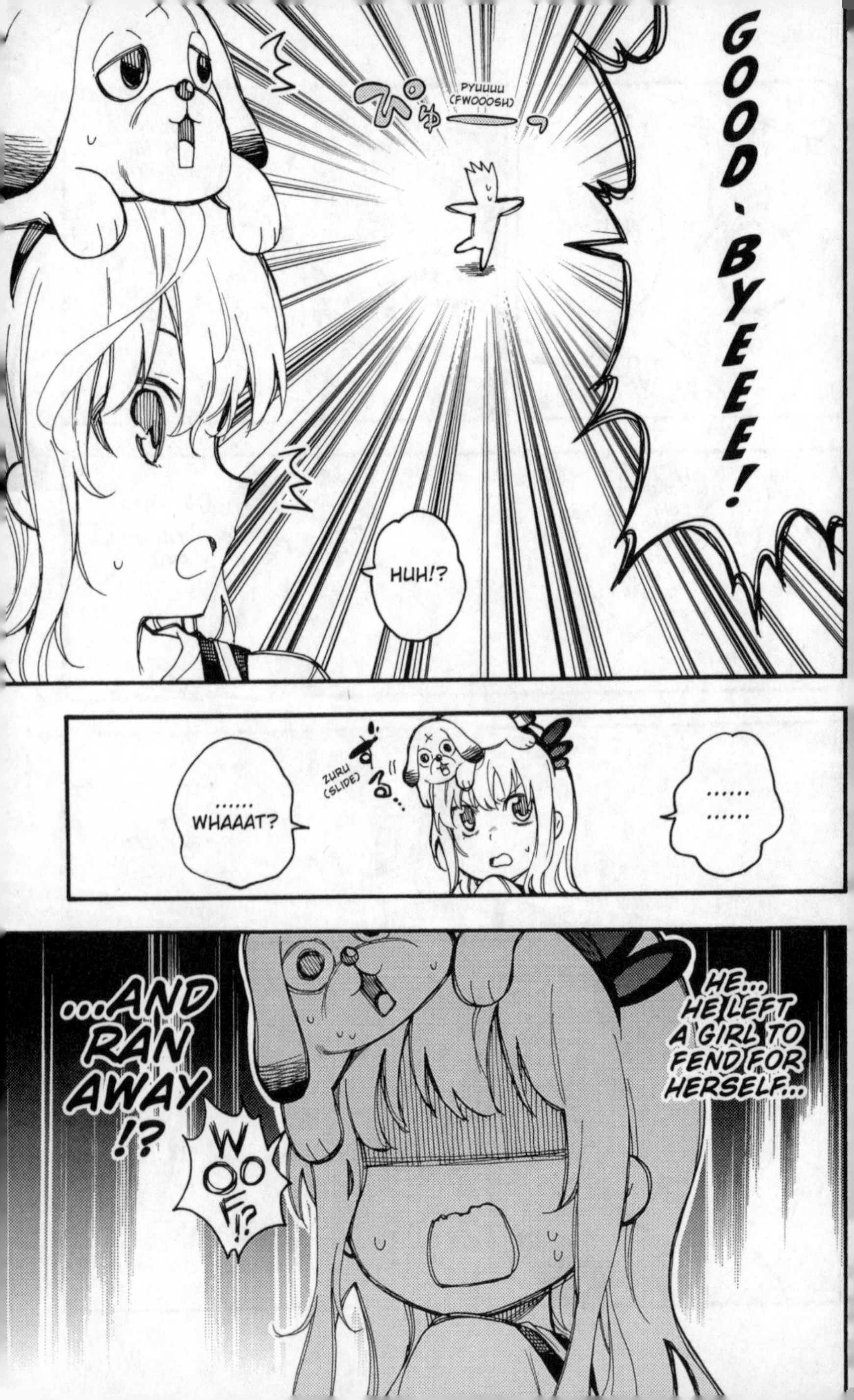
GOOD-BYEEEE!
PYUUUU (FWOOOSH)
HUH!?
......
......
ZURU (SLIDE)
......
WHAAAT?
HE... HE LEFT A GIRL TO FEND FOR HERSELF...
...AND RAN AWAY!?
WOOF!?

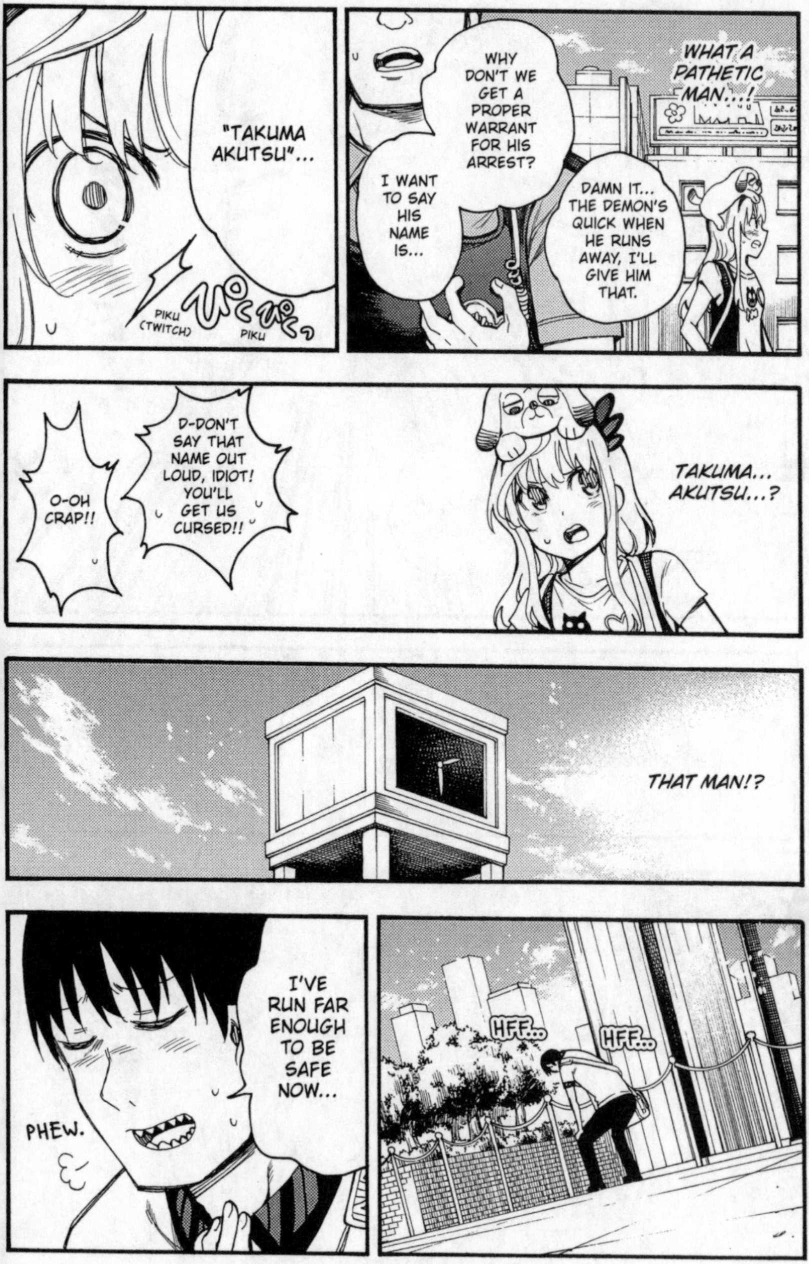
WHAT A PATHETIC MAN...!
DAMN IT... THE DEMON'S QUICK WHEN HE RUNS AWAY, I'LL GIVE HIM THAT.
WHY DON'T WE GET A PROPER WARRANT FOR HIS ARREST?
I WANT TO SAY HIS NAME IS...
"TAKUMA AKUTSU"...
ぴくぴくっ
PIKU PIKU (TWITCH)
TAKUMA... AKUTSU...?
D-DON'T SAY THAT NAME OUT LOUD, IDIOT! YOU'LL GET US CURSED!!
O-OH CRAP!!
THAT MAN!?
HFF...
HFF...
I'VE RUN FAR ENOUGH TO BE SAFE NOW...
PHEW.

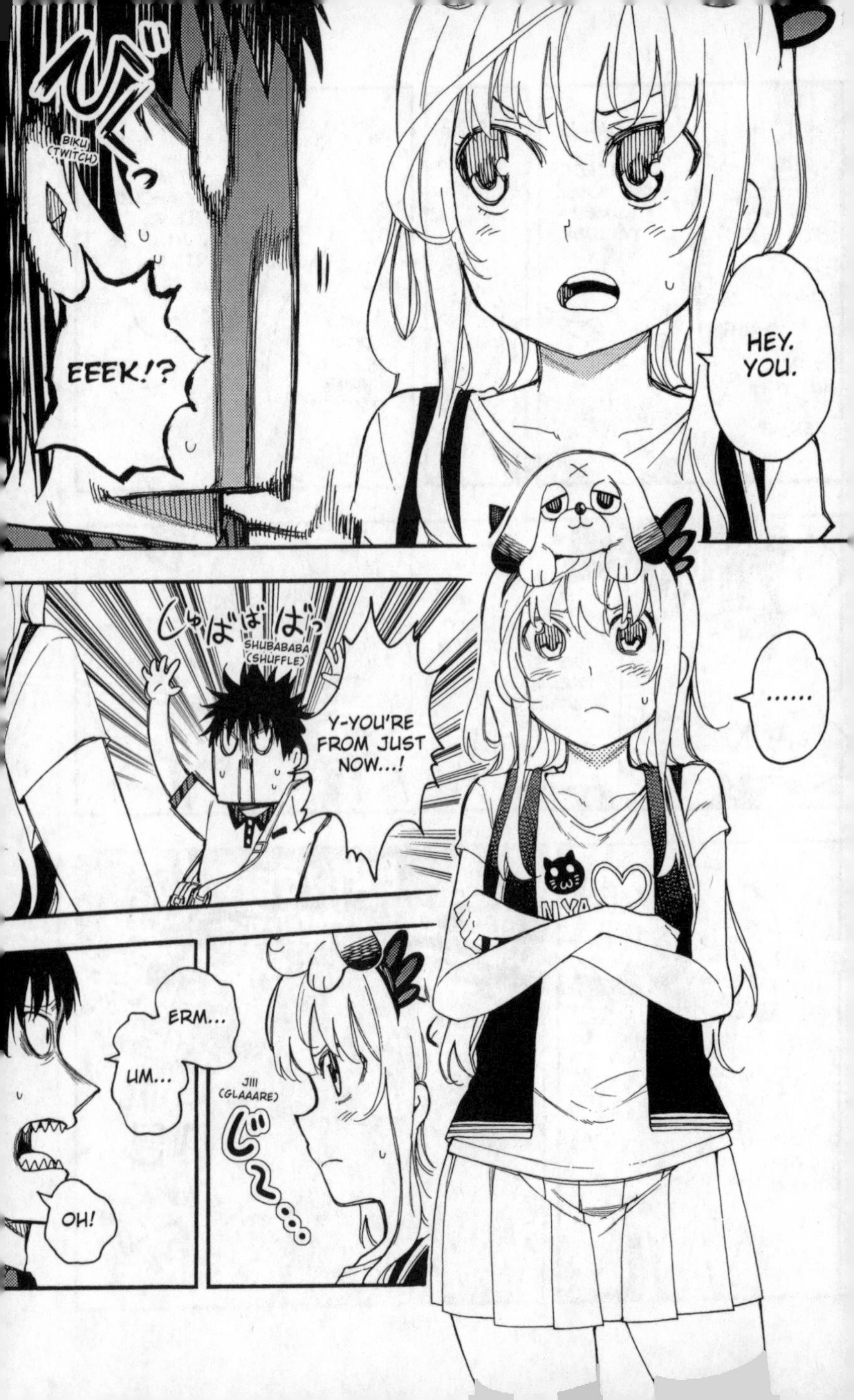
HEY. YOU.
BIKU (TWITCH)
EEEK!?
......
SHUBABABA (SHUFFLE)
Y-YOU'RE FROM JUST NOW...!
JIII (GLAAARE)
ERM...
UM...
OH!

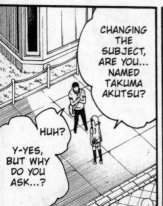

CHANGING THE SUBJECT, ARE YOU... NAMED TAKUMA AKUTSU?

HUH?

Y-YES, BUT WHY DO YOU ASK...?

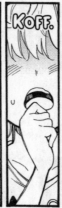

KOFF.

YOU DON'T NEED TO BRING THAT UP!

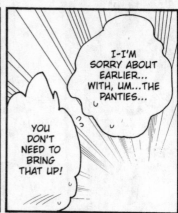

I-I'M SORRY ABOUT EARLIER... WITH, UM...THE PANTIES...

...?

...!?

HE'S TAKUMA AKUTSU...

SO IT IS HIM.

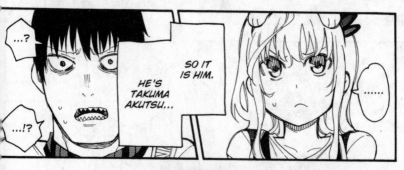

....

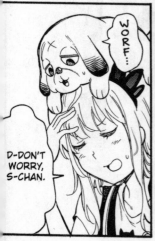

WORF!...

D-DON'T WORRY, S-CHAN.

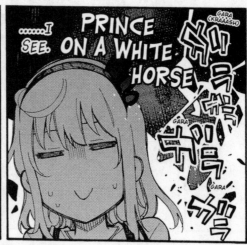

......I SEE.

PRINCE ON A WHITE HORSE

GARA (KRAAASH)

GARA

GARA

106

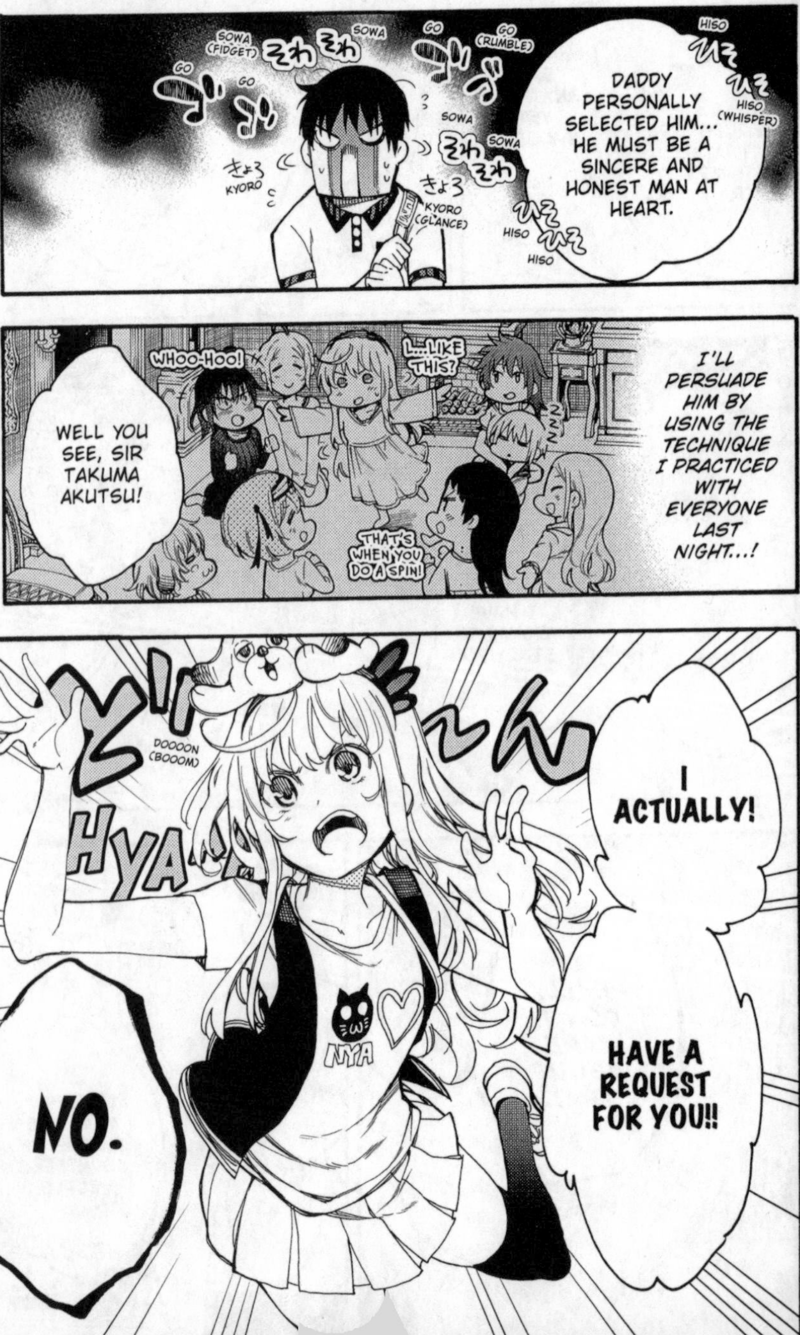

HISO
HISO (WHISPER)
DADDY PERSONALLY SELECTED HIM... HE MUST BE A SINCERE AND HONEST MAN AT HEART.
HISO
HISO
GO
GO (RUMBLE)
SOWA
SOWA (FIDGET)
SOWA
SOWA
GO
GO
きょろ
KYORO (GLANCE)
きょろ
KYORO
I'LL PERSUADE HIM BY USING THE TECHNIQUE I PRACTICED WITH EVERYONE LAST NIGHT...!
L...LIKE THIS?
WHOO-HOO!
THAT'S WHEN YOU DO A SPIN!
WELL YOU SEE, SIR TAKUMA AKUTSU!
I ACTUALLY!
HAVE A REQUEST FOR YOU!!
DOOOON (BOOOM)
HYA
NYA
NO.

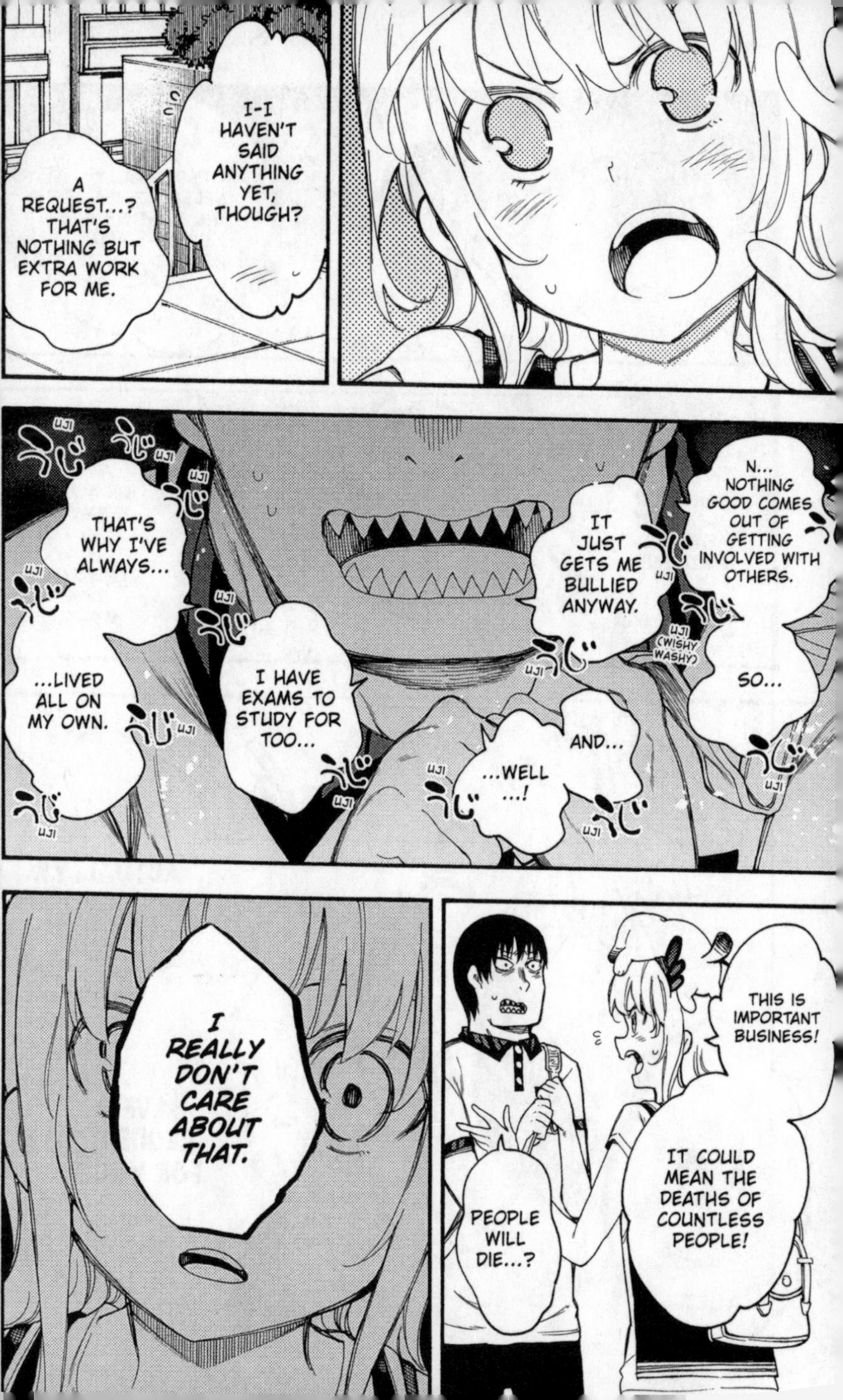
I-I HAVEN'T SAID ANYTHING YET, THOUGH?
A REQUEST...? THAT'S NOTHING BUT EXTRA WORK FOR ME.
N... NOTHING GOOD COMES OUT OF GETTING INVOLVED WITH OTHERS.
IT JUST GETS ME BULLIED ANYWAY.
うじ UJI (WISHY WASHY)
SO...
AND...
...WELL ...!
I HAVE EXAMS TO STUDY FOR TOO...
THAT'S WHY I'VE ALWAYS...
...LIVED ALL ON MY OWN.
うじ UJI
THIS IS IMPORTANT BUSINESS!
IT COULD MEAN THE DEATHS OF COUNTLESS PEOPLE!
PEOPLE WILL DIE...?
I REALLY DON'T CARE ABOUT THAT.

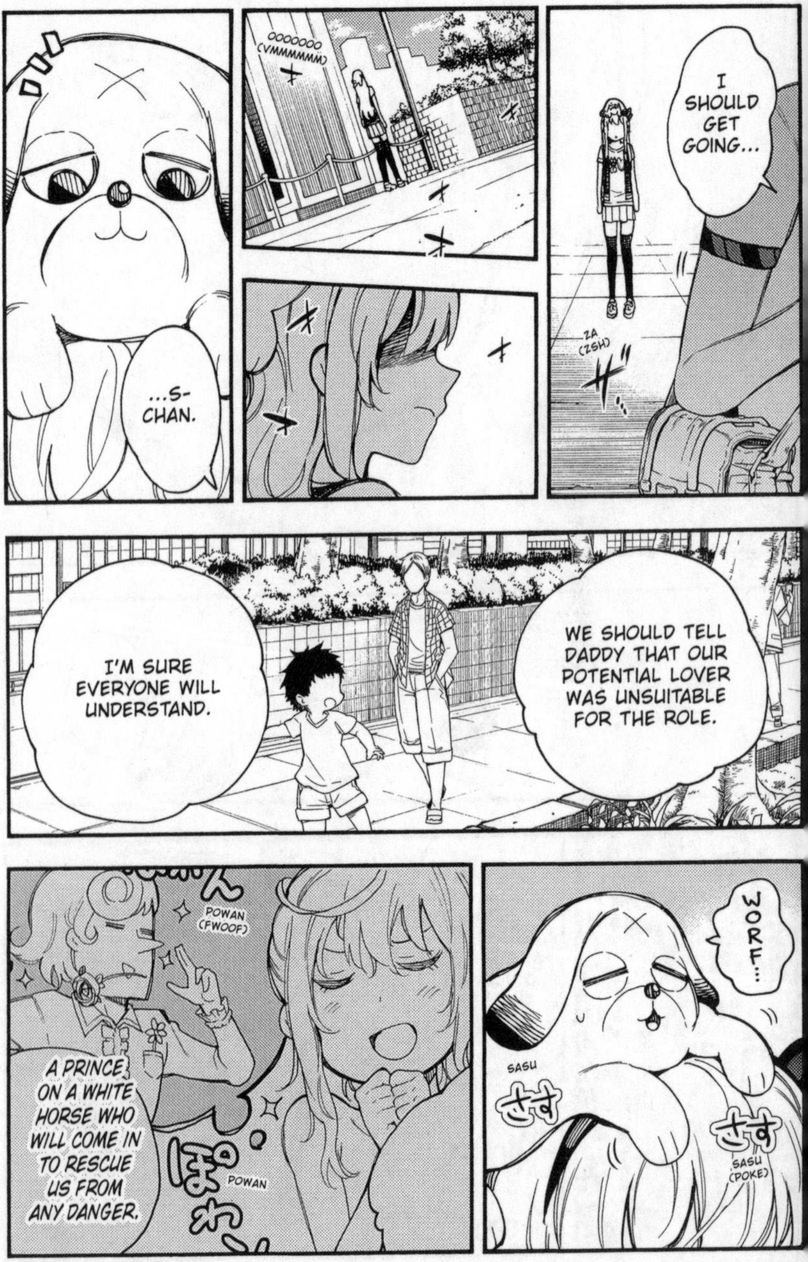
I SHOULD GET GOING...
ZA (ZSH)
OOOOOOO (VMMMMMM)
...S-CHAN.
WE SHOULD TELL DADDY THAT OUR POTENTIAL LOVER WAS UNSUITABLE FOR THE ROLE.
I'M SURE EVERYONE WILL UNDERSTAND.
WORF...
さす
SASU
さす
SASU (POKE)
POWAN (FWOOF)
A PRINCE ON A WHITE HORSE WHO WILL COME IN TO RESCUE US FROM ANY DANGER.
POWAN

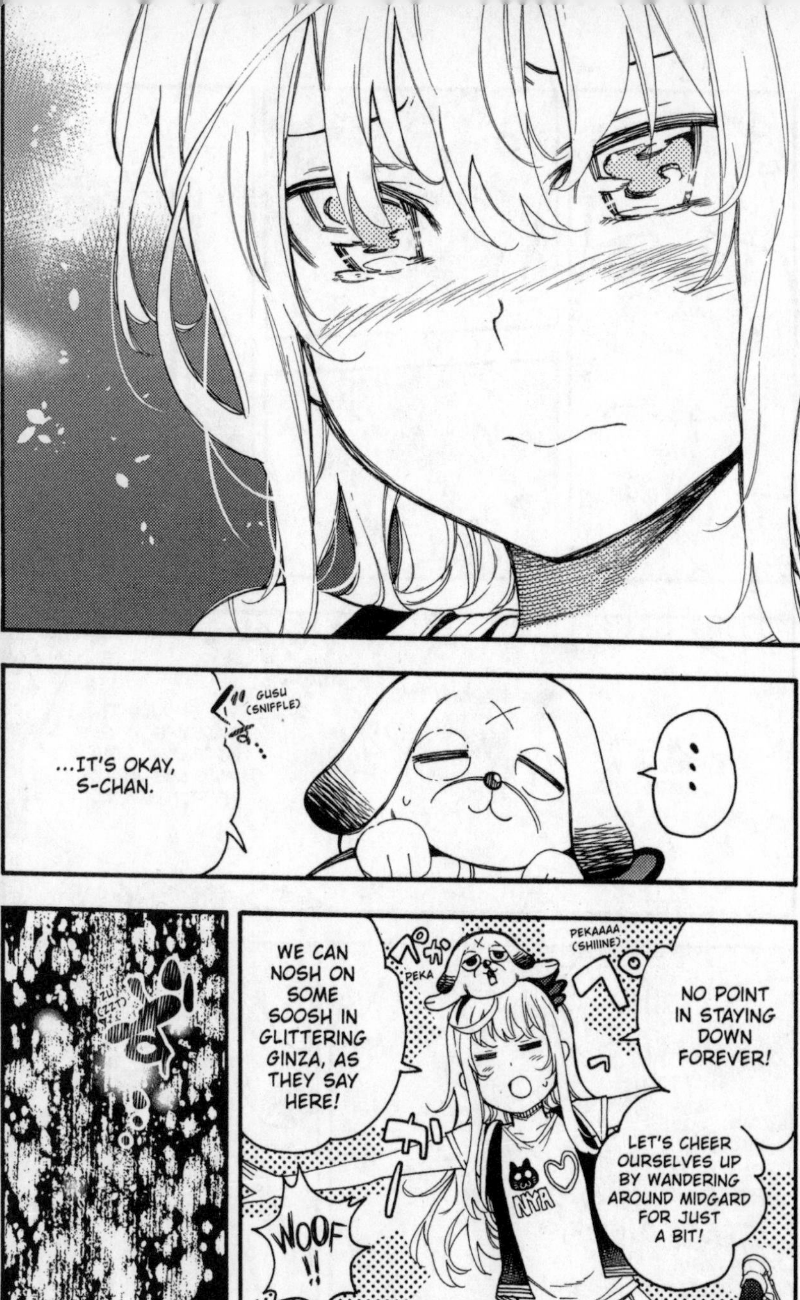

...
GUSU (SNIFFLE)
...IT'S OKAY, S-CHAN.
PEKAAAA (SHIIINE)
NO POINT IN STAYING DOWN FOREVER!
PEKA
WE CAN NOSH ON SOME SOOSH IN GLITTERING GINZA, AS THEY SAY HERE!
LET'S CHEER OURSELVES UP BY WANDERING AROUND MIDGARD FOR JUST A BIT!
WOOF !!
ZU (ZZT)

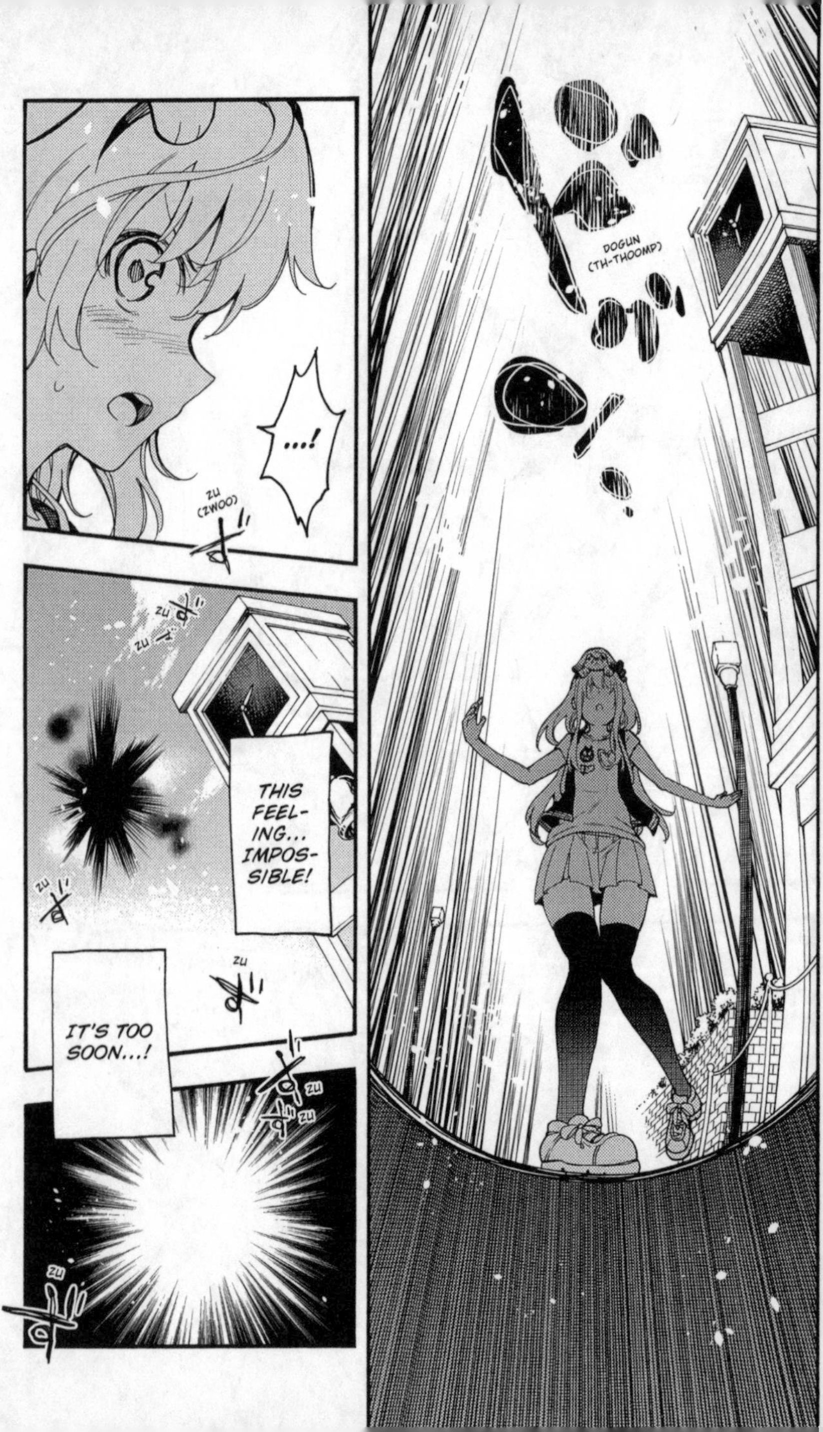
DOGUN
(TH-THOOMP)
...!
ZU
(ZWOO)
ZU
ZU
THIS FEELING... IMPOSSIBLE!
ZU
ZU
IT'S TOO SOON...!
ZU
ZU
ZU

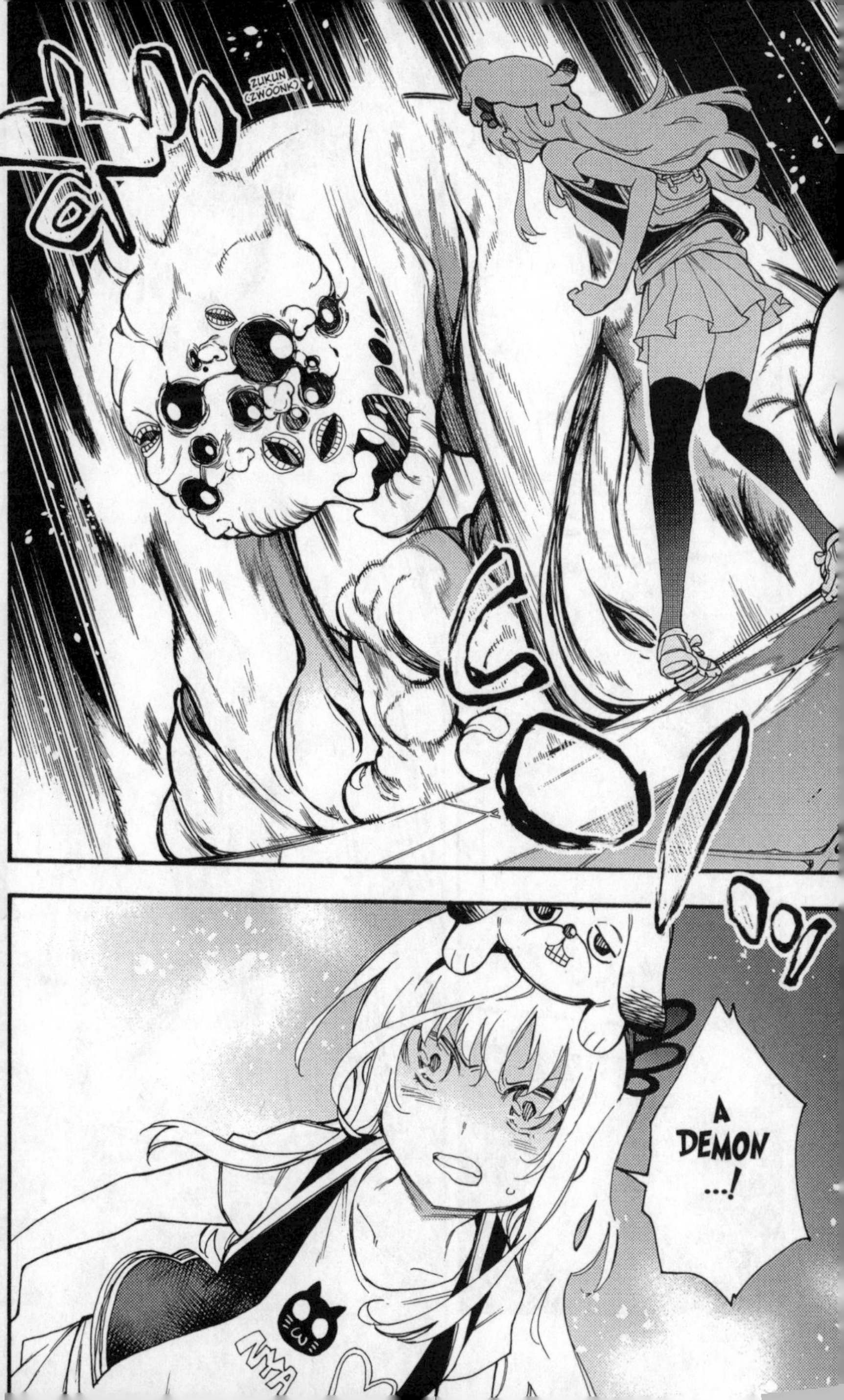
ZUKUN
(ZWOONK)
A DEMON ...!

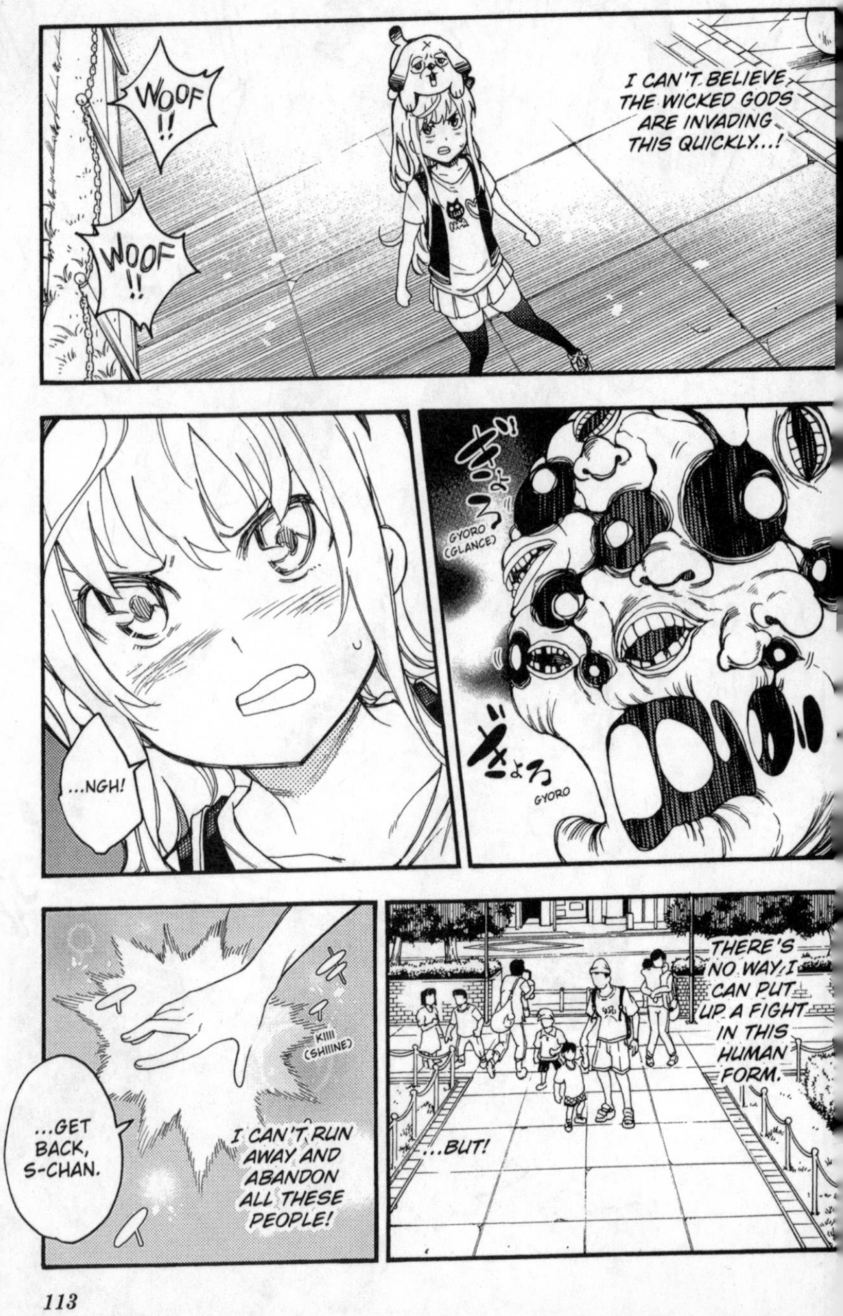
I CAN'T BELIEVE THE WICKED GODS ARE INVADING THIS QUICKLY...!
WOOF!!
WOOF!!
ぎょろ
GYORO (GLANCE)
ぎょろ
GYORO
...NGH!
THERE'S NO WAY I CAN PUT UP A FIGHT IN THIS HUMAN FORM.
...BUT!
KIIII (SHIIINE)
I CAN'T RUN AWAY AND ABANDON ALL THESE PEOPLE!
...GET BACK, S-CHAN.

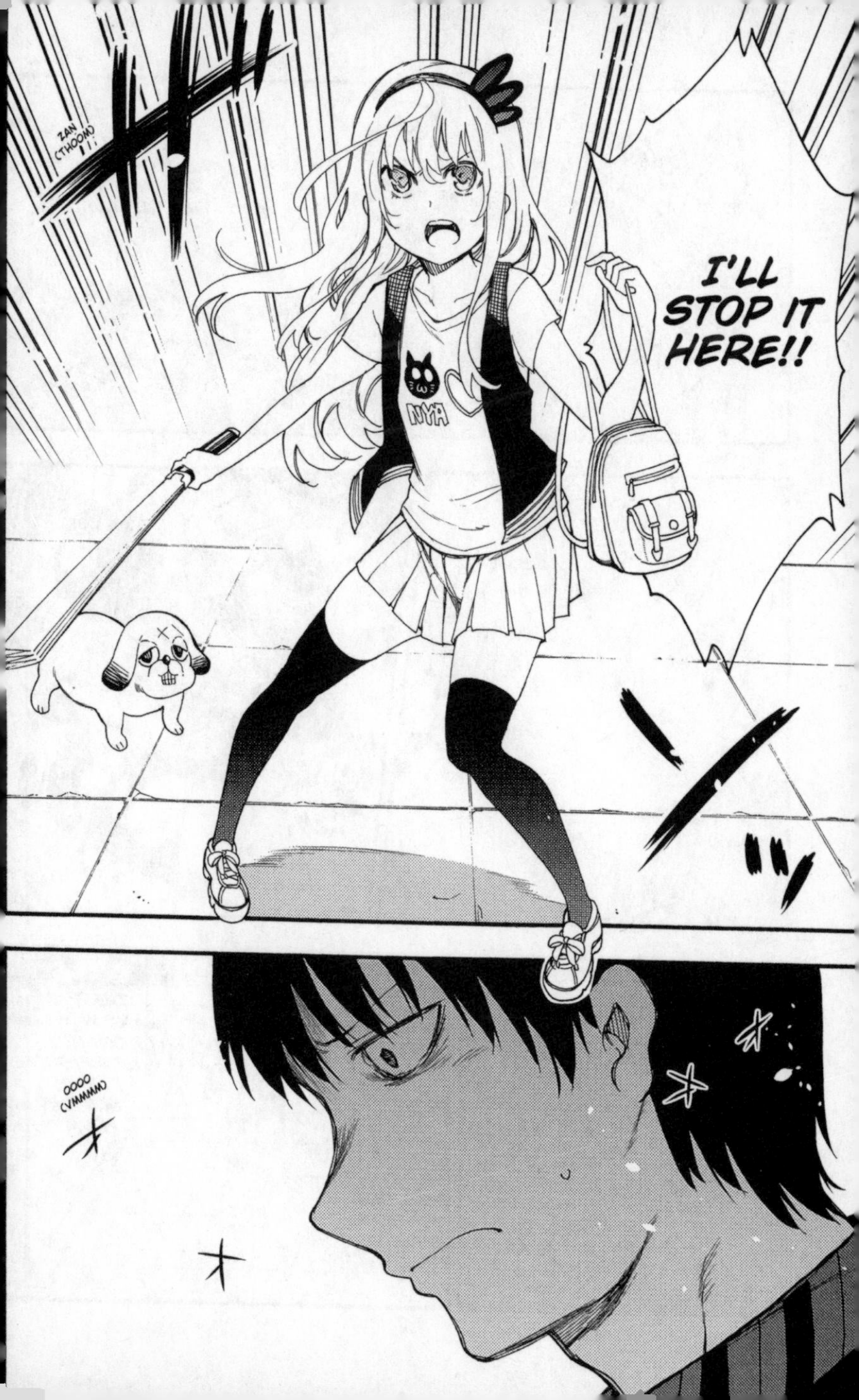
ZAN
(THOOM)
I'LL STOP IT HERE!!
OOOO
(VMMMM)

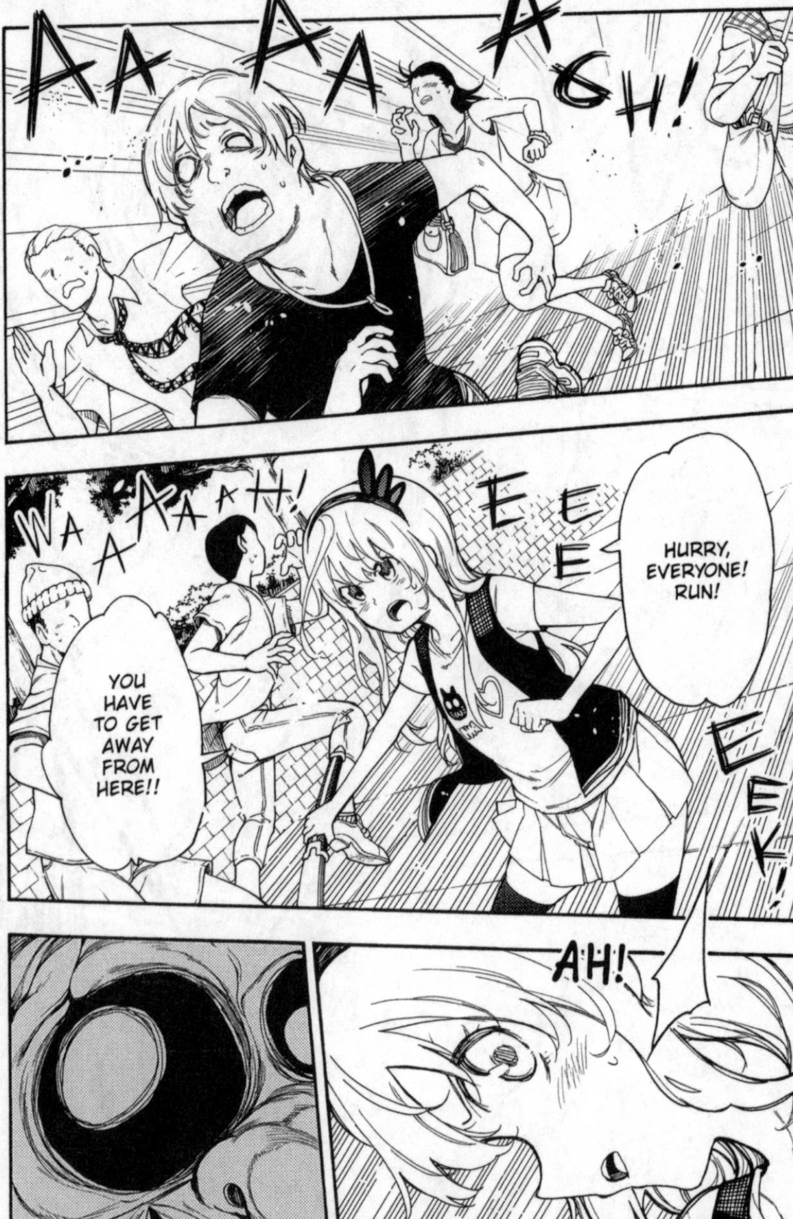
AAAAAGH!
HURRY, EVERYONE! RUN!
EEEEEEK!
WAAAAAH!
YOU HAVE TO GET AWAY FROM HERE!!
AH!

Chapter 53: The Kissing Maiden

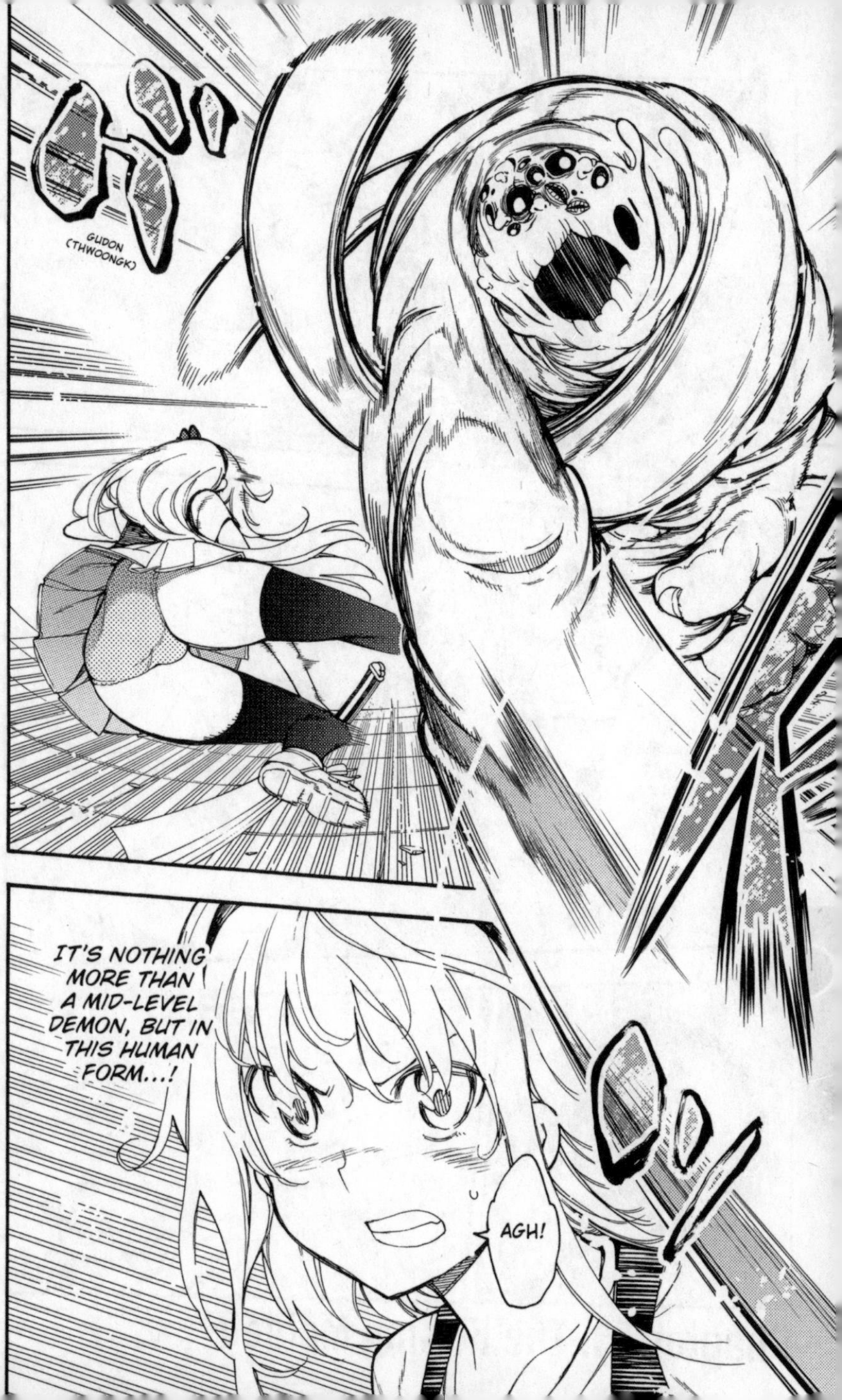
GUDON (THWOONGK)
IT'S NOTHING MORE THAN A MID-LEVEL DEMON, BUT IN THIS HUMAN FORM...!
AGH!

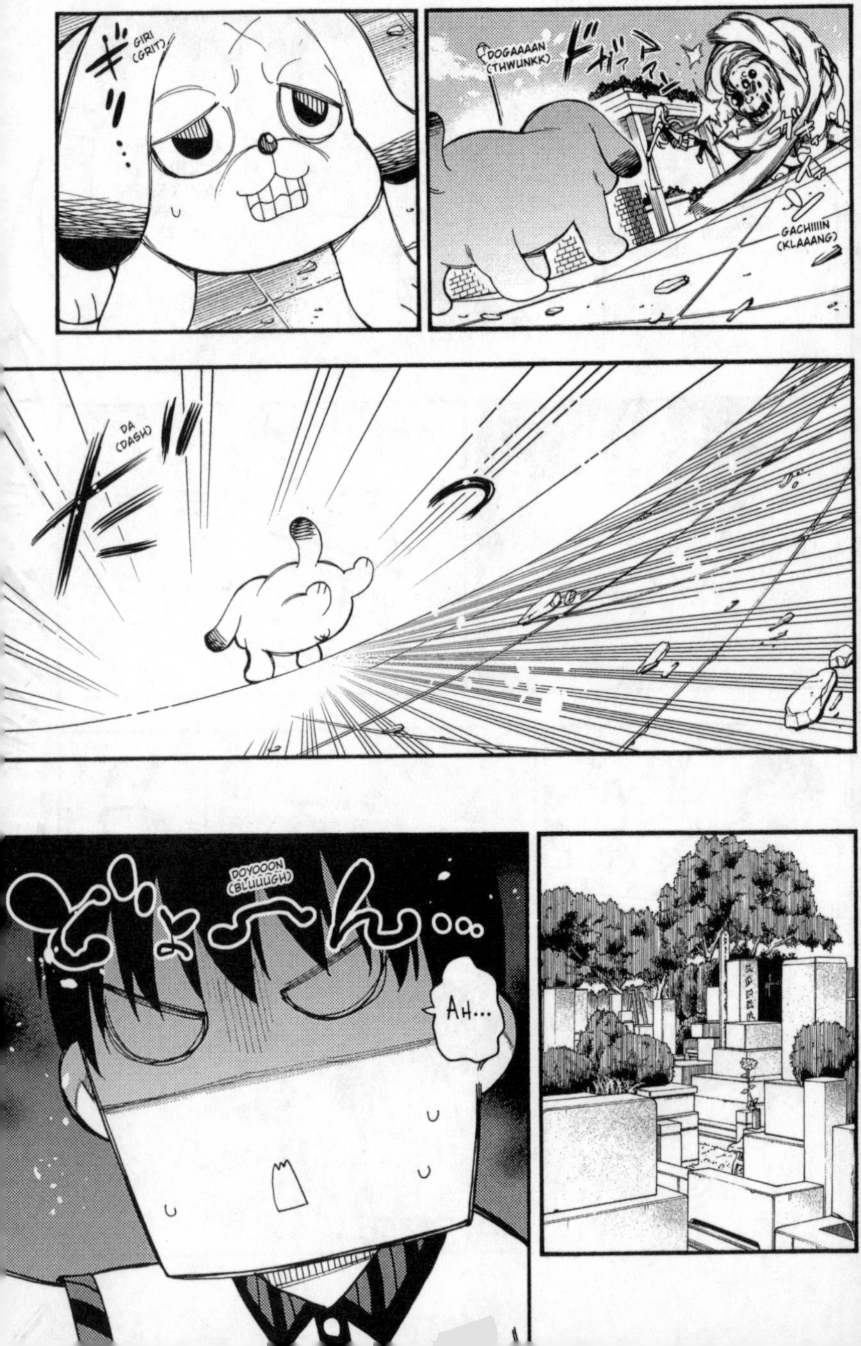
DOGAAAAN (THWUNKK)
GACHIIIIIN (KLAAANG)
GIRI (GRIT)
DA (DASH)
DOYOOON (BLUUUGH)
AH...

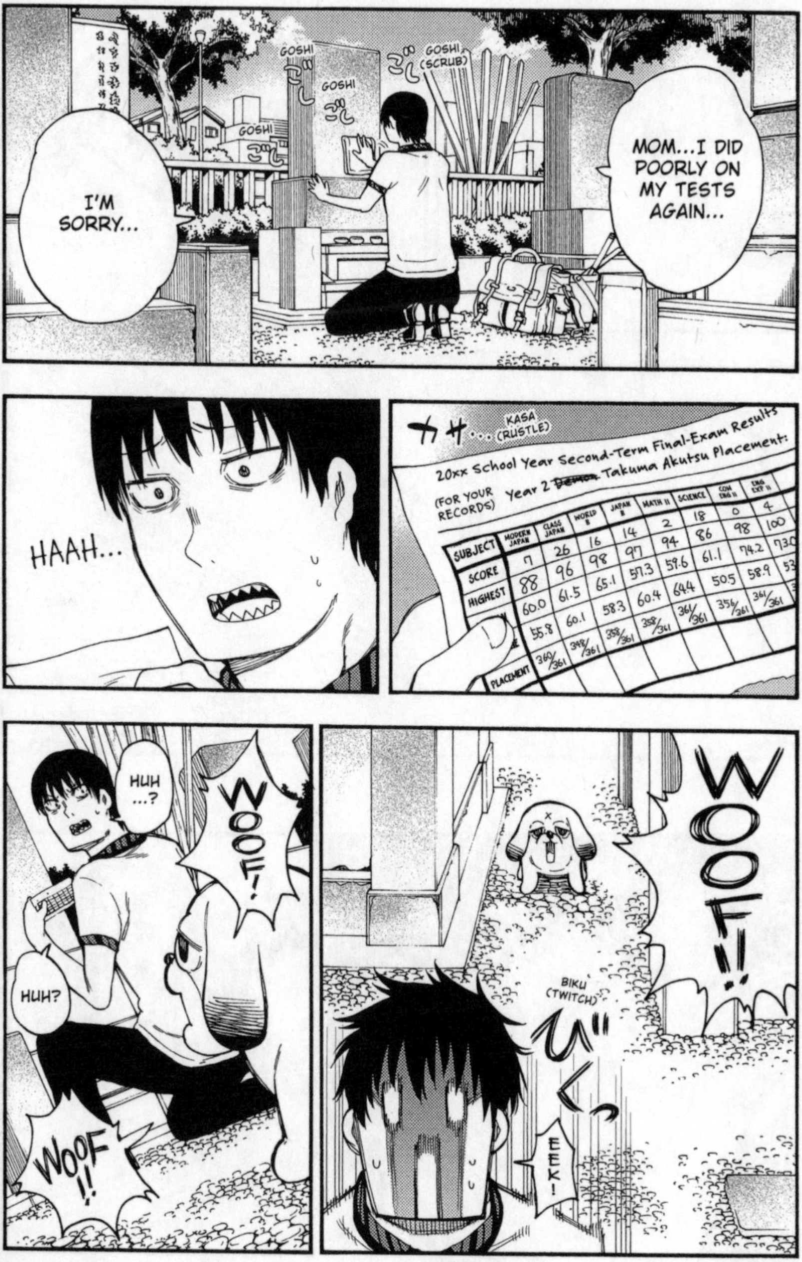
MOM...I DID POORLY ON MY TESTS AGAIN...
GOSHI (SCRUB)
GOSHI
GOSHI
GOSHI
I'M SORRY...
KASA... (RUSTLE)
20xx School Year Second-Term Final-Exam Results
Year 2 Demon Takuma Akutsu Placement:
(FOR YOUR RECORDS)
SUBJECT
SCORE
HIGHEST
PLACEMENT
MODERN JAPAN 7 88 60.0 55.8 360/361
CLASS JAPAN 26 96 61.5 60.1 348/361
WORLD H 16 98 65.1 58.3 358/361
JAPAN H 14 97 57.3 60.4 358/361
MATH II 2 94 59.6 64.4 361/361
SCIENCE 18 86 61.1 50.5 356/361
COM ENG II 0 98 74.2 58.9 361/361
ENG EXP II 4 100 73.0 53
HAAH...
WOOF!!
BIKU (TWITCH)
EEK!
HUH...?
WOOF!
HUH?
WOOF!!

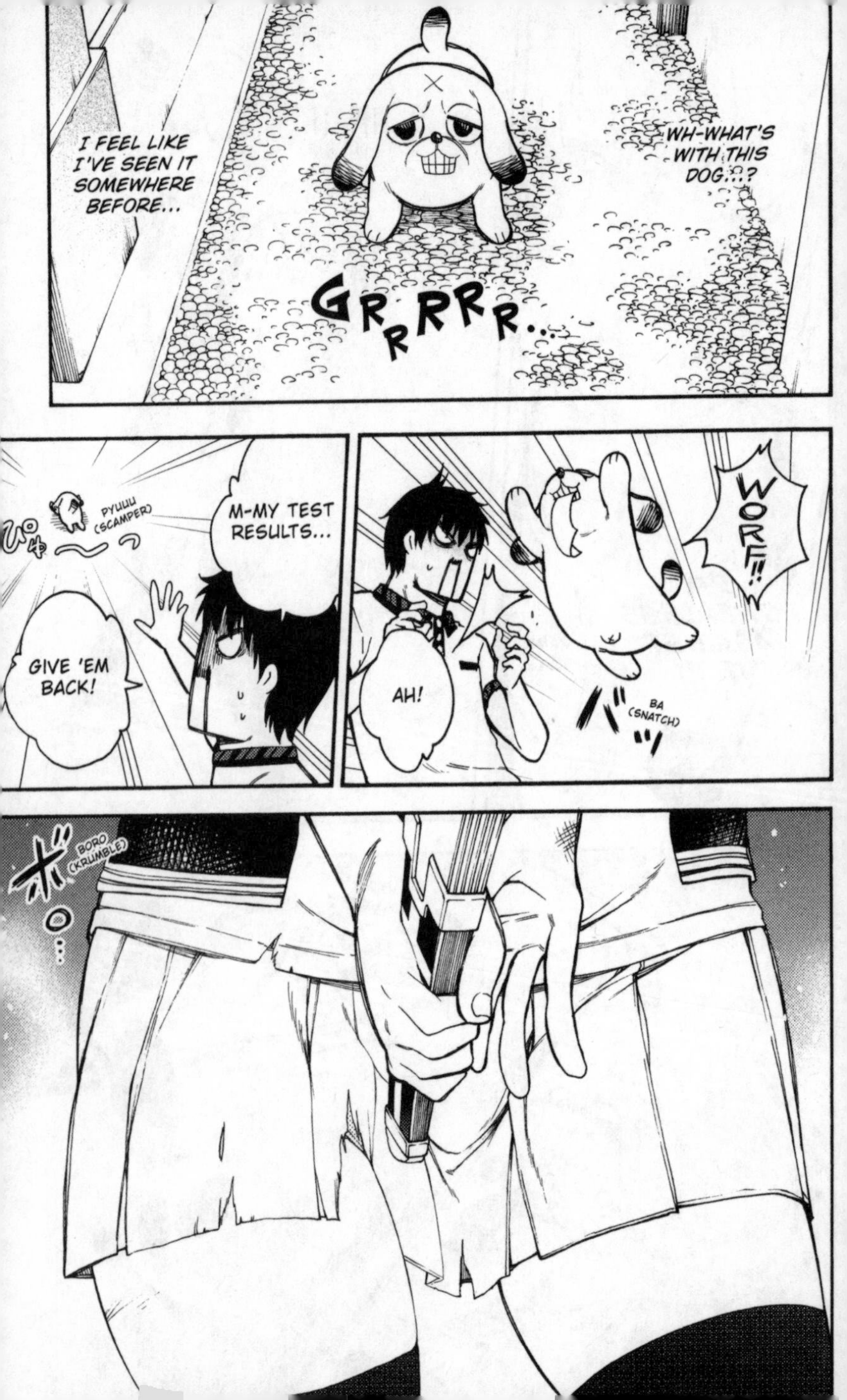
WH-WHAT'S WITH THIS DOG...?
I FEEL LIKE I'VE SEEN IT SOMEWHERE BEFORE...
GRRRRR...
WORF!!
AH!
BA (SNATCH)
M-MY TEST RESULTS...
PYUUU (SCAMPER)
GIVE 'EM BACK!
BORO (KRUMBLE)

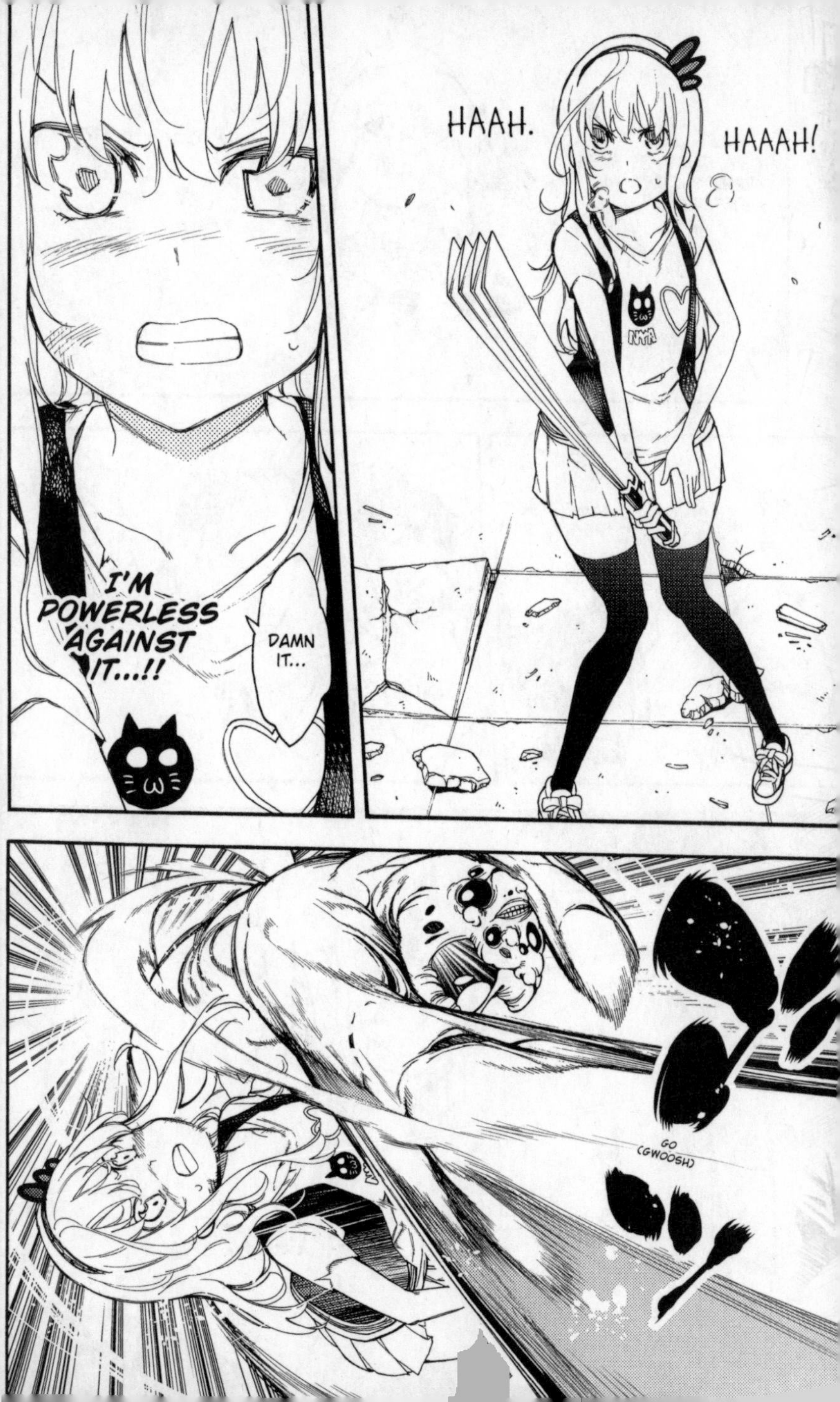
HAAAH!
HAAH.
DAMN IT...
I'M POWERLESS AGAINST IT...!!
GO (GWOOSH)

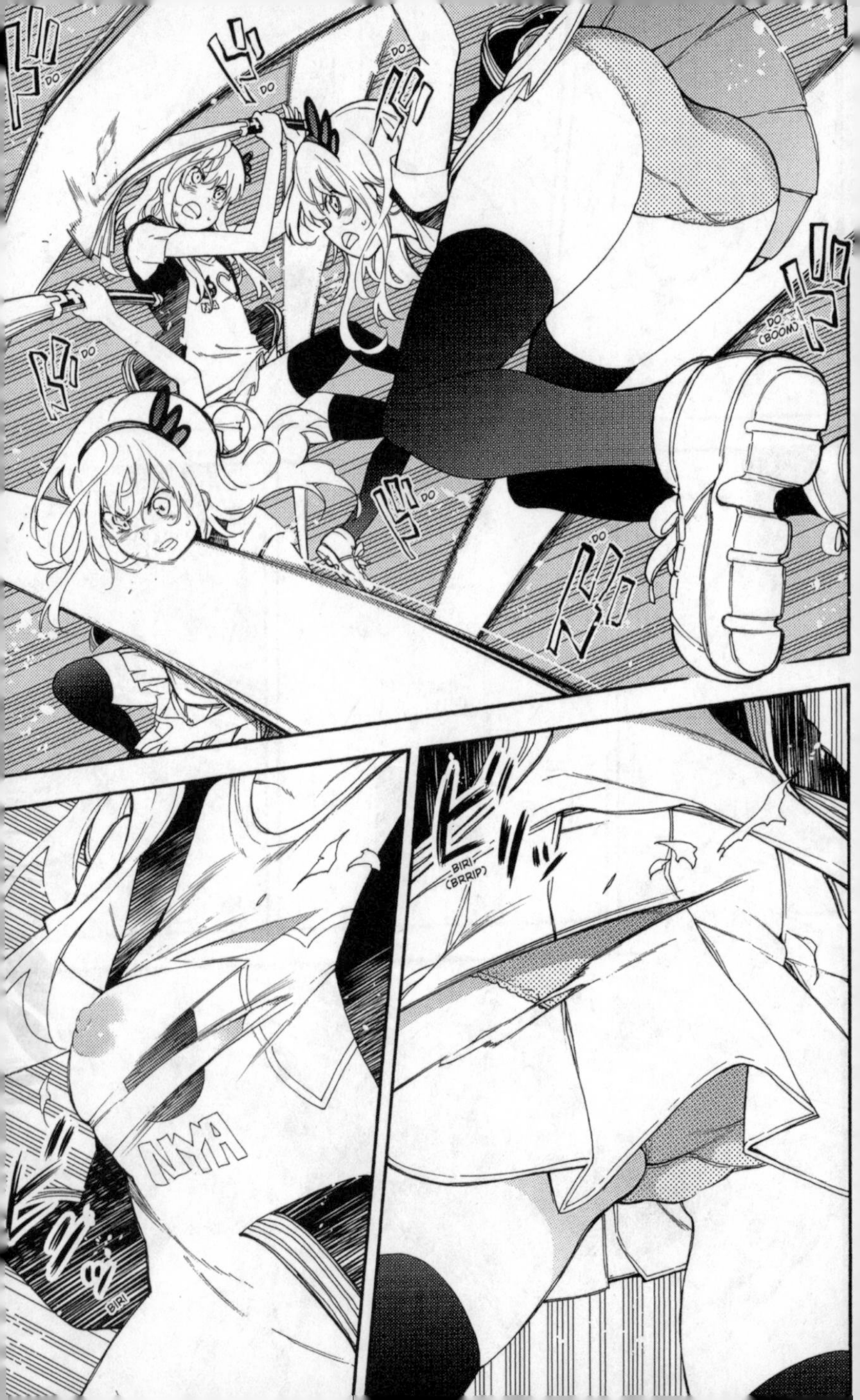
DO
(BOOM)
DO
DO
DO
DO
DO
DO
BIRI
(BRRIP)
NYA
BIRI

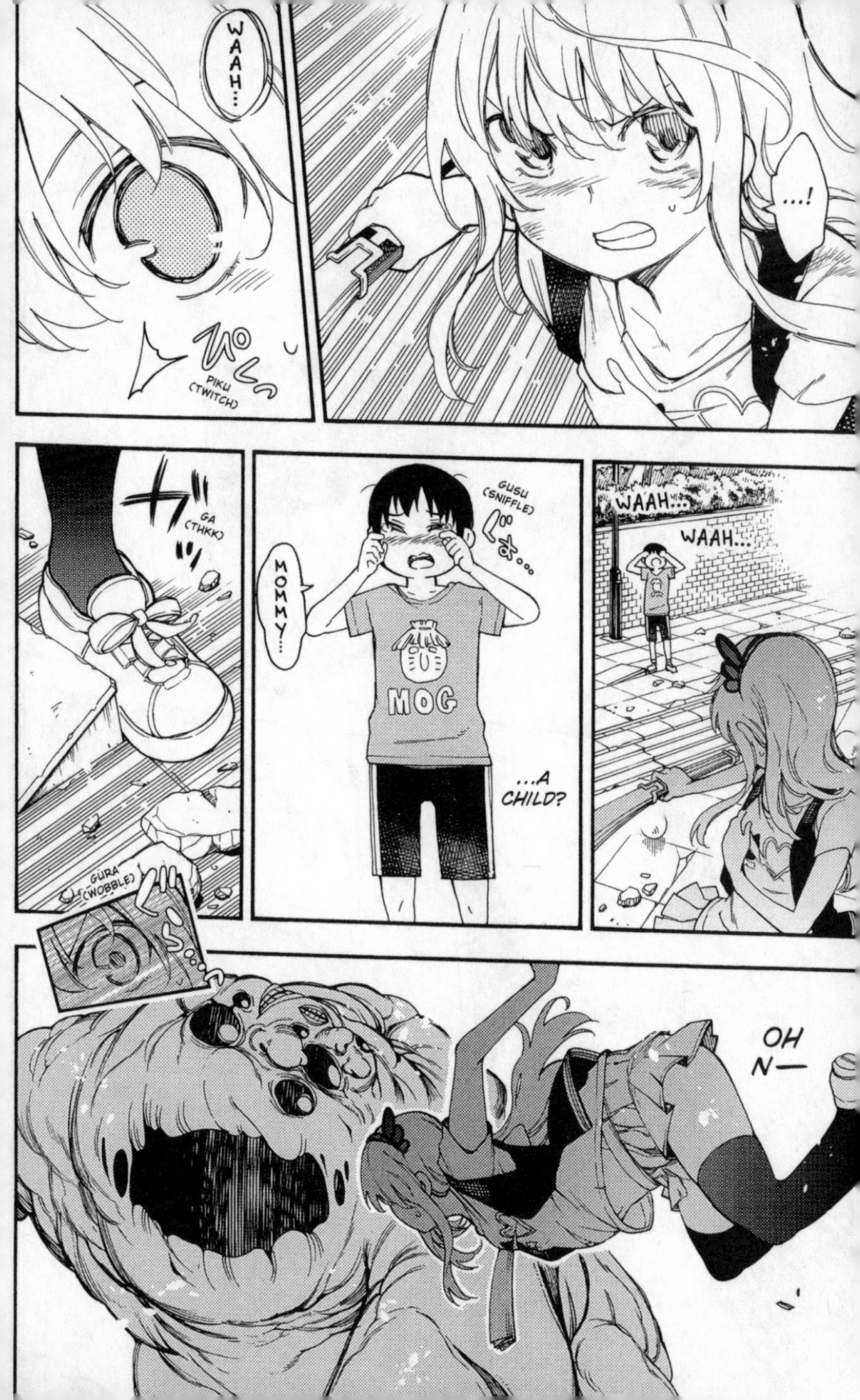
...!
WAAH...
PIKU (TWITCH)
WAAH...
WAAH...
GUSU (SNIFFLE)
MOMMY...
...A CHILD?
GA (THKK)
GURA (WOBBLE)
OH N—

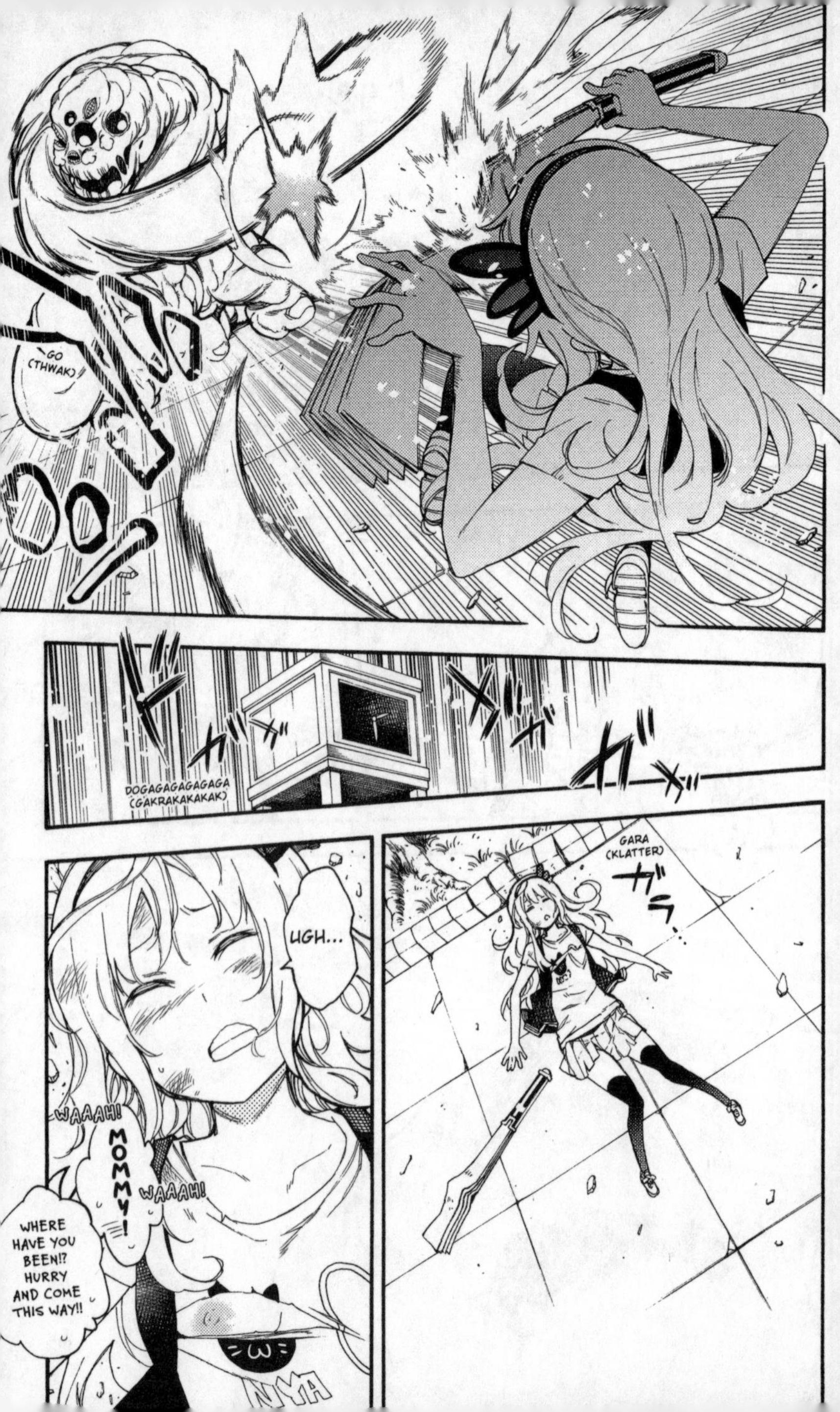
GO
(THWAK)
DOGAGAGAGAGAGA
(GAKRAKAKAKAK)
GARA
(KLATTER)
UGH...
WAAAH!
MOMMY!
WAAAH!
WHERE HAVE YOU BEEN!? HURRY AND COME THIS WAY!!
NYA

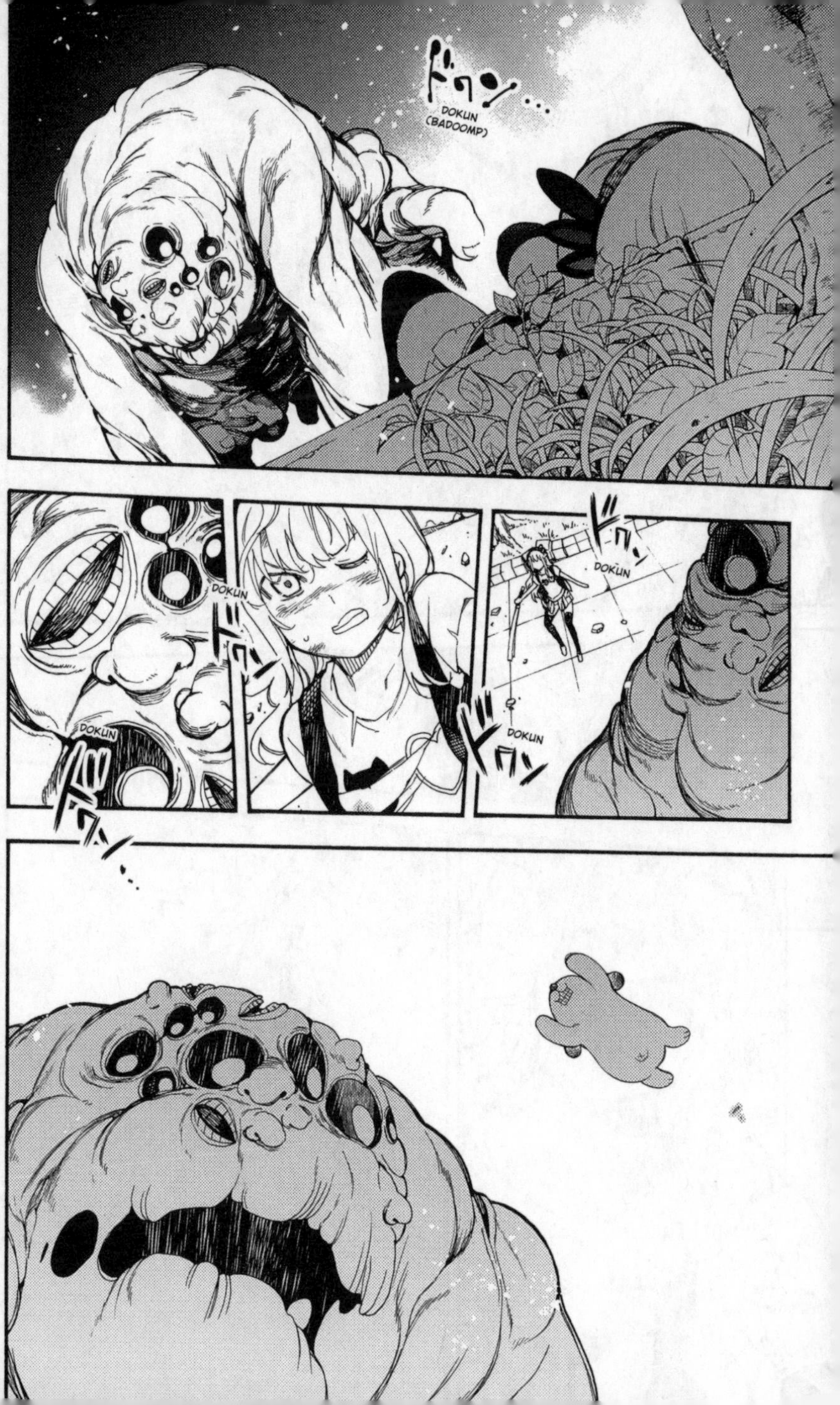

DOKUN
(BADOOMP)
DOKUN
DOKUN
DOKUN
DOKUN

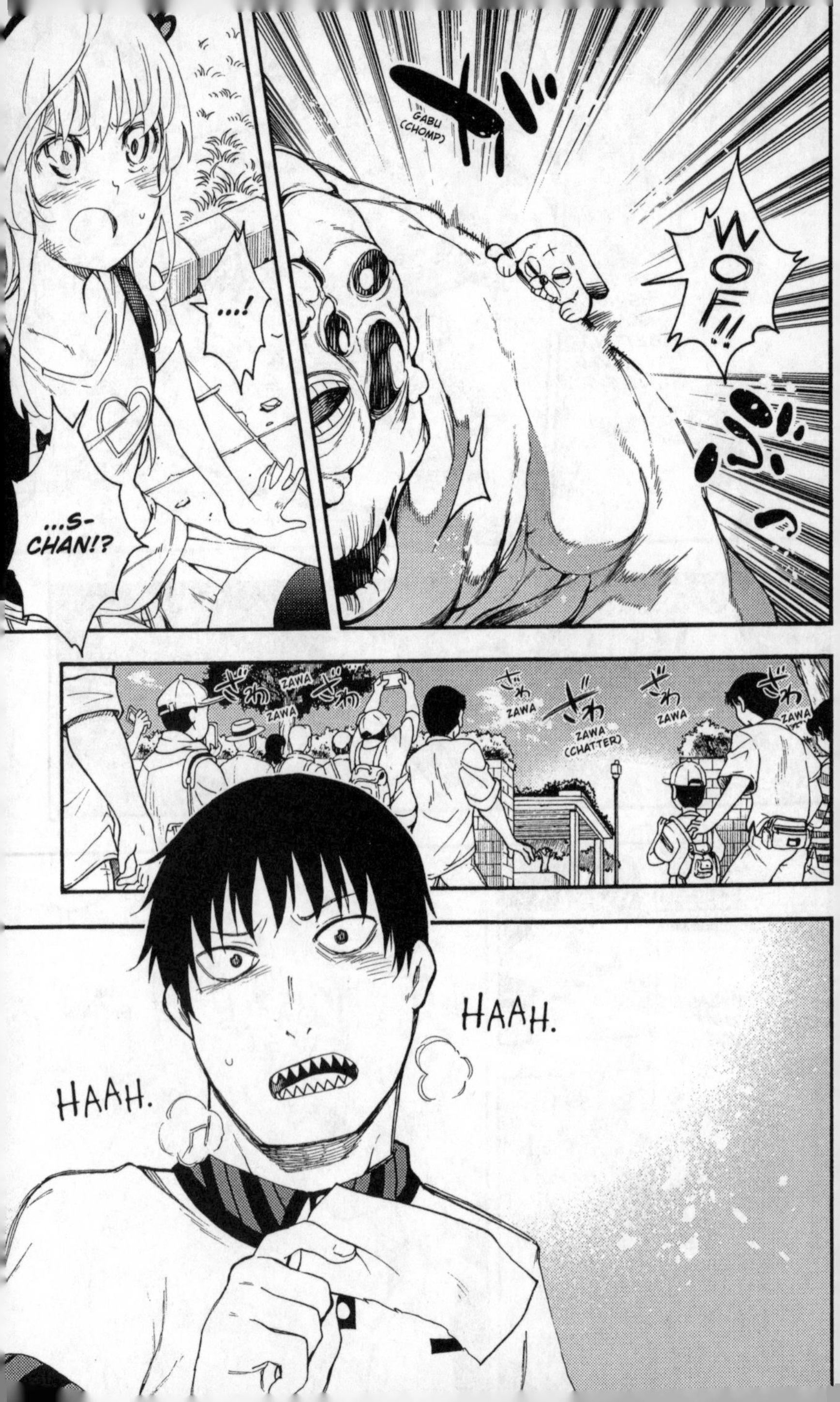
GABU (CHOMP)
WOF!!
...!
...S-CHAN!?
ZAWA
ZAWA
ZAWA (CHATTER)
ZAWA
ZAWA
ZAWA
HAAH.
HAAH.

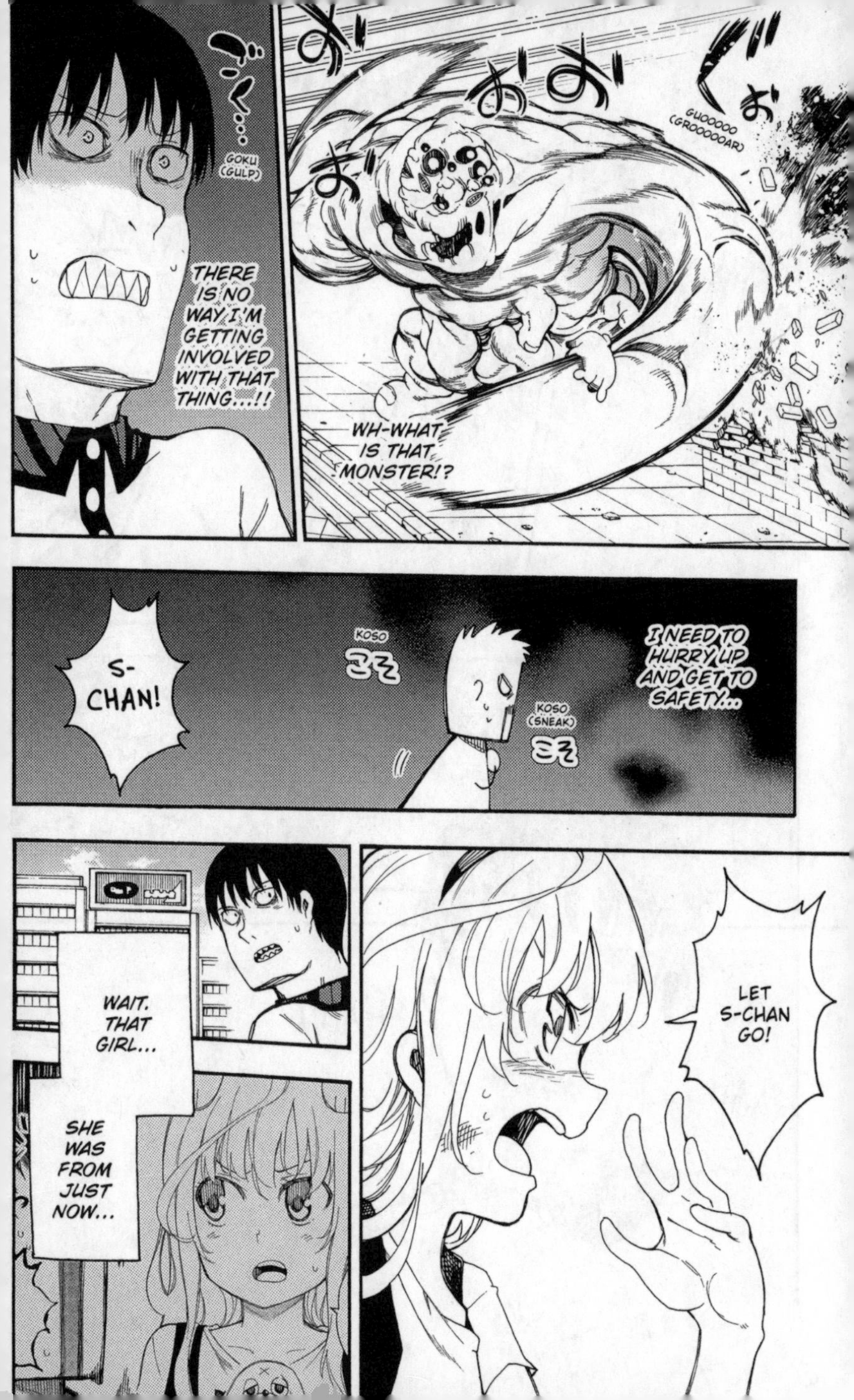
GUOOOOO (GROOOOOAR)
WH-WHAT IS THAT MONSTER!?
GOKU (GULP)
THERE IS NO WAY I'M GETTING INVOLVED WITH THAT THING...!!
I NEED TO HURRY UP AND GET TO SAFETY...
KOSO (SNEAK)
こそ
KOSO
こそ
S-CHAN!
LET S-CHAN GO!
WAIT. THAT GIRL...
SHE WAS FROM JUST NOW...

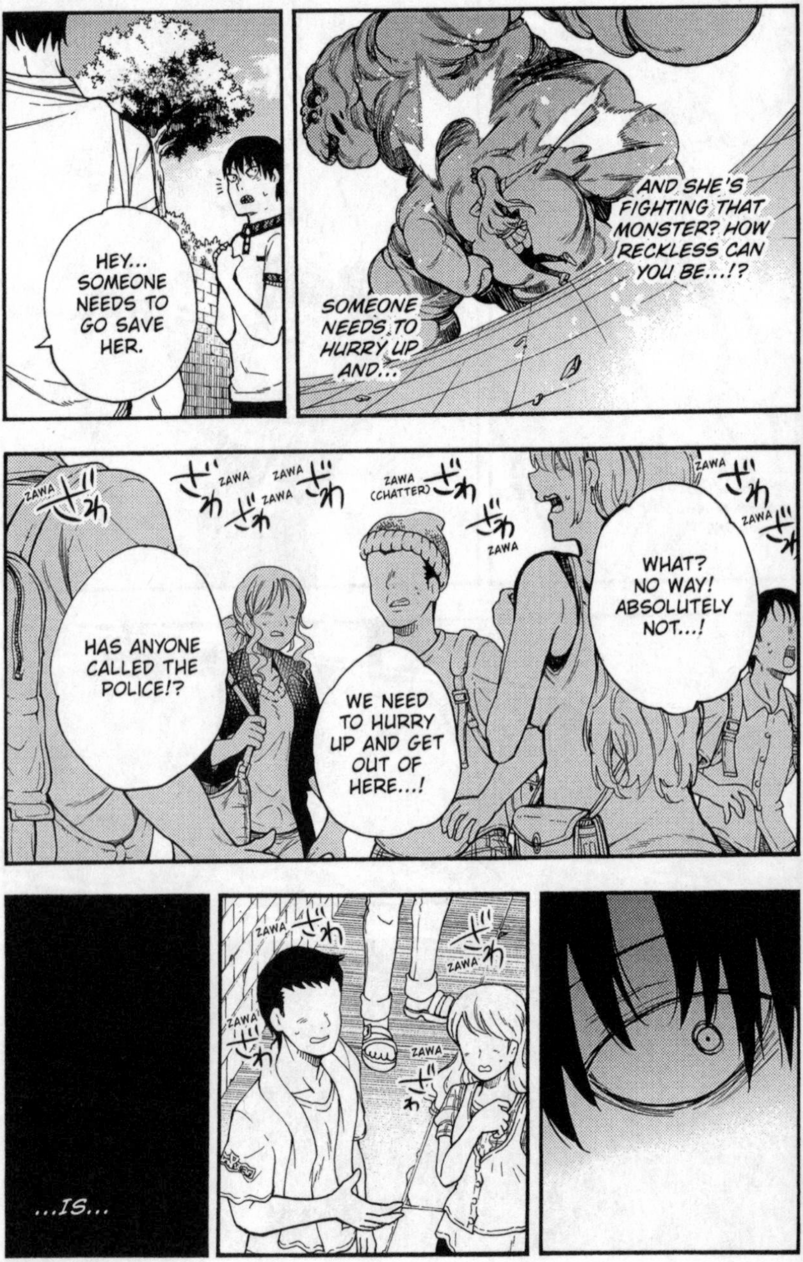
AND SHE'S FIGHTING THAT MONSTER? HOW RECKLESS CAN YOU BE...!?
SOMEONE NEEDS TO HURRY UP AND...
HEY... SOMEONE NEEDS TO GO SAVE HER.
ざわ ZAWA
ざわ ZAWA
ざわ ZAWA
ZAWA (CHATTER) ざわ
WHAT? NO WAY! ABSOLUTELY NOT...!
WE NEED TO HURRY UP AND GET OUT OF HERE...!
ざわ ZAWA
ざわ ZAWA
ざわ ZAWA
ざわ ZAWA
HAS ANYONE CALLED THE POLICE!?
ざわ ZAWA
ざわ ZAWA
ざわ ZAWA
ざわ ZAWA
...IS...

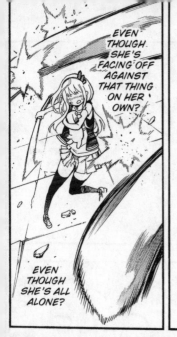

EVEN THOUGH SHE'S FACING OFF AGAINST THAT THING ON HER OWN?

EVEN THOUGH SHE'S ALL ALONE?

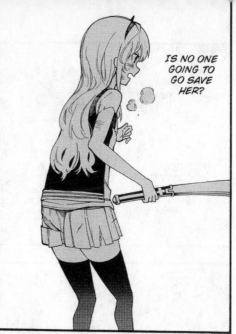

IS NO ONE GOING TO GO SAVE HER?

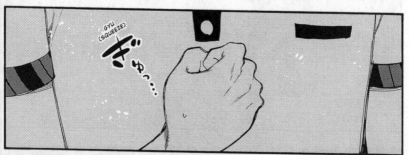

GYU (SQUEEZE)

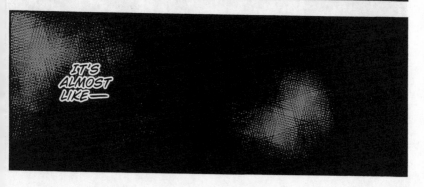

IT'S ALMOST LIKE—

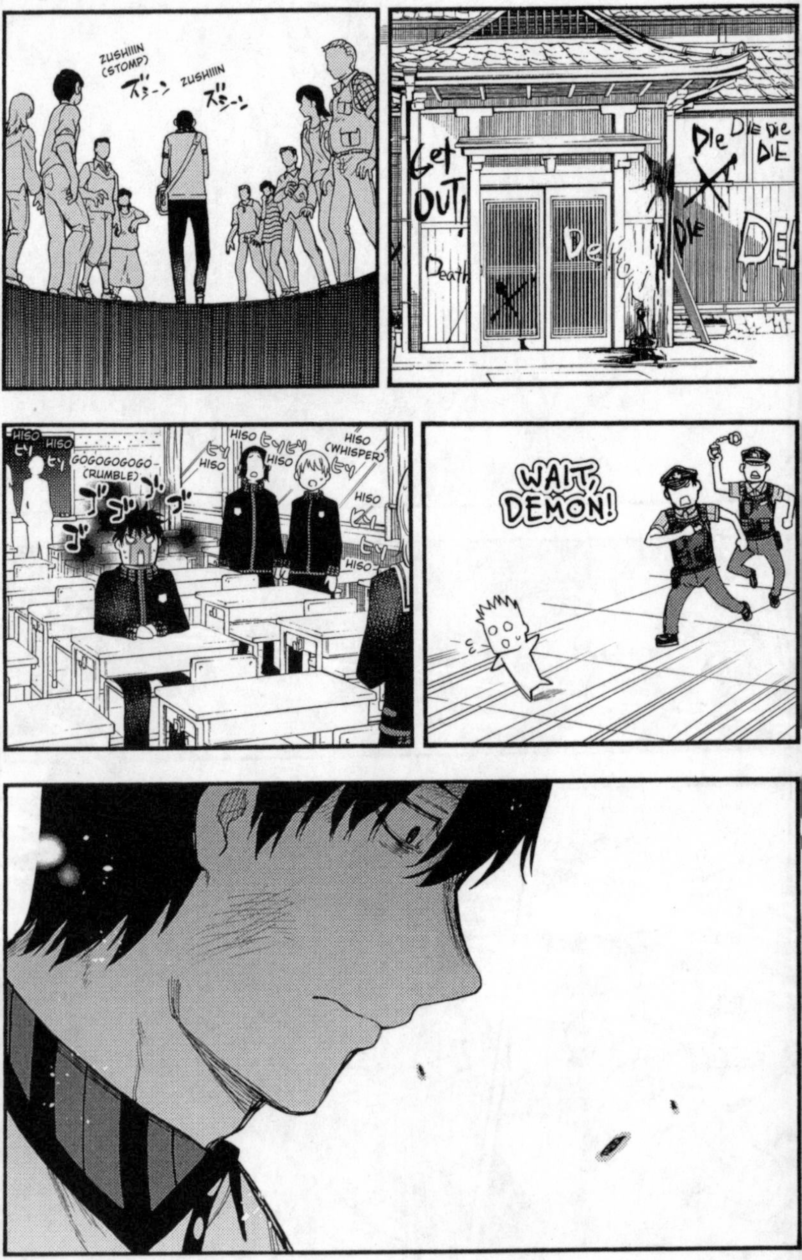
Die Die Die
DIE
Get OUT!
Death
De
DIE
DE
ZUSHIIN (STOMP)
ズシーン
ZUSHIIN
ズシーン
WAIT, DEMON!
HISO (WHISPER)
ヒソ
HISO
ヒソヒソ
HISO
HISO
ヒソ
HISO
HISO
ヒソ
HISO
ヒソ
GOGOGOGOGO (RUMBLE)
ゴゴゴゴゴ

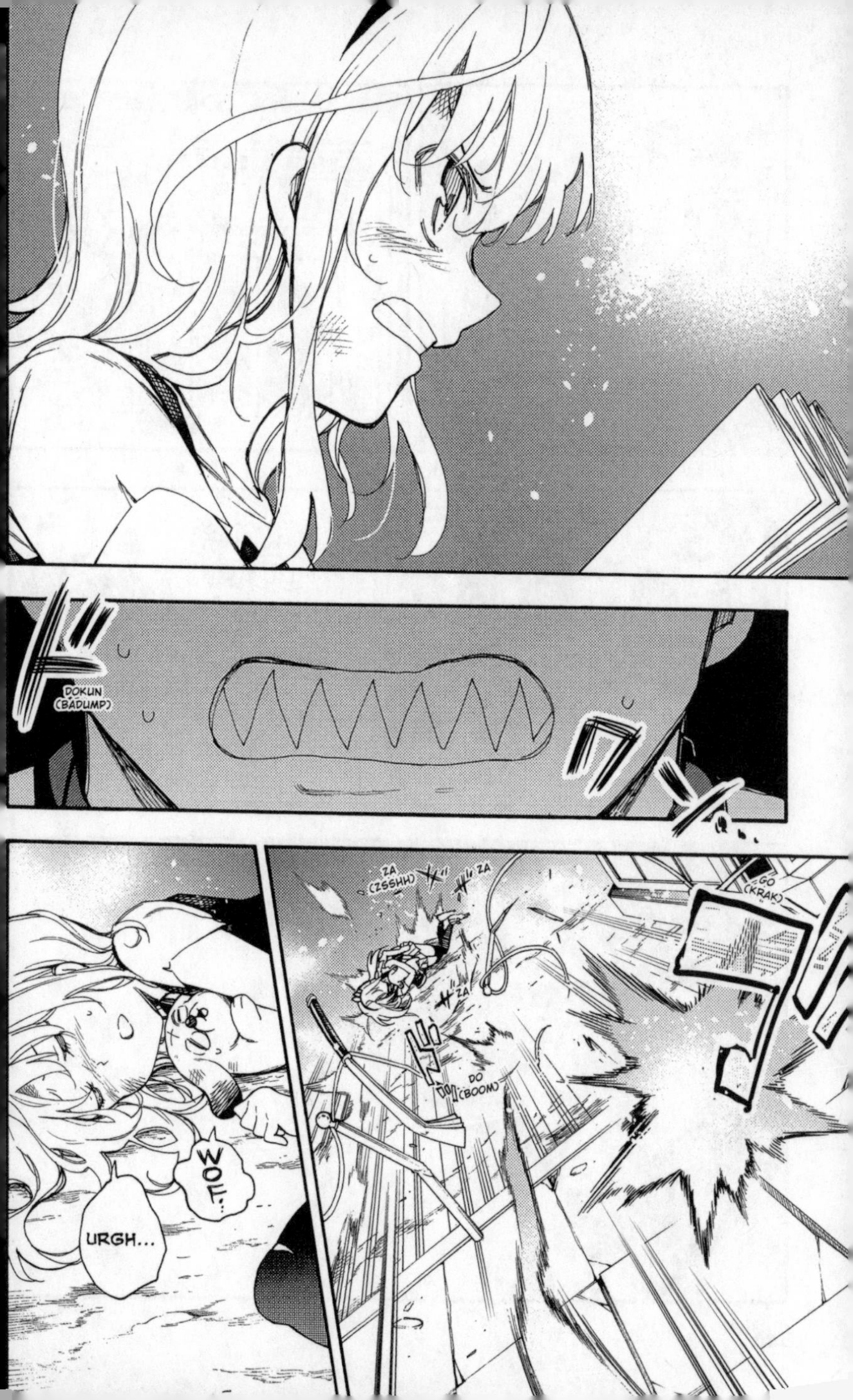
DOKUN (BADUMP)
GO (KRAK)
ZA
ZA (ZSSHH)
ZA
DO (BOOM)
WOF...
URGH...

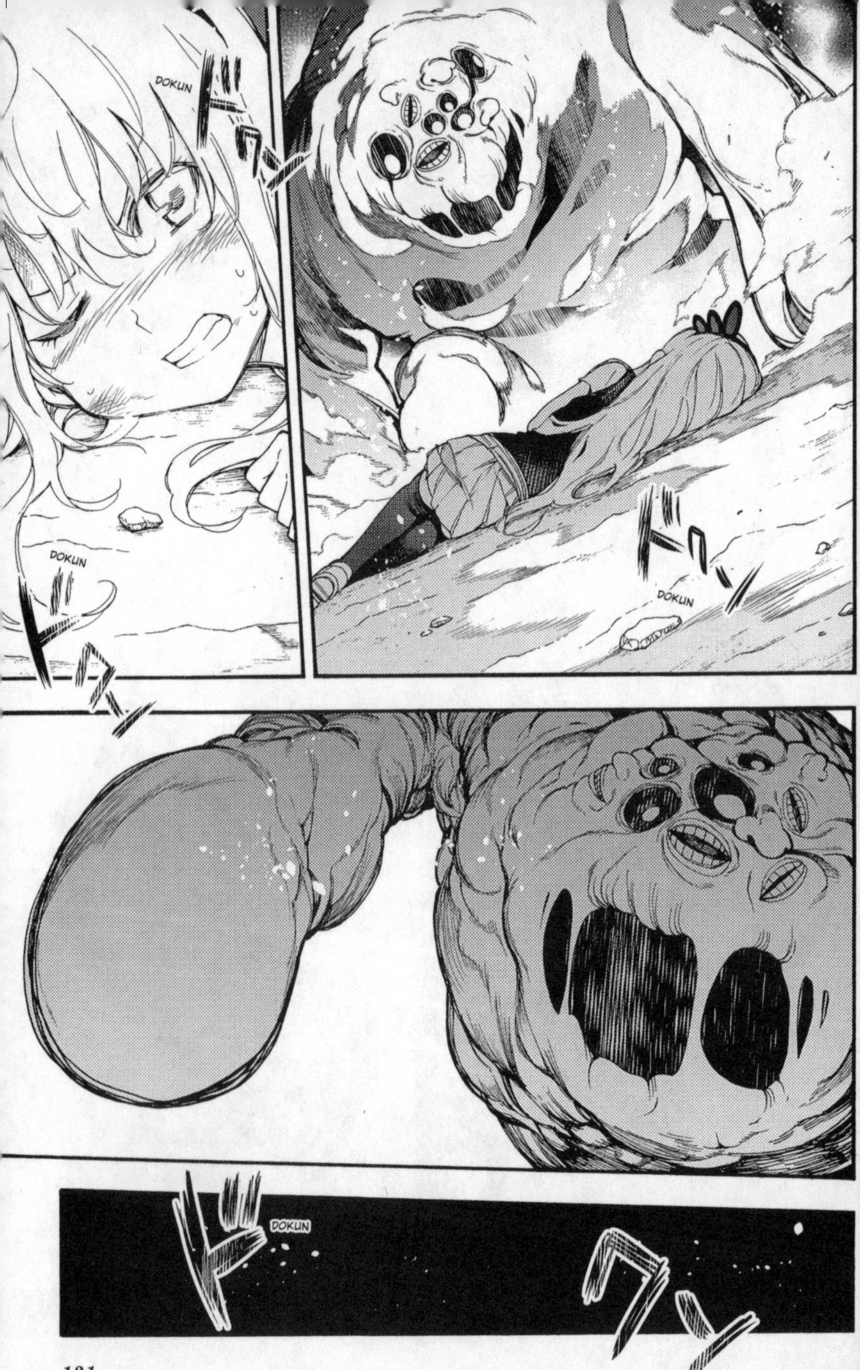
DOKUN
DOKUN
DOKUN
DOKUN

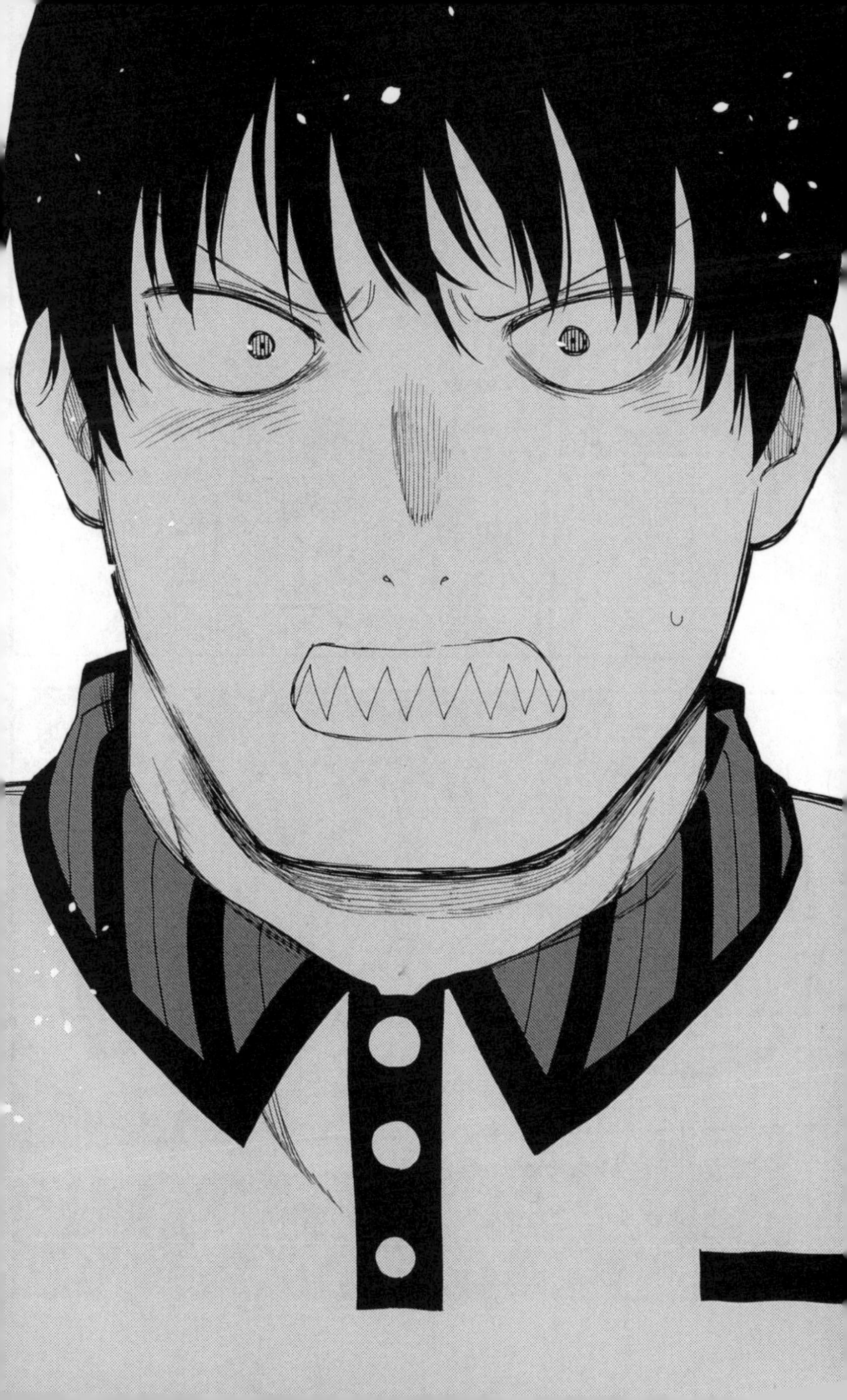

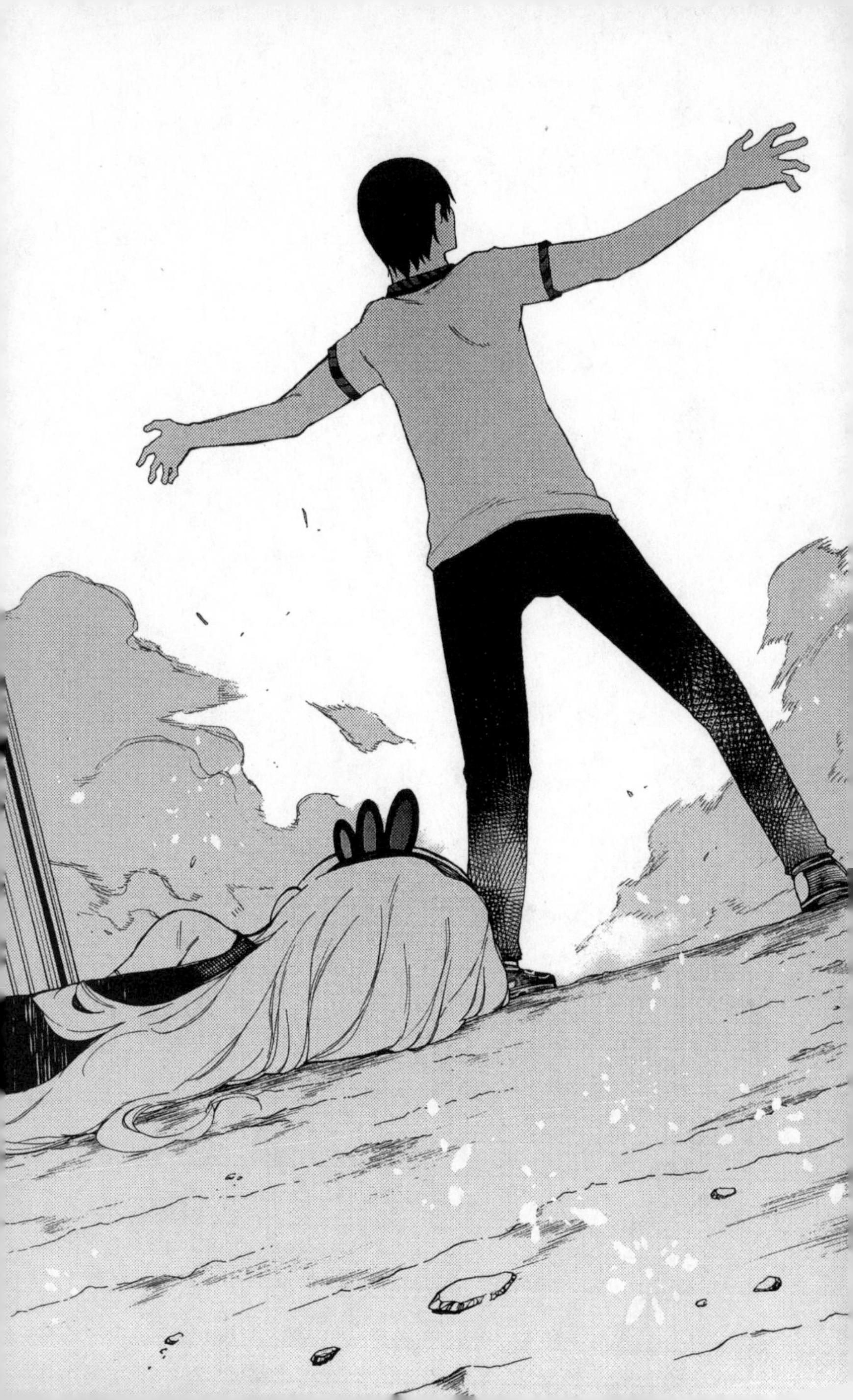

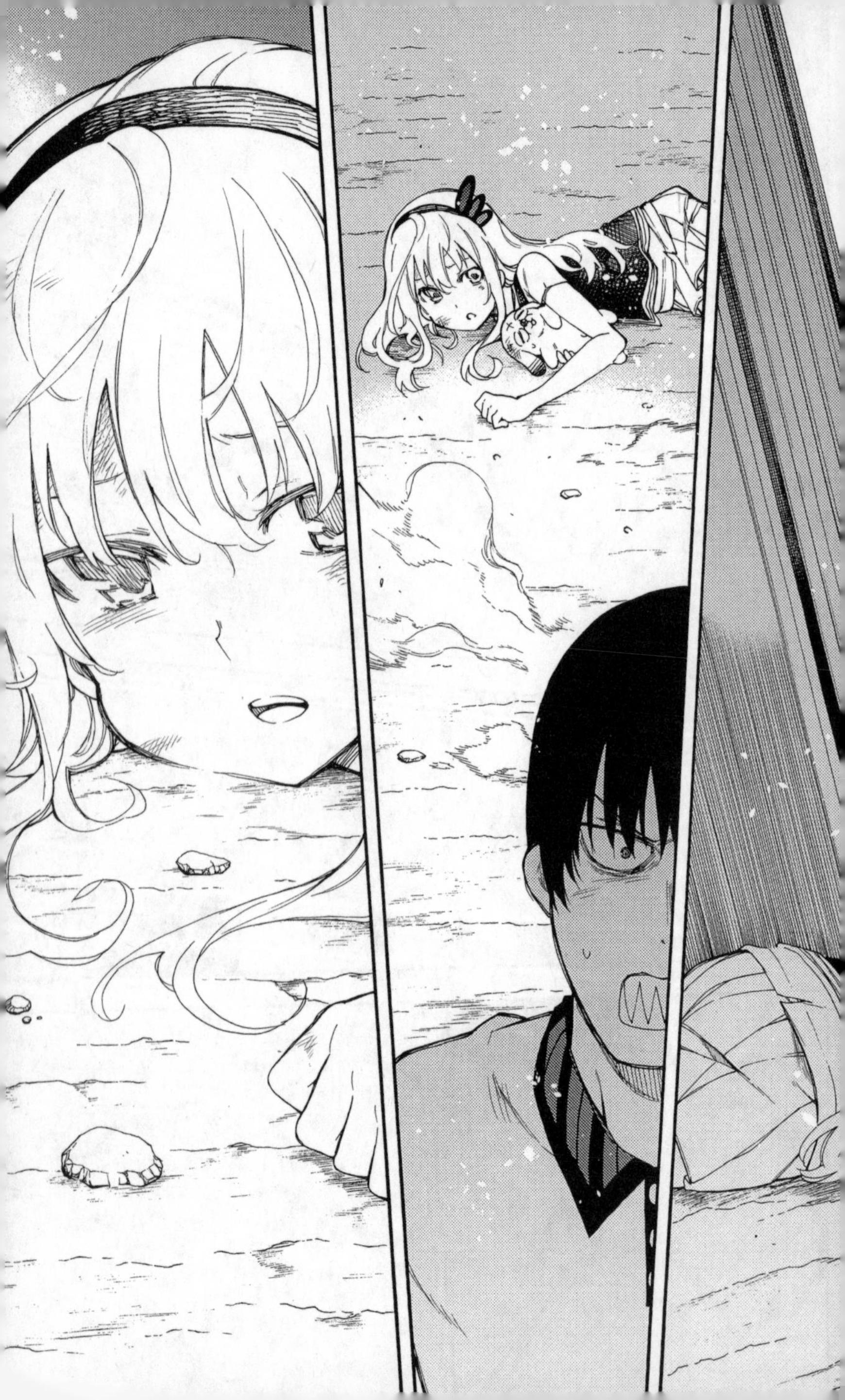

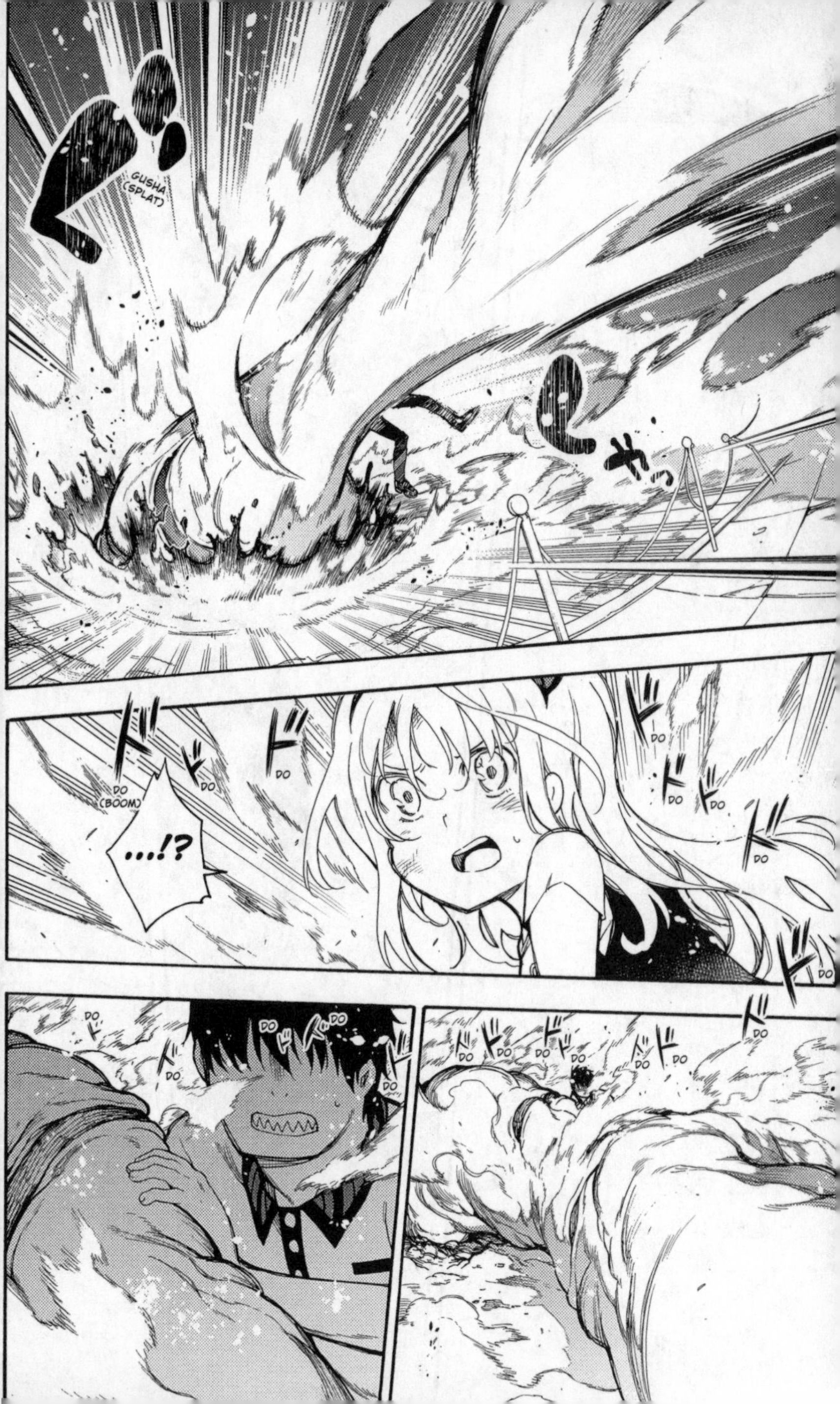
GUSHA (SPLAT)
DO DO DO DO DO DO DO
DO (BOOM) DO DO
...!?
DO DO DO DO DO DO DO
DO DO DO DO

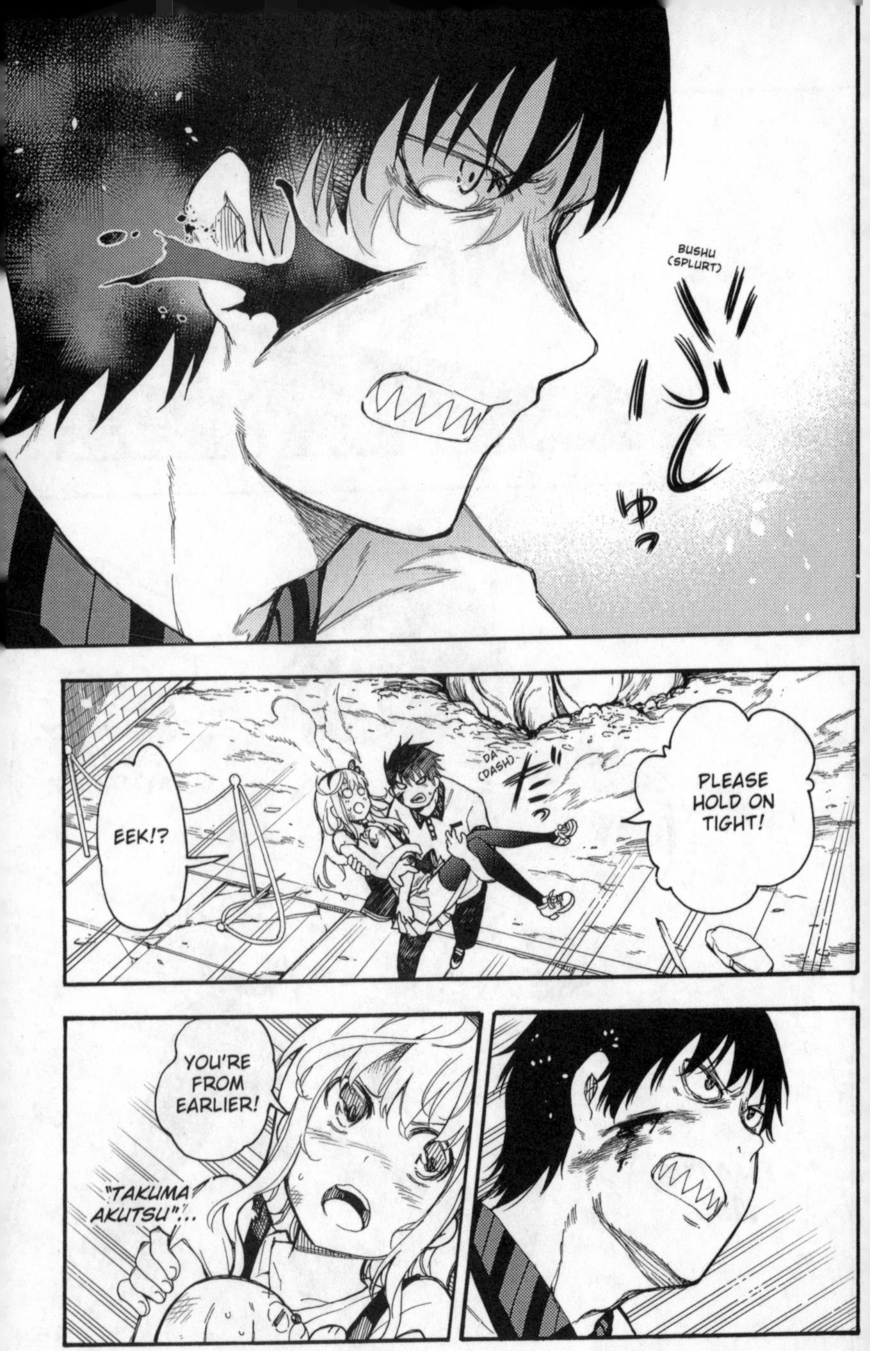
BUSHU (SPLURT)
ぶしゅっ
PLEASE HOLD ON TIGHT!
DA (DASH)
ダッ
EEK!?
YOU'RE FROM EARLIER!
"TAKUMA AKUTSU"...

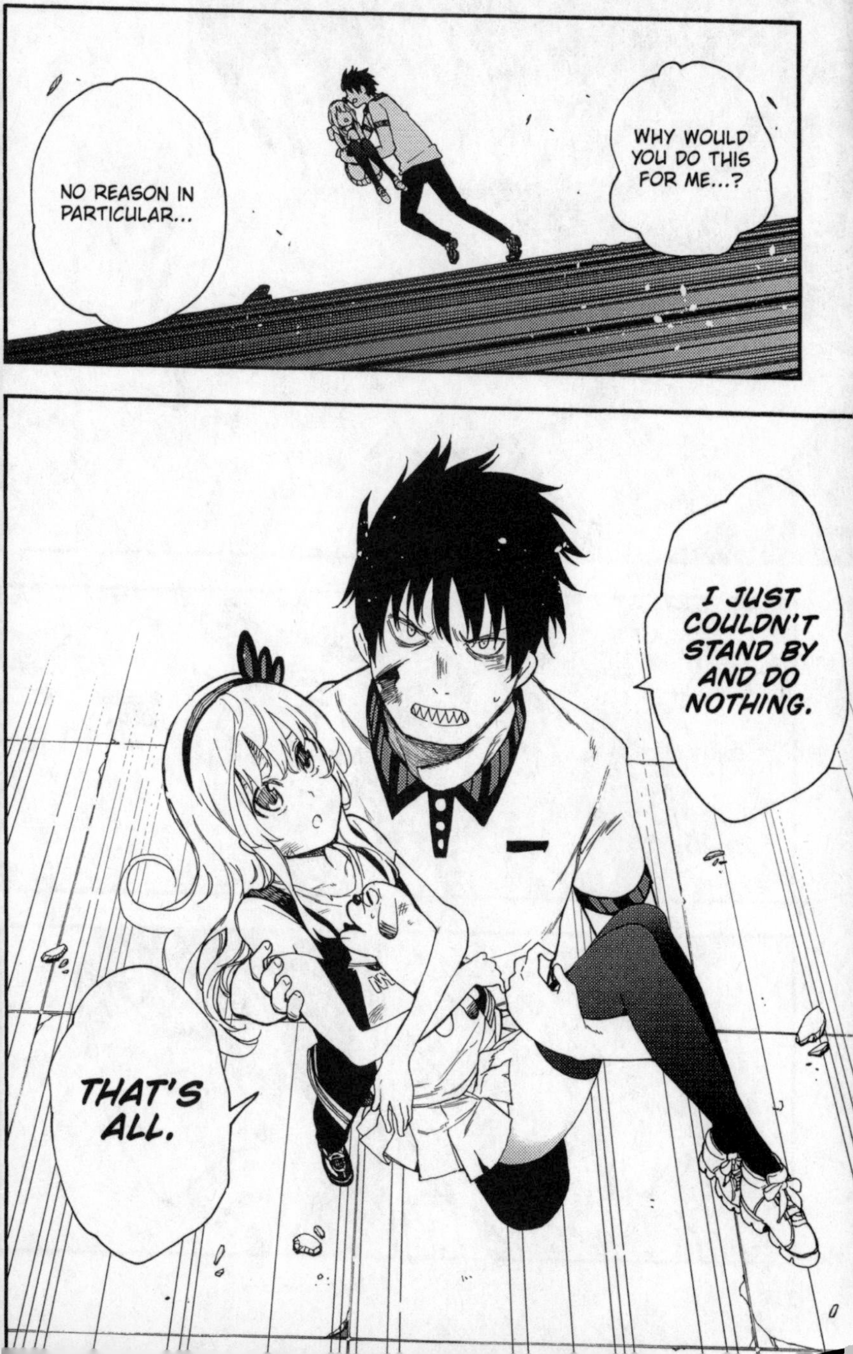
WHY WOULD YOU DO THIS FOR ME...?
NO REASON IN PARTICULAR...
I JUST COULDN'T STAND BY AND DO NOTHING.
THAT'S ALL.

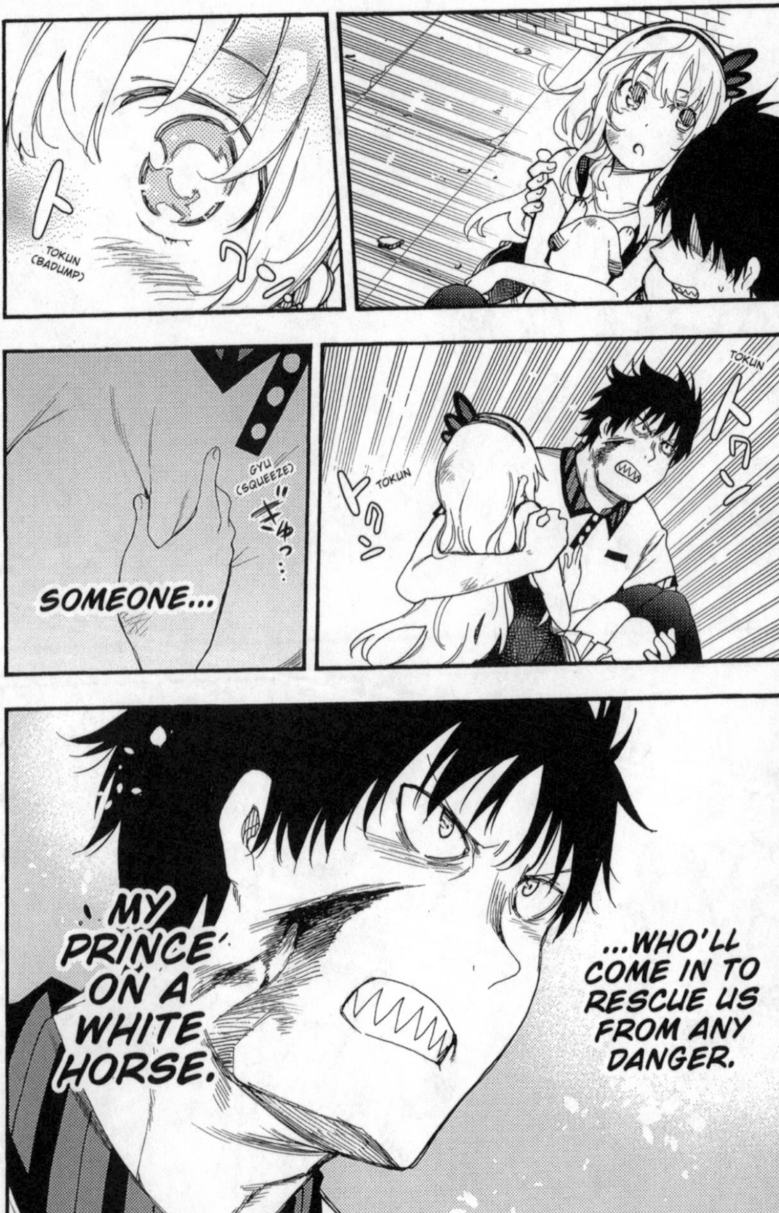
TOKUN (BADUMP)
トクン
TOKUN
トクン
TOKUN
トクン
GYU (SQUEEZE)
ぎゅっ…
SOMEONE...
...WHO'LL COME IN TO RESCUE US FROM ANY DANGER.
MY PRINCE ON A WHITE HORSE.

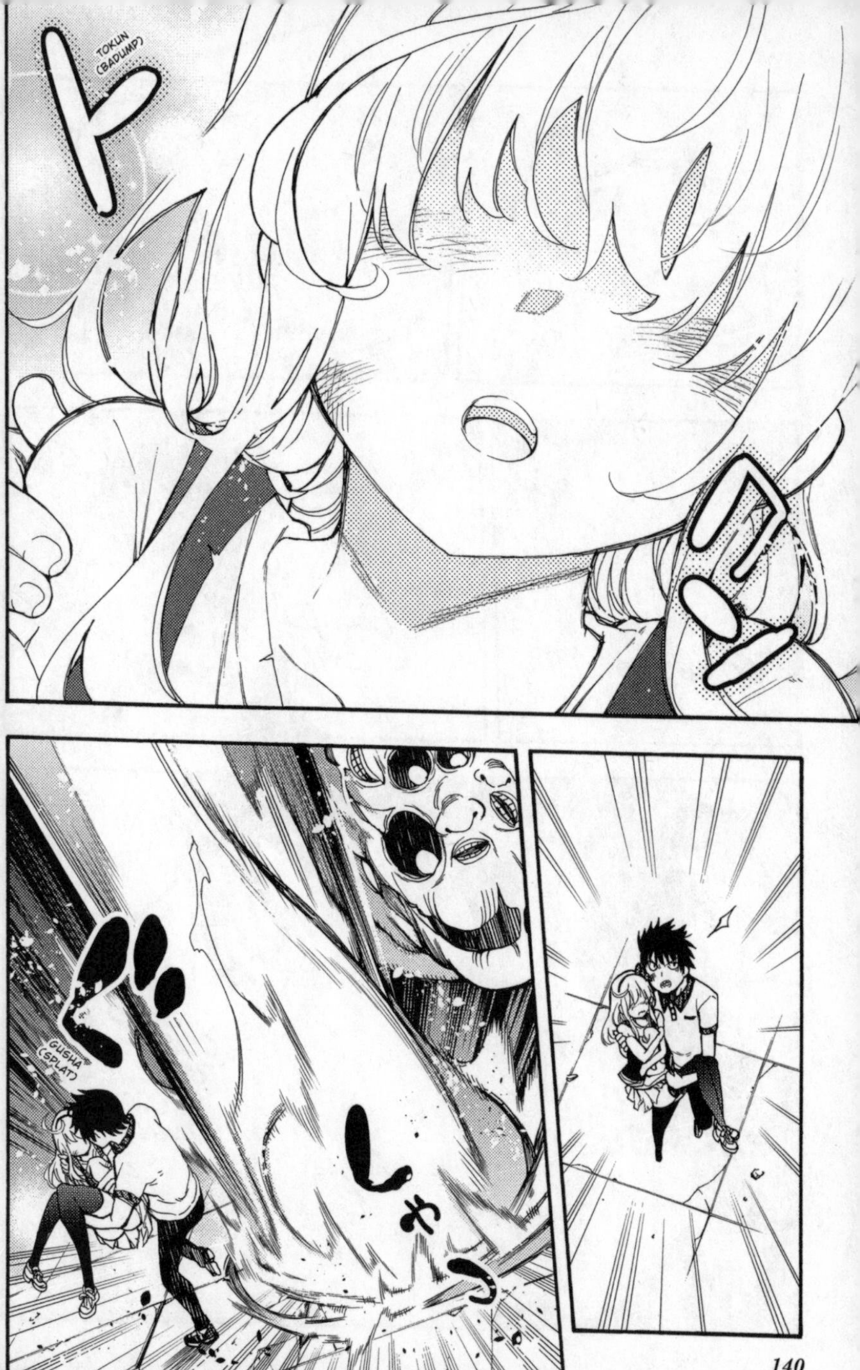
TOKUN
(BADUMP)
GUSHA
(SPLAT)

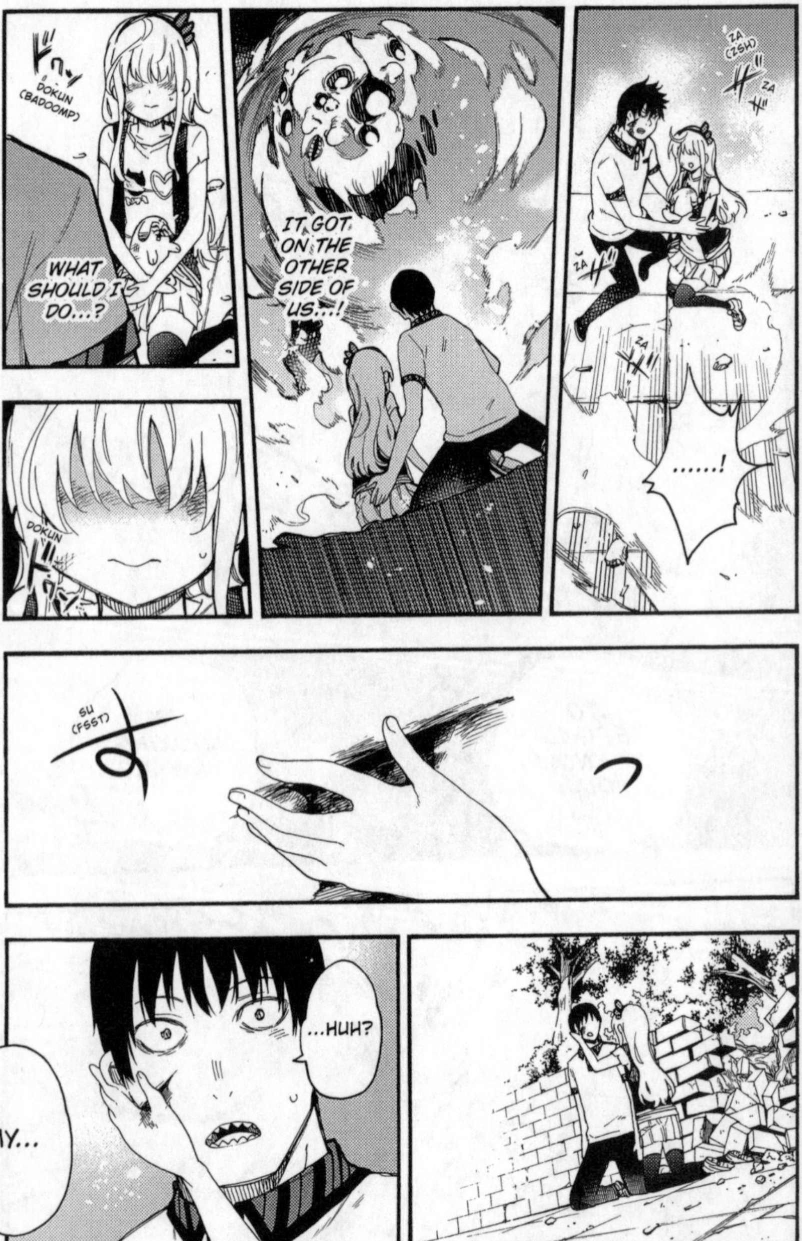
ZA (ZSH)
ZA
ZA
ZA
......!
IT GOT ON THE OTHER SIDE OF US...!
DOKUN (BADOOMP)
WHAT SHOULD I DO...?
DOKUN
SU (FSST)
...HUH?
MY...

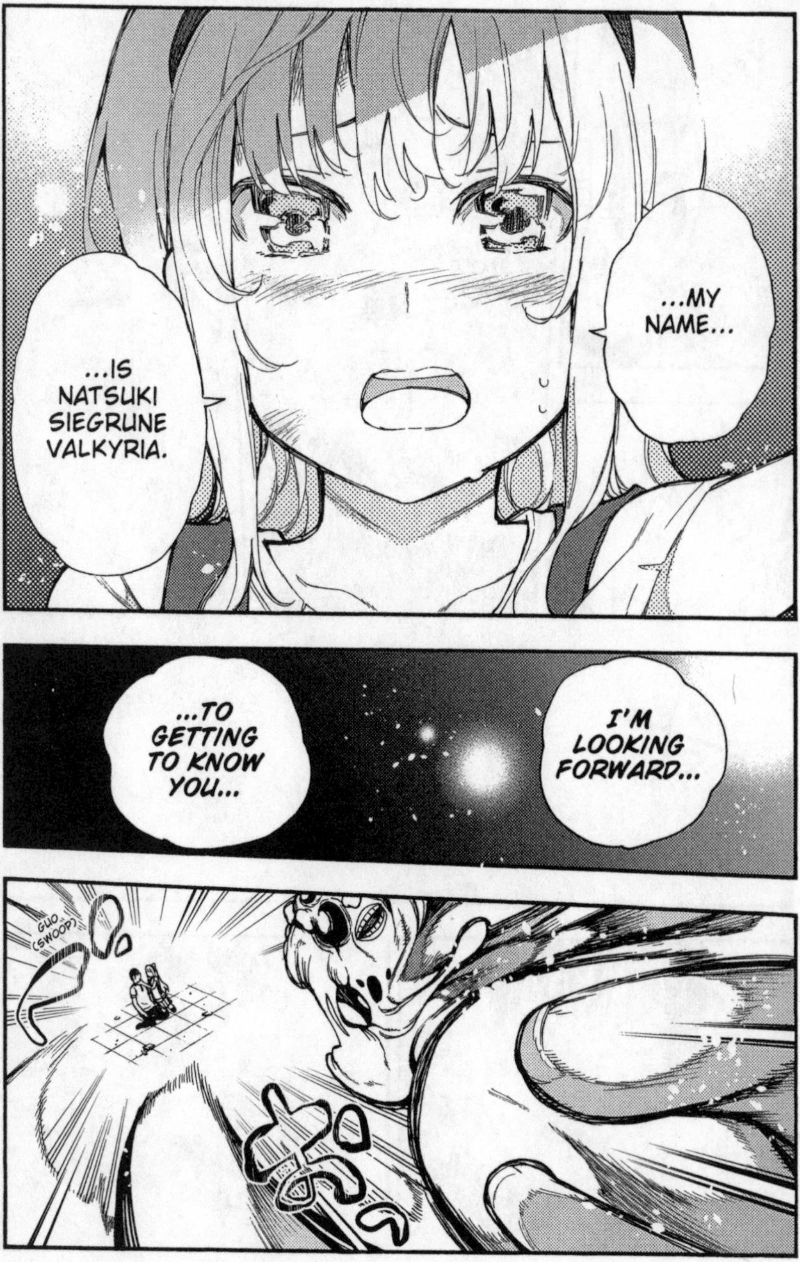
...MY NAME...
...IS NATSUKI SIEGRUNE VALKYRIA.
I'M LOOKING FORWARD...
...TO GETTING TO KNOW YOU...
GUO (SWOOP)

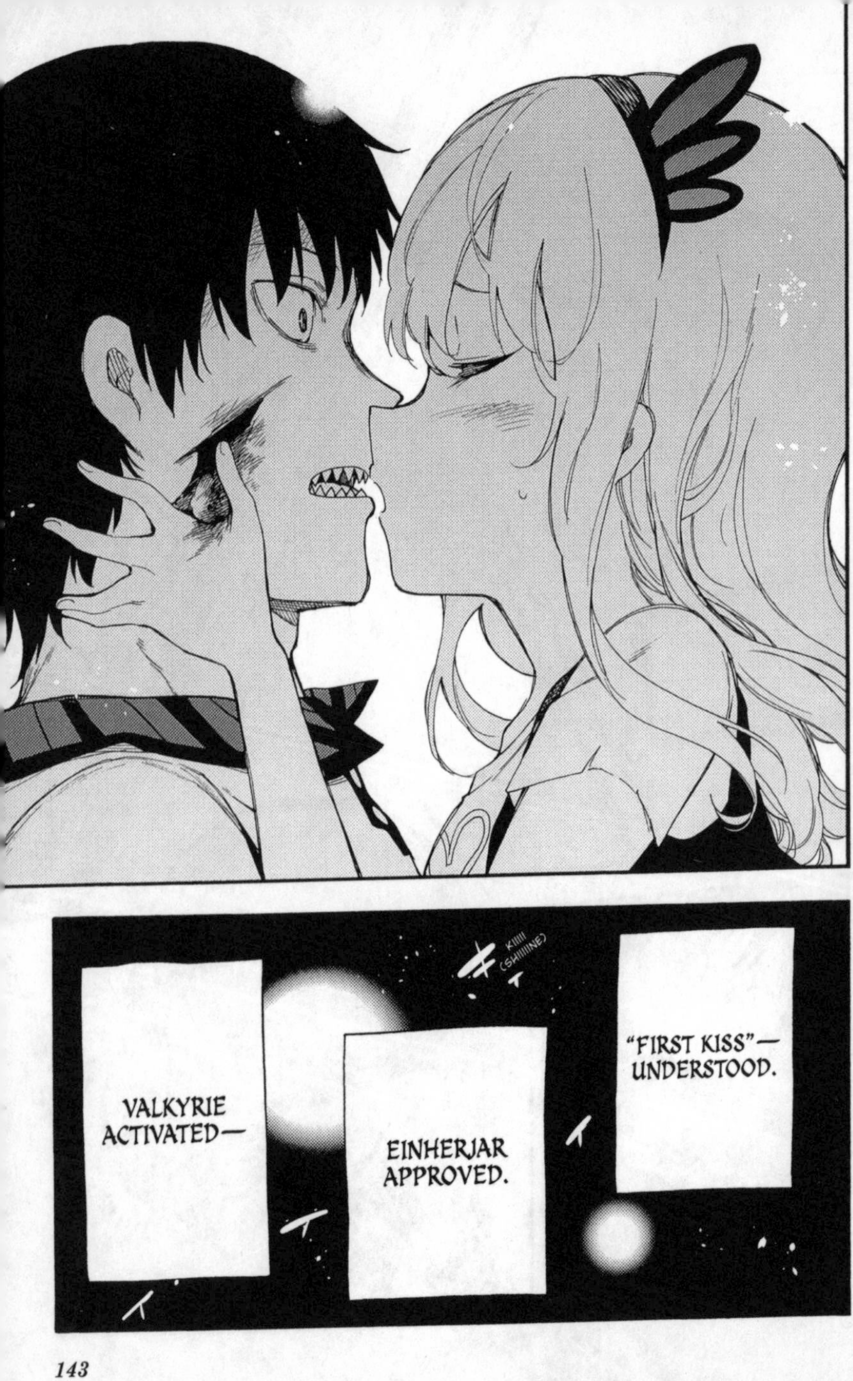
"FIRST KISS"—UNDERSTOOD.
KIIIII (SHIIIINE)
EINHERJAR APPROVED.
VALKYRIE ACTIVATED—

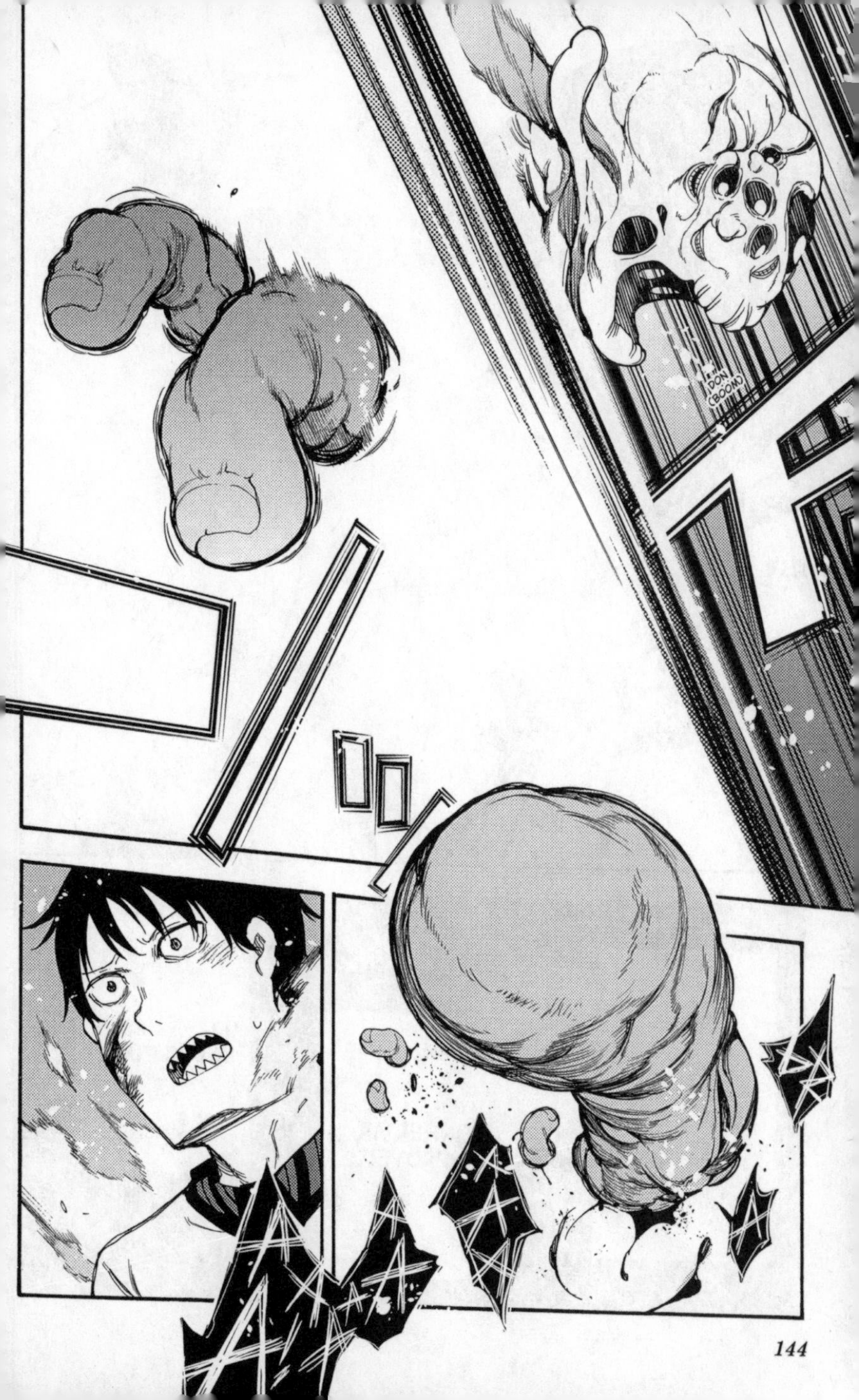
DON
(BOOM)

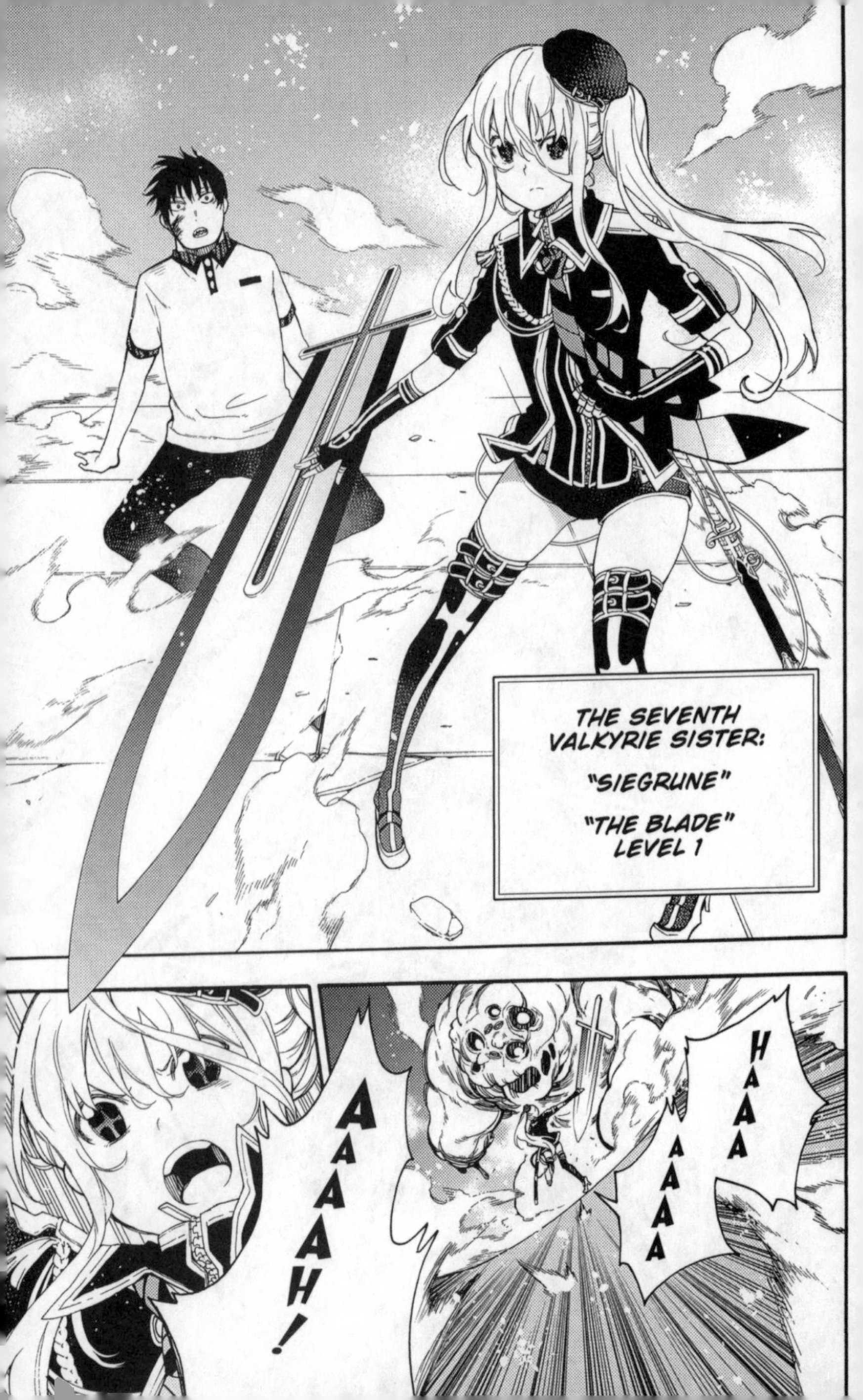
THE SEVENTH VALKYRIE SISTER:
"SIEGRUNE"
"THE BLADE" LEVEL 1
HAAAAAAAA
AAAAAH!

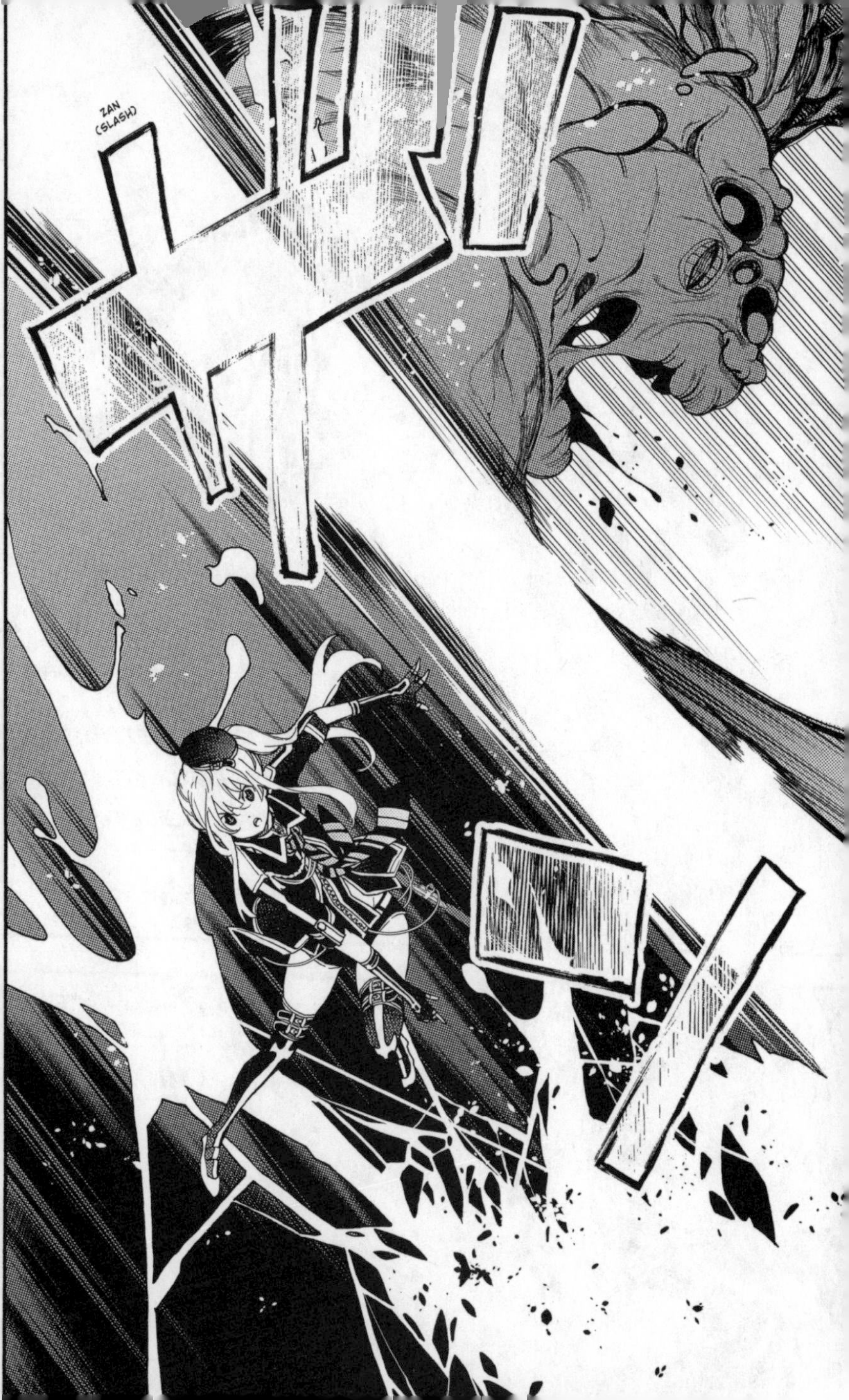
ZAN
(SLASH)

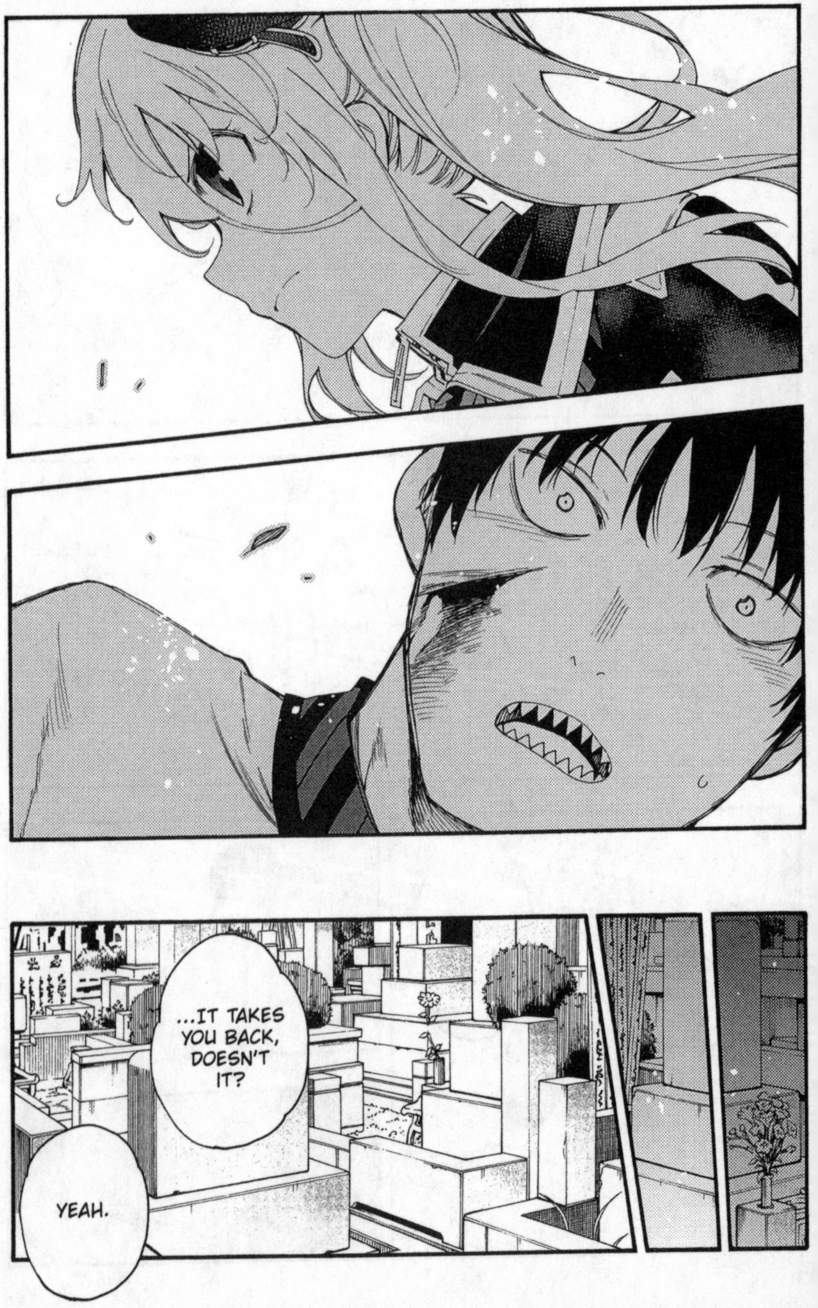
...IT TAKES YOU BACK, DOESN'T IT?
YEAH.

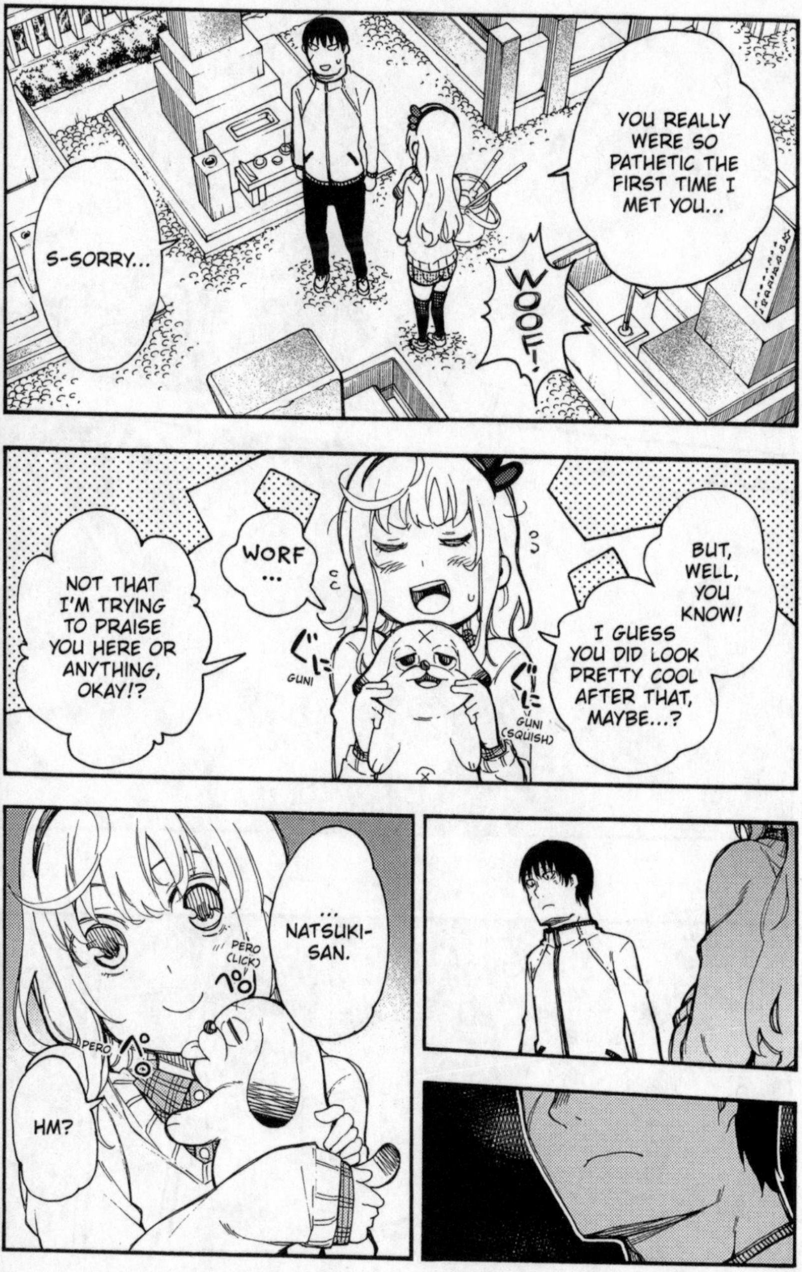
YOU REALLY WERE SO PATHETIC THE FIRST TIME I MET YOU...
WOOF!
S-SORRY...
BUT, WELL, YOU KNOW!
I GUESS YOU DID LOOK PRETTY COOL AFTER THAT, MAYBE...?
GUNI (SQUISH)
WORF ...
GUNI
NOT THAT I'M TRYING TO PRAISE YOU HERE OR ANYTHING, OKAY!?
... NATSUKI-SAN.
PERO (LICK)
PERO
HM?

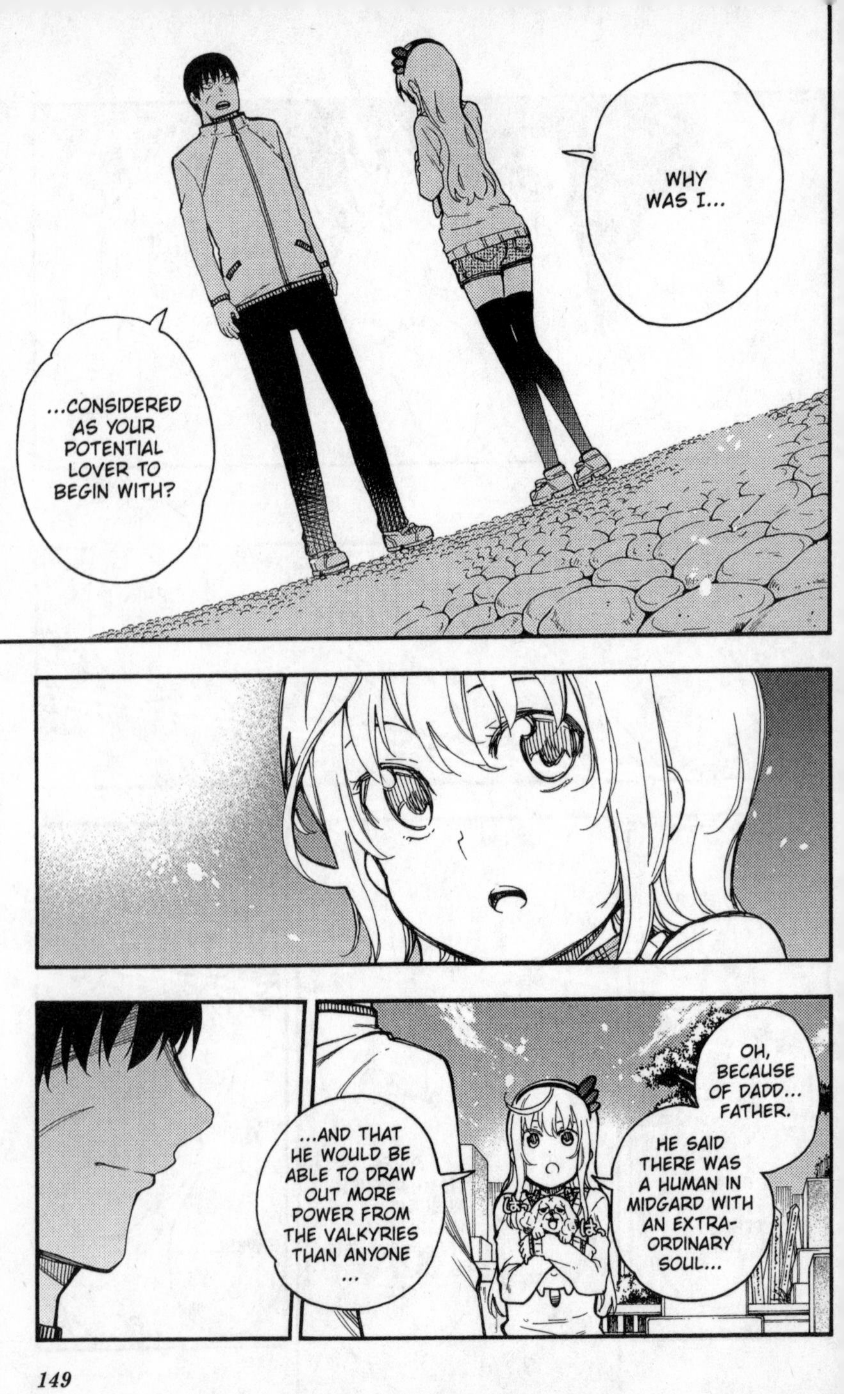
WHY WAS I...
...CONSIDERED AS YOUR POTENTIAL LOVER TO BEGIN WITH?
OH, BECAUSE OF DADD... FATHER.
HE SAID THERE WAS A HUMAN IN MIDGARD WITH AN EXTRA-ORDINARY SOUL...
...AND THAT HE WOULD BE ABLE TO DRAW OUT MORE POWER FROM THE VALKYRIES THAN ANYONE ...

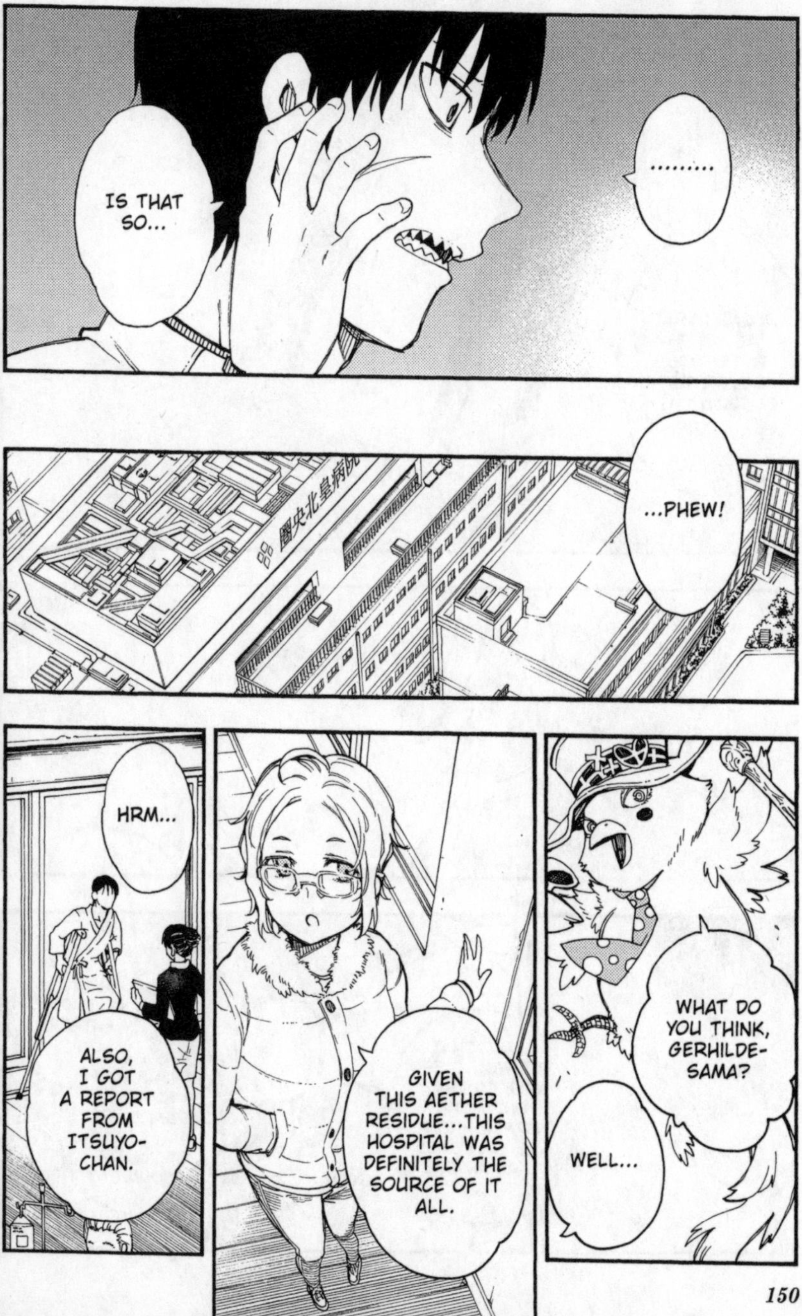
....
IS THAT SO...
...PHEW!
WHAT DO YOU THINK, GERHILDE-SAMA?
WELL...
GIVEN THIS AETHER RESIDUE...THIS HOSPITAL WAS DEFINITELY THE SOURCE OF IT ALL.
HRM...
ALSO, I GOT A REPORT FROM ITSUYO-CHAN.

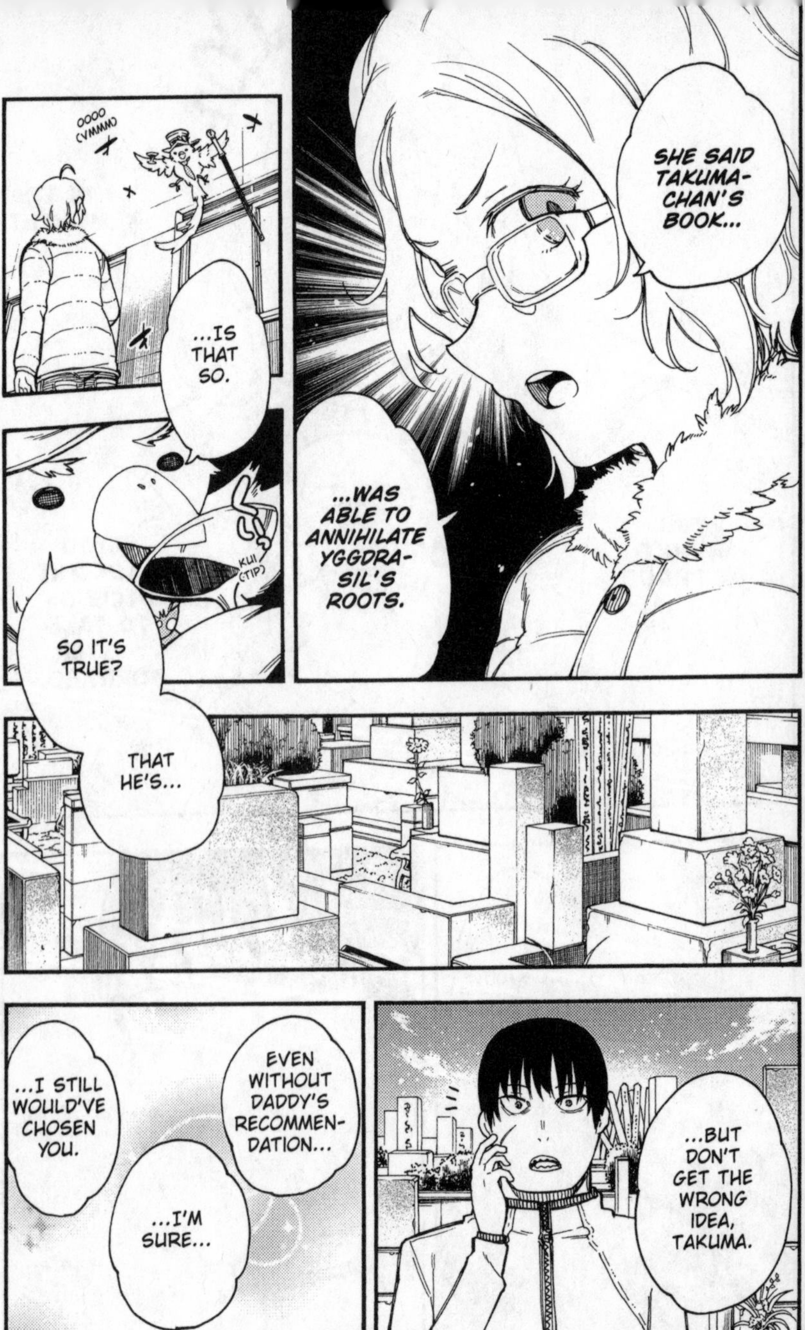
SHE SAID TAKUMA-CHAN'S BOOK...
...WAS ABLE TO ANNIHILATE YGGDRASIL'S ROOTS.
OOOO (VMMM)
...IS THAT SO.
KUI (TIP)
SO IT'S TRUE?
THAT HE'S...
...BUT DON'T GET THE WRONG IDEA, TAKUMA.
EVEN WITHOUT DADDY'S RECOMMENDATION...
...I STILL WOULD'VE CHOSEN YOU.
...I'M SURE...

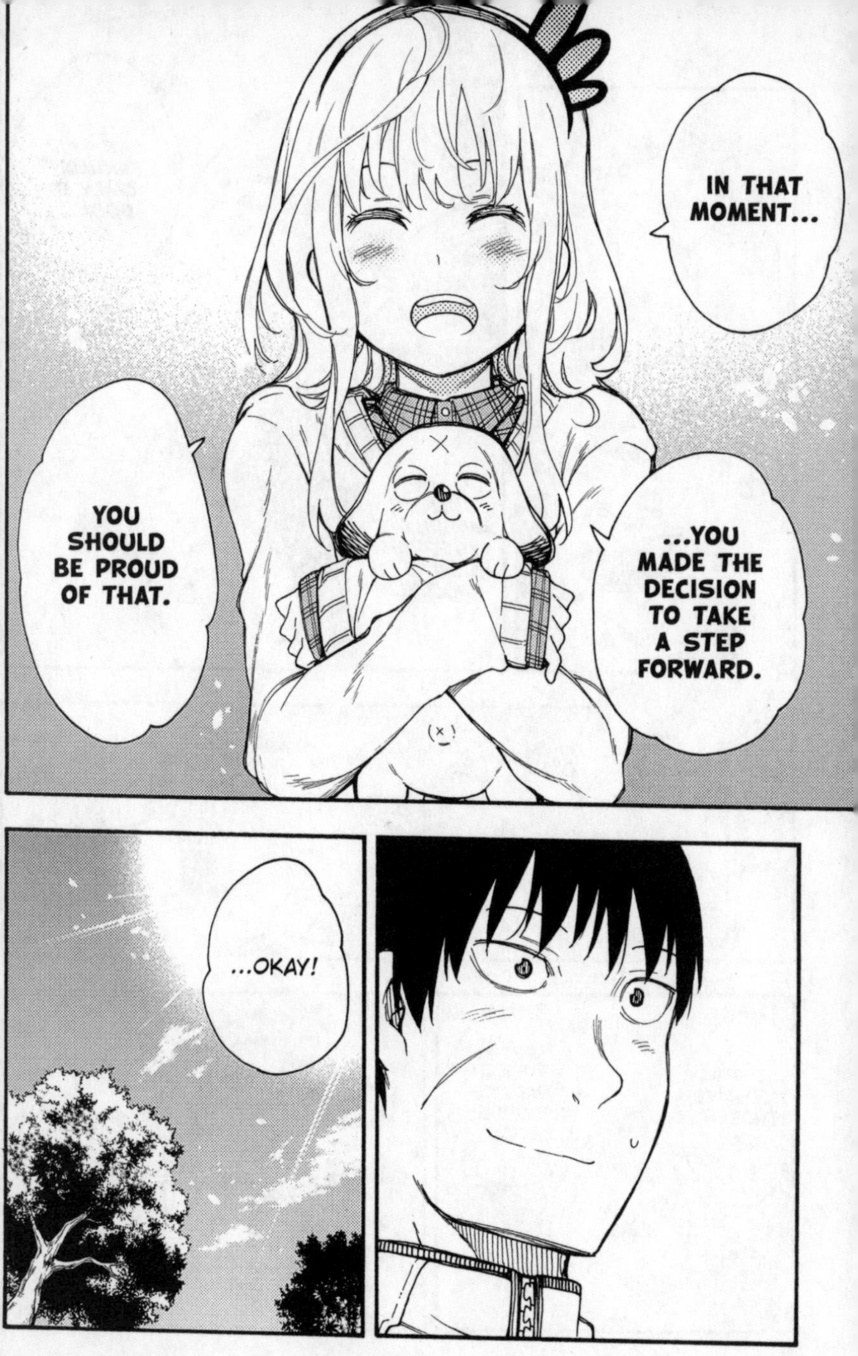
IN THAT MOMENT...
...YOU MADE THE DECISION TO TAKE A STEP FORWARD.
YOU SHOULD BE PROUD OF THAT.
...OKAY!

Val×Löve

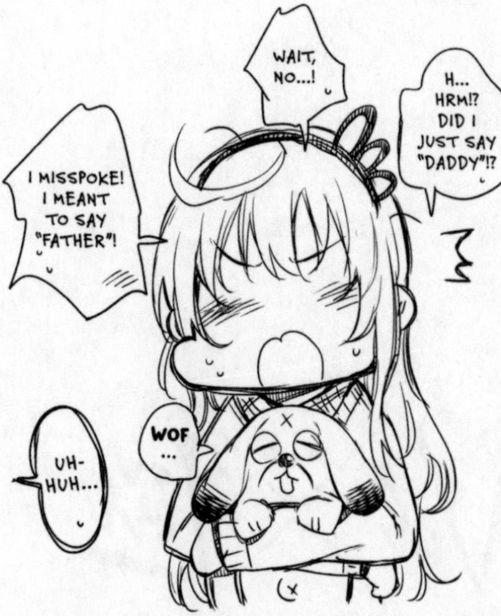
H... HRM!? DID I JUST SAY "DADDY"!?
WAIT, NO...!
I MISSPOKE! I MEANT TO SAY "FATHER"!
WOF...
UH-HUH...

Chapter 54

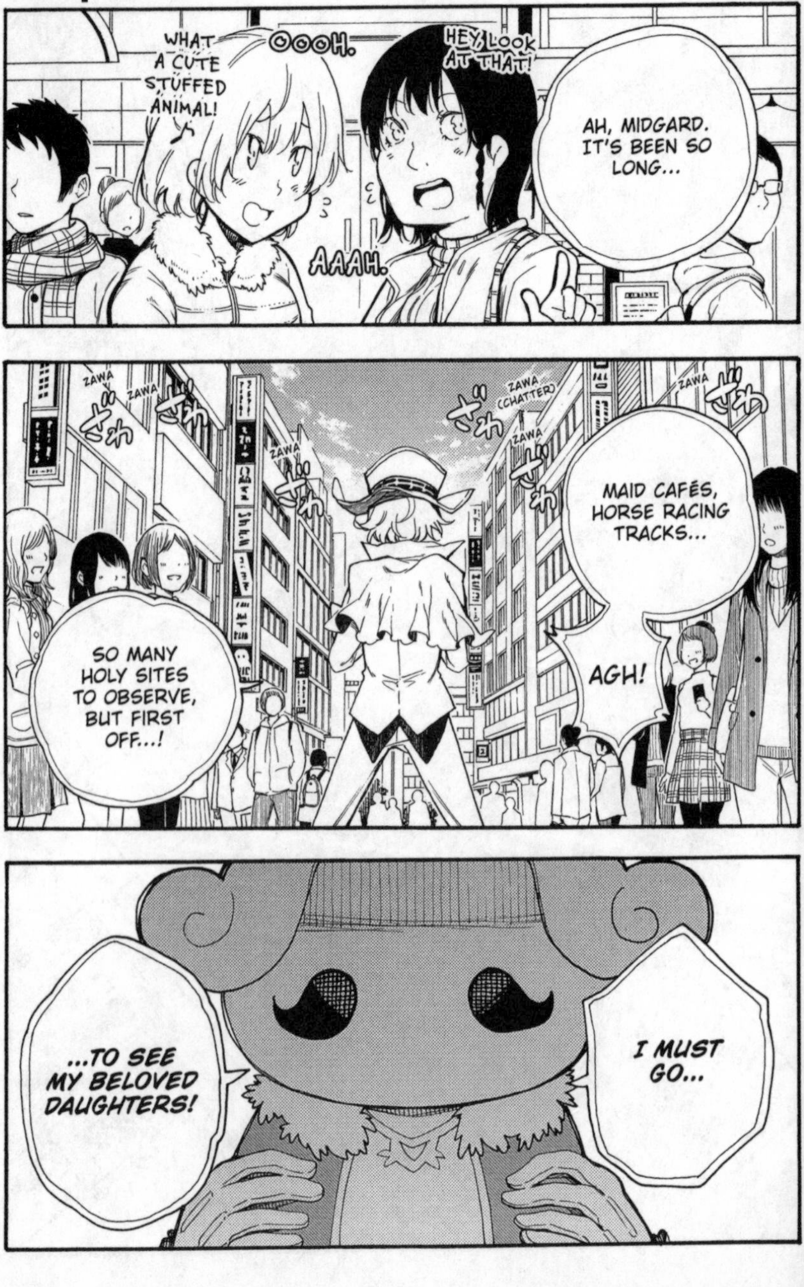

AH, MIDGARD. IT'S BEEN SO LONG...
HEY, LOOK AT THAT!
OOOH.
WHAT A CUTE STUFFED ANIMAL!
AAAH.
ZAWA
ZAWA (CHATTER)
ZAWA
MAID CAFÉS, HORSE RACING TRACKS...
AGH!
ZAWA
ZAWA
ZAWA
SO MANY HOLY SITES TO OBSERVE, BUT FIRST OFF...!
I MUST GO...
...TO SEE MY BELOVED DAUGHTERS!

Chapter 54: A Lover's Resolve

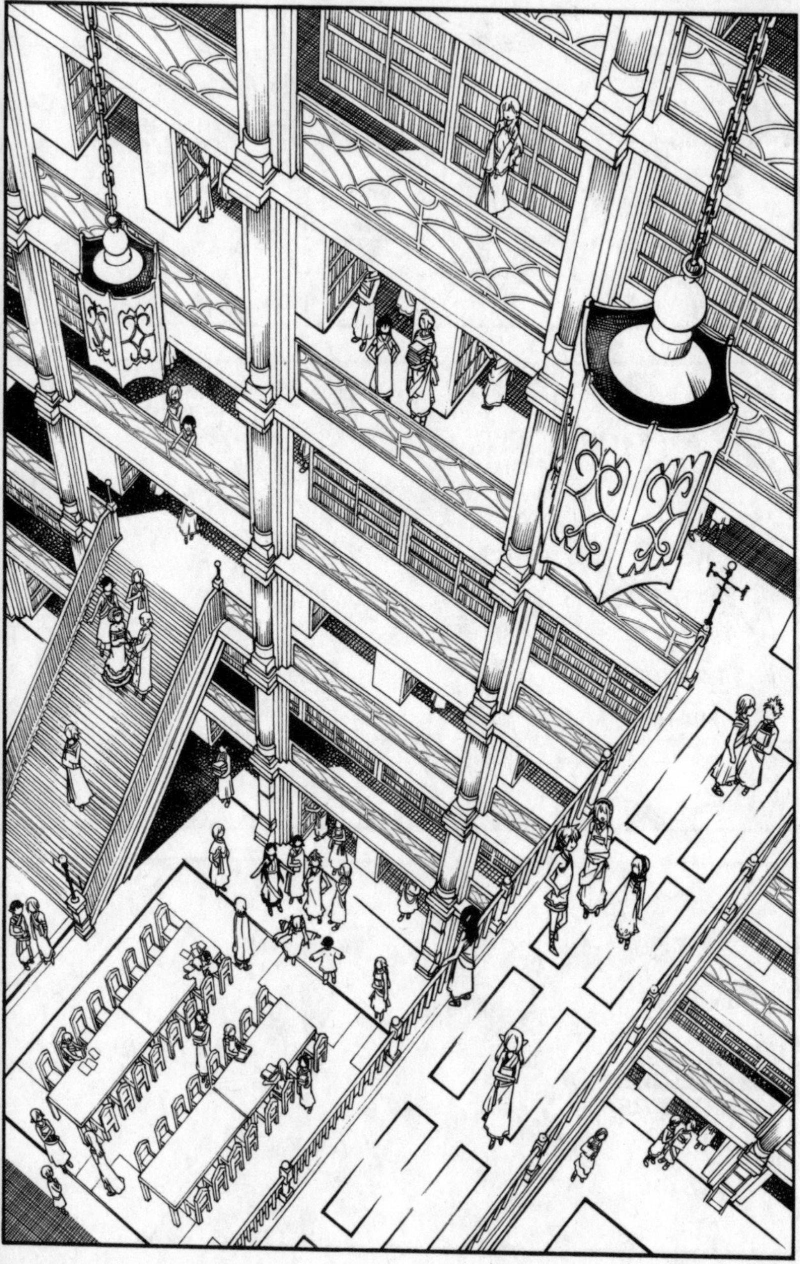

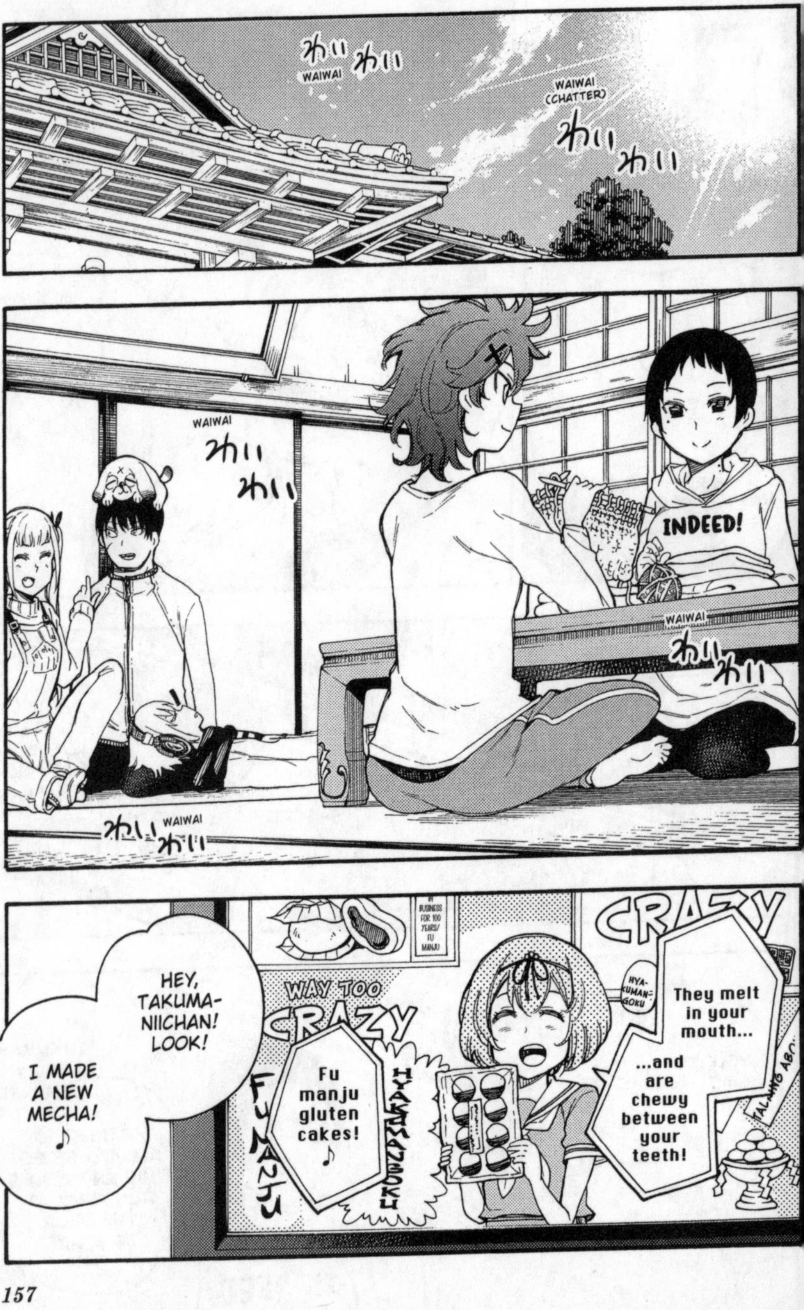
わいわい
WAIWAI
WAIWAI (CHATTER)
わいわい
INDEED!
WAIWAI
わいわい
WAIWAI
わいわい
WAIWAI
わいわい
CRAZY
HYAKUMANGOKU
They melt in your mouth...
...and are chewy between your teeth!
IN BUSINESS FOR 100 YEARS/ FU MANJU
WAY TOO CRAZY
Fu manju gluten cakes! ♪
HYAKUMANGOKU
FU MANJU
HEY, TAKUMA-NIICHAN! LOOK!
I MADE A NEW MECHA! ♪

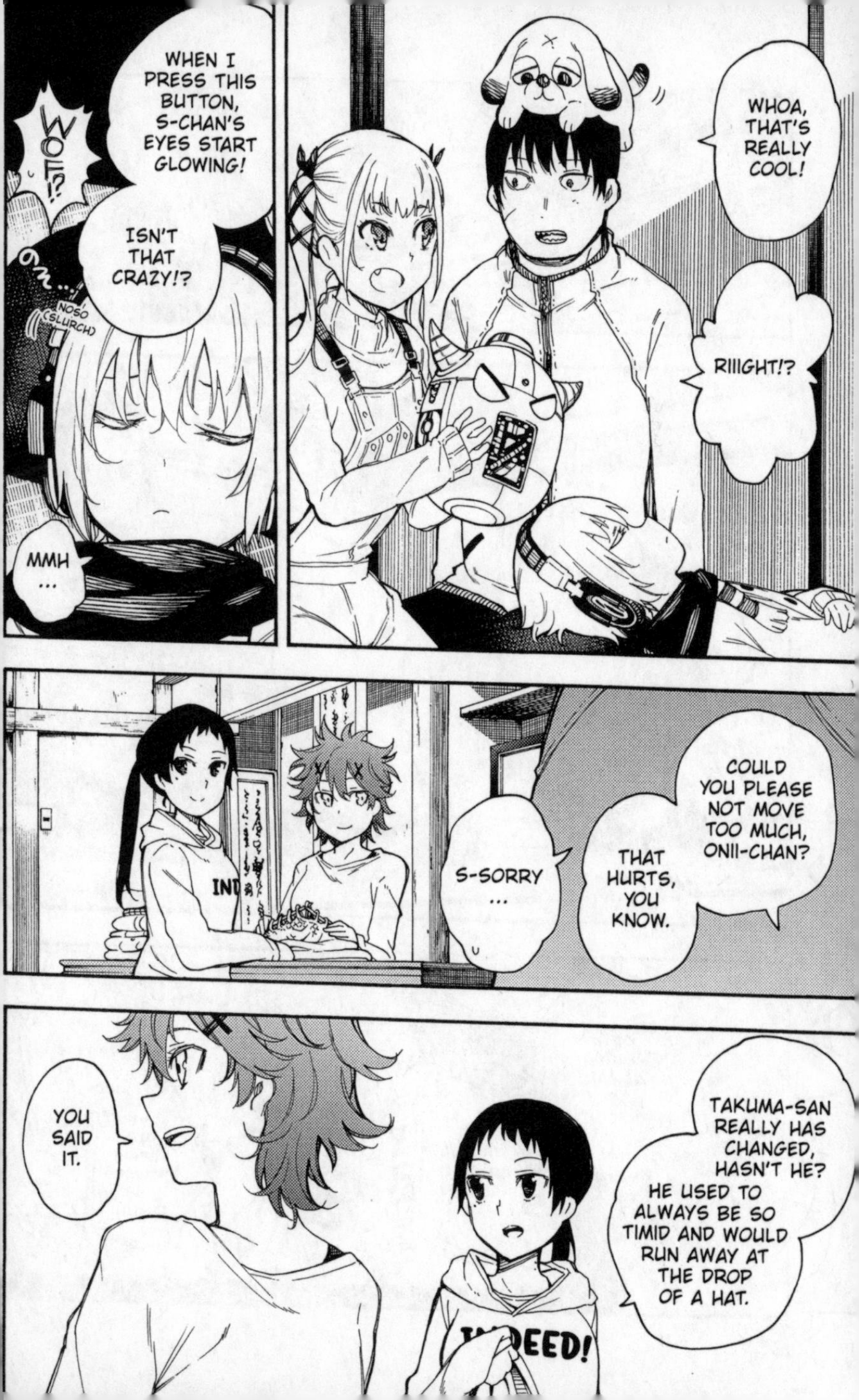
WHEN I PRESS THIS BUTTON, S-CHAN'S EYES START GLOWING!
ISN'T THAT CRAZY!?
WHOA, THAT'S REALLY COOL!
RIIIGHT!?
WOF!?
NOSO (SLURCH)
MMH ...
COULD YOU PLEASE NOT MOVE TOO MUCH, ONII-CHAN?
THAT HURTS, YOU KNOW.
S-SORRY ...
TAKUMA-SAN REALLY HAS CHANGED, HASN'T HE?
HE USED TO ALWAYS BE SO TIMID AND WOULD RUN AWAY AT THE DROP OF A HAT.
YOU SAID IT.

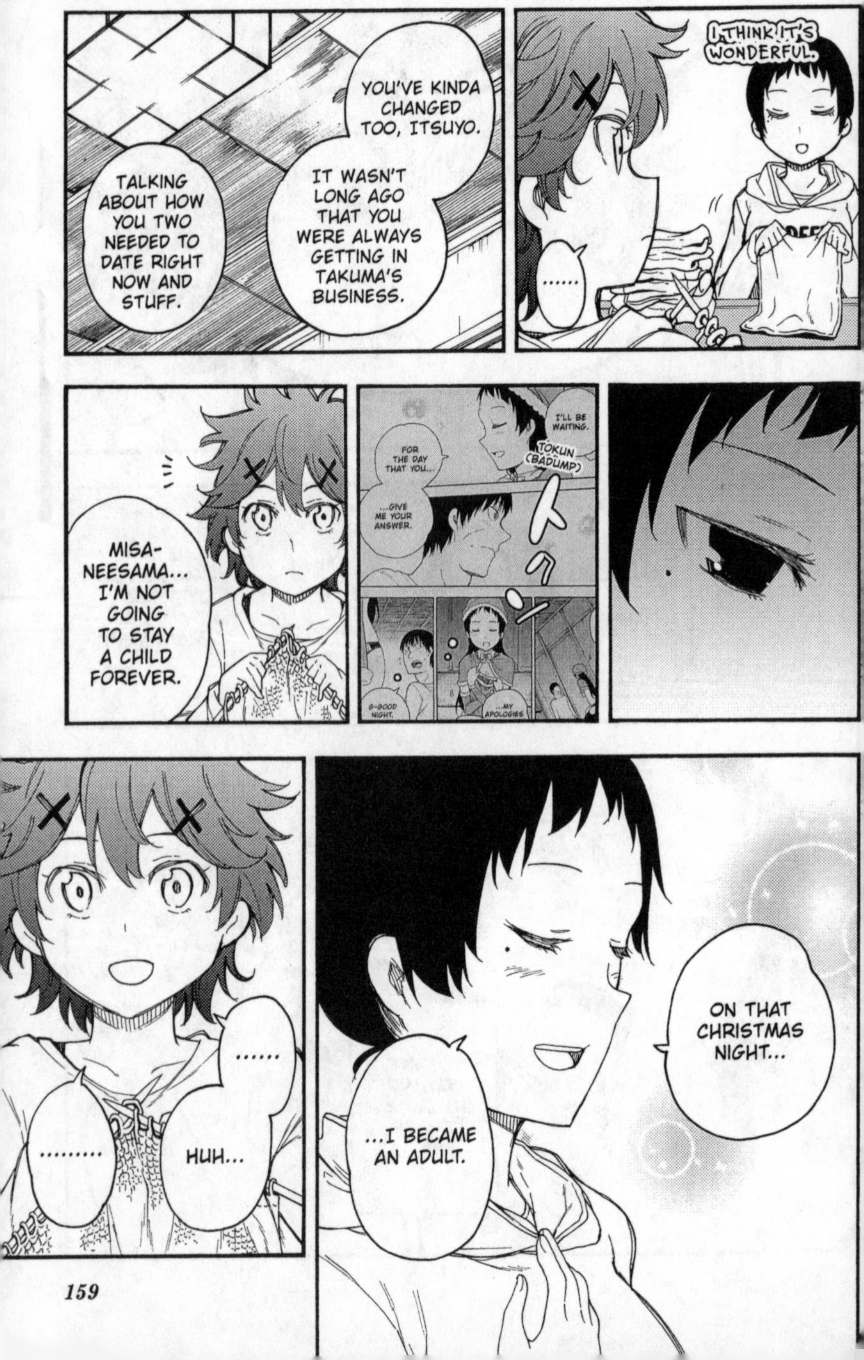
I THINK IT'S WONDERFUL.
......
YOU'VE KINDA CHANGED TOO, ITSUYO.
IT WASN'T LONG AGO THAT YOU WERE ALWAYS GETTING IN TAKUMA'S BUSINESS.
TALKING ABOUT HOW YOU TWO NEEDED TO DATE RIGHT NOW AND STUFF.
I'LL BE WAITING.
FOR THE DAY THAT YOU...
TOKUN (BADUMP)
...GIVE ME YOUR ANSWER.
...MY APOLOGIES
G-GOOD NIGHT.
MISA-NEESAMA... I'M NOT GOING TO STAY A CHILD FOREVER.
ON THAT CHRISTMAS NIGHT...
...I BECAME AN ADULT.
......
HUH...
....

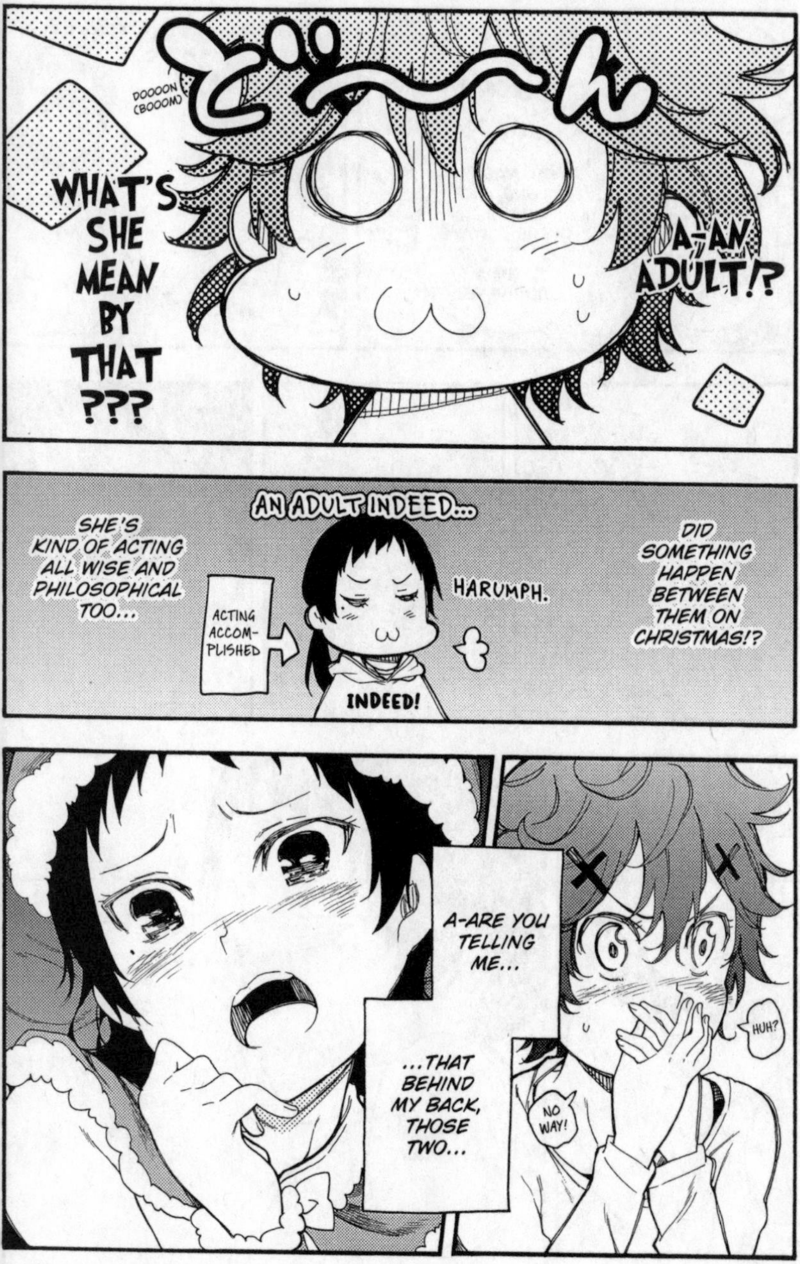
どーん
DOOOON (BOOOM)
A-AN ADULT!?
WHAT'S SHE MEAN BY THAT???
DID SOMETHING HAPPEN BETWEEN THEM ON CHRISTMAS!?
HARUMPH.
AN ADULT INDEED...
SHE'S KIND OF ACTING ALL WISE AND PHILOSOPHICAL TOO...
ACTING ACCOMPLISHED
INDEED!
HUH?
NO WAY!
A-ARE YOU TELLING ME...
...THAT BEHIND MY BACK, THOSE TWO...

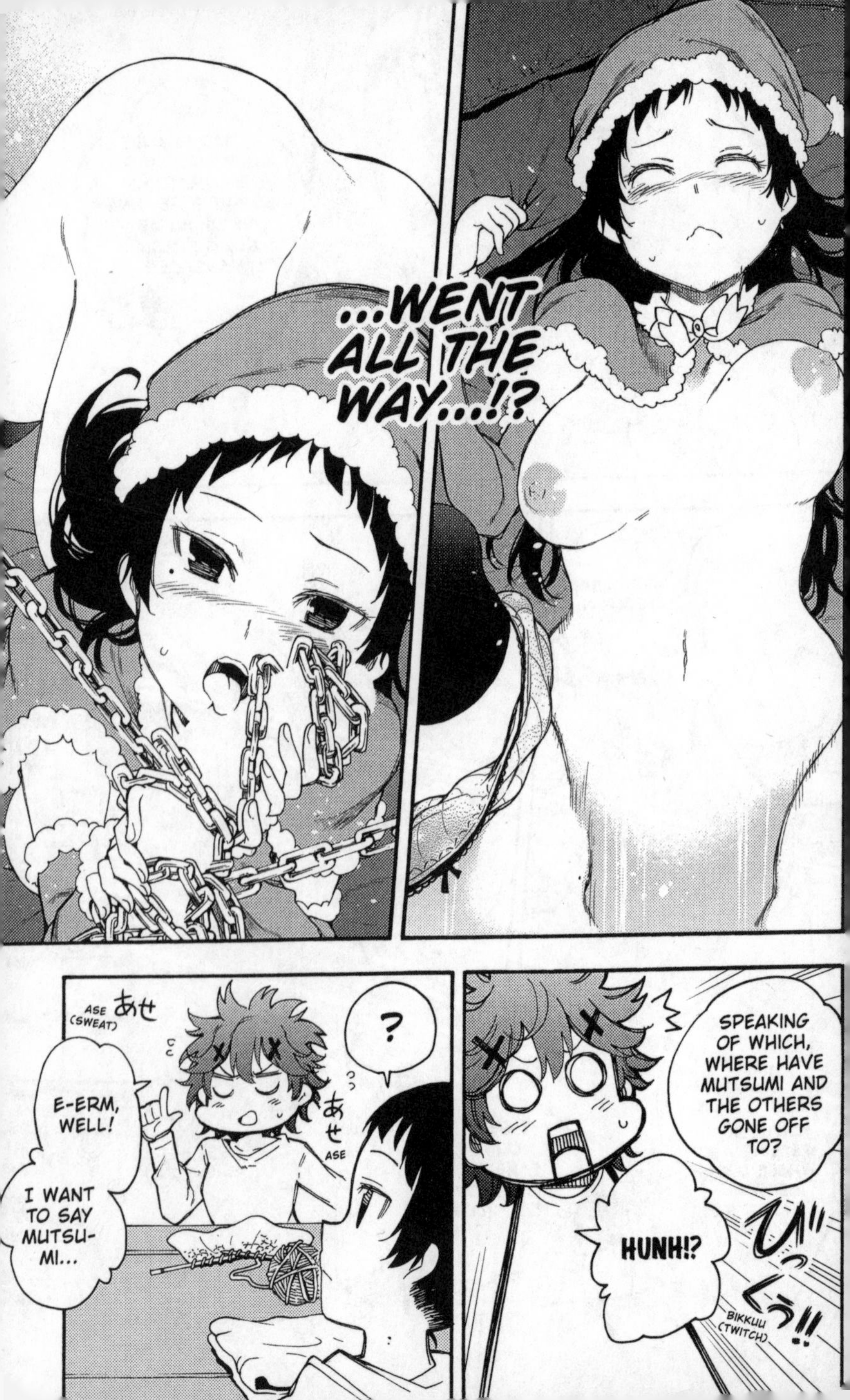
...WENT ALL THE WAY...!?
SPEAKING OF WHICH, WHERE HAVE MUTSUMI AND THE OTHERS GONE OFF TO?
HUNH!?
びっくぅ!!
BIKKUU (TWITCH)
?
ASE あせ (SWEAT)
あせ ASE
E-ERM, WELL!
I WANT TO SAY MUTSU-MI...

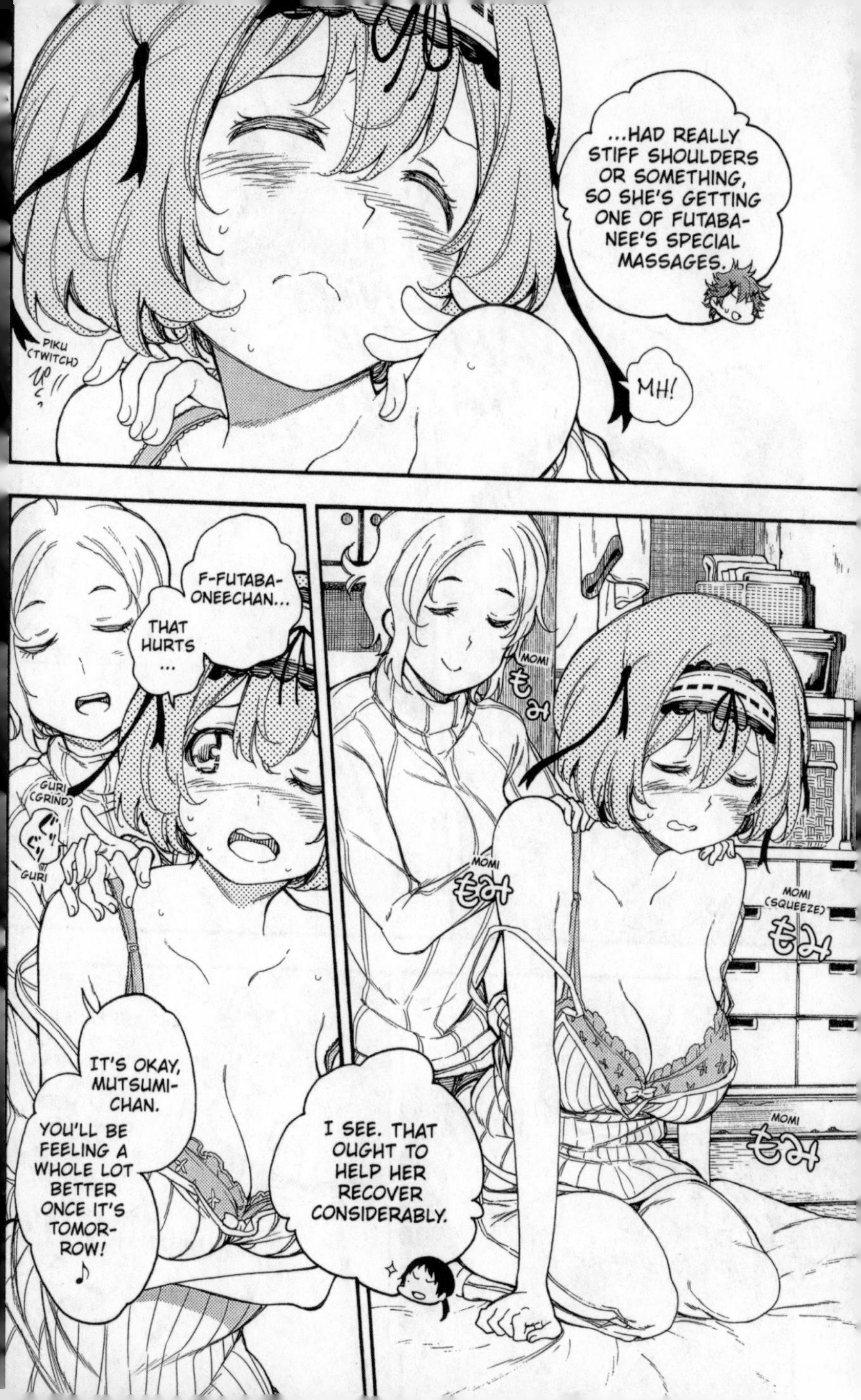

...HAD REALLY STIFF SHOULDERS OR SOMETHING, SO SHE'S GETTING ONE OF FUTABA-NEE'S SPECIAL MASSAGES.
MH!
PIKU (TWITCH)
MOMI
MOMI
MOMI (SQUEEZE)
MOMI
I SEE. THAT OUGHT TO HELP HER RECOVER CONSIDERABLY.
F-FUTABA-ONEECHAN...
THAT HURTS...
GURI (GRIND)
GURI
IT'S OKAY, MUTSUMI-CHAN.
YOU'LL BE FEELING A WHOLE LOT BETTER ONCE IT'S TOMORROW! ♪

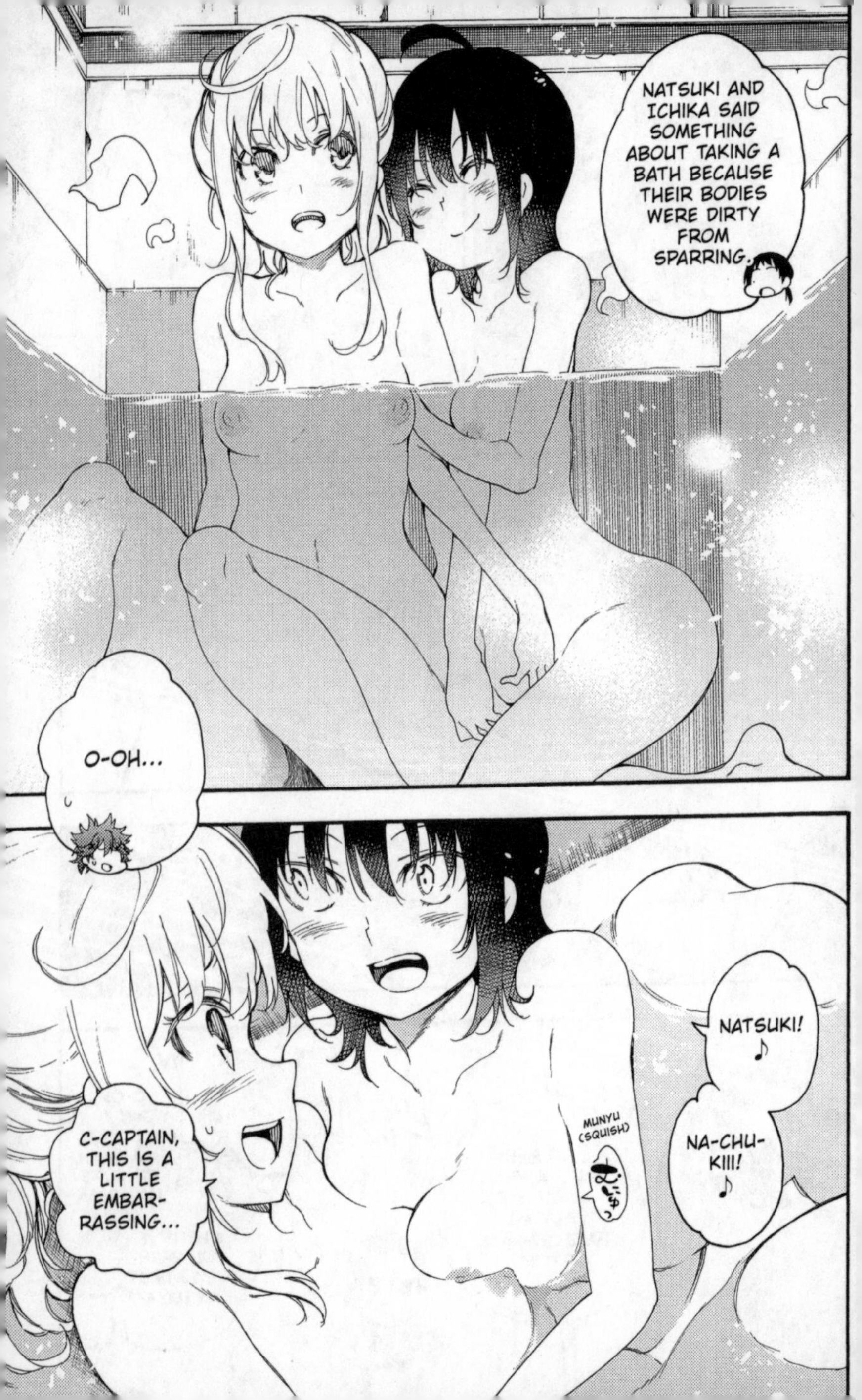
NATSUKI AND ICHIKA SAID SOMETHING ABOUT TAKING A BATH BECAUSE THEIR BODIES WERE DIRTY FROM SPARRING.
O-OH...
NATSUKI! ♪
NA-CHU-KIII! ♪
MUNYU (SQUISH)
C-CAPTAIN, THIS IS A LITTLE EMBAR-RASSING...

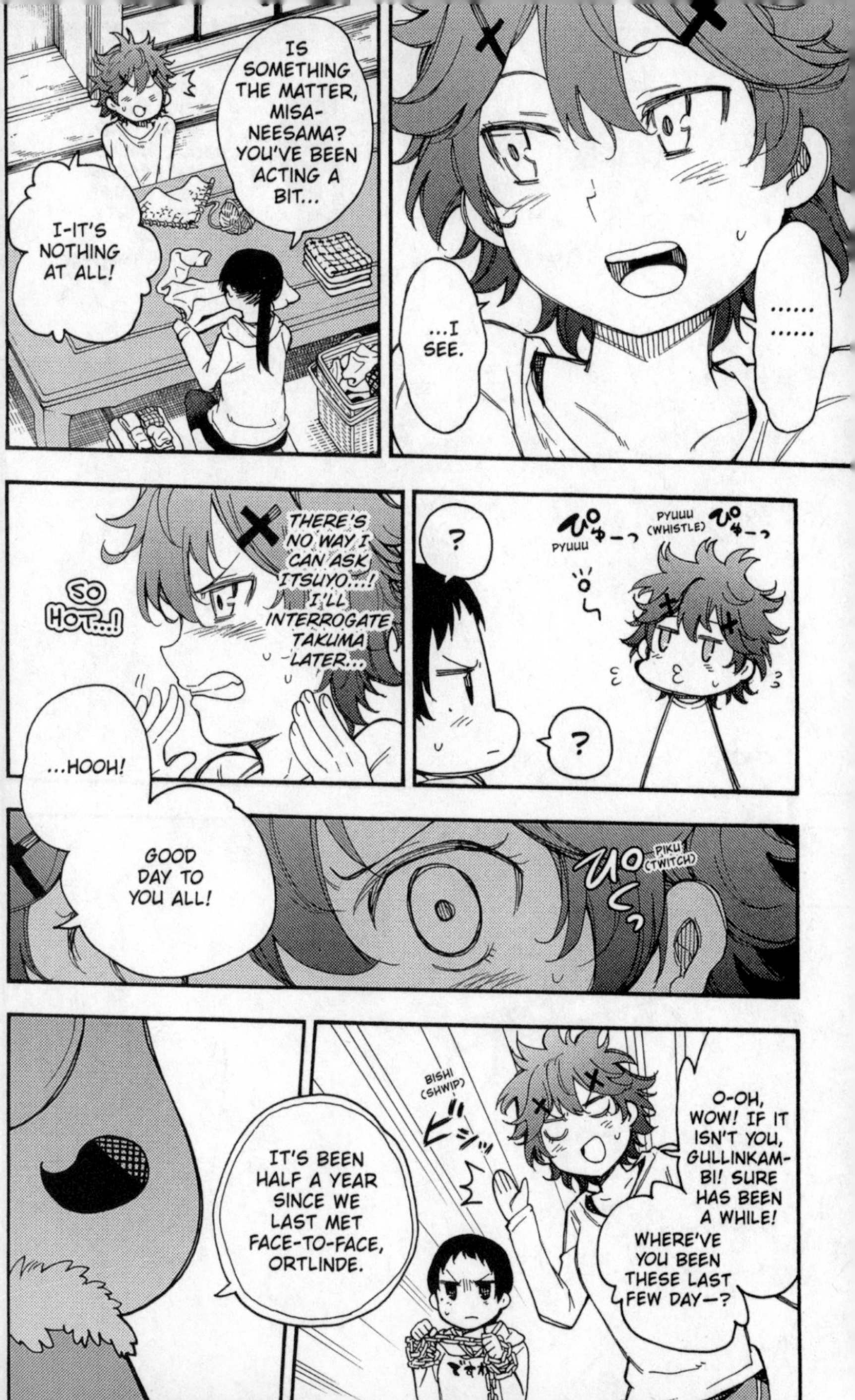
......
......
...I SEE.
IS SOMETHING THE MATTER, MISA-NEESAMA? YOU'VE BEEN ACTING A BIT...
I-IT'S NOTHING AT ALL!
?
PYUUU (WHISTLE)
PYUUU
?
THERE'S NO WAY I CAN ASK ITSUYO...! I'LL INTERROGATE TAKUMA LATER...
SO HOT...!
...HOOH!
PIKU (TWITCH)
GOOD DAY TO YOU ALL!
O-OH, WOW! IF IT ISN'T YOU, GULLINKAMBI! SURE HAS BEEN A WHILE!
WHERE'VE YOU BEEN THESE LAST FEW DAY—?
BISHI (SHWIP)
IT'S BEEN HALF A YEAR SINCE WE LAST MET FACE-TO-FACE, ORTLINDE.

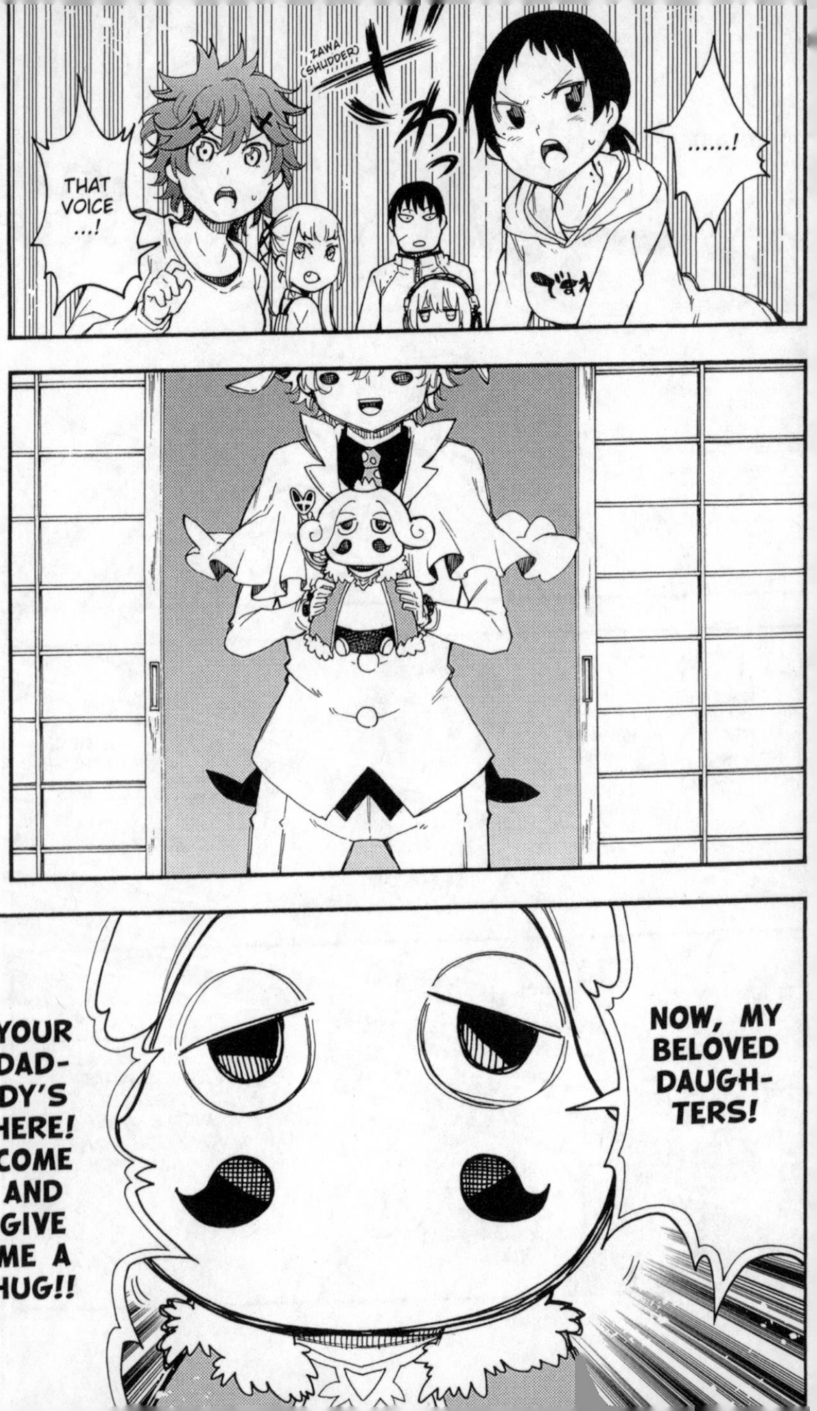
......!
ZAWA (SHUDDER)
THAT VOICE ...!
NOW, MY BELOVED DAUGH-TERS!
YOUR DAD-DY'S HERE! COME AND GIVE ME A HUG!!

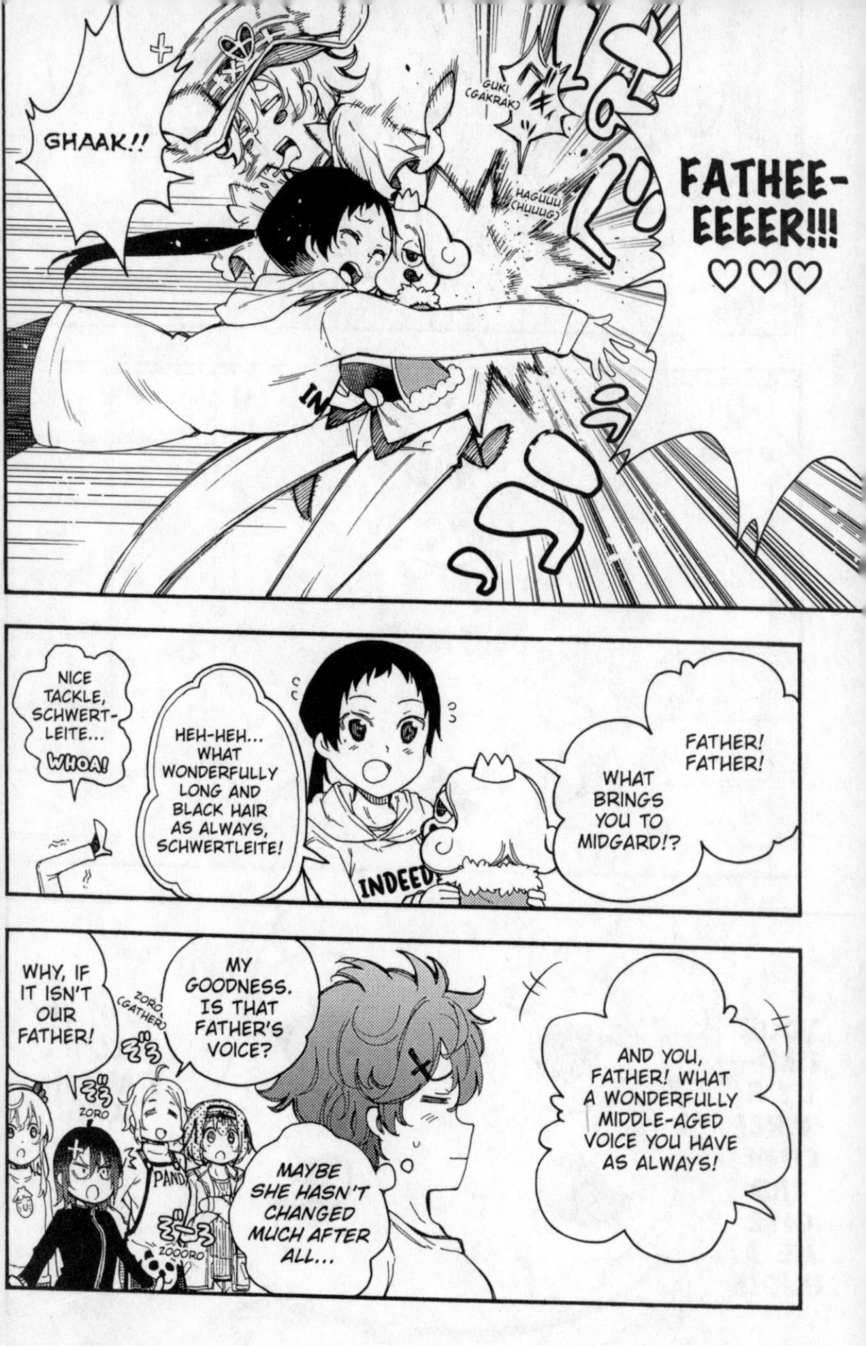
FATHEE-EEEER!!! ♡♡♡
GUKI (GAKRAK)
HAGUUU (CHUUUG)
GHAAK!!
IN
FATHER! FATHER!
WHAT BRINGS YOU TO MIDGARD!?
INDEED
HEH-HEH... WHAT WONDERFULLY LONG AND BLACK HAIR AS ALWAYS, SCHWERTLEITE!
NICE TACKLE, SCHWERTLEITE... WHOA!
AND YOU, FATHER! WHAT A WONDERFULLY MIDDLE-AGED VOICE YOU HAVE AS ALWAYS!
MAYBE SHE HASN'T CHANGED MUCH AFTER ALL...
MY GOODNESS. IS THAT FATHER'S VOICE?
ZORO (GATHER)
WHY, IF IT ISN'T OUR FATHER!
ZORO
PAND
ZOOORO

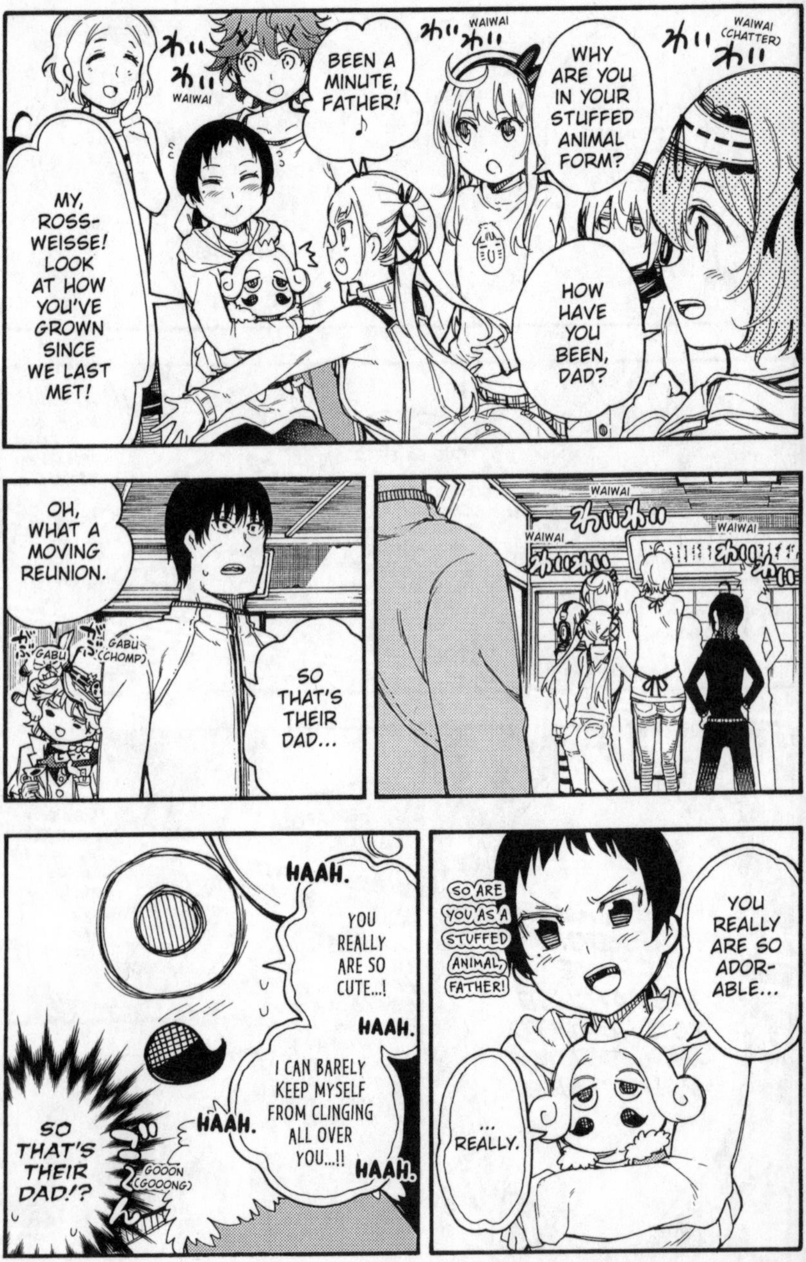
WAIWAI (CHATTER)
HOW HAVE YOU BEEN, DAD?
WHY ARE YOU IN YOUR STUFFED ANIMAL FORM?
WAIWAI
BEEN A MINUTE, FATHER! ♪
WAIWAI
MY, ROSSWEISSE! LOOK AT HOW YOU'VE GROWN SINCE WE LAST MET!
WAIWAI
WAIWAI
WAIWAI
OH, WHAT A MOVING REUNION.
SO THAT'S THEIR DAD...
GABU (CHOMP)
GABU
YOU REALLY ARE SO ADORABLE...
SO ARE YOU AS A STUFFED ANIMAL, FATHER!
...REALLY.
HAAH.
YOU REALLY ARE SO CUTE...!
HAAH.
I CAN BARELY KEEP MYSELF FROM CLINGING ALL OVER YOU...!!
HAAH.
HAAH.
SO THAT'S THEIR DAD!?
GOOON (GOOONG)

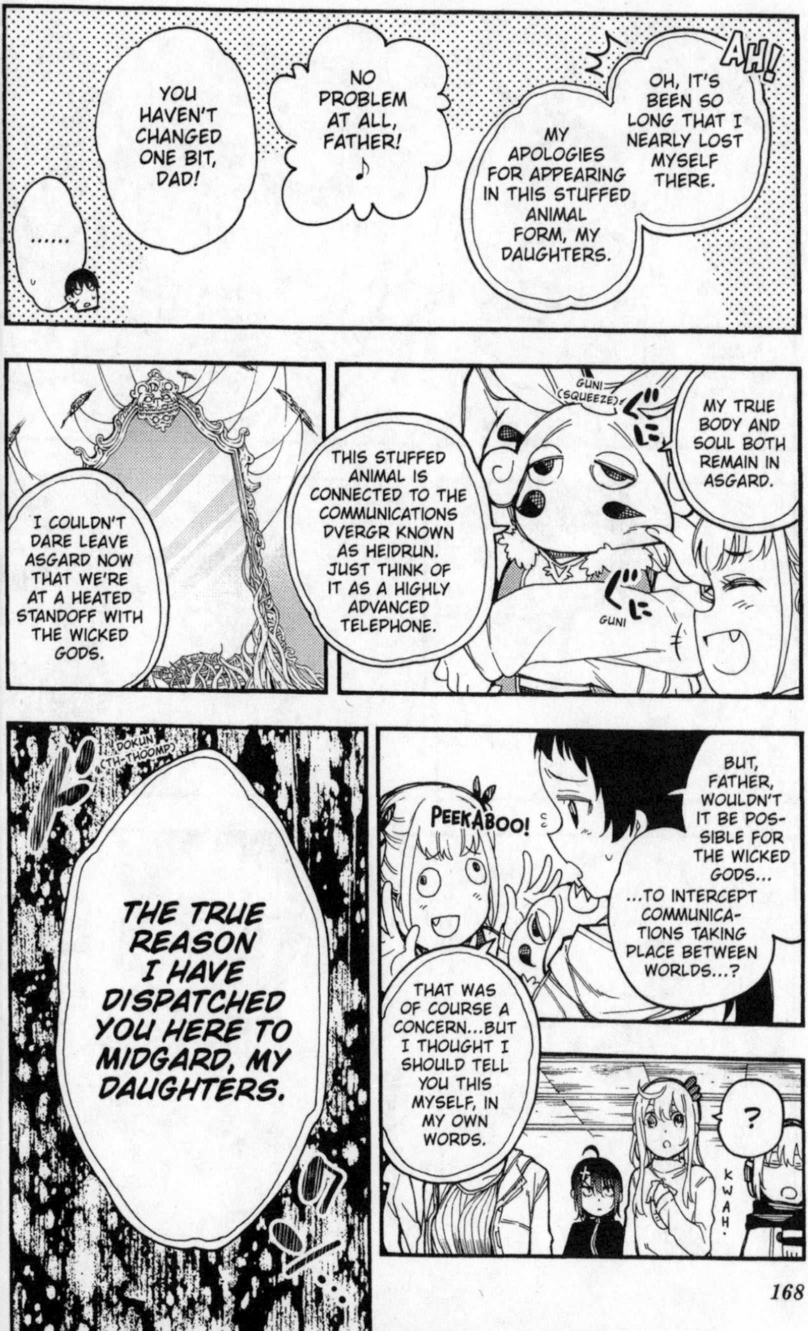
AH!
OH, IT'S BEEN SO LONG THAT I NEARLY LOST MYSELF THERE.
MY APOLOGIES FOR APPEARING IN THIS STUFFED ANIMAL FORM, MY DAUGHTERS.
NO PROBLEM AT ALL, FATHER! ♪
YOU HAVEN'T CHANGED ONE BIT, DAD!
......
GUNI (SQUEEZE)
MY TRUE BODY AND SOUL BOTH REMAIN IN ASGARD.
THIS STUFFED ANIMAL IS CONNECTED TO THE COMMUNICATIONS DVERGR KNOWN AS HEIDRUN. JUST THINK OF IT AS A HIGHLY ADVANCED TELEPHONE.
GUNI
I COULDN'T DARE LEAVE ASGARD NOW THAT WE'RE AT A HEATED STANDOFF WITH THE WICKED GODS.
BUT, FATHER, WOULDN'T IT BE POSSIBLE FOR THE WICKED GODS...
...TO INTERCEPT COMMUNICATIONS TAKING PLACE BETWEEN WORLDS...?
PEEKABOO!
THAT WAS OF COURSE A CONCERN...BUT I THOUGHT I SHOULD TELL YOU THIS MYSELF, IN MY OWN WORDS.
?
KWAH.
DOKUN (TH-THOOMP)
THE TRUE REASON I HAVE DISPATCHED YOU HERE TO MIDGARD, MY DAUGHTERS.

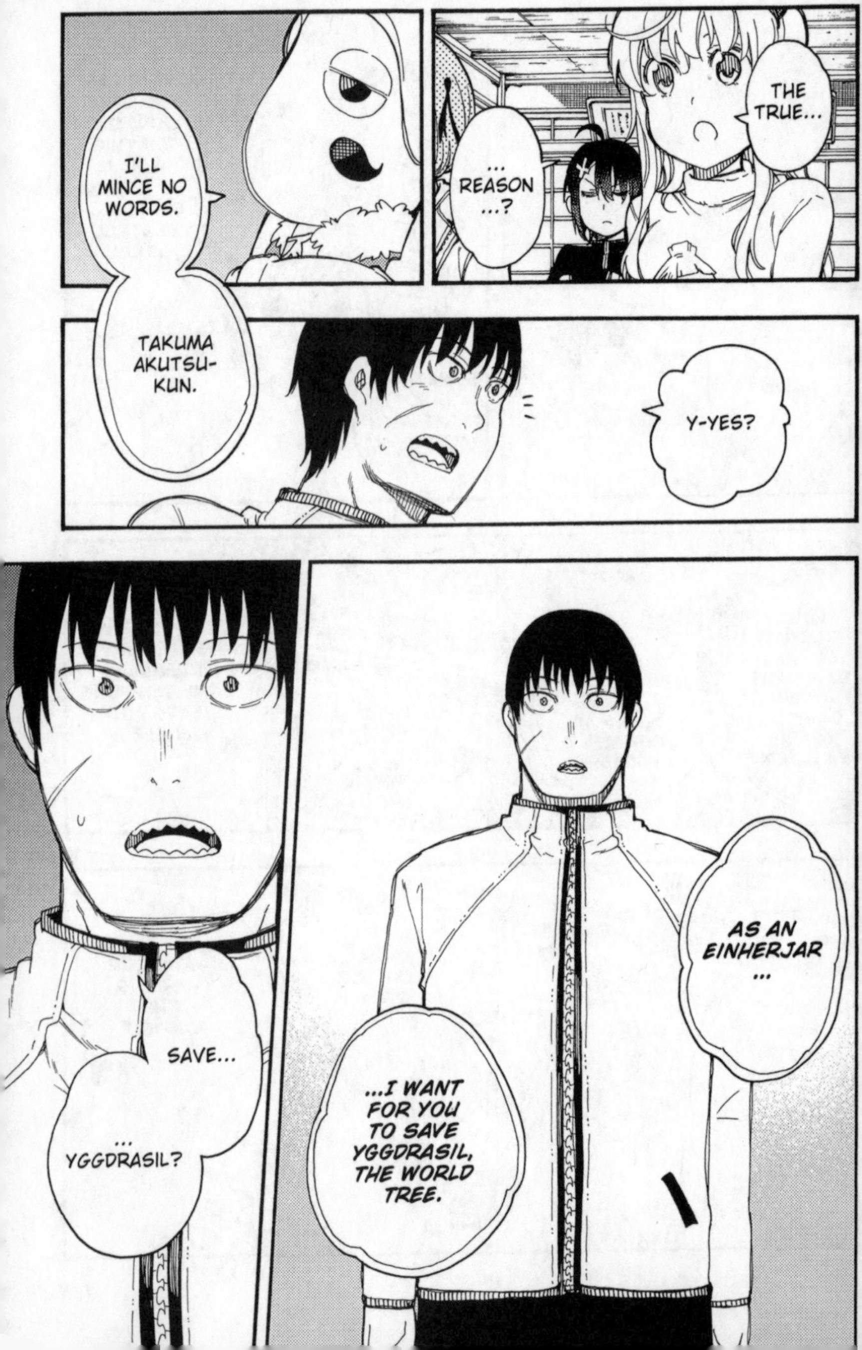
THE TRUE...
...REASON...?
I'LL MINCE NO WORDS.
TAKUMA AKUTSU-KUN.
Y-YES?
AS AN EINHERJAR...
...I WANT FOR YOU TO SAVE YGGDRASIL, THE WORLD TREE.
SAVE...
...YGGDRASIL?

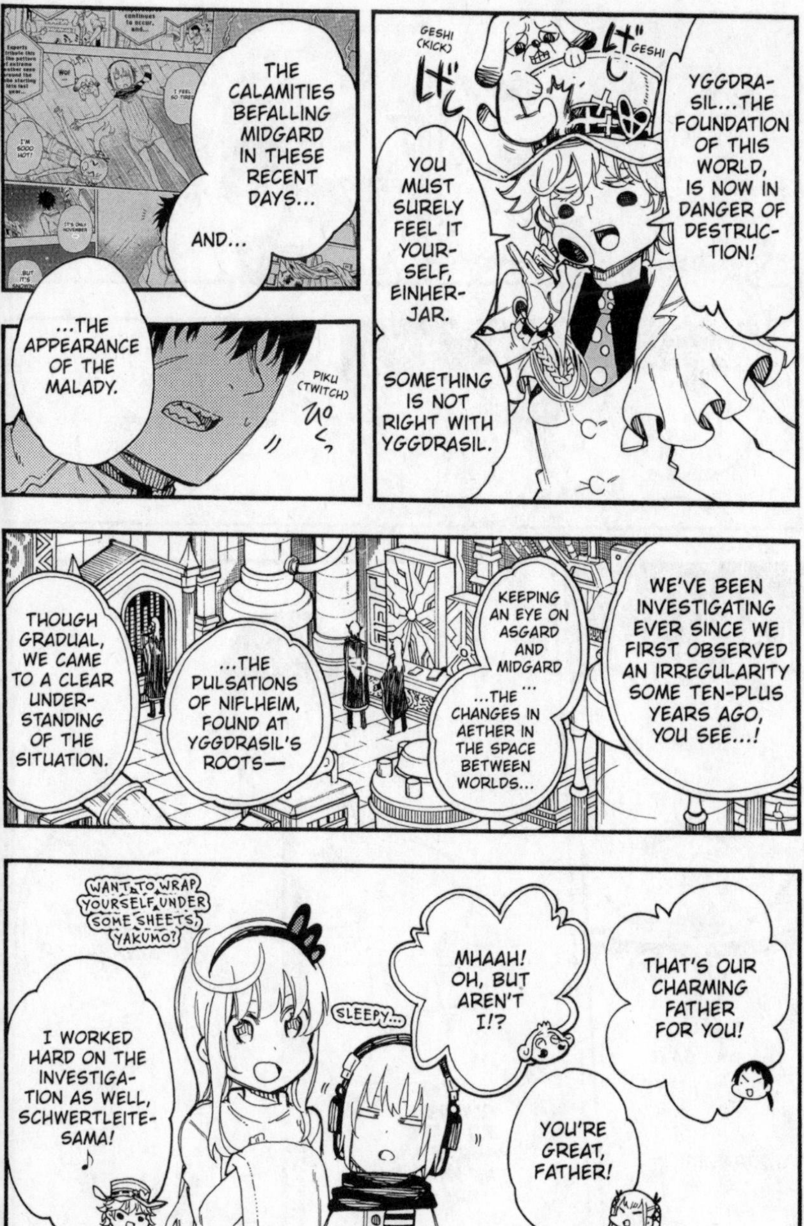
GESHI (KICK)
GESHI
YGGDRA-SIL...THE FOUNDATION OF THIS WORLD, IS NOW IN DANGER OF DESTRUC-TION!
YOU MUST SURELY FEEL IT YOUR-SELF, EINHER-JAR.
SOMETHING IS NOT RIGHT WITH YGGDRASIL.
THE CALAMITIES BEFALLING MIDGARD IN THESE RECENT DAYS...
AND...
I'M SOOO HOT!
...THE APPEARANCE OF THE MALADY.
PIKU (TWITCH)
WE'VE BEEN INVESTIGATING EVER SINCE WE FIRST OBSERVED AN IRREGULARITY SOME TEN-PLUS YEARS AGO, YOU SEE...!
KEEPING AN EYE ON ASGARD AND MIDGARD...
...THE CHANGES IN AETHER IN THE SPACE BETWEEN WORLDS...
...THE PULSATIONS OF NIFLHEIM, FOUND AT YGGDRASIL'S ROOTS—
THOUGH GRADUAL, WE CAME TO A CLEAR UNDER-STANDING OF THE SITUATION.
THAT'S OUR CHARMING FATHER FOR YOU!
YOU'RE GREAT, FATHER!
MHAAH! OH, BUT AREN'T I!?
SLEEPY...
WANT TO WRAP YOURSELF UNDER SOME SHEETS, YAKUMO?
I WORKED HARD ON THE INVESTIGA-TION AS WELL, SCHWERTLEITE-SAMA! ♪

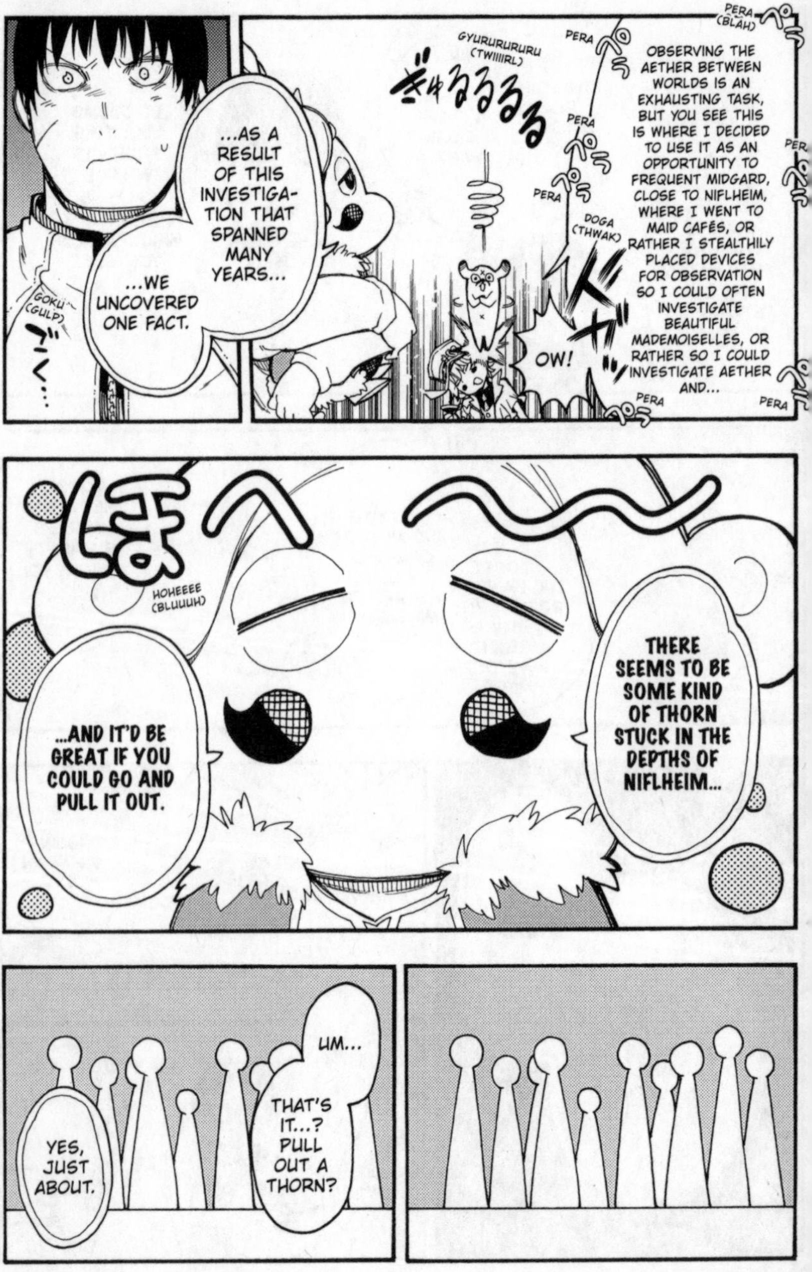
PERA (BLAH)
OBSERVING THE AETHER BETWEEN WORLDS IS AN EXHAUSTING TASK, BUT YOU SEE THIS IS WHERE I DECIDED TO USE IT AS AN OPPORTUNITY TO FREQUENT MIDGARD, CLOSE TO NIFLHEIM, WHERE I WENT TO MAID CAFÉS, OR RATHER I STEALTHILY PLACED DEVICES FOR OBSERVATION SO I COULD OFTEN INVESTIGATE BEAUTIFUL MADEMOISELLES, OR RATHER SO I COULD INVESTIGATE AETHER AND...
PERA
PERA
PERA
PERA
PERA
GYURURURURU (TWIIIIRL)
ぎゅるるるる
DOGA (THWAK)
OW!
...AS A RESULT OF THIS INVESTIGATION THAT SPANNED MANY YEARS...
...WE UNCOVERED ONE FACT.
GOKU (GULP)
ゴく…
HOHEEEE (BLUUUH)
ほへ〜〜
THERE SEEMS TO BE SOME KIND OF THORN STUCK IN THE DEPTHS OF NIFLHEIM...
...AND IT'D BE GREAT IF YOU COULD GO AND PULL IT OUT.
UM...
THAT'S IT...? PULL OUT A THORN?
YES, JUST ABOUT.

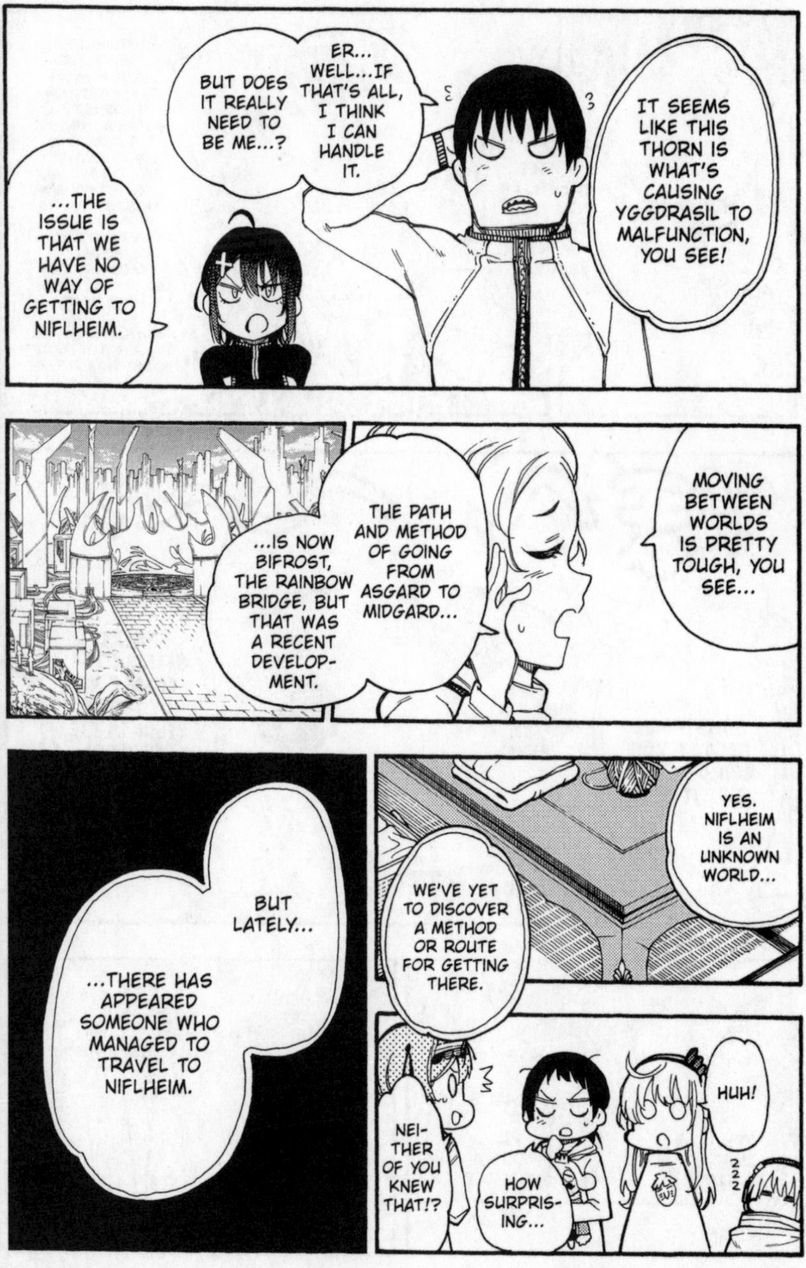
IT SEEMS LIKE THIS THORN IS WHAT'S CAUSING YGGDRASIL TO MALFUNCTION, YOU SEE!
ER... WELL...IF THAT'S ALL, I THINK I CAN HANDLE IT.
BUT DOES IT REALLY NEED TO BE ME...?
...THE ISSUE IS THAT WE HAVE NO WAY OF GETTING TO NIFLHEIM.
MOVING BETWEEN WORLDS IS PRETTY TOUGH, YOU SEE...
THE PATH AND METHOD OF GOING FROM ASGARD TO MIDGARD...
...IS NOW BIFROST, THE RAINBOW BRIDGE, BUT THAT WAS A RECENT DEVELOP-MENT.
YES. NIFLHEIM IS AN UNKNOWN WORLD...
WE'VE YET TO DISCOVER A METHOD OR ROUTE FOR GETTING THERE.
HUH!
HOW SURPRIS-ING...
NEI-THER OF YOU KNEW THAT!?
BUT LATELY...
...THERE HAS APPEARED SOMEONE WHO MANAGED TO TRAVEL TO NIFLHEIM.

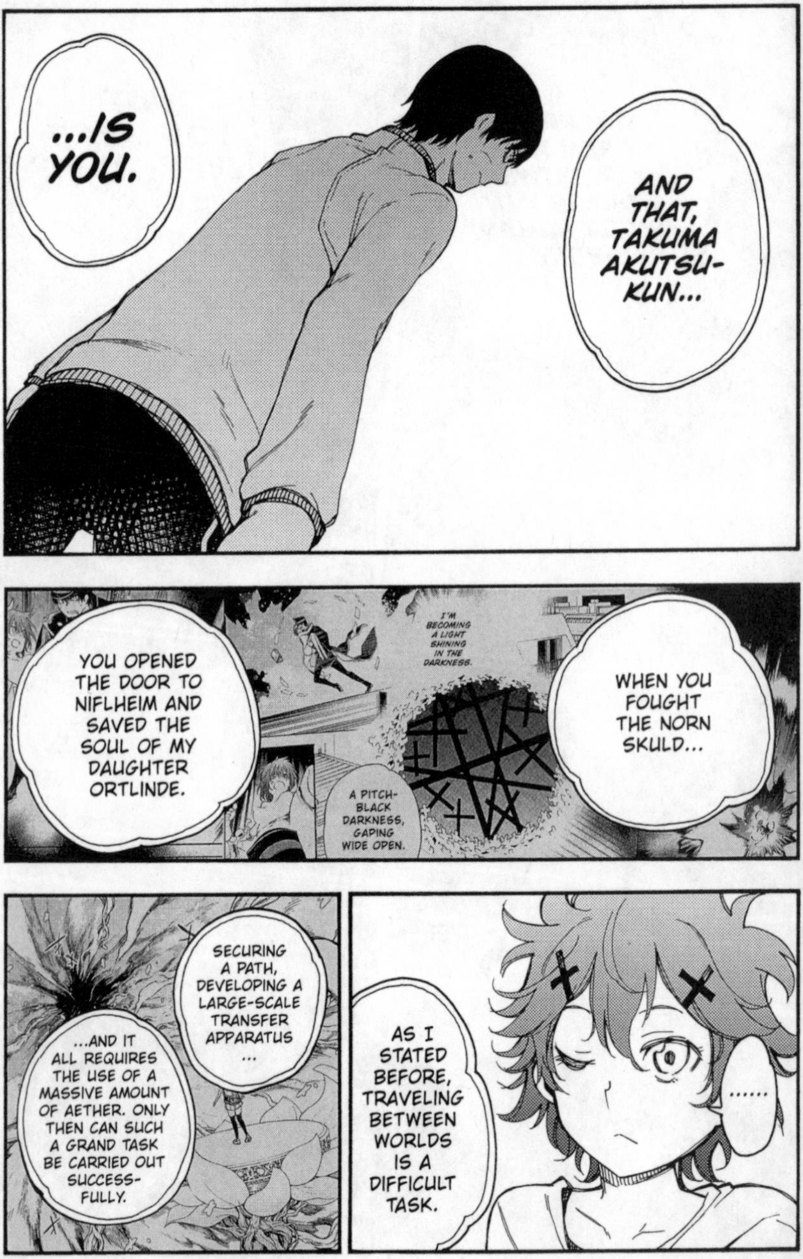
AND THAT, TAKUMA AKUTSU-KUN...
...IS YOU.
WHEN YOU FOUGHT THE NORN SKULD...
I'M BECOMING A LIGHT SHINING IN THE DARKNESS.
A PITCH-BLACK DARKNESS, GAPING WIDE OPEN.
YOU OPENED THE DOOR TO NIFLHEIM AND SAVED THE SOUL OF MY DAUGHTER ORTLINDE.
......
AS I STATED BEFORE, TRAVELING BETWEEN WORLDS IS A DIFFICULT TASK.
SECURING A PATH, DEVELOPING A LARGE-SCALE TRANSFER APPARATUS...
...AND IT ALL REQUIRES THE USE OF A MASSIVE AMOUNT OF AETHER. ONLY THEN CAN SUCH A GRAND TASK BE CARRIED OUT SUCCESSFULLY.

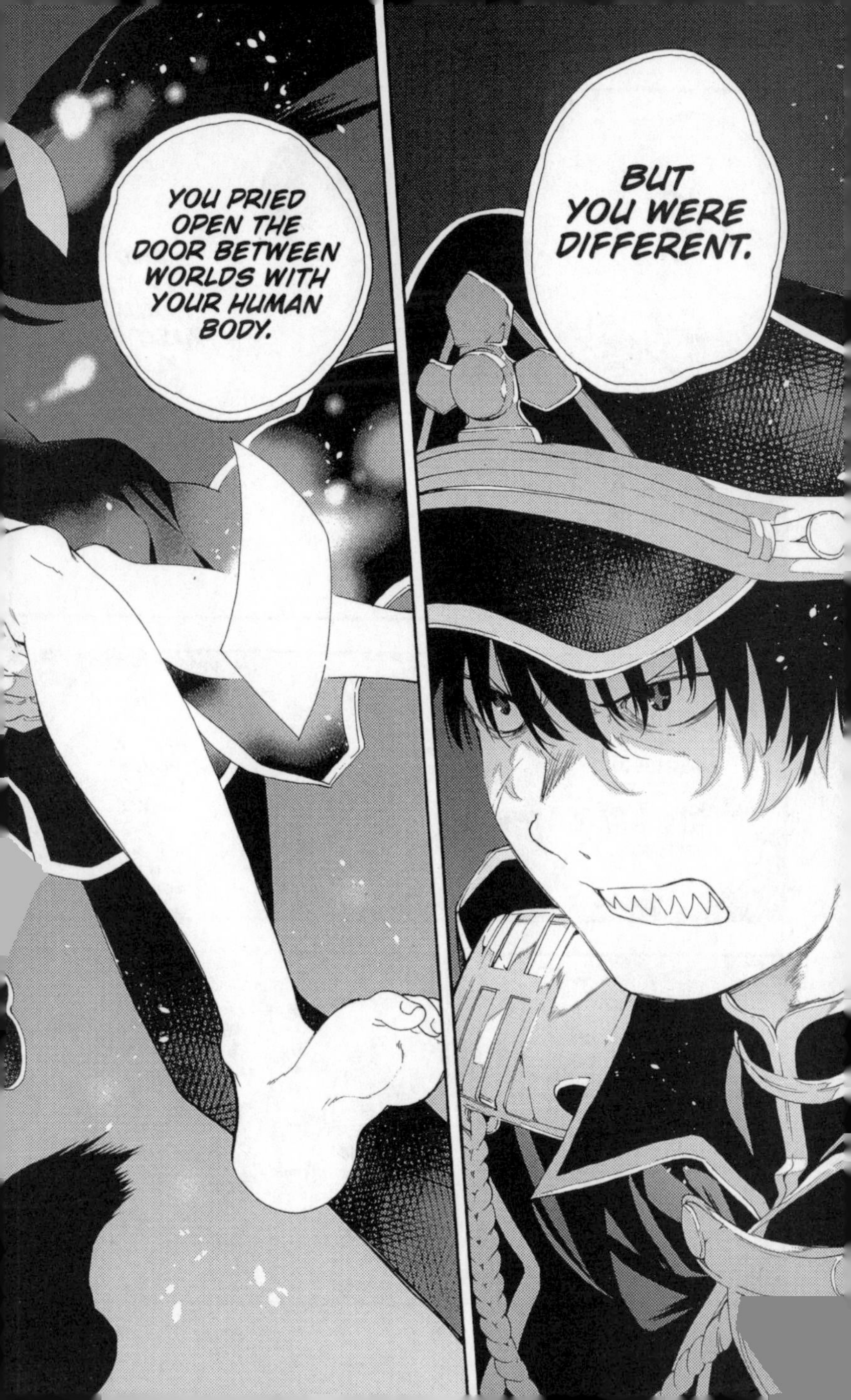
BUT YOU WERE DIFFERENT.
YOU PRIED OPEN THE DOOR BETWEEN WORLDS WITH YOUR HUMAN BODY.

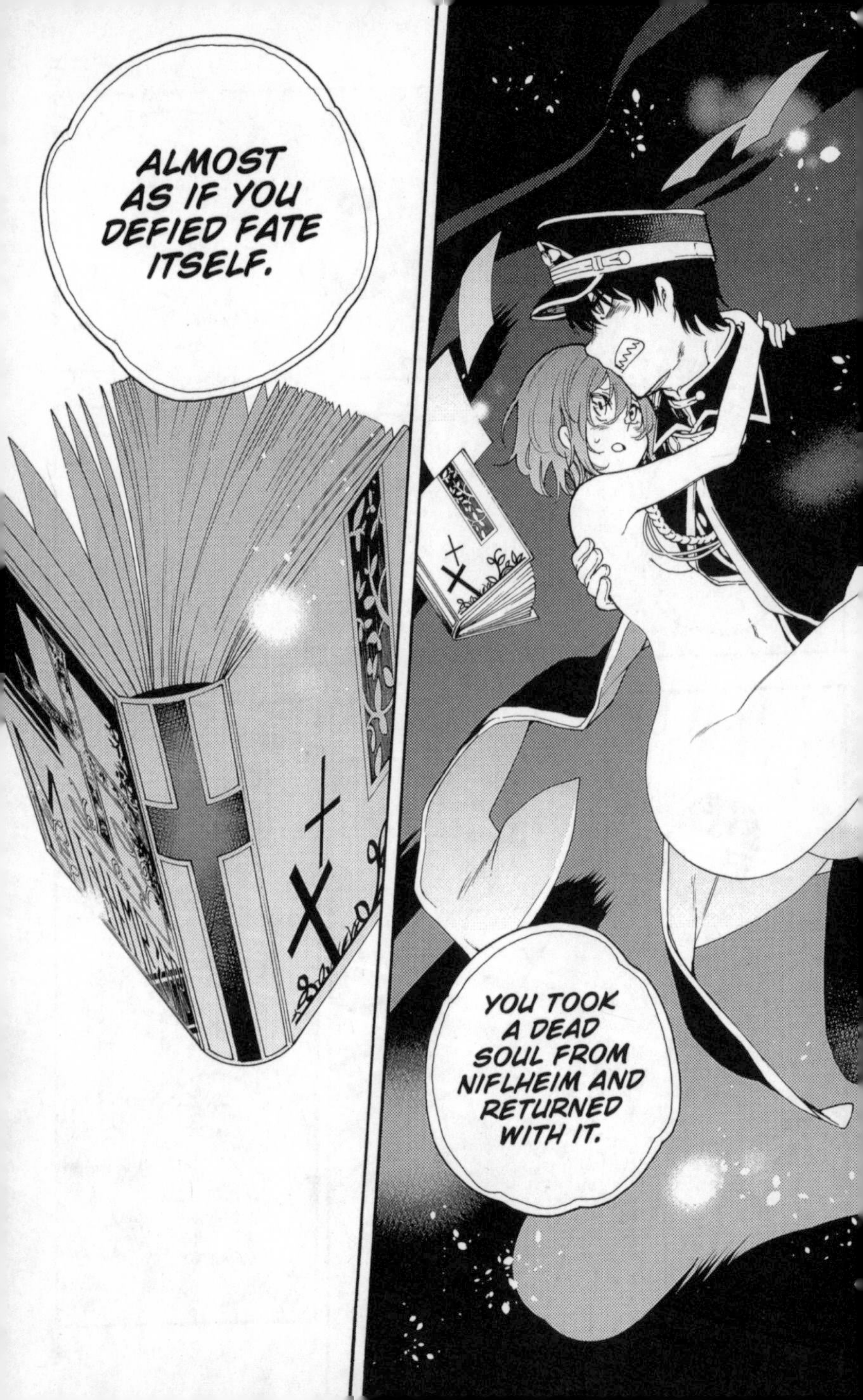
YOU TOOK A DEAD SOUL FROM NIFLHEIM AND RETURNED WITH IT.
ALMOST AS IF YOU DEFIED FATE ITSELF.

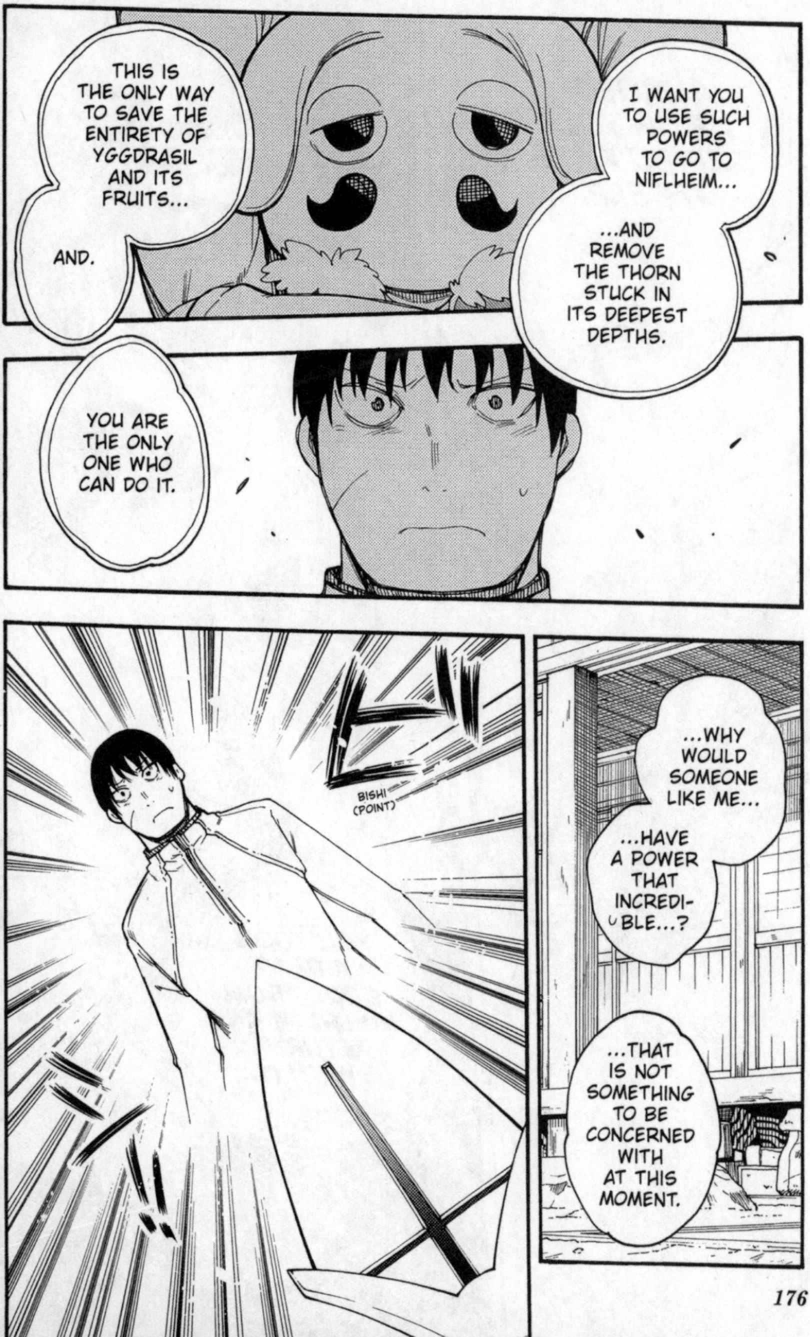
I WANT YOU TO USE SUCH POWERS TO GO TO NIFLHEIM...
...AND REMOVE THE THORN STUCK IN ITS DEEPEST DEPTHS.
THIS IS THE ONLY WAY TO SAVE THE ENTIRETY OF YGGDRASIL AND ITS FRUITS...
AND.
YOU ARE THE ONLY ONE WHO CAN DO IT.
...WHY WOULD SOMEONE LIKE ME...
...HAVE A POWER THAT INCREDI-BLE...?
...THAT IS NOT SOMETHING TO BE CONCERNED WITH AT THIS MOMENT.
BISHI (POINT)

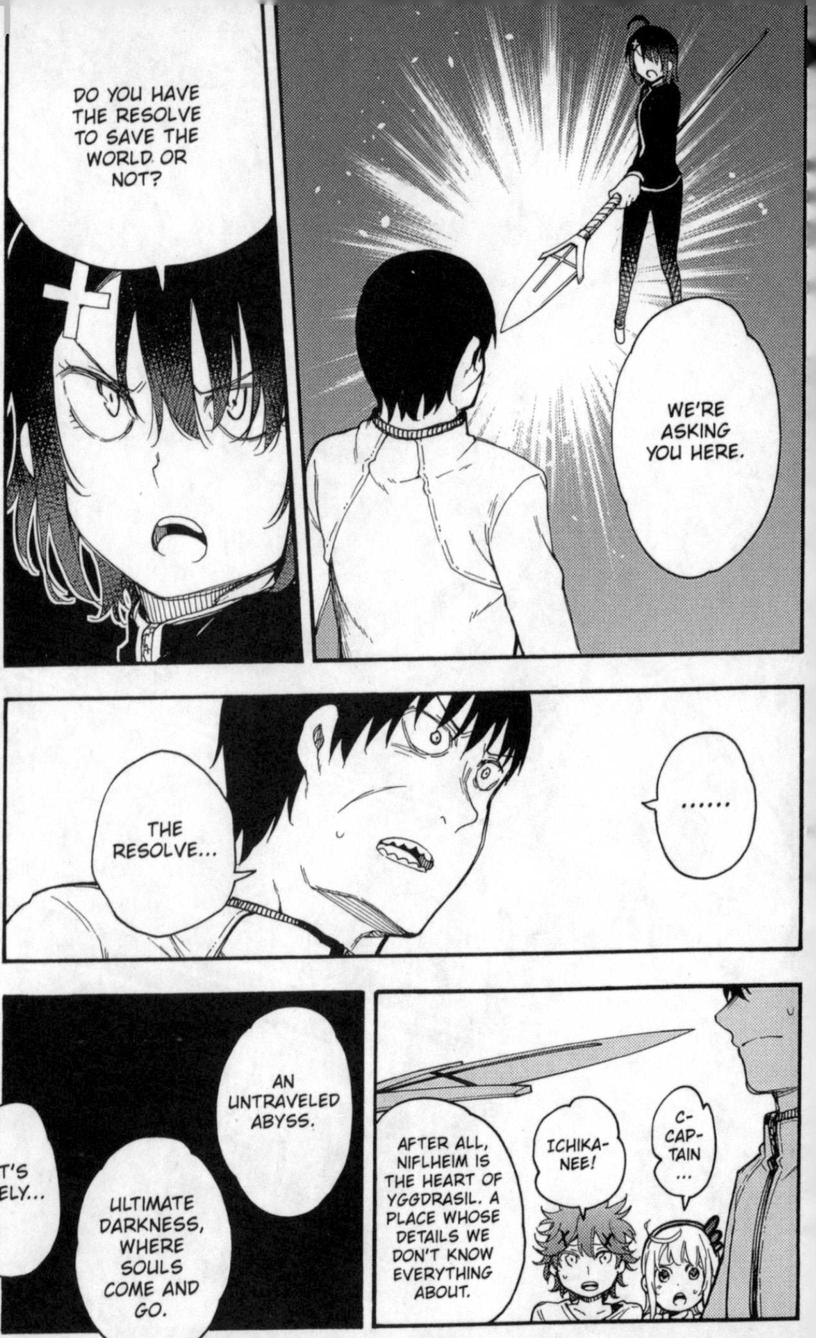
WE'RE ASKING YOU HERE.
DO YOU HAVE THE RESOLVE TO SAVE THE WORLD OR NOT?
......
THE RESOLVE...
C-CAPTAIN...
ICHIKA-NEE!
AFTER ALL, NIFLHEIM IS THE HEART OF YGGDRASIL. A PLACE WHOSE DETAILS WE DON'T KNOW EVERYTHING ABOUT.
AN UNTRAVELED ABYSS.
ULTIMATE DARKNESS, WHERE SOULS COME AND GO.
IT'S LIKELY...

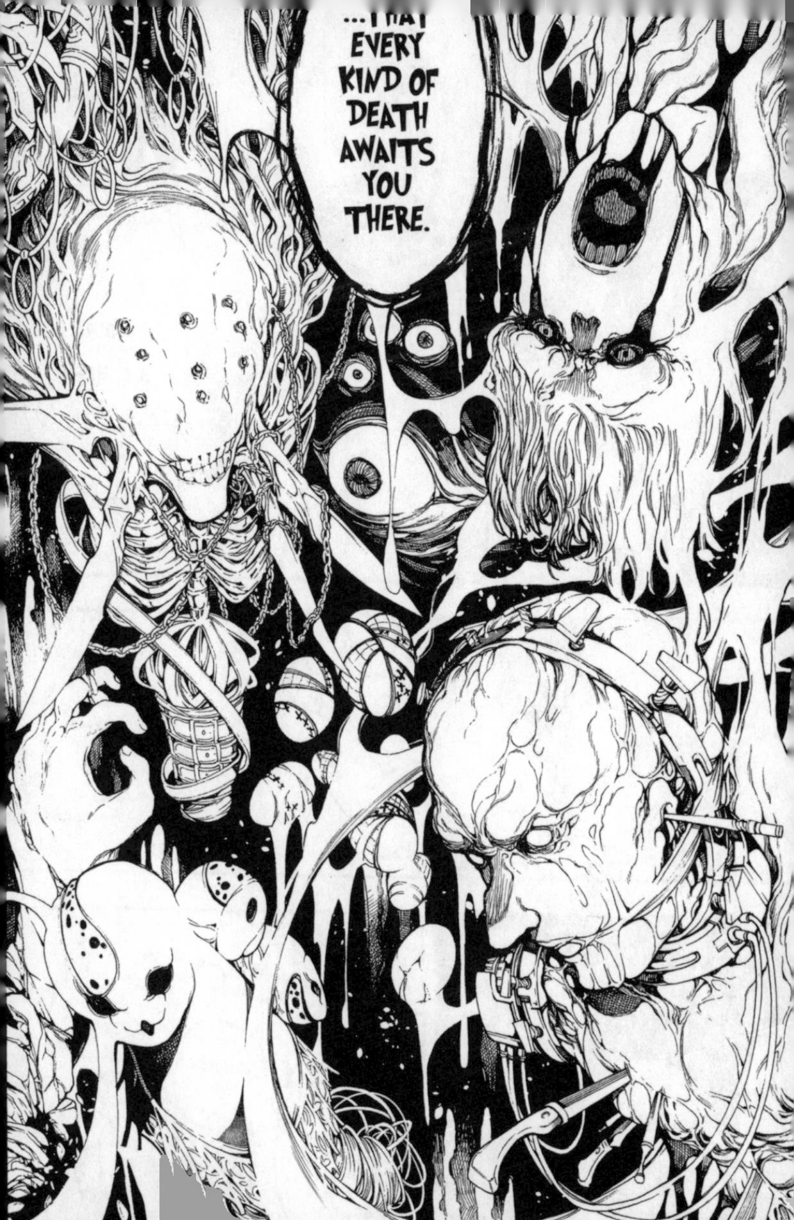
...THAT EVERY KIND OF DEATH AWAITS YOU THERE.

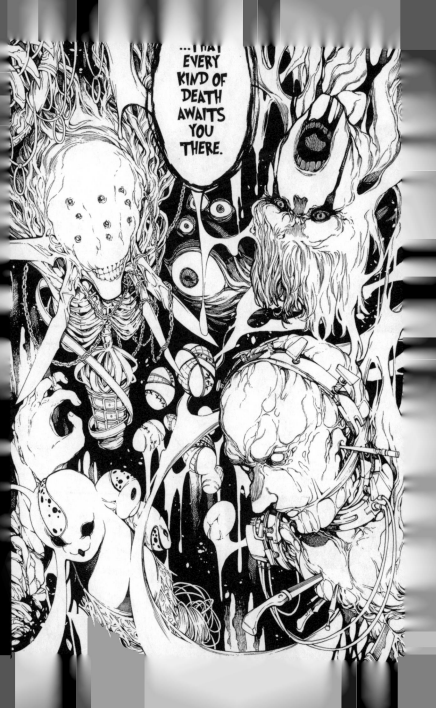

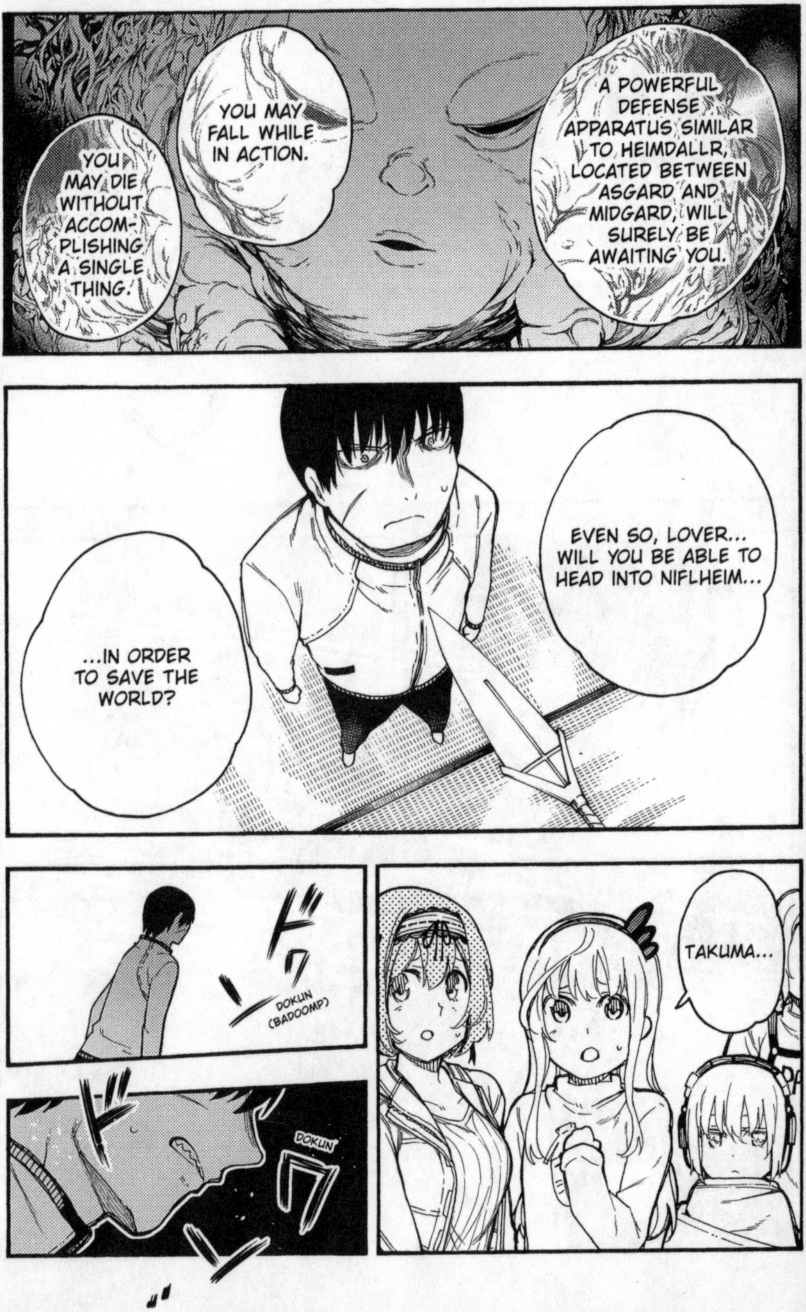
A POWERFUL DEFENSE APPARATUS SIMILAR TO HEIMDALLR, LOCATED BETWEEN ASGARD AND MIDGARD, WILL SURELY BE AWAITING YOU.
YOU MAY FALL WHILE IN ACTION.
YOU MAY DIE WITHOUT ACCOM-PLISHING A SINGLE THING.
EVEN SO, LOVER... WILL YOU BE ABLE TO HEAD INTO NIFLHEIM...
...IN ORDER TO SAVE THE WORLD?
TAKUMA...
DOKUN (BADOOMP)
DOKUN

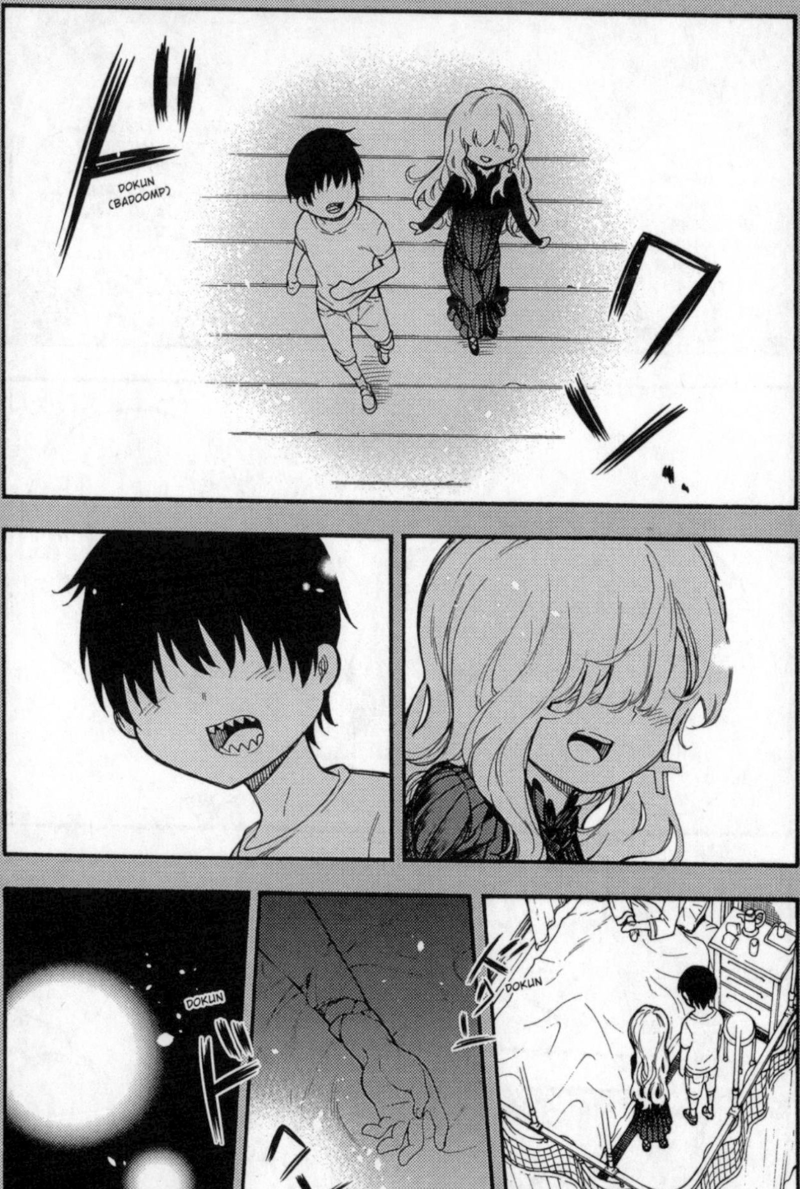
DOKUN
(BADOOMP)
DOKUN
DOKUN

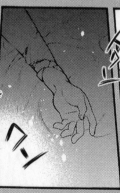

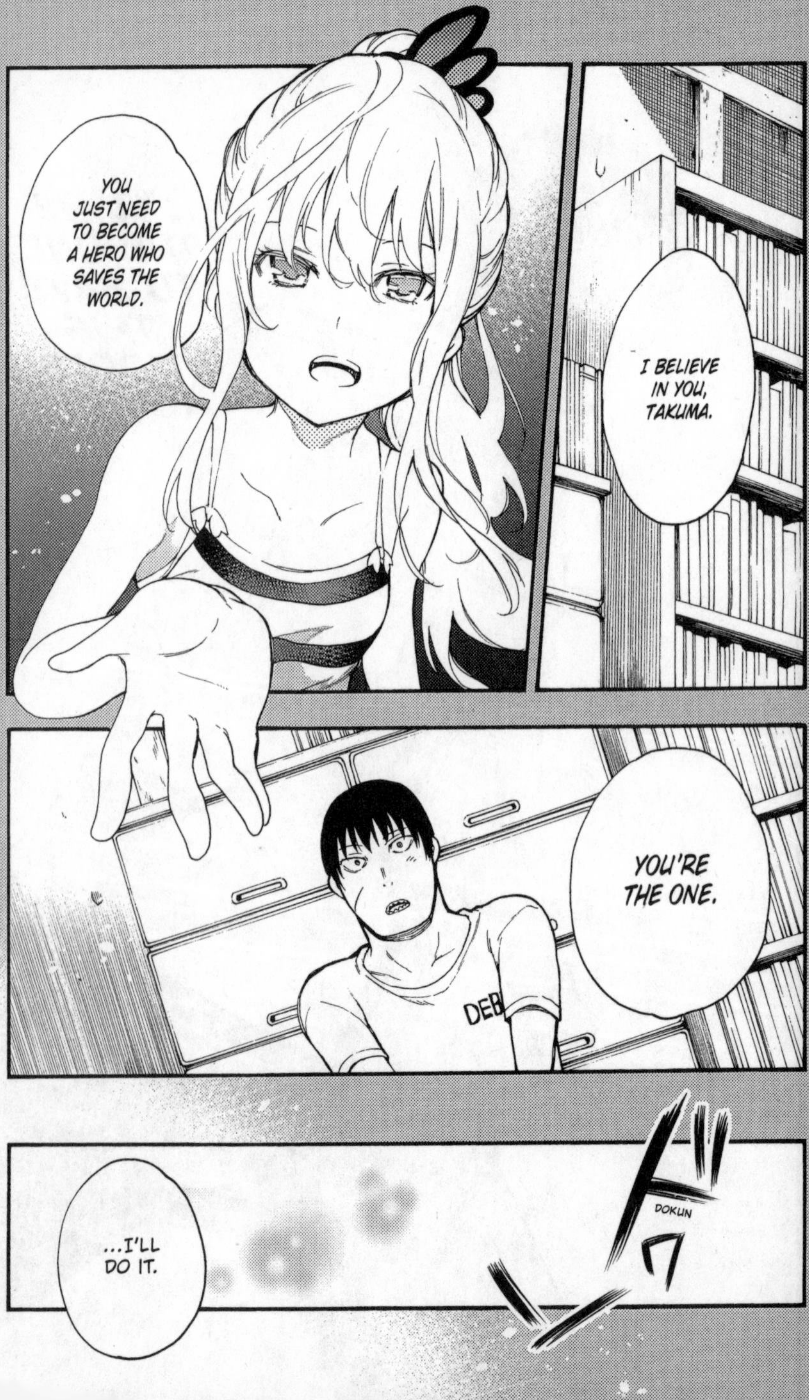
I BELIEVE IN YOU, TAKUMA.
YOU JUST NEED TO BECOME A HERO WHO SAVES THE WORLD.
YOU'RE THE ONE.
DEB
DOKUN
...I'LL DO IT.

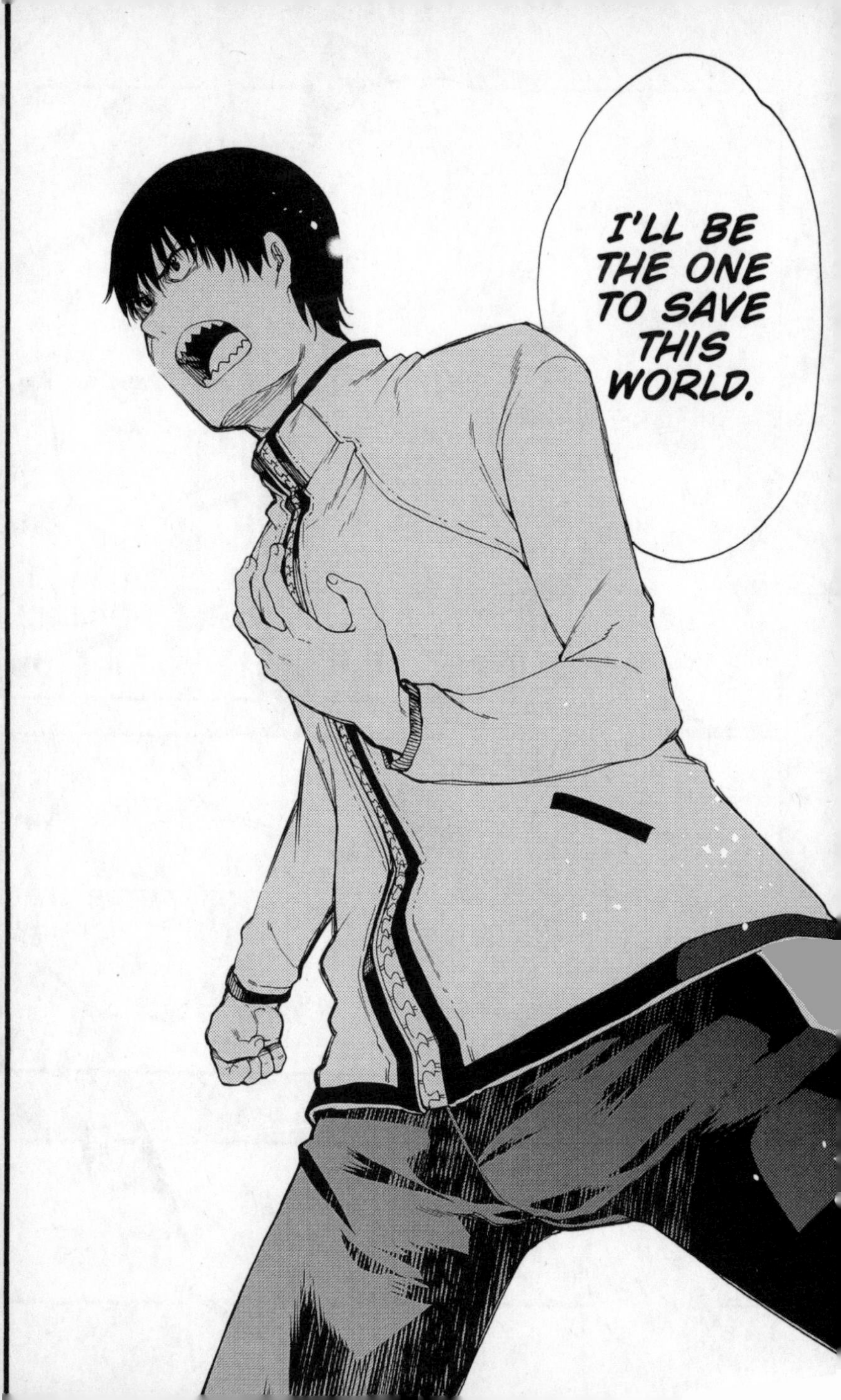
I'LL BE THE ONE TO SAVE THIS WORLD.

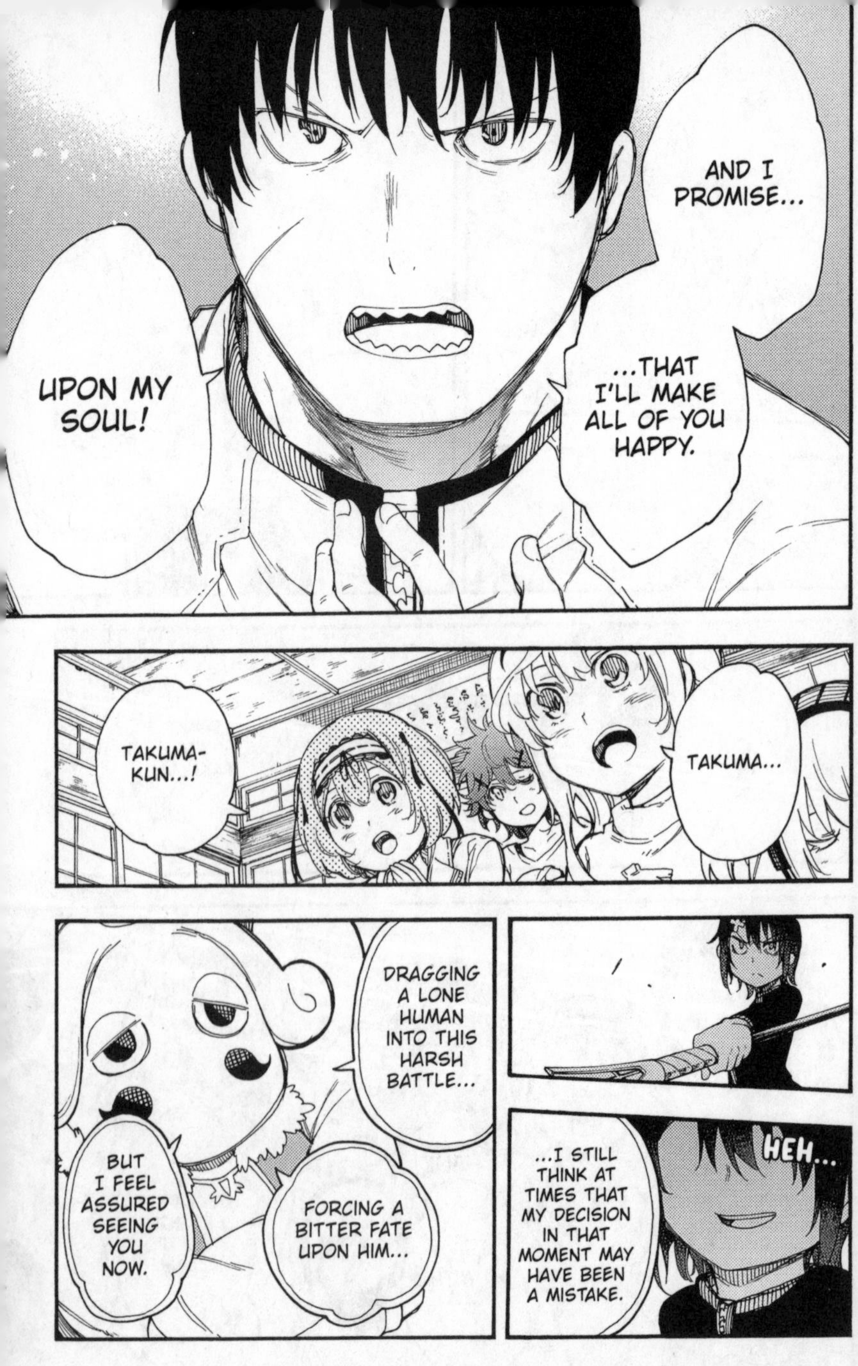
AND I PROMISE...
...THAT I'LL MAKE ALL OF YOU HAPPY.
UPON MY SOUL!
TAKUMA...
TAKUMA-KUN...!
HEH...
...I STILL THINK AT TIMES THAT MY DECISION IN THAT MOMENT MAY HAVE BEEN A MISTAKE.
DRAGGING A LONE HUMAN INTO THIS HARSH BATTLE...
FORCING A BITTER FATE UPON HIM...
BUT I FEEL ASSURED SEEING YOU NOW.

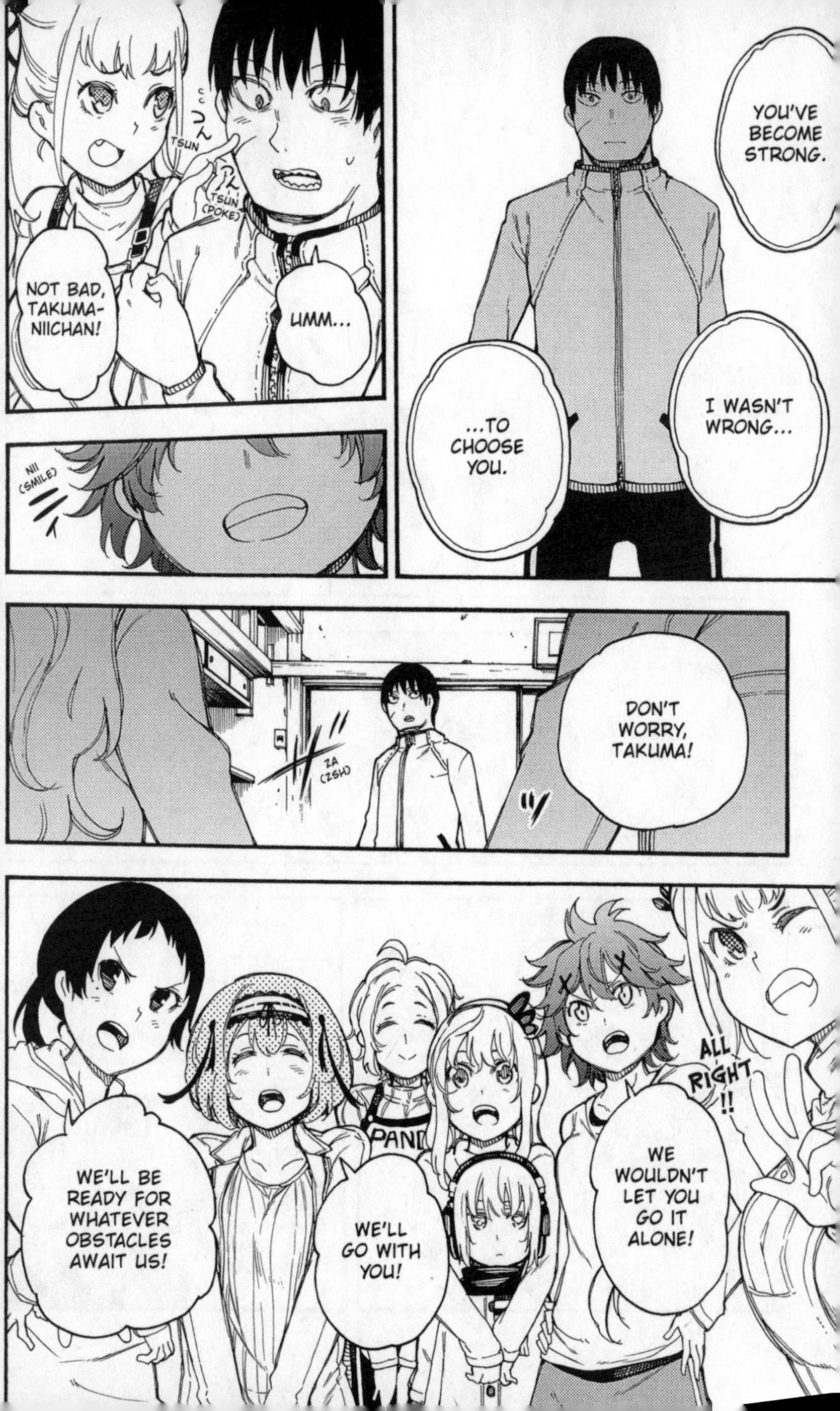
YOU'VE BECOME STRONG.
I WASN'T WRONG...
...TO CHOOSE YOU.
TSUN
TSUN (POKE)
UMM...
NOT BAD, TAKUMA-NIICHAN!
NII (SMILE)
DON'T WORRY, TAKUMA!
ZA (ZSH)
ALL RIGHT!!
WE WOULDN'T LET YOU GO IT ALONE!
WE'LL GO WITH YOU!
WE'LL BE READY FOR WHATEVER OBSTACLES AWAIT US!

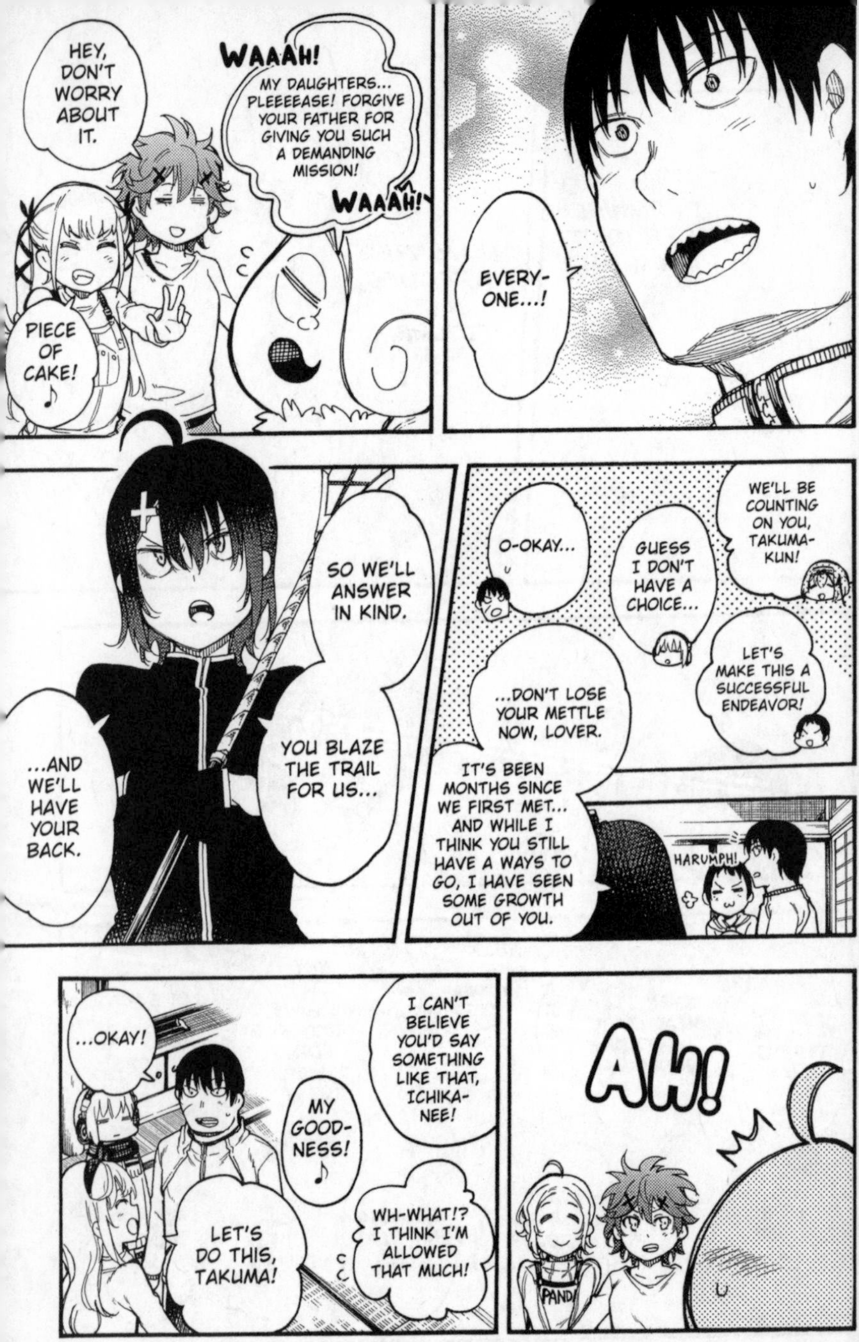
EVERY-ONE...!
WAAAH!
MY DAUGHTERS... PLEEEEASE! FORGIVE YOUR FATHER FOR GIVING YOU SUCH A DEMANDING MISSION!
WAAAH!
HEY, DON'T WORRY ABOUT IT.
PIECE OF CAKE! ♪
WE'LL BE COUNTING ON YOU, TAKUMA-KUN!
GUESS I DON'T HAVE A CHOICE...
O-OKAY...
LET'S MAKE THIS A SUCCESSFUL ENDEAVOR!
...DON'T LOSE YOUR METTLE NOW, LOVER.
HARUMPH!
IT'S BEEN MONTHS SINCE WE FIRST MET... AND WHILE I THINK YOU STILL HAVE A WAYS TO GO, I HAVE SEEN SOME GROWTH OUT OF YOU.
SO WE'LL ANSWER IN KIND.
YOU BLAZE THE TRAIL FOR US...
...AND WE'LL HAVE YOUR BACK.
AH!
I CAN'T BELIEVE YOU'D SAY SOMETHING LIKE THAT, ICHIKA-NEE!
MY GOODNESS! ♪
WH-WHAT!? I THINK I'M ALLOWED THAT MUCH!
...OKAY!
LET'S DO THIS, TAKUMA!

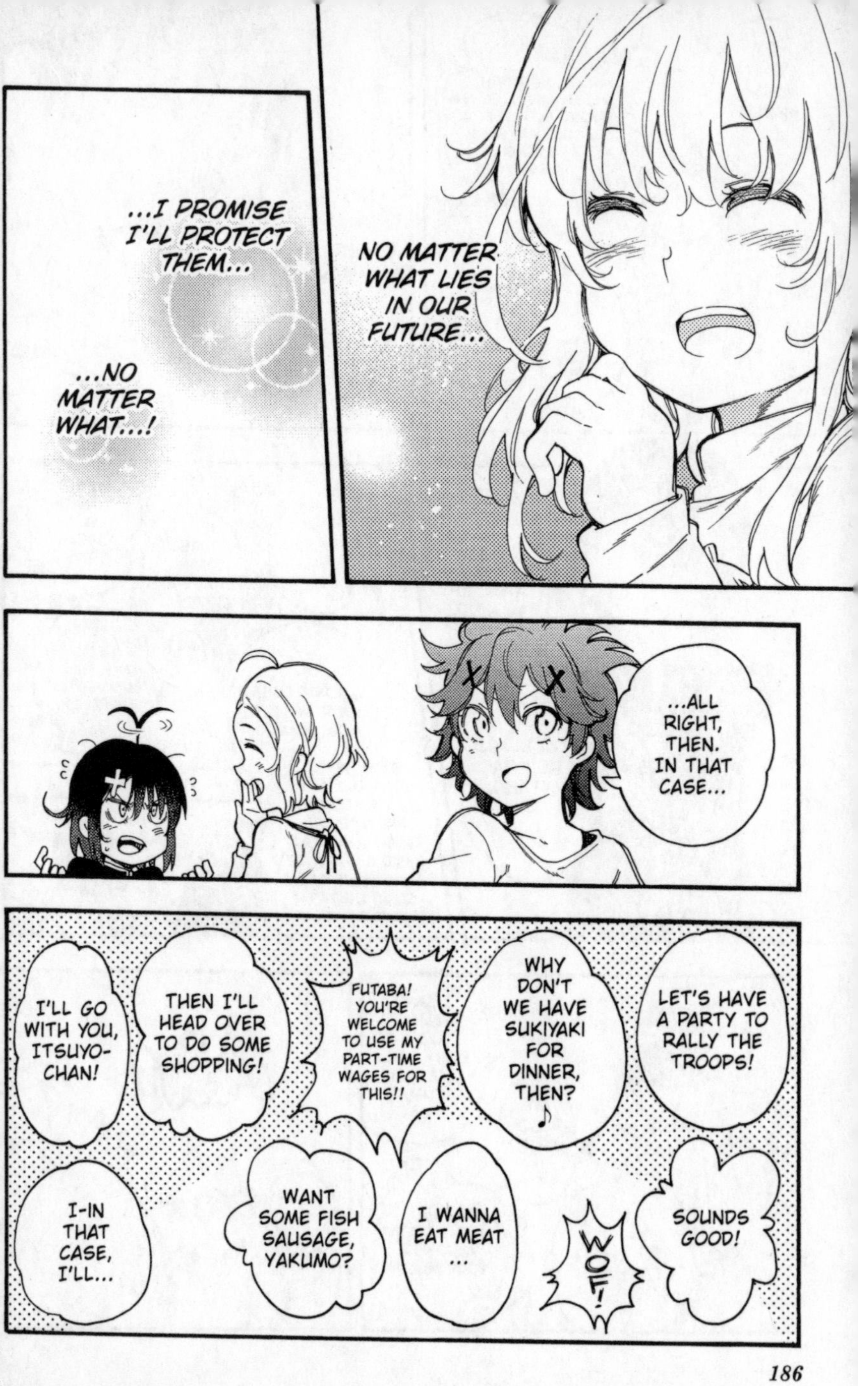
NO MATTER WHAT LIES IN OUR FUTURE...
...I PROMISE I'LL PROTECT THEM...
...NO MATTER WHAT...!
...ALL RIGHT, THEN. IN THAT CASE...
LET'S HAVE A PARTY TO RALLY THE TROOPS!
WHY DON'T WE HAVE SUKIYAKI FOR DINNER, THEN? ♪
FUTABA! YOU'RE WELCOME TO USE MY PART-TIME WAGES FOR THIS!!
THEN I'LL HEAD OVER TO DO SOME SHOPPING!
I'LL GO WITH YOU, ITSUYO-CHAN!
SOUNDS GOOD!
WOF!
I WANNA EAT MEAT ...
WANT SOME FISH SAUSAGE, YAKUMO?
I-IN THAT CASE, I'LL...

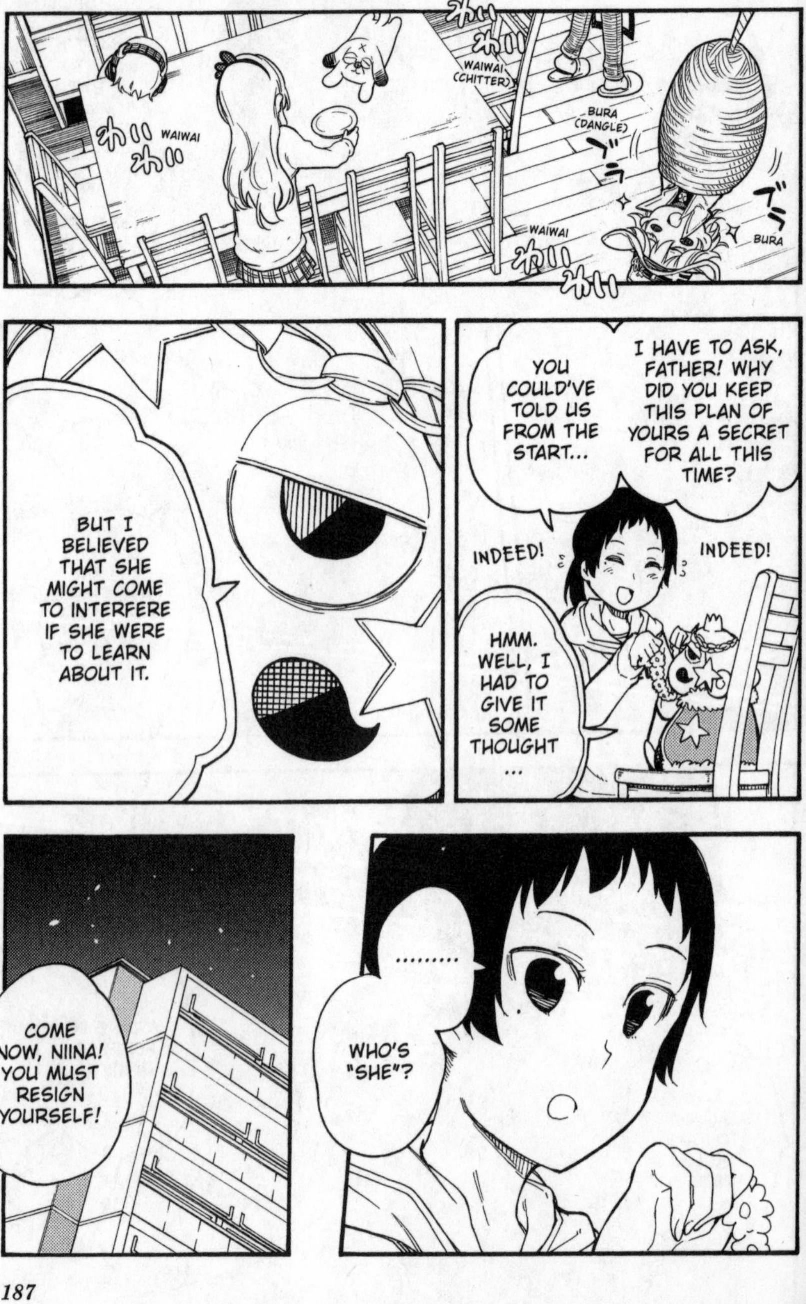
WAIWAI (CHITTER)
BURA (DANGLE)
BURA
WAIWAI
WAIWAI
I HAVE TO ASK, FATHER! WHY DID YOU KEEP THIS PLAN OF YOURS A SECRET FOR ALL THIS TIME?
YOU COULD'VE TOLD US FROM THE START...
INDEED!
INDEED!
HMM. WELL, I HAD TO GIVE IT SOME THOUGHT ...
BUT I BELIEVED THAT SHE MIGHT COME TO INTERFERE IF SHE WERE TO LEARN ABOUT IT.
....
WHO'S "SHE"?
COME NOW, NIINA! YOU MUST RESIGN YOURSELF!

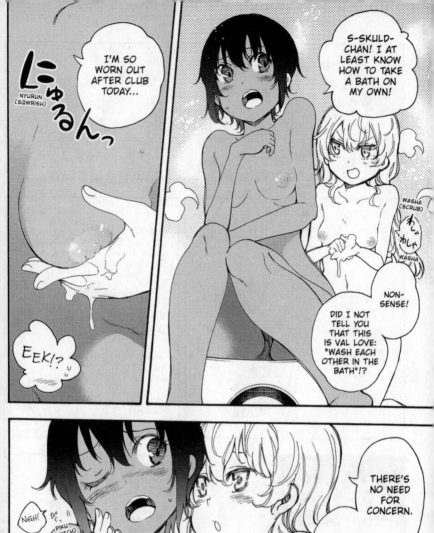

I'M SO WORN OUT AFTER CLUB TODAY...

にゅるんっ
NYURUN (SQWRISH)

S-SKULD-CHAN! I AT LEAST KNOW HOW TO TAKE A BATH ON MY OWN!

WASHA (SCRUB)
わしゃ
わしゃ
WASHA

EEK!?

NON-SENSE!

DID I NOT TELL YOU THAT THIS IS VAL LOVE: "WASH EACH OTHER IN THE BATH"!?

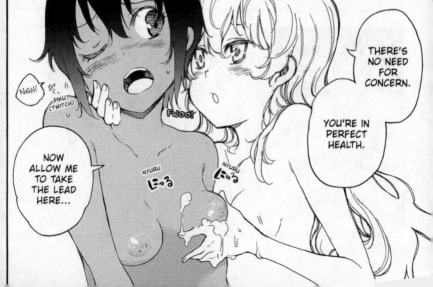

NGH!
ぴく、
PIKU (TWITCH)

FWOO!

THERE'S NO NEED FOR CONCERN.

YOU'RE IN PERFECT HEALTH.

NOW ALLOW ME TO TAKE THE LEAD HERE...

NYURU
にゅる

NYURU
にゅる

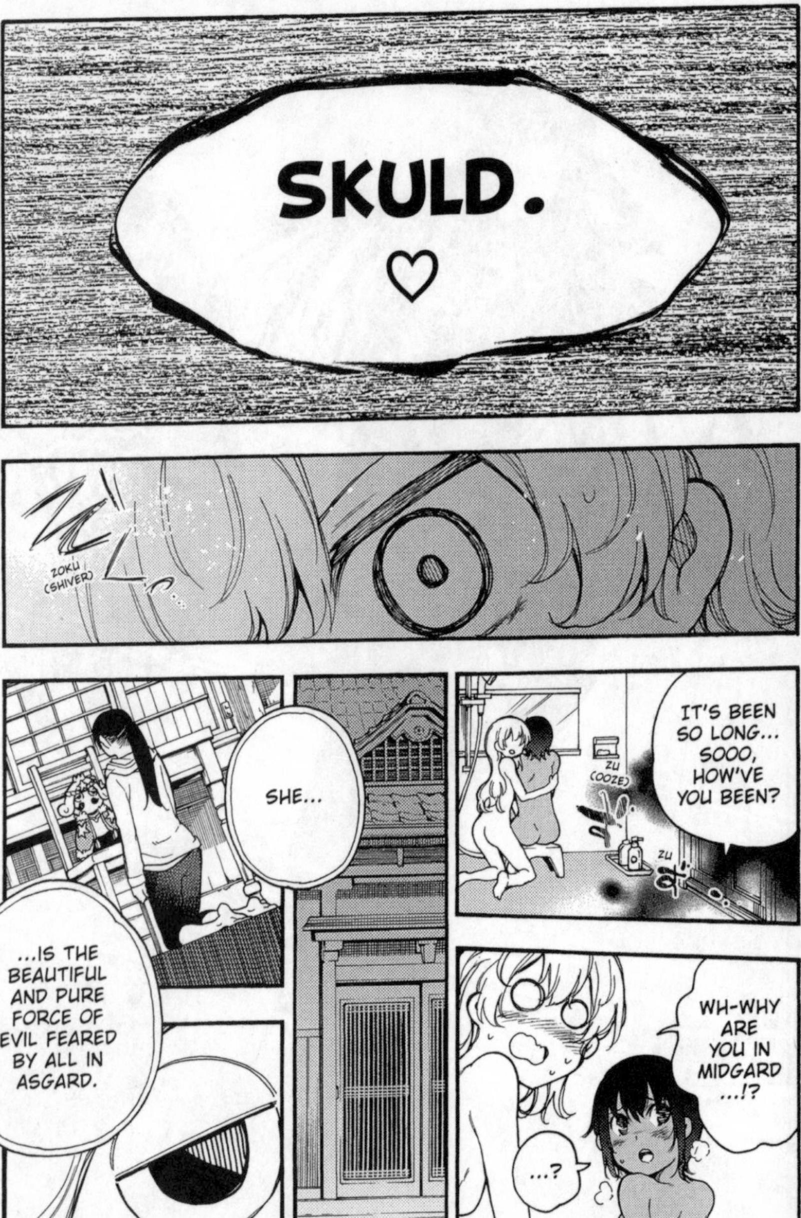
SKULD. ♡
ZOKU (SHIVER)
IT'S BEEN SO LONG... SOOO, HOW'VE YOU BEEN?
ZU (OOZE)
ZU
WH-WHY ARE YOU IN MIDGARD ...!?
...?
SHE...
...IS THE BEAUTIFUL AND PURE FORCE OF EVIL FEARED BY ALL IN ASGARD.

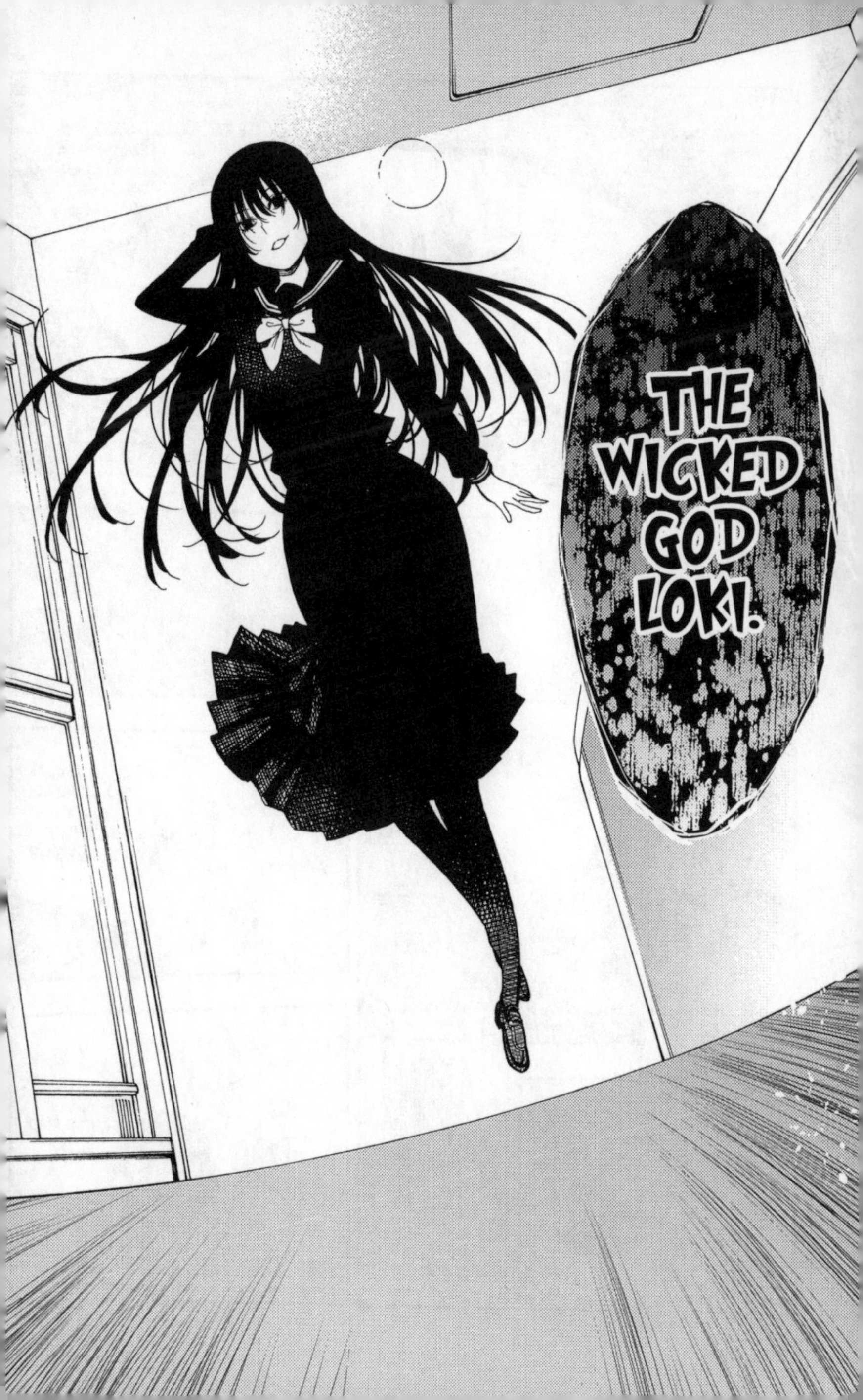
THE WICKED GOD LOKI.

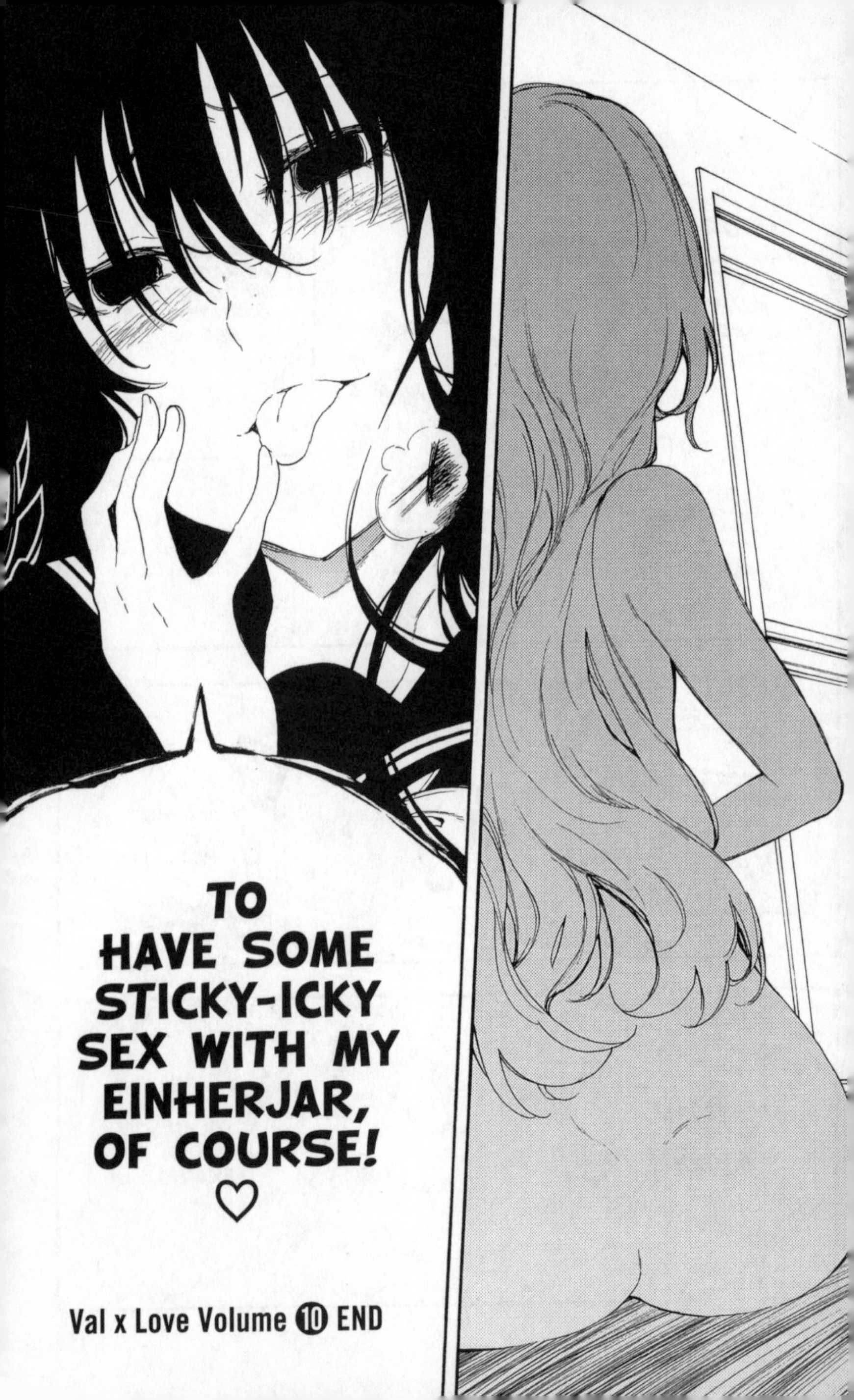
TO HAVE SOME STICKY-ICKY SEX WITH MY EINHERJAR, OF COURSE! ♡

Val x Love Volume ⑩ END

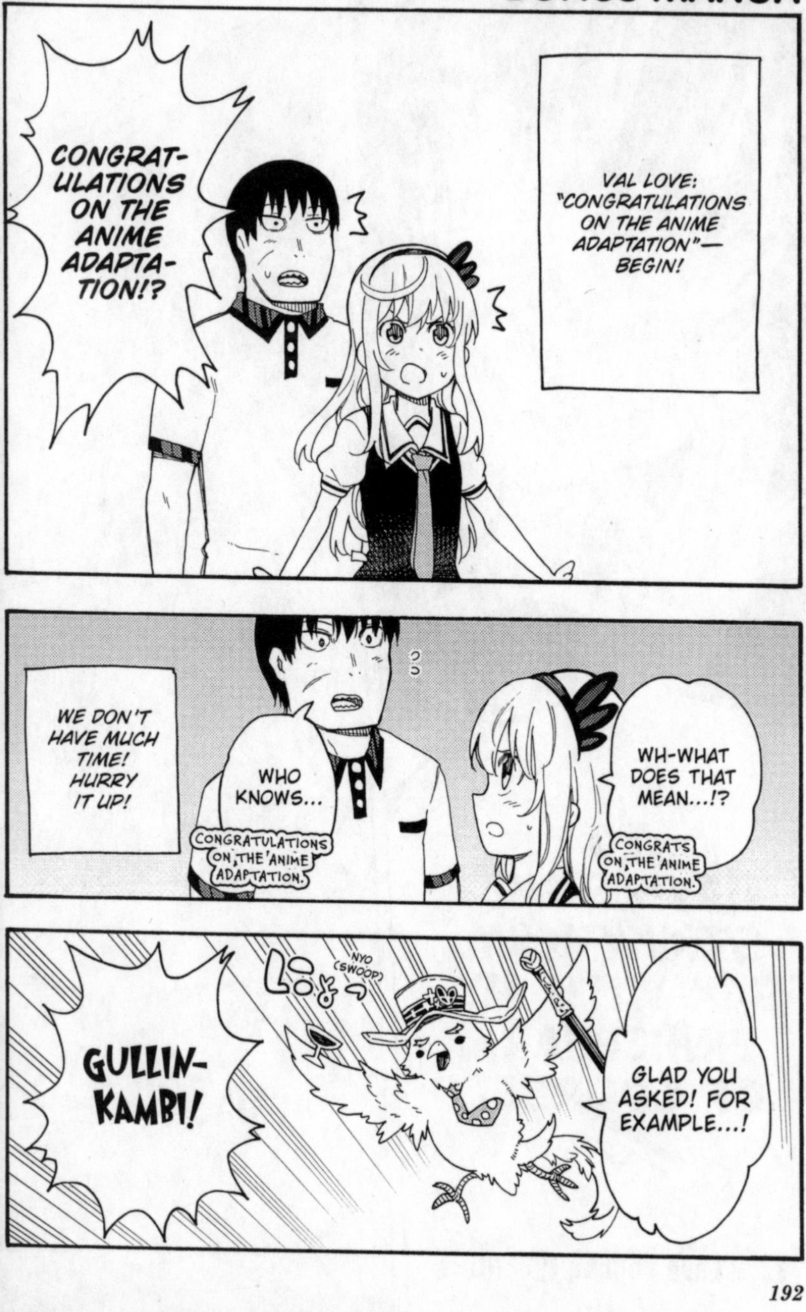
VAL LOVE: "CONGRATULATIONS ON THE ANIME ADAPTATION"—BEGIN!
CONGRAT-ULATIONS ON THE ANIME ADAPTA-TION!?
WH-WHAT DOES THAT MEAN...!?
CONGRATS ON THE ANIME ADAPTATION.
WHO KNOWS...
CONGRATULATIONS ON THE ANIME ADAPTATION.
WE DON'T HAVE MUCH TIME! HURRY IT UP!
GLAD YOU ASKED! FOR EXAMPLE...!
NYO (SWOOP)
GULLIN-KAMBI!

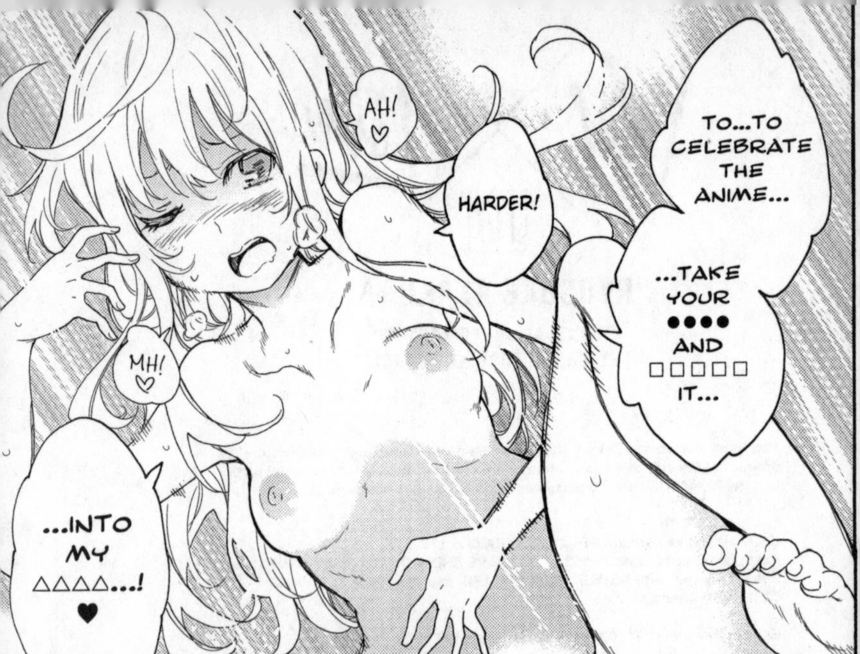
TO...TO CELEBRATE THE ANIME...
...TAKE YOUR ●●●● AND □□□□□ IT...
HARDER!
AH! ♡
MH! ♡
...INTO MY △△△△...! ♥

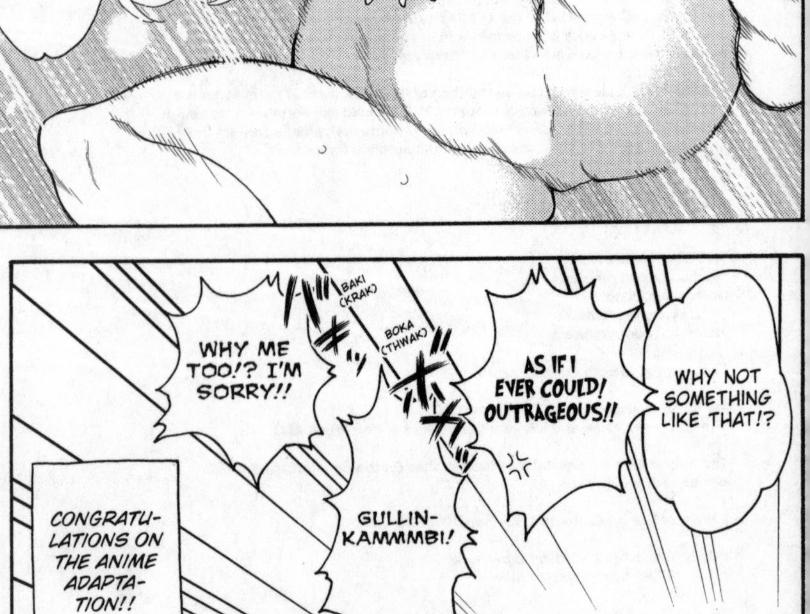
WHY NOT SOMETHING LIKE THAT!?
AS IF I EVER COULD! OUTRAGEOUS!!
BAKI (KRAK)
BOKA (THWAK)
WHY ME TOO!? I'M SORRY!!
GULLIN-KAMMMBI!
CONGRATU-LATIONS ON THE ANIME ADAPTA-TION!!

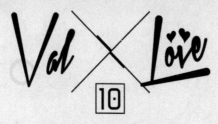

VAL ✕ LOVE 10

RYOSUKE ASAKURA

TRANSLATION: KO RANSOM
LETTERING: ROCHELLE GANCIO

VAL LOVE vol. 10
©2020 Ryosuke Asakura / SQUARE ENIX CO., LTD.
First published in Japan in 2020 by SQUARE ENIX CO., LTD. English translation rights arranged with SQUARE ENIX CO., LTD. and Yen Press, LLC through Tuttle-Mori Agency, Inc.

English translation © 2021 by SQUARE ENIX CO., LTD.

Yen Press
150 West 30th Street, 19th Floor
New York, NY 10001

Visit us at yenpress.com
facebook.com/yenpress
twitter.com/yenpress
yenpress.tumblr.com
instagram.com/yenpress

First Yen Press Edition: October 2021

Yen Press is an imprint of Yen Press, LLC.
The Yen Press name and logo are trademarks of Yen Press, LLC.

The publisher is not responsible for websites (or their content) that are not owned by the publisher.

Library of Congress Control Number: 2017954705

ISBNs: 978-1-9753-3562-5 (paperback)
        978-1-9753-3563-2 (ebook)

10 9 8 7 6 5 4 3 2 1

BVG

Printed in the United States of America